合法ドラッグ

LEGAL DRUG

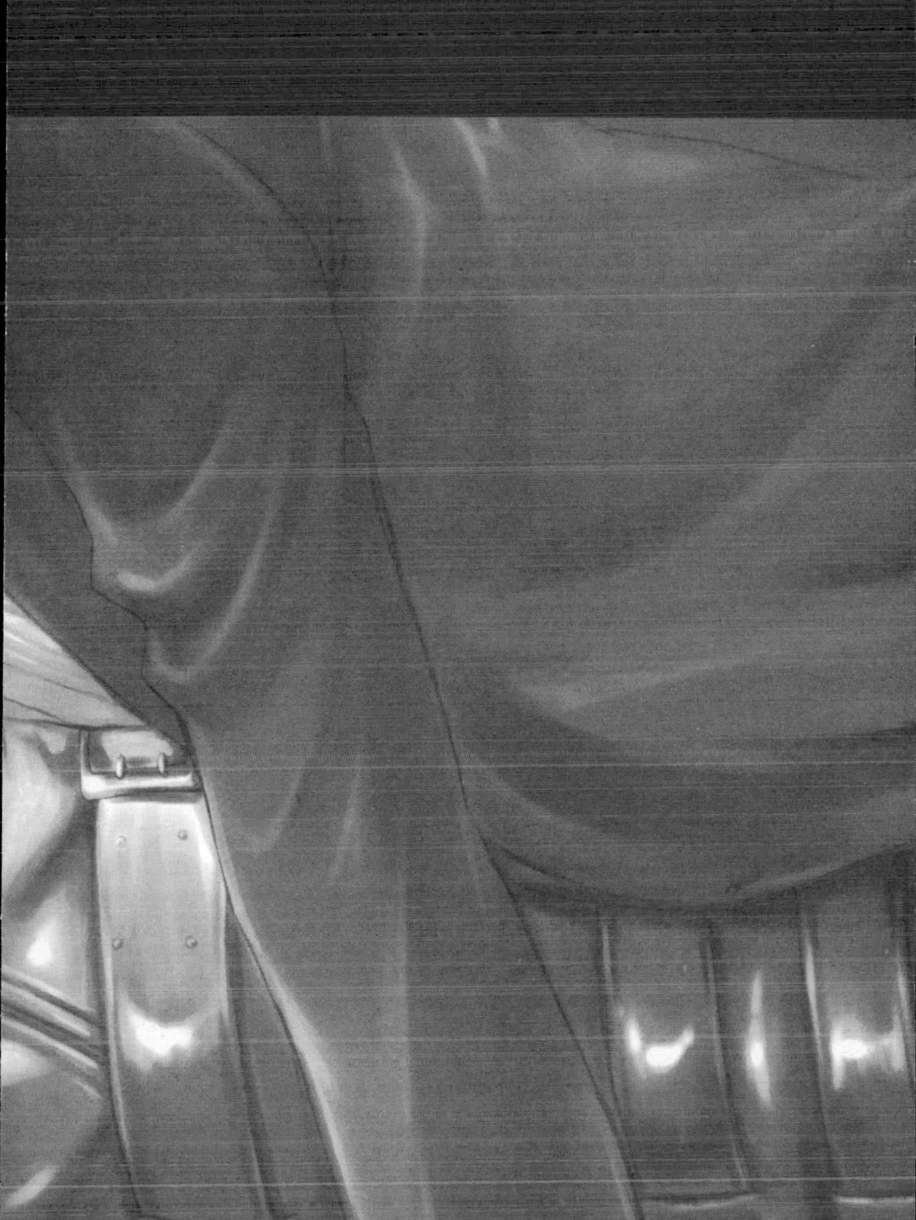

DRUG NO.11

Daily use of the drug may cause poisoning.

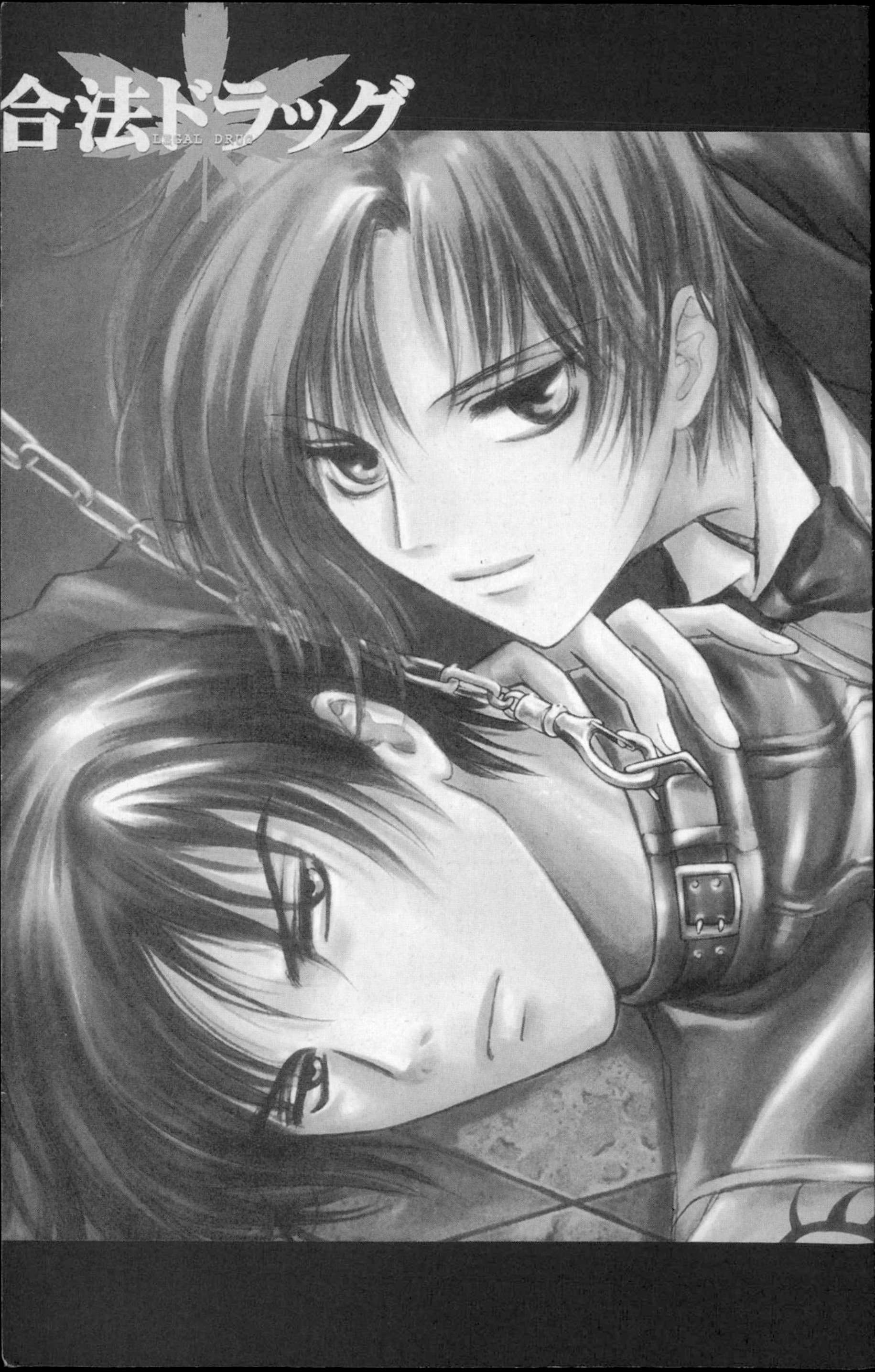
合法ドラッグ
LEGAL DRUG

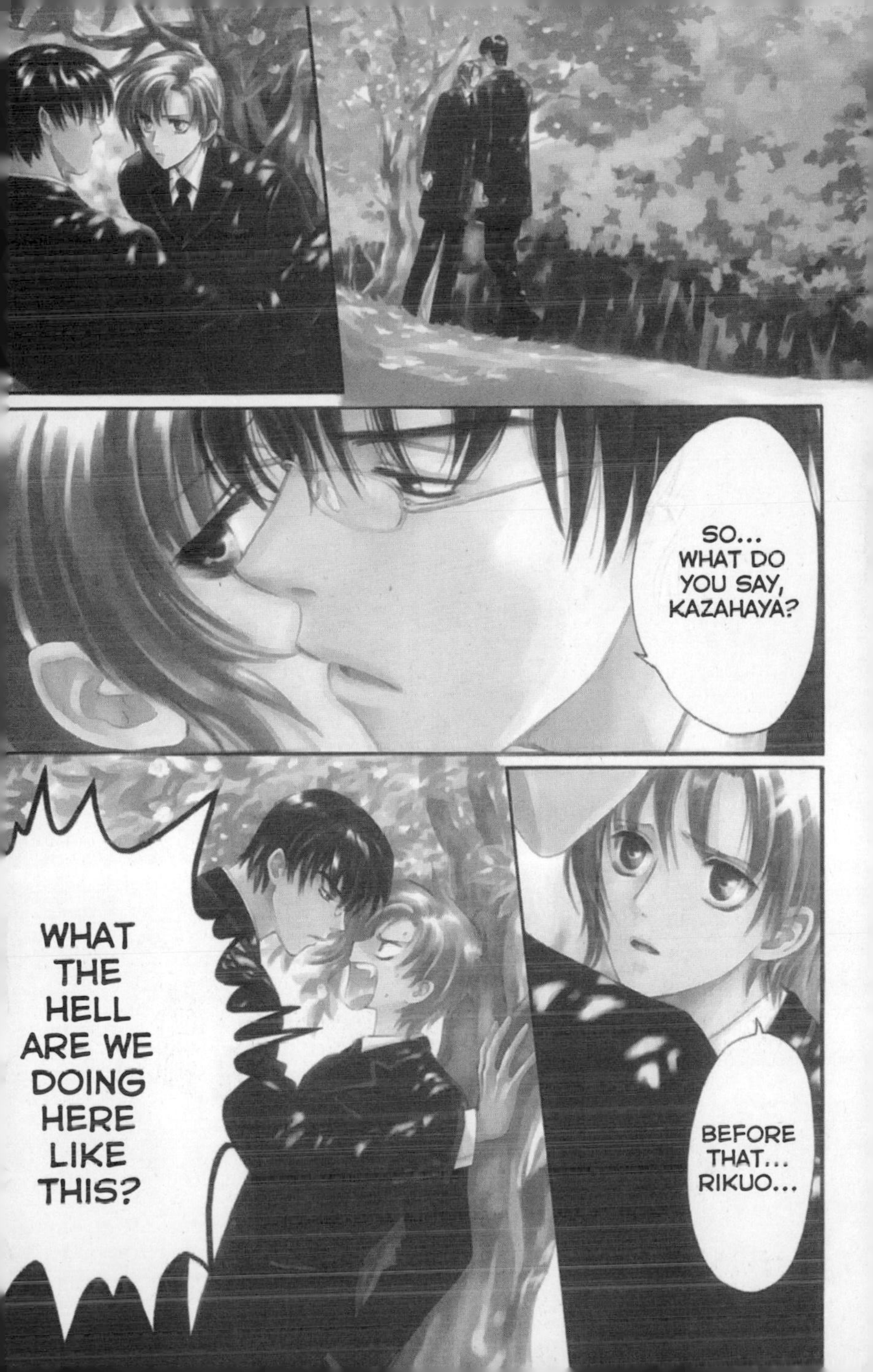
SO... WHAT DO YOU SAY, KAZAHAYA?
BEFORE THAT... RIKUO...
WHAT THE HELL ARE WE DOING HERE LIKE THIS?

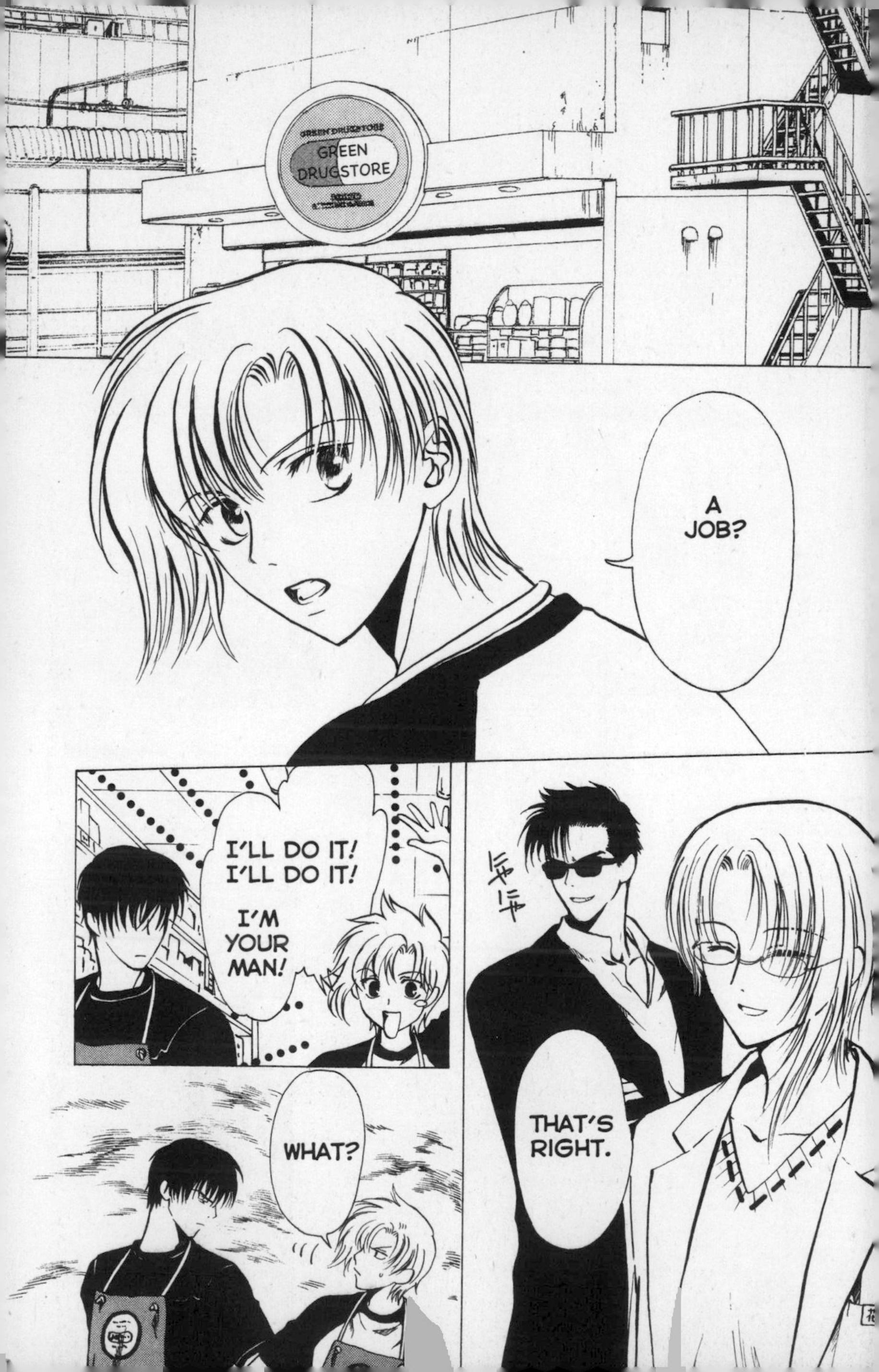
GREEN DRUGSTORE
A JOB?
ニヤニヤ
THAT'S RIGHT.
I'LL DO IT! I'LL DO IT!
I'M YOUR MAN!
WHAT?

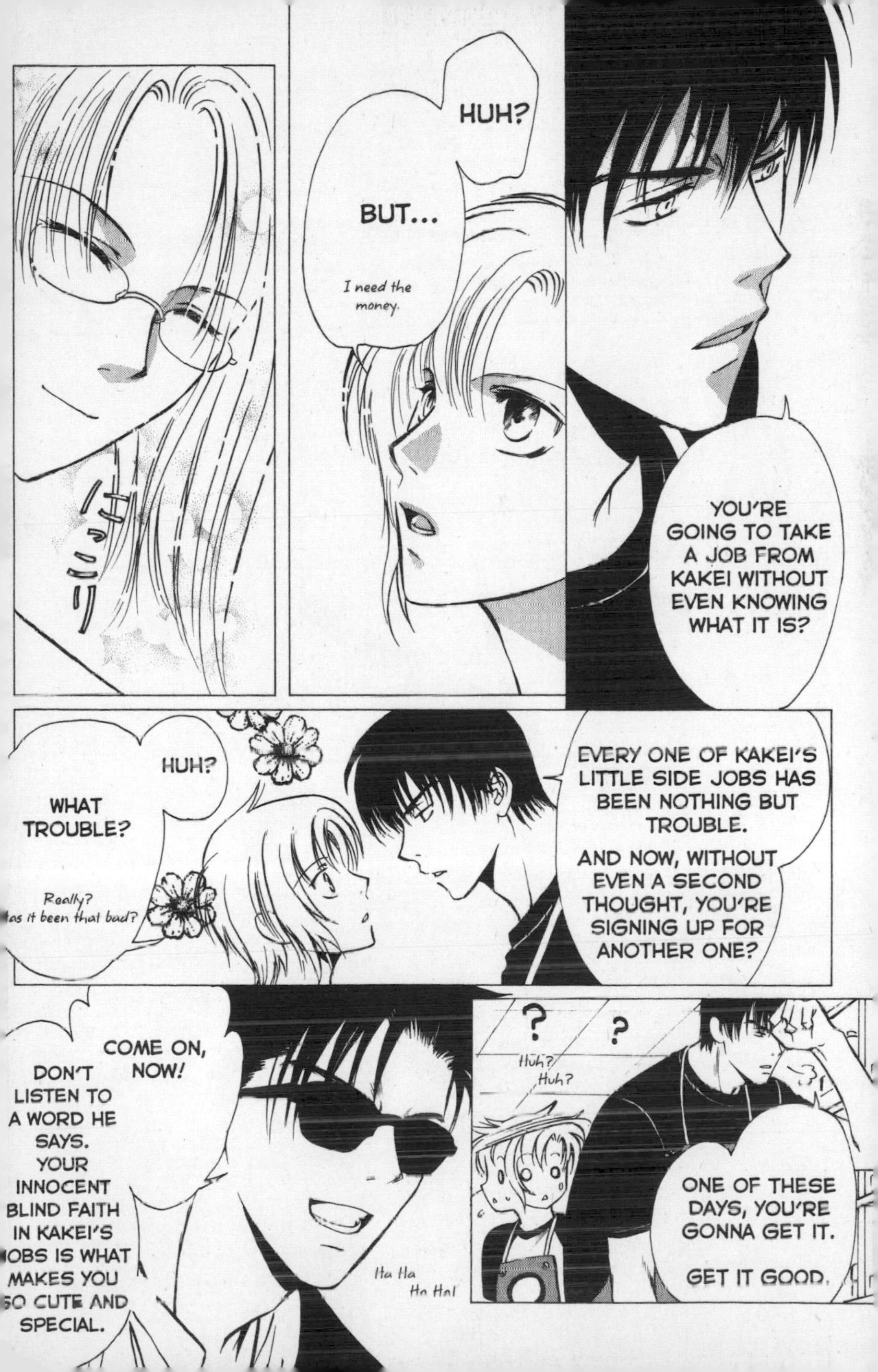

YOU'RE GOING TO TAKE A JOB FROM KAKEI WITHOUT EVEN KNOWING WHAT IT IS?
HUH?
BUT...
I need the money.
ニッコリ
EVERY ONE OF KAKEI'S LITTLE SIDE JOBS HAS BEEN NOTHING BUT TROUBLE.
AND NOW, WITHOUT EVEN A SECOND THOUGHT, YOU'RE SIGNING UP FOR ANOTHER ONE?
HUH?
WHAT TROUBLE?
Really? as it been that bad?
? ?
Huh? Huh?
ONE OF THESE DAYS, YOU'RE GONNA GET IT.
GET IT GOOD.
COME ON, NOW!
DON'T LISTEN TO A WORD HE SAYS. YOUR INNOCENT BLIND FAITH IN KAKEI'S JOBS IS WHAT MAKES YOU SO CUTE AND SPECIAL.
Ha Ha Ha Ha!

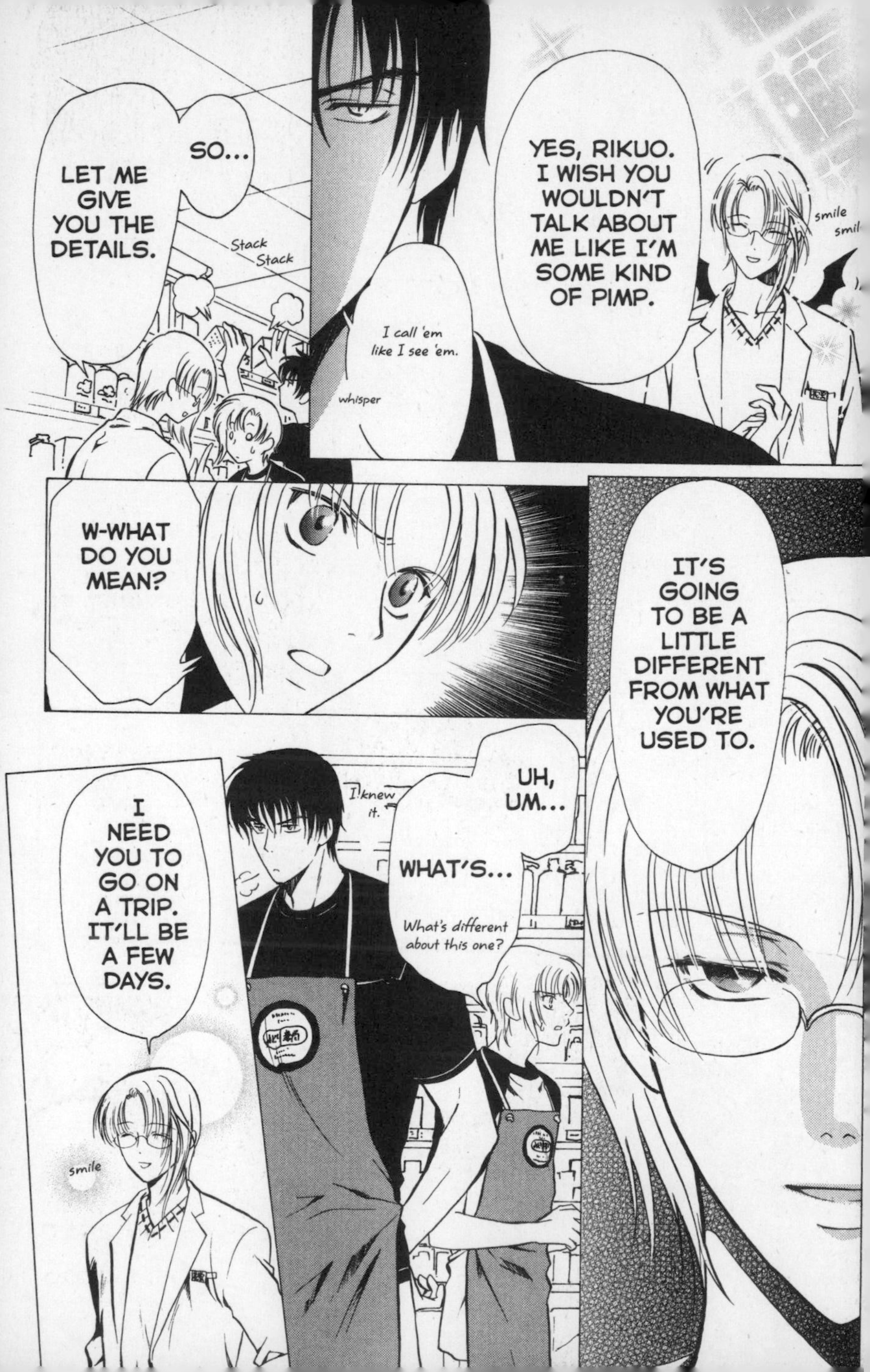
YES, RIKUO. I WISH YOU WOULDN'T TALK ABOUT ME LIKE I'M SOME KIND OF PIMP.
smile
smil
I call 'em like I see 'em.
whisper
SO...
LET ME GIVE YOU THE DETAILS.
Stack
Stack
IT'S GOING TO BE A LITTLE DIFFERENT FROM WHAT YOU'RE USED TO.
W-WHAT DO YOU MEAN?
UH, UM...
WHAT'S...
What's different about this one?
I knew it.
I NEED YOU TO GO ON A TRIP. IT'LL BE A FEW DAYS.
smile

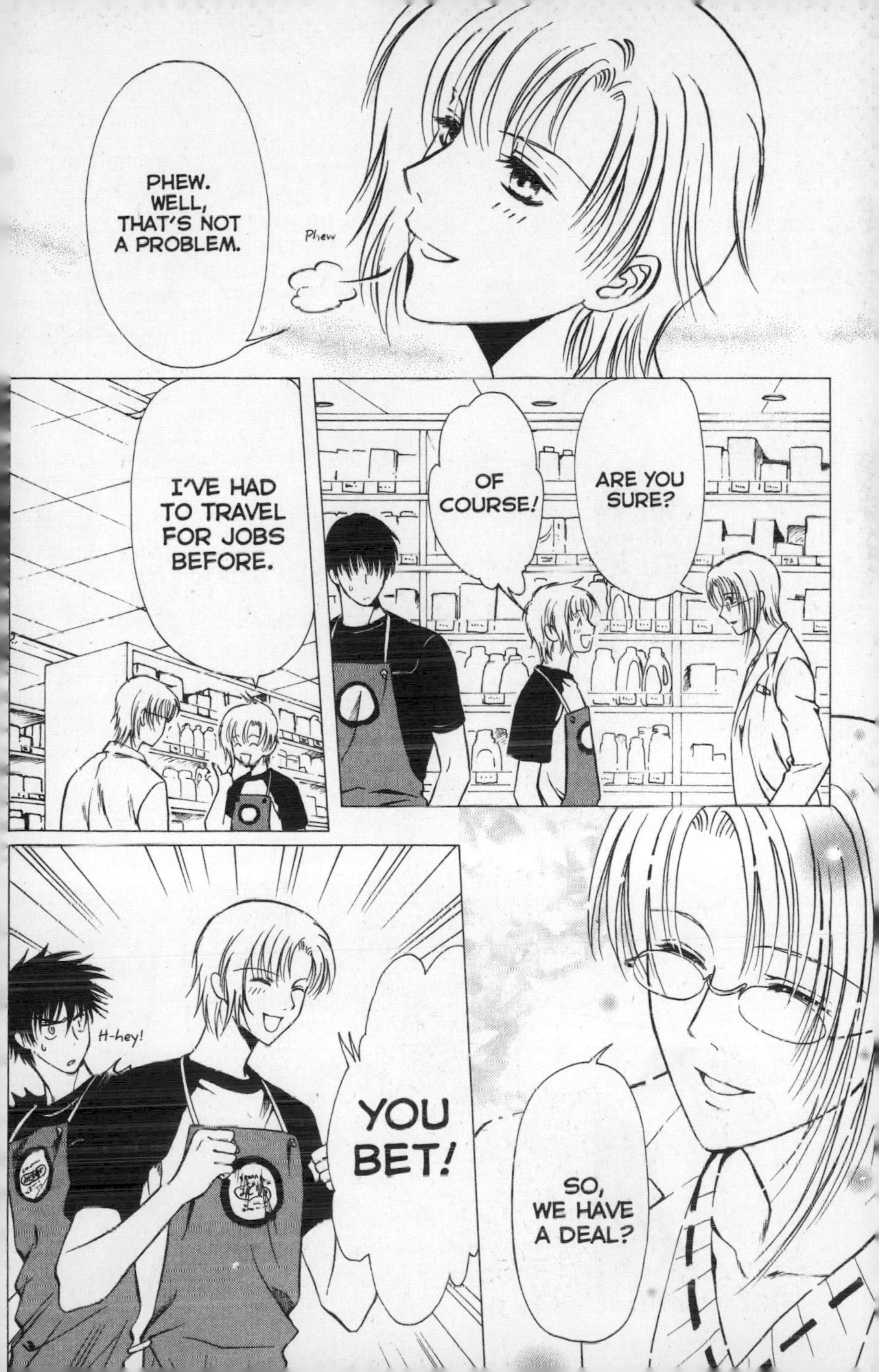
Phew
PHEW. WELL, THAT'S NOT A PROBLEM.
ARE YOU SURE?
OF COURSE!
I'VE HAD TO TRAVEL FOR JOBS BEFORE.
SO, WE HAVE A DEAL?
YOU BET!
H-hey!

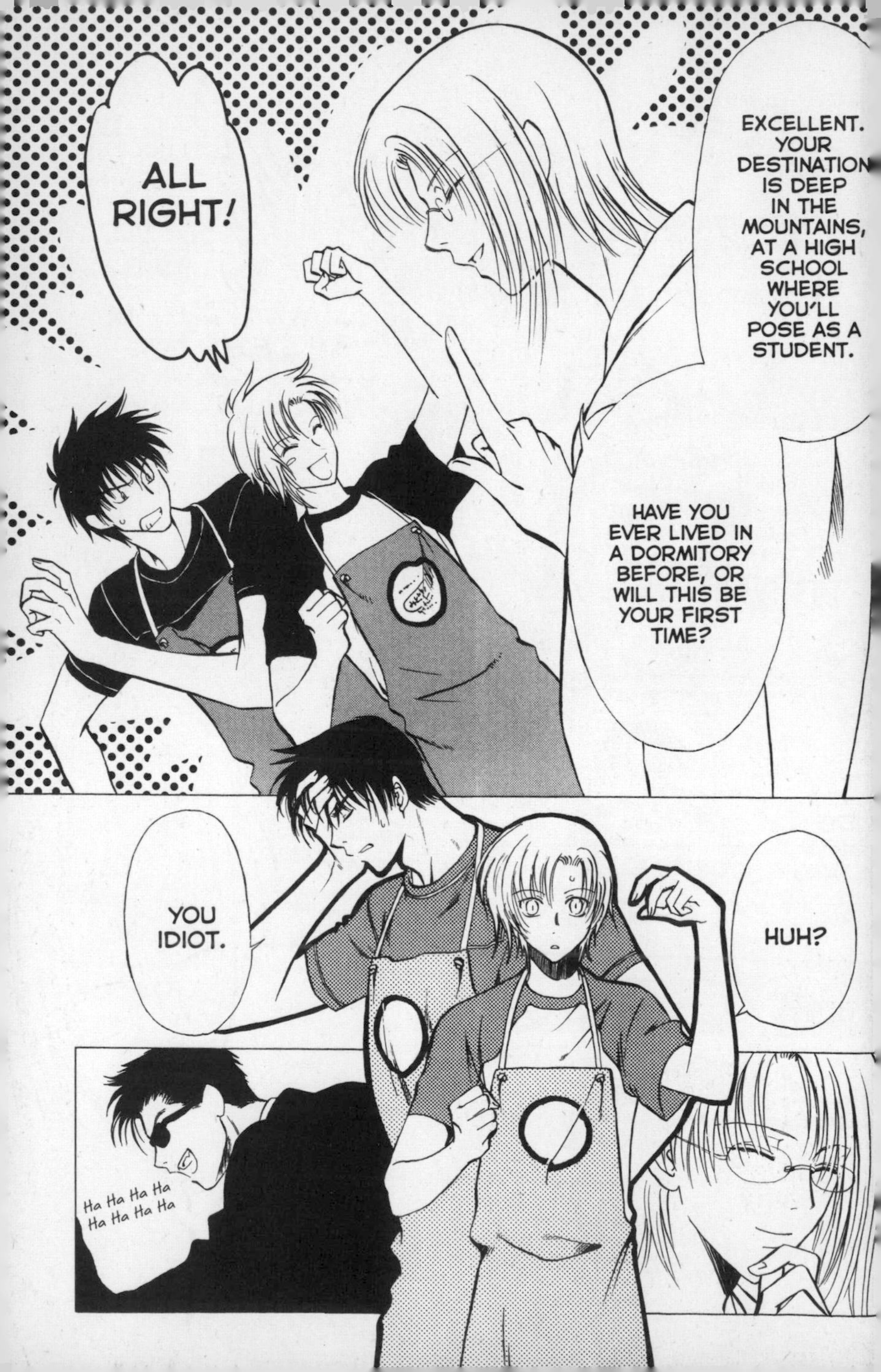
EXCELLENT. YOUR DESTINATION IS DEEP IN THE MOUNTAINS, AT A HIGH SCHOOL WHERE YOU'LL POSE AS A STUDENT.
ALL RIGHT!
HAVE YOU EVER LIVED IN A DORMITORY BEFORE, OR WILL THIS BE YOUR FIRST TIME?
HUH?
YOU IDIOT.
Ha Ha Ha Ha Ha Ha Ha Ha Ha

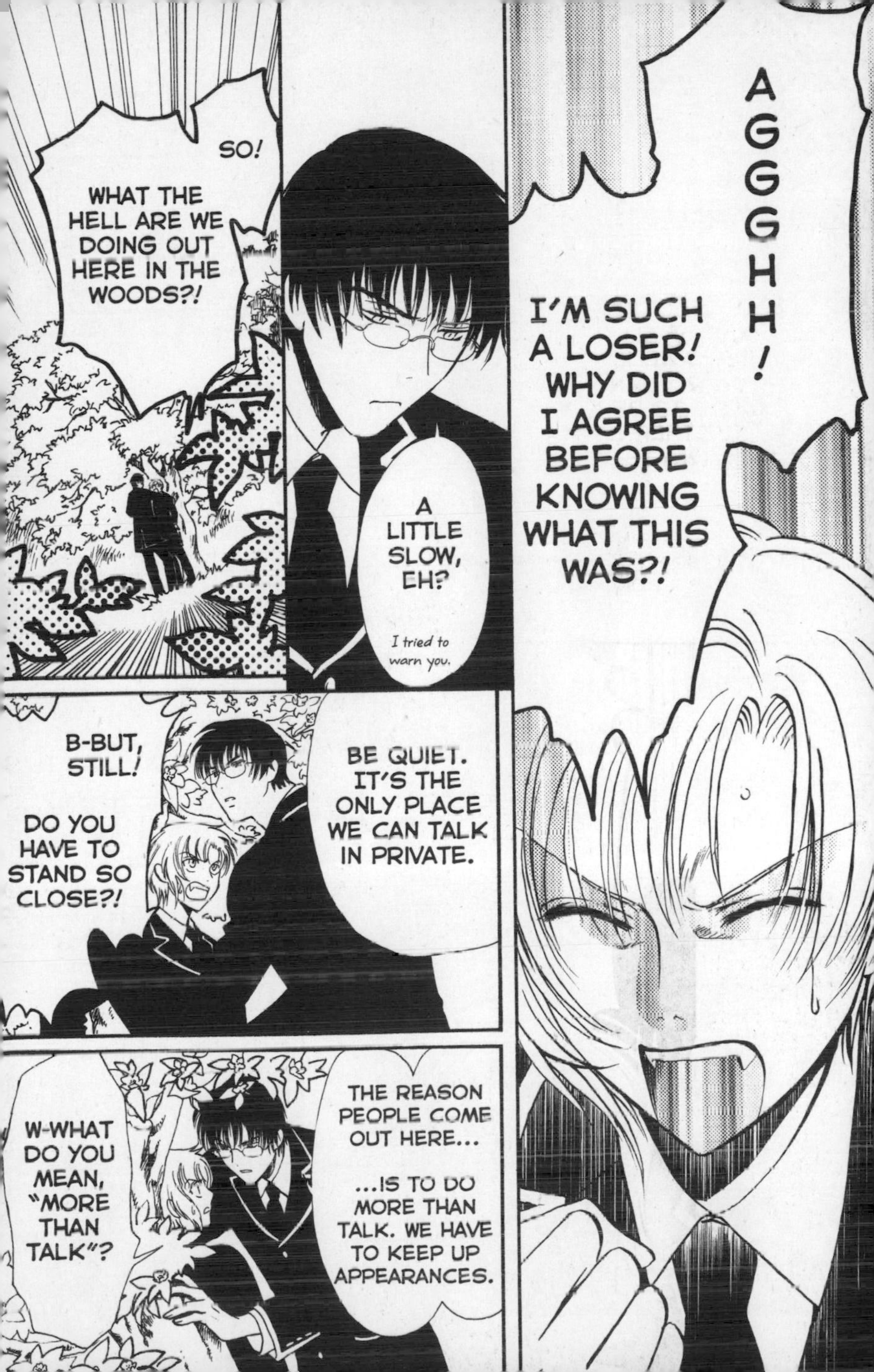
AGGGH!
I'M SUCH A LOSER! WHY DID I AGREE BEFORE KNOWING WHAT THIS WAS?!
A LITTLE SLOW, EH?
I tried to warn you.
SO!
WHAT THE HELL ARE WE DOING OUT HERE IN THE WOODS?!
BE QUIET. IT'S THE ONLY PLACE WE CAN TALK IN PRIVATE.
B-BUT, STILL!
DO YOU HAVE TO STAND SO CLOSE?!
THE REASON PEOPLE COME OUT HERE...
...IS TO DO MORE THAN TALK. WE HAVE TO KEEP UP APPEARANCES.
W-WHAT DO YOU MEAN, "MORE THAN TALK"?

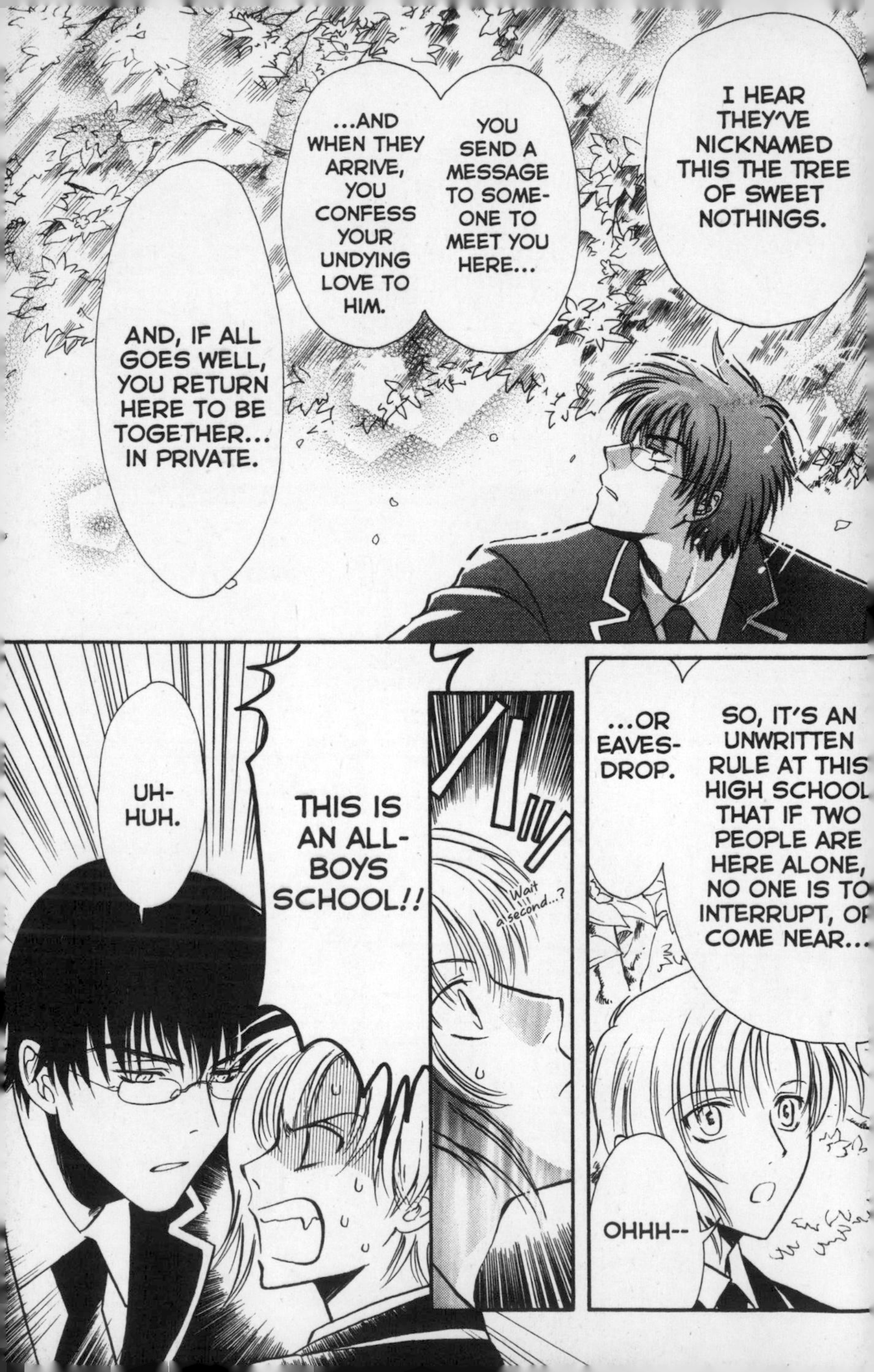
I HEAR THEY'VE NICKNAMED THIS THE TREE OF SWEET NOTHINGS.
YOU SEND A MESSAGE TO SOME-ONE TO MEET YOU HERE...
...AND WHEN THEY ARRIVE, YOU CONFESS YOUR UNDYING LOVE TO HIM.
AND, IF ALL GOES WELL, YOU RETURN HERE TO BE TOGETHER... IN PRIVATE.
SO, IT'S AN UNWRITTEN RULE AT THIS HIGH SCHOOL THAT IF TWO PEOPLE ARE HERE ALONE, NO ONE IS TO INTERRUPT, OR COME NEAR...
...OR EAVES-DROP.
OHHH--
Wait a second...?
THIS IS AN ALL-BOYS SCHOOL!!
UH-HUH.

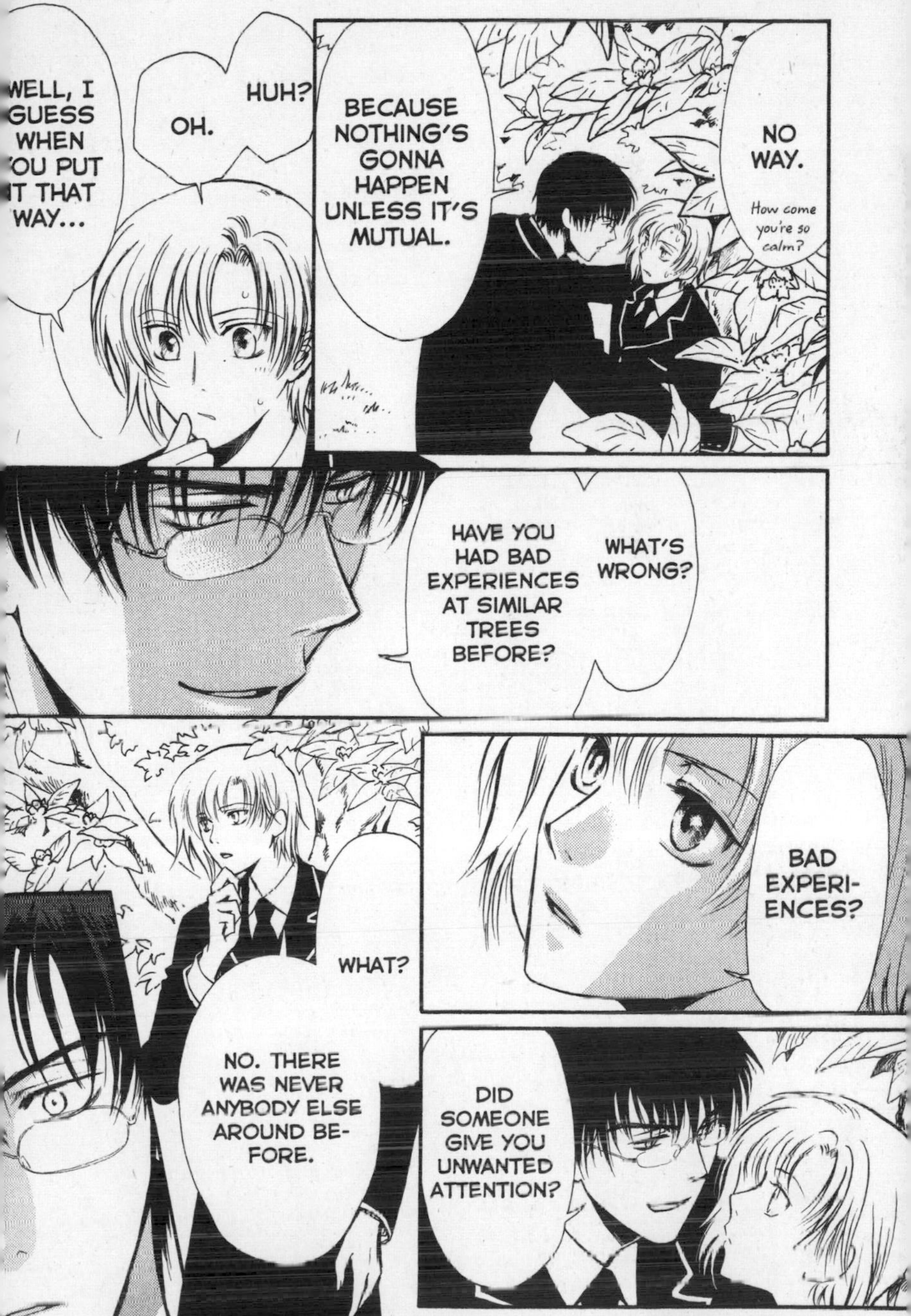
NO WAY.
How come you're so calm?
BECAUSE NOTHING'S GONNA HAPPEN UNLESS IT'S MUTUAL.
HUH?
OH.
WELL, I GUESS WHEN YOU PUT IT THAT WAY...
WHAT'S WRONG?
HAVE YOU HAD BAD EXPERIENCES AT SIMILAR TREES BEFORE?
BAD EXPERI-ENCES?
DID SOMEONE GIVE YOU UNWANTED ATTENTION?
WHAT?
NO. THERE WAS NEVER ANYBODY ELSE AROUND BE-FORE.

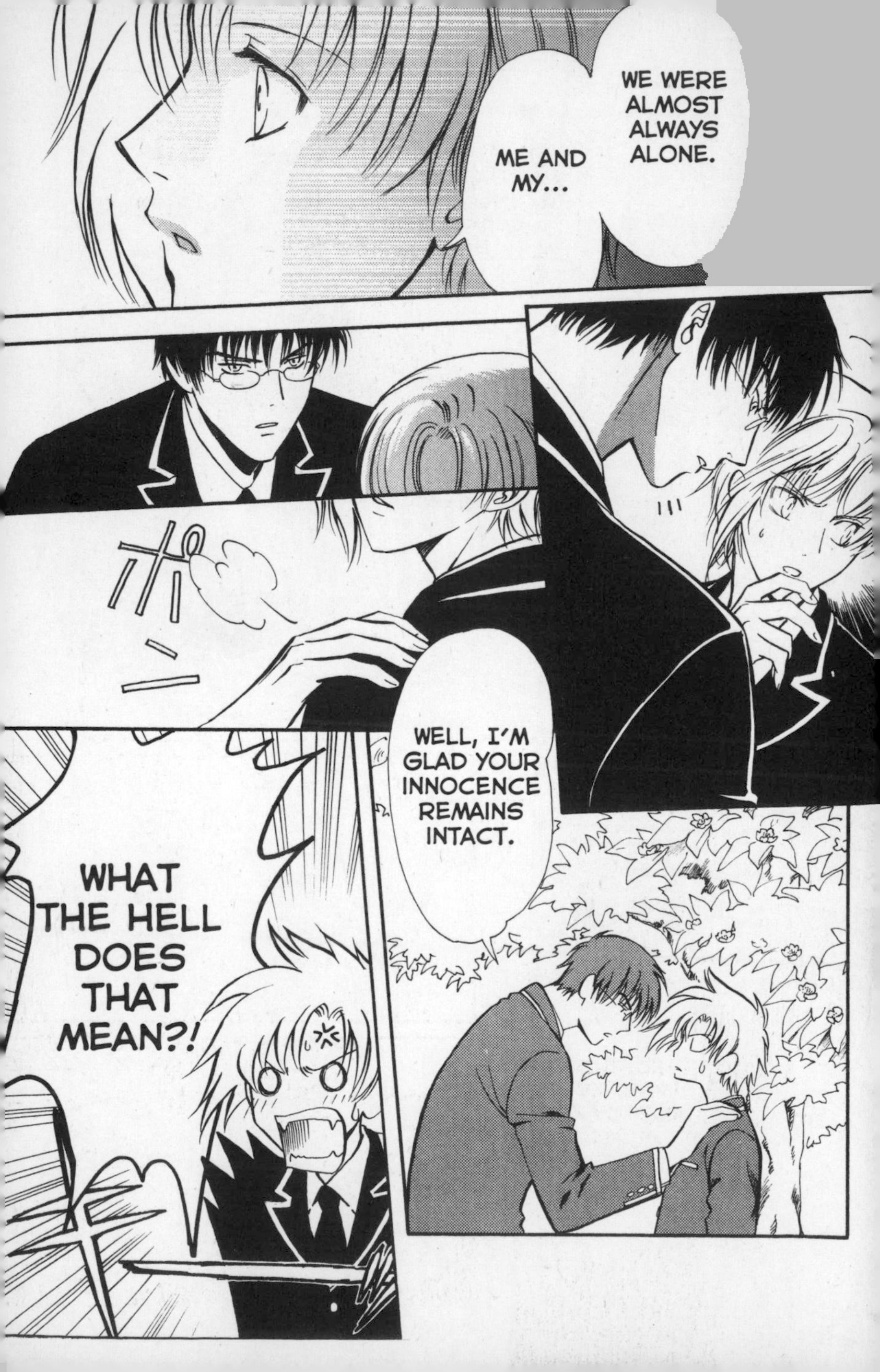
ME AND MY...
WE WERE ALMOST ALWAYS ALONE.
WELL, I'M GLAD YOUR INNOCENCE REMAINS INTACT.
WHAT THE HELL DOES THAT MEAN?!

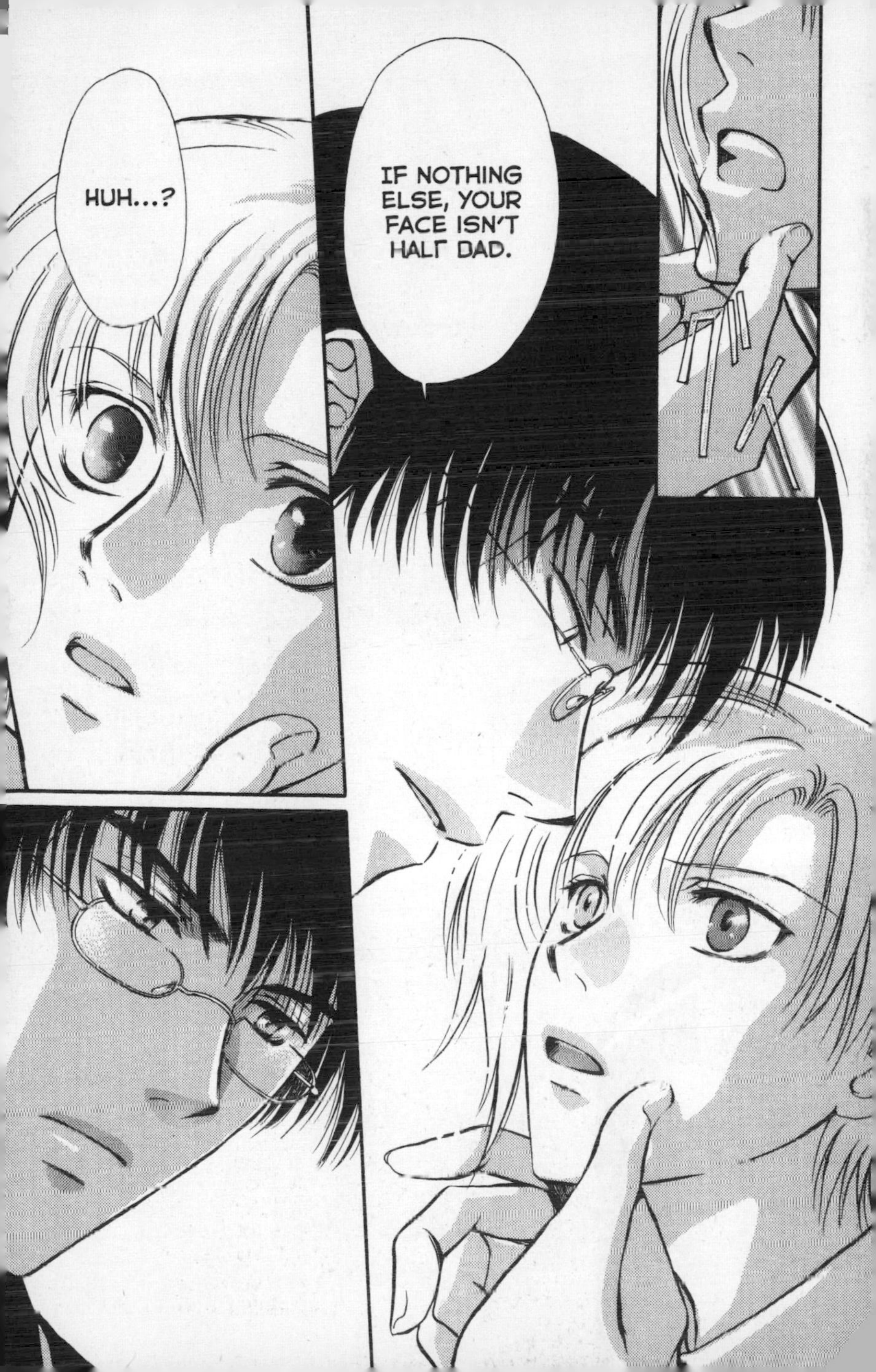
IF NOTHING ELSE, YOUR FACE ISN'T HALF BAD.
HUH...?

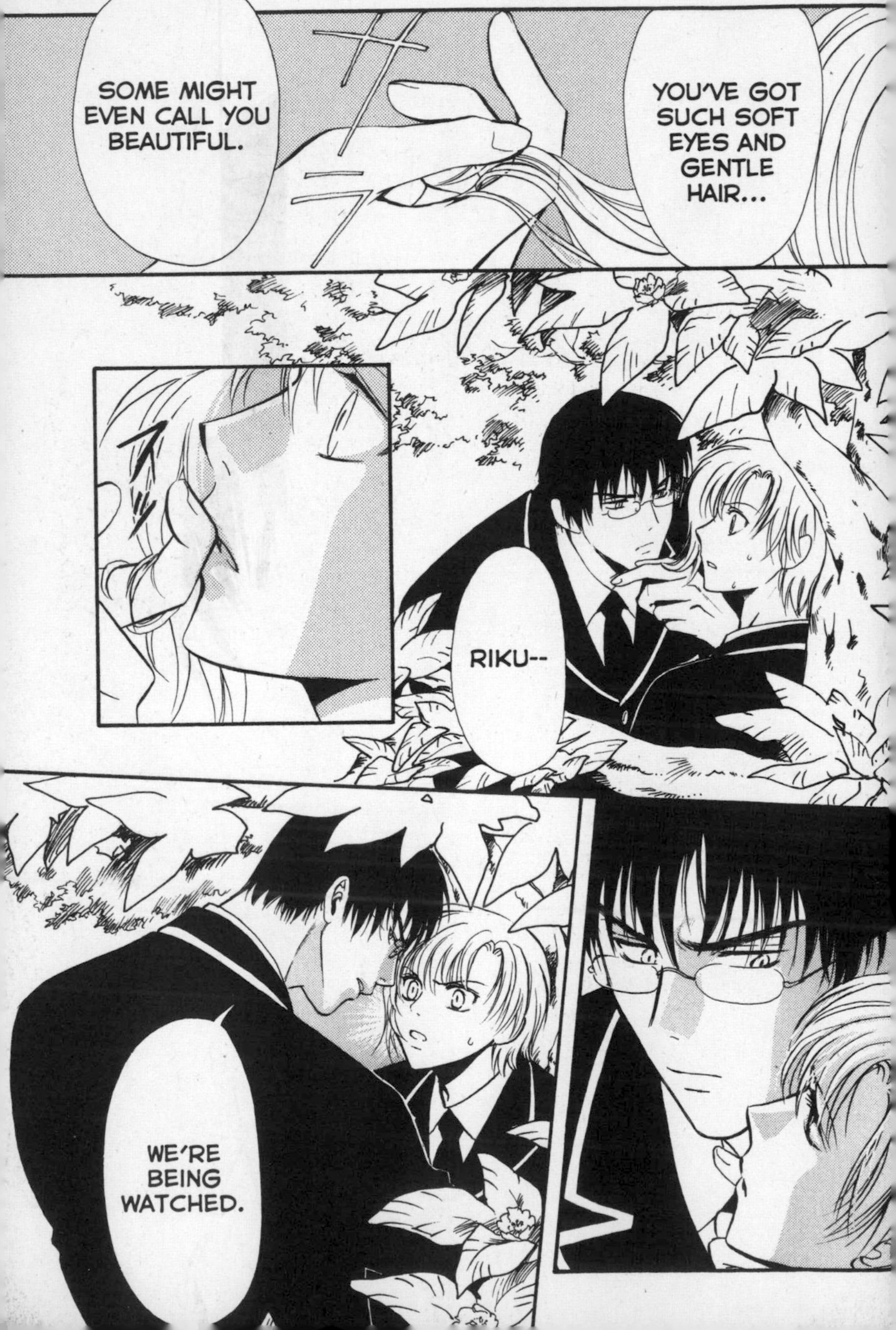
YOU'VE GOT SUCH SOFT EYES AND GENTLE HAIR...
SOME MIGHT EVEN CALL YOU BEAUTIFUL.
RIKU--
WE'RE BEING WATCHED.

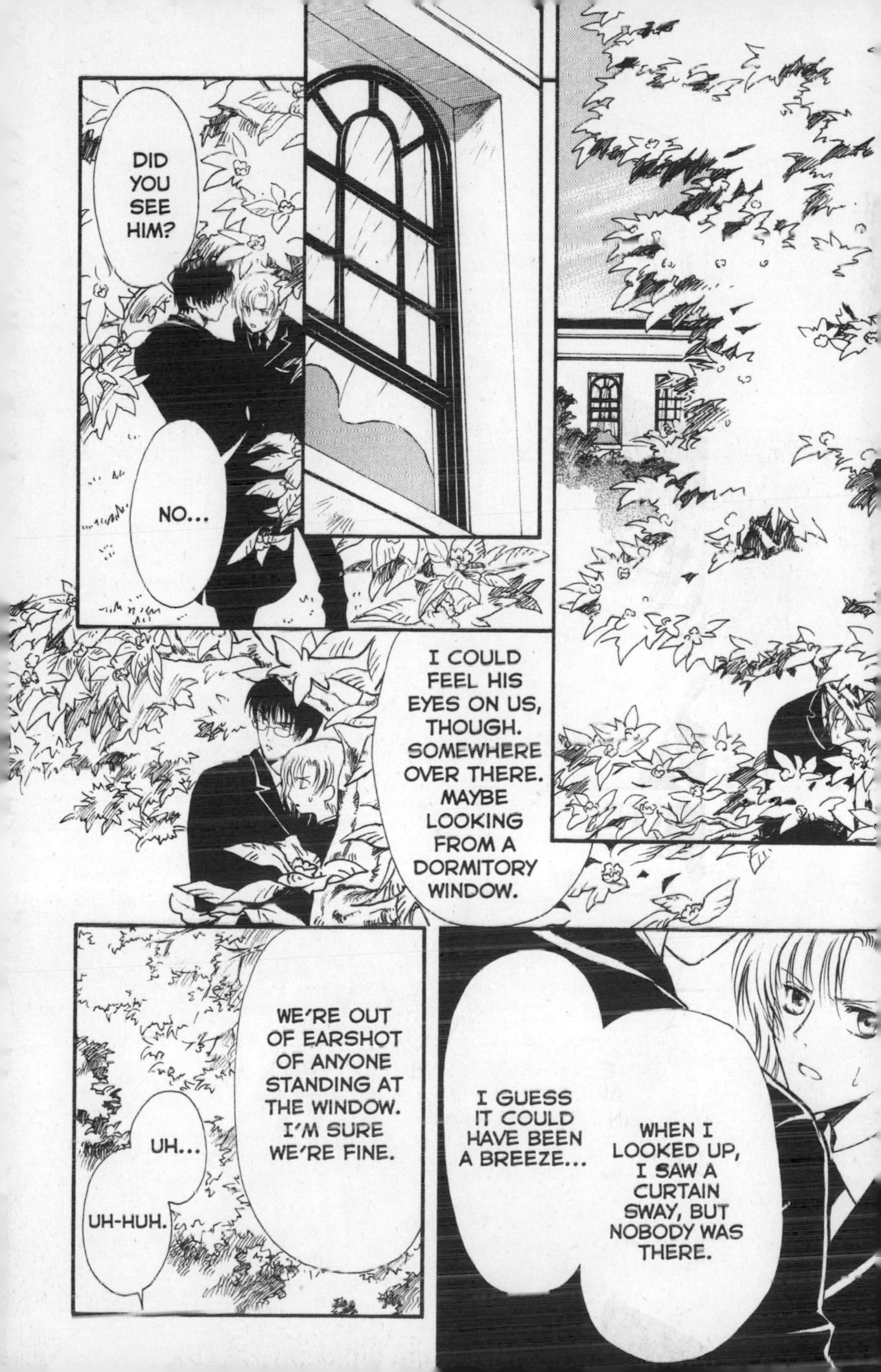
DID YOU SEE HIM?
NO...
I COULD FEEL HIS EYES ON US, THOUGH. SOMEWHERE OVER THERE. MAYBE LOOKING FROM A DORMITORY WINDOW.
WHEN I LOOKED UP, I SAW A CURTAIN SWAY, BUT NOBODY WAS THERE.
I GUESS IT COULD HAVE BEEN A BREEZE...
WE'RE OUT OF EARSHOT OF ANYONE STANDING AT THE WINDOW. I'M SURE WE'RE FINE.
UH...
UH-HUH.

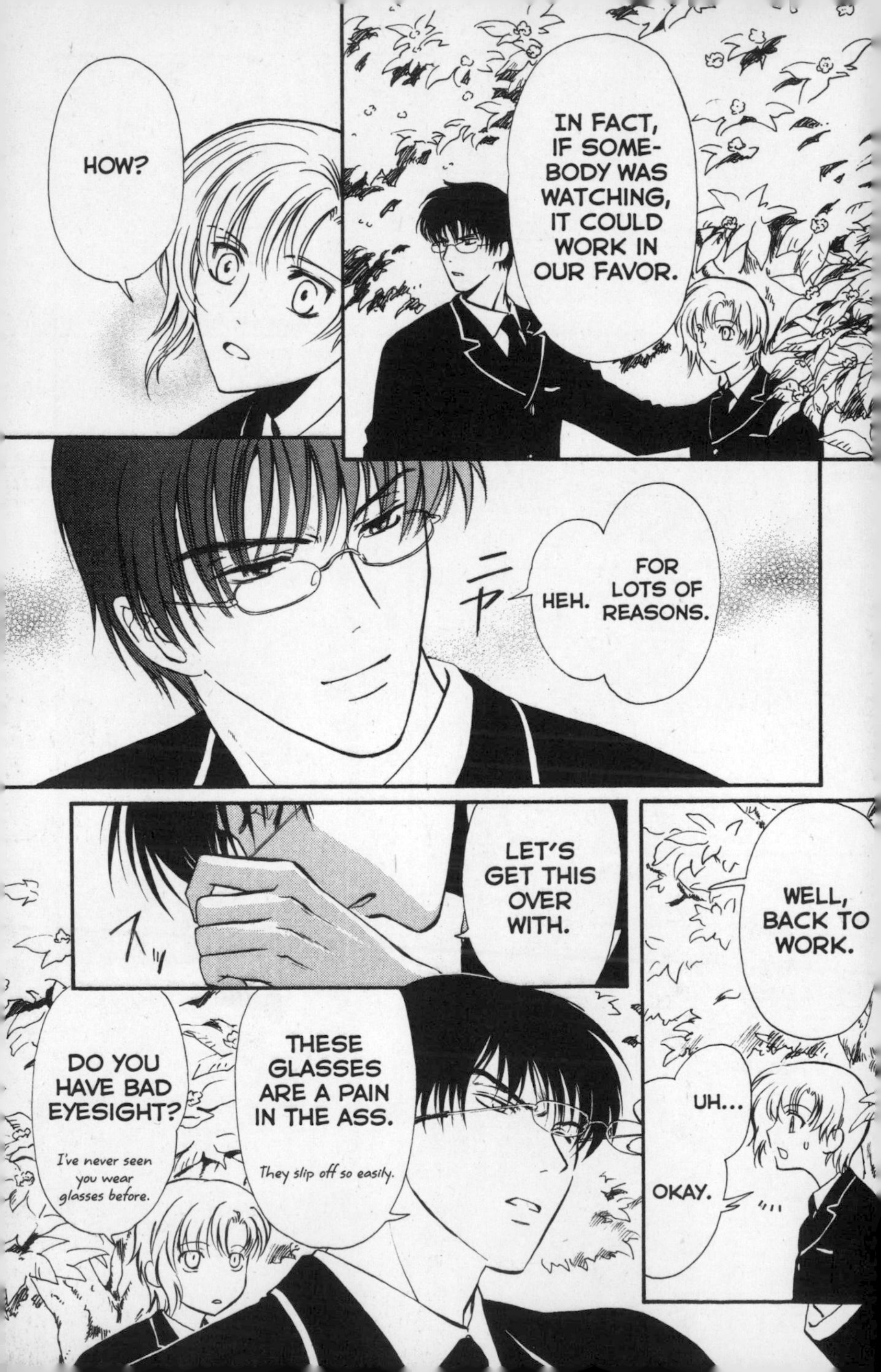
IN FACT, IF SOMEBODY WAS WATCHING, IT COULD WORK IN OUR FAVOR.
HOW?
ニヤ
HEH.
FOR LOTS OF REASONS.
WELL, BACK TO WORK.
UH...
OKAY.
LET'S GET THIS OVER WITH.
スッ
THESE GLASSES ARE A PAIN IN THE ASS.
They slip off so easily.
DO YOU HAVE BAD EYESIGHT?
I've never seen you wear glasses before.

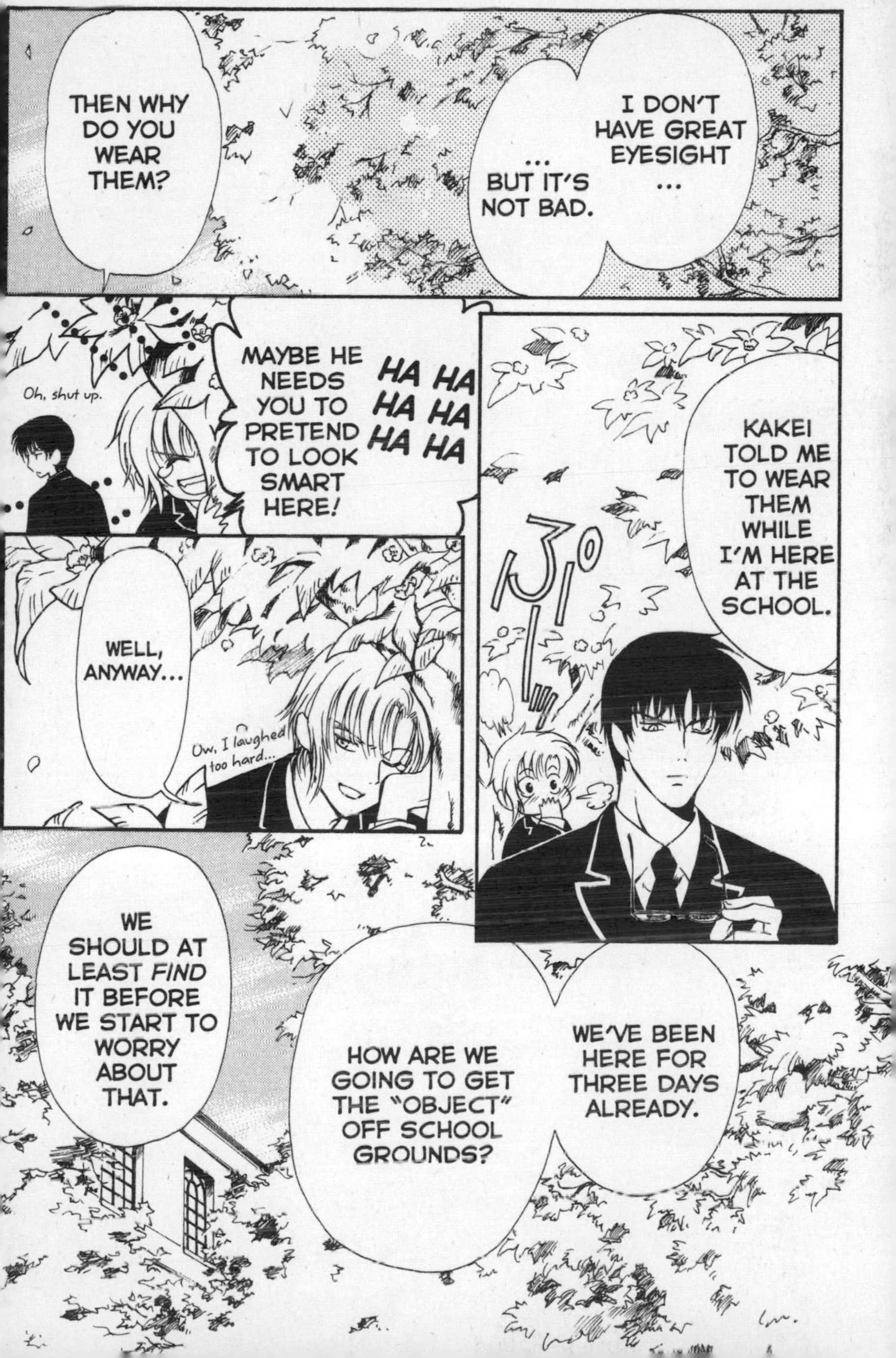
I DON'T HAVE GREAT EYESIGHT ...
... BUT IT'S NOT BAD.
THEN WHY DO YOU WEAR THEM?
KAKEI TOLD ME TO WEAR THEM WHILE I'M HERE AT THE SCHOOL.
ぷ
MAYBE HE NEEDS YOU TO PRETEND TO LOOK SMART HERE!
HA HA HA HA HA HA
Oh, shut up.
WELL, ANYWAY...
Ow, I laughed too hard...
WE'VE BEEN HERE FOR THREE DAYS ALREADY.
HOW ARE WE GOING TO GET THE "OBJECT" OFF SCHOOL GROUNDS?
WE SHOULD AT LEAST *FIND* IT BEFORE WE START TO WORRY ABOUT THAT.

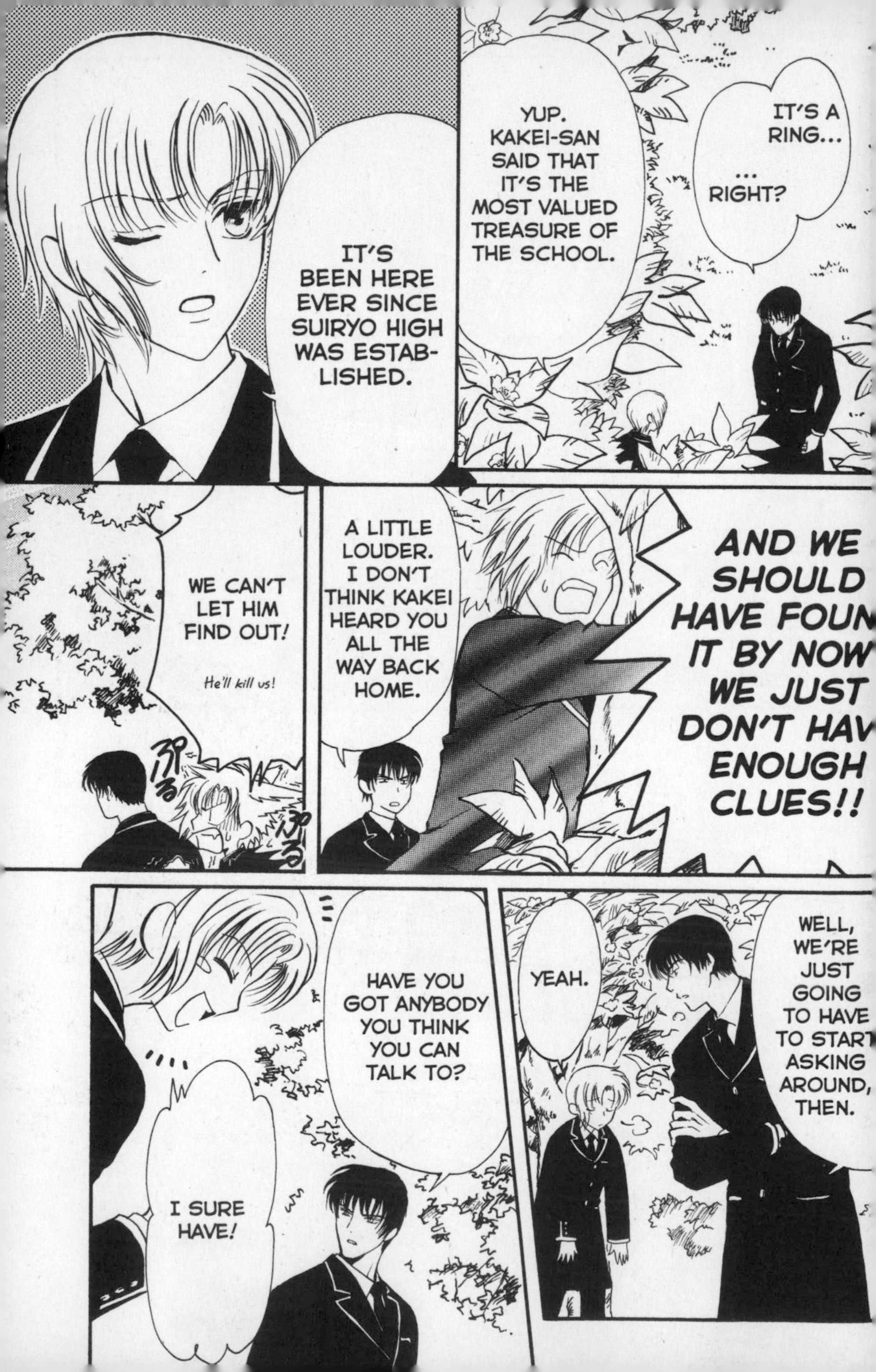
IT'S A RING... ... RIGHT?
YUP. KAKEI-SAN SAID THAT IT'S THE MOST VALUED TREASURE OF THE SCHOOL.
IT'S BEEN HERE EVER SINCE SUIRYO HIGH WAS ESTAB-LISHED.
AND WE SHOULD HAVE FOUN IT BY NOW WE JUST DON'T HAV ENOUGH CLUES!!
A LITTLE LOUDER. I DON'T THINK KAKEI HEARD YOU ALL THE WAY BACK HOME.
WE CAN'T LET HIM FIND OUT!
He'll kill us!
WELL, WE'RE JUST GOING TO HAVE TO START ASKING AROUND, THEN.
YEAH.
HAVE YOU GOT ANYBODY YOU THINK YOU CAN TALK TO?
...
I SURE HAVE!

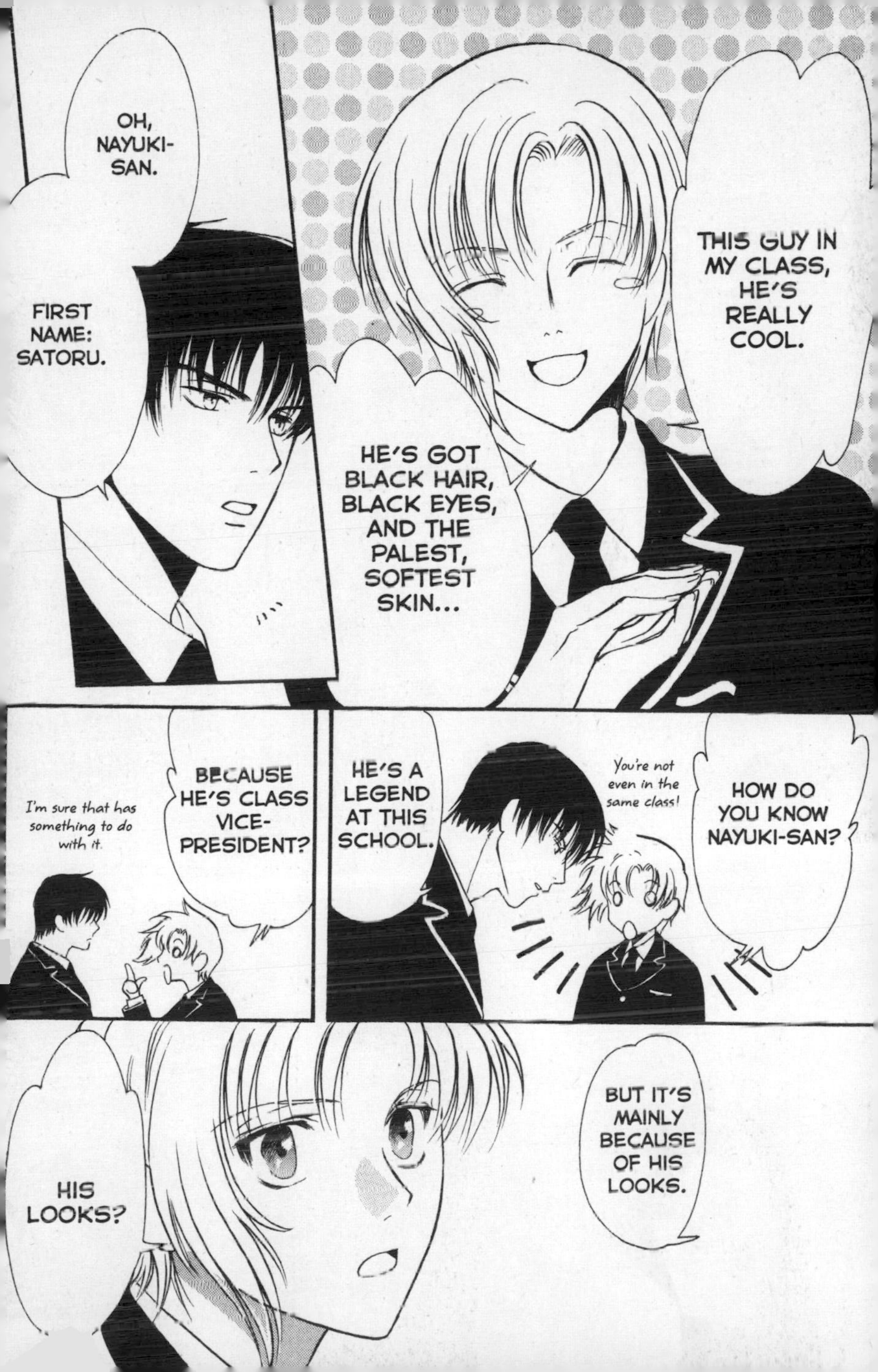
THIS GUY IN MY CLASS, HE'S REALLY COOL.
HE'S GOT BLACK HAIR, BLACK EYES, AND THE PALEST, SOFTEST SKIN...
OH, NAYUKI-SAN.
FIRST NAME: SATORU.
HOW DO YOU KNOW NAYUKI-SAN?
You're not even in the same class!
HE'S A LEGEND AT THIS SCHOOL.
BECAUSE HE'S CLASS VICE-PRESIDENT?
I'm sure that has something to do with it.
BUT IT'S MAINLY BECAUSE OF HIS LOOKS.
HIS LOOKS?

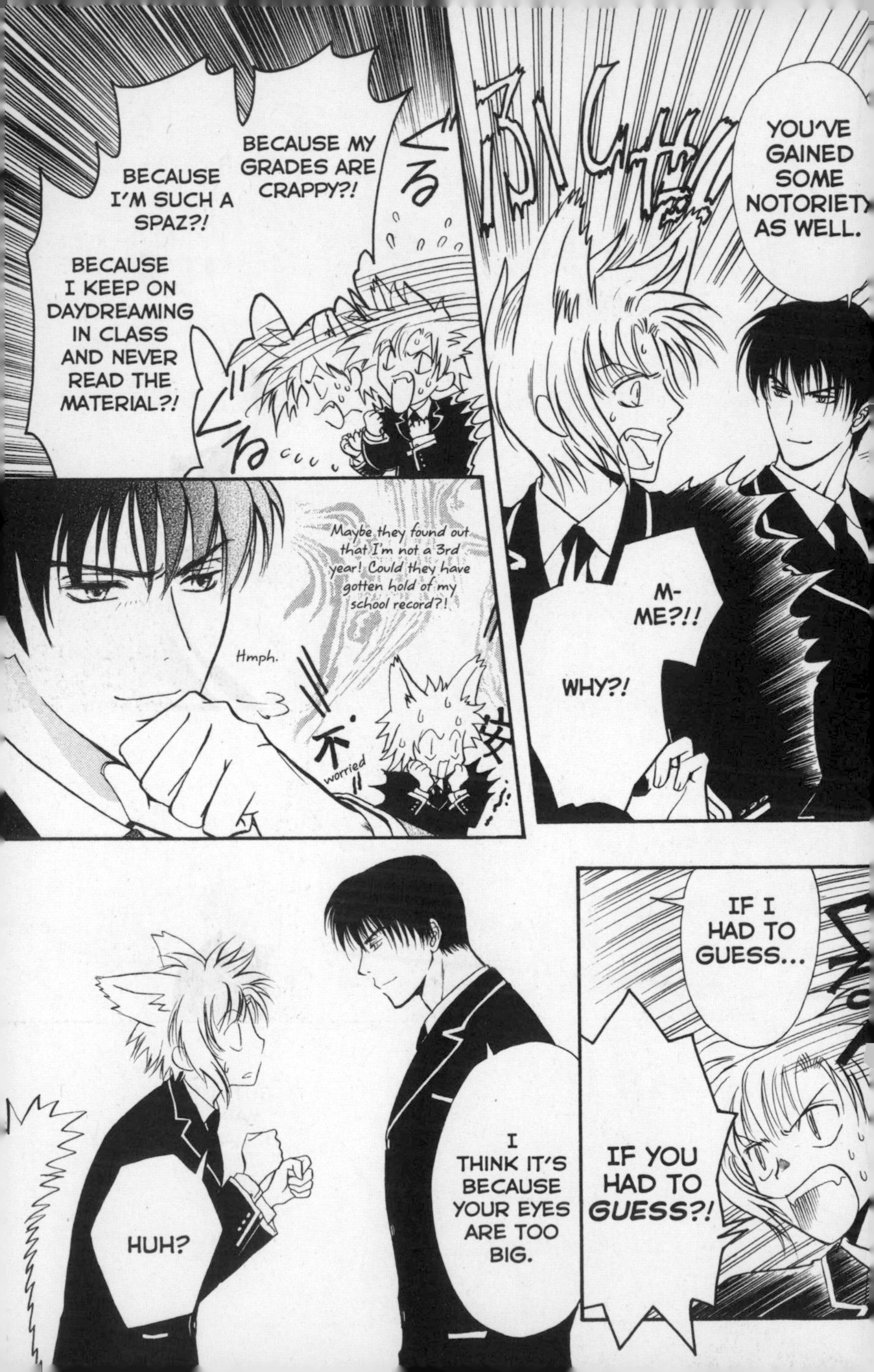
YOU'VE GAINED SOME NOTORIETY AS WELL.
M-ME?!!
WHY?!
BECAUSE MY GRADES ARE CRAPPY?!
BECAUSE I'M SUCH A SPAZ?!
BECAUSE I KEEP ON DAYDREAMING IN CLASS AND NEVER READ THE MATERIAL?!
Maybe they found out that I'm not a 3rd year! Could they have gotten hold of my school record?!
Hmph.
worried
IF I HAD TO GUESS...
IF YOU HAD TO GUESS?!
I THINK IT'S BECAUSE YOUR EYES ARE TOO BIG.
HUH?

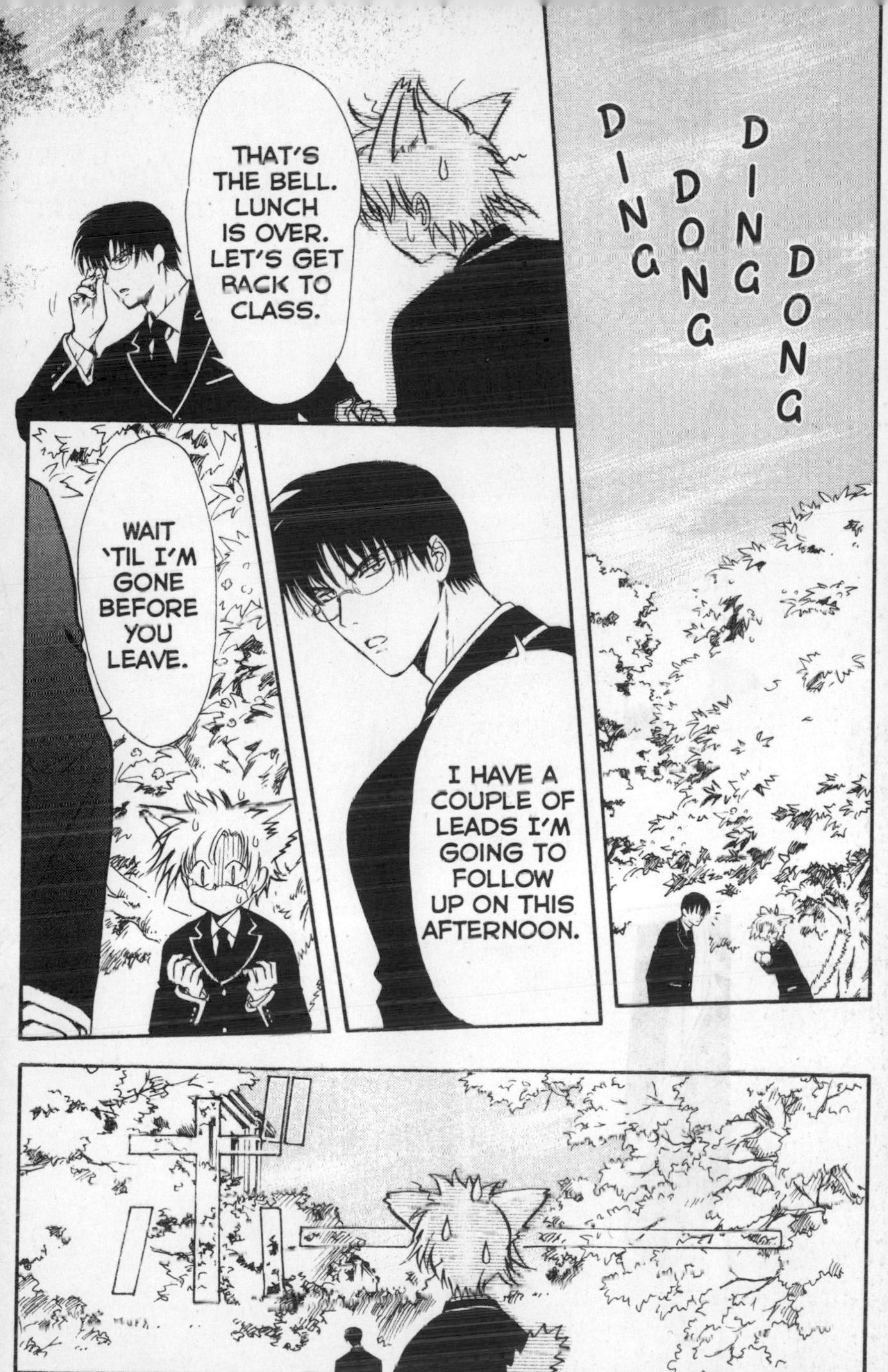
DING
DONG
DING
DONG
THAT'S THE BELL. LUNCH IS OVER. LET'S GET RACK TO CLASS.
I HAVE A COUPLE OF LEADS I'M GOING TO FOLLOW UP ON THIS AFTERNOON.
WAIT 'TIL I'M GONE BEFORE YOU LEAVE.

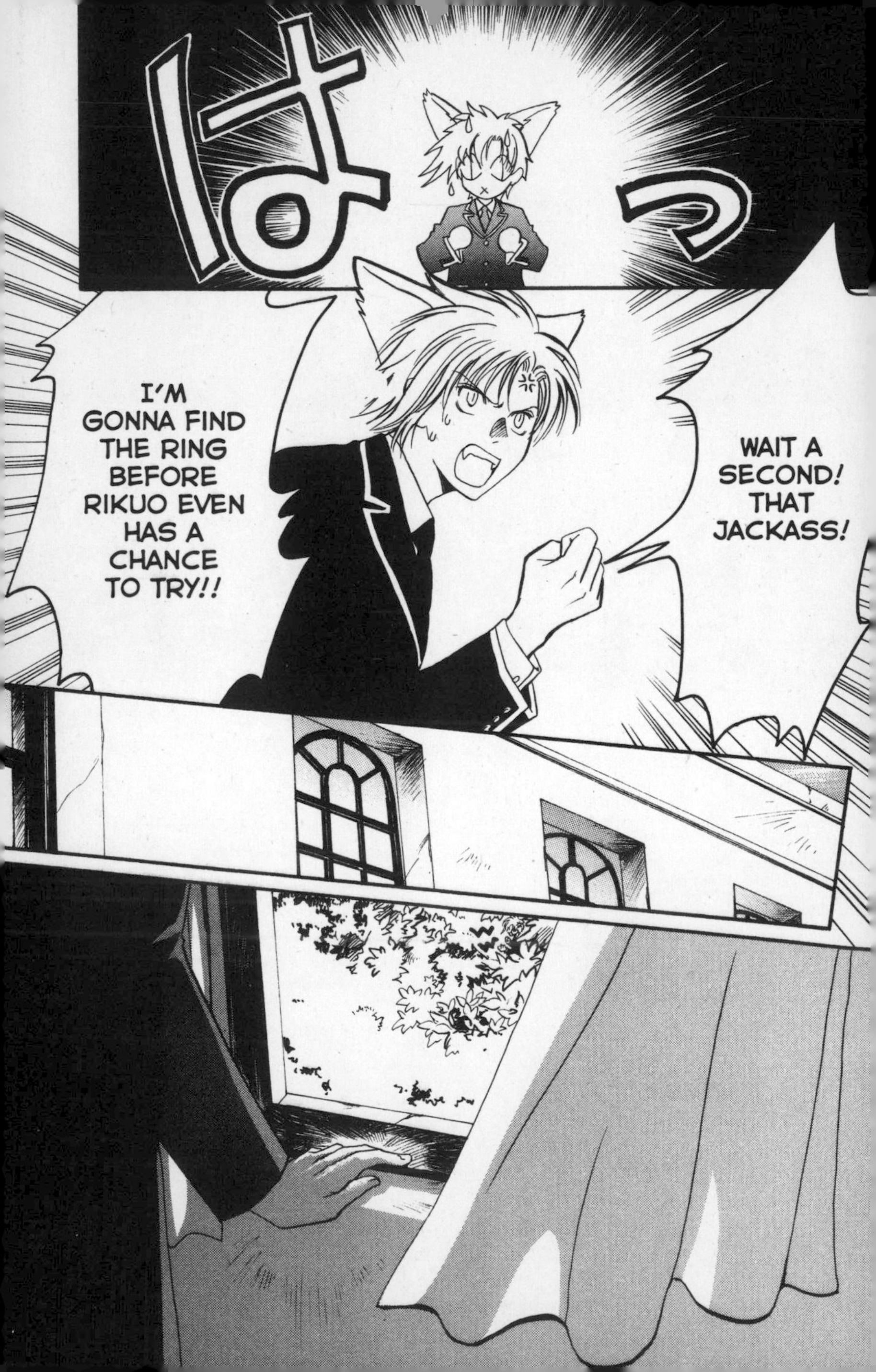
はっ
WAIT A SECOND! THAT JACKASS!
I'M GONNA FIND THE RING BEFORE RIKUO EVEN HAS A CHANCE TO TRY!!

合法ドラッグ
LEGAL DRUG

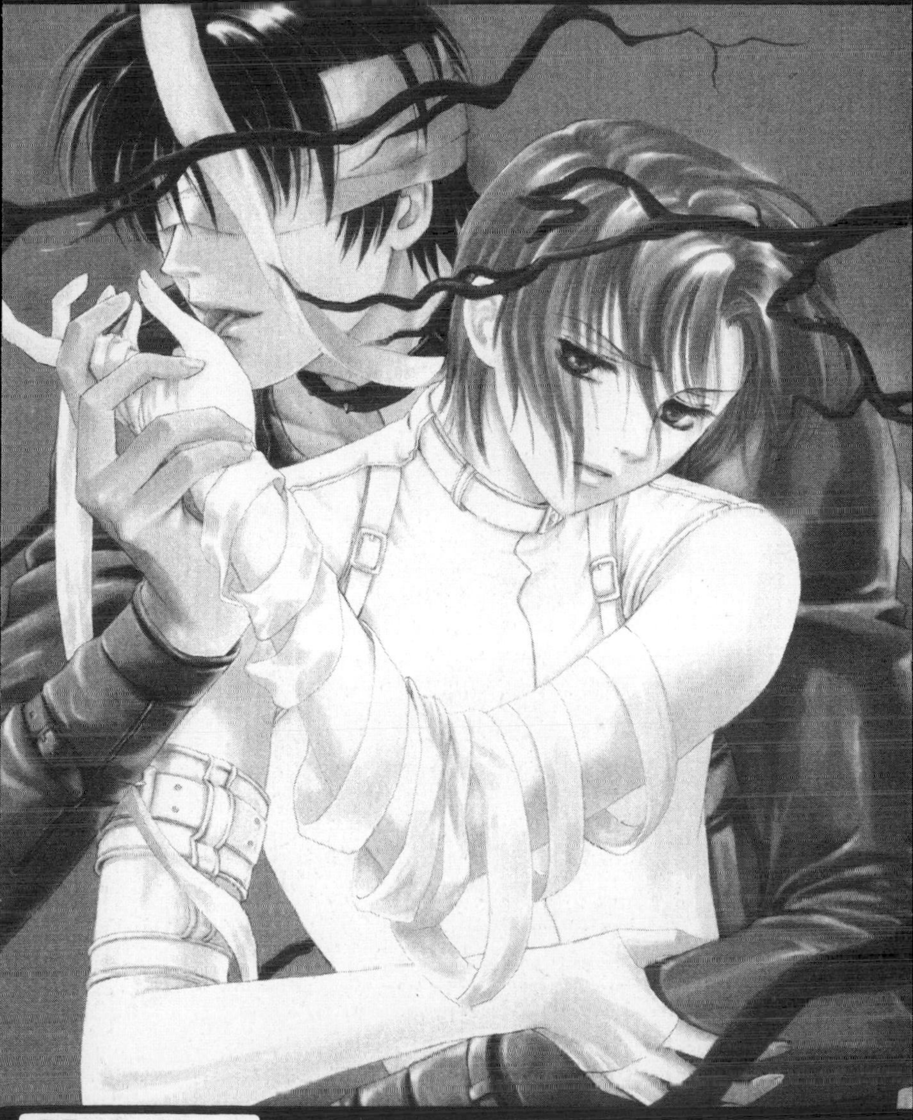

DRUG NO.12 Daily use of the drug may cause poisoning.

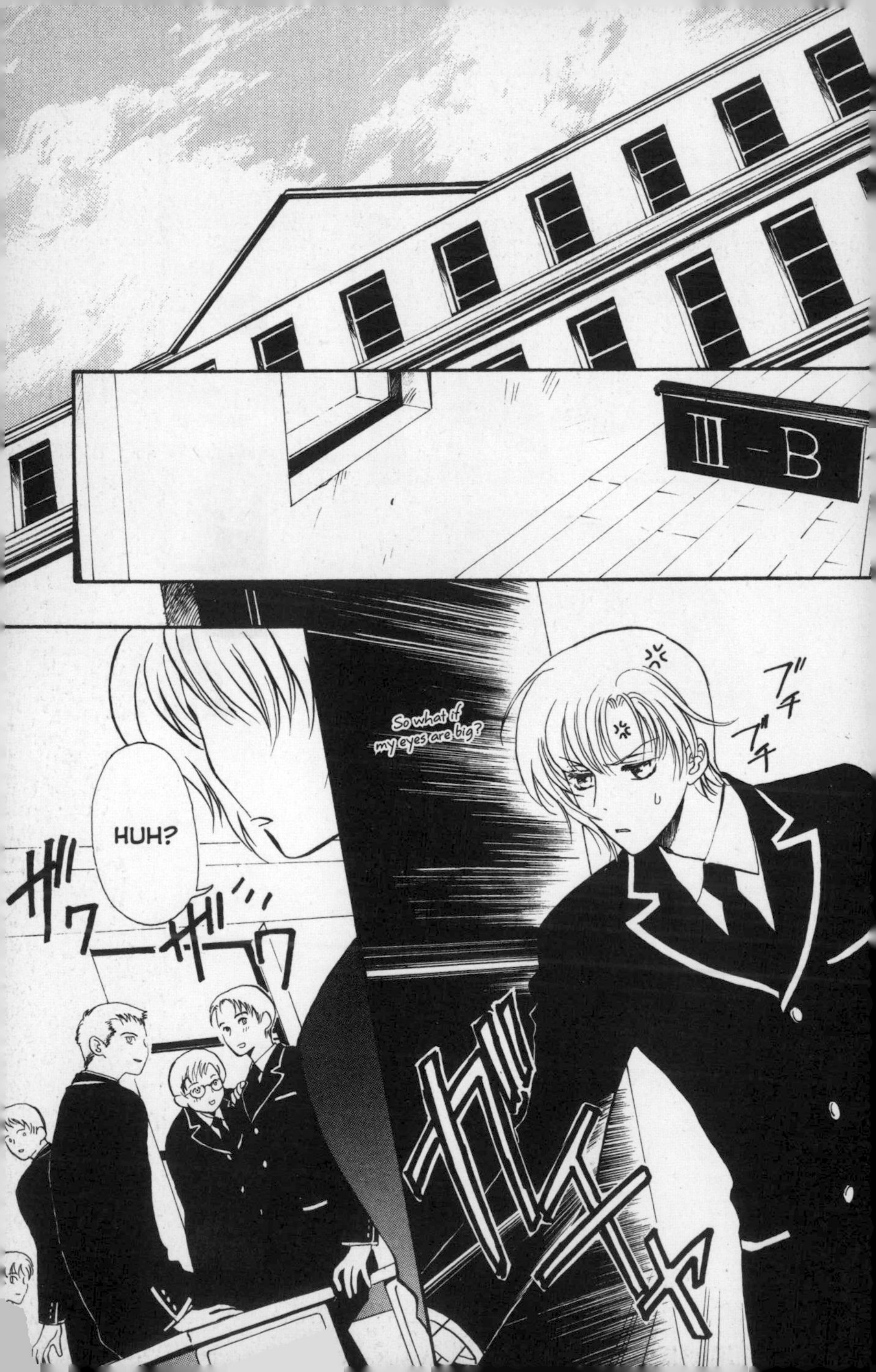
III-B
ブチ ブチ
So what if my eyes are big?
HUH?
ザワー ザワ

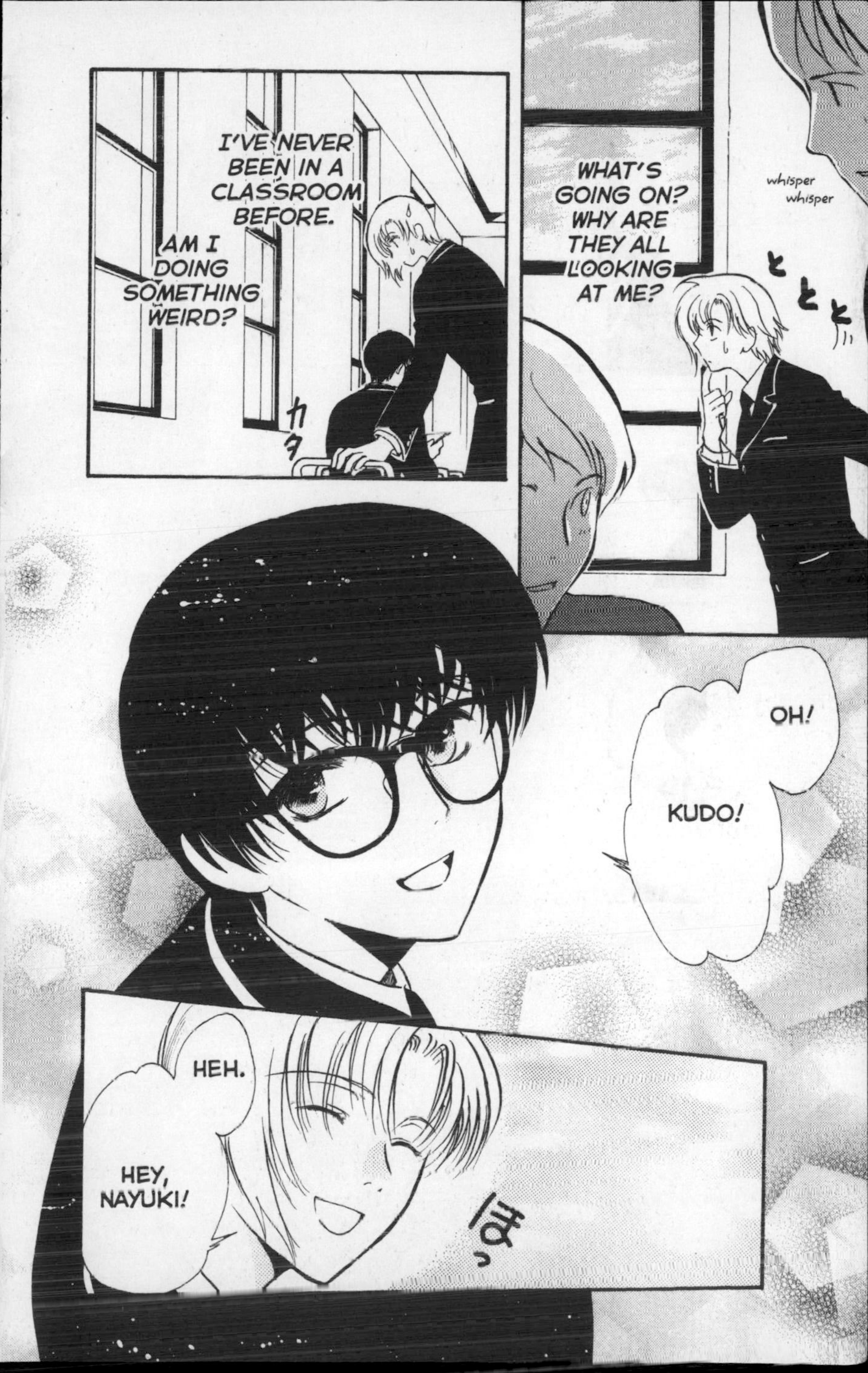
whisper whisper
WHAT'S GOING ON? WHY ARE THEY ALL LOOKING AT ME?
とととと
I'VE NEVER BEEN IN A CLASSROOM BEFORE.
AM I DOING SOMETHING WEIRD?
カタ
OH!
KUDO!
HEH.
HEY, NAYUKI!
ほっ

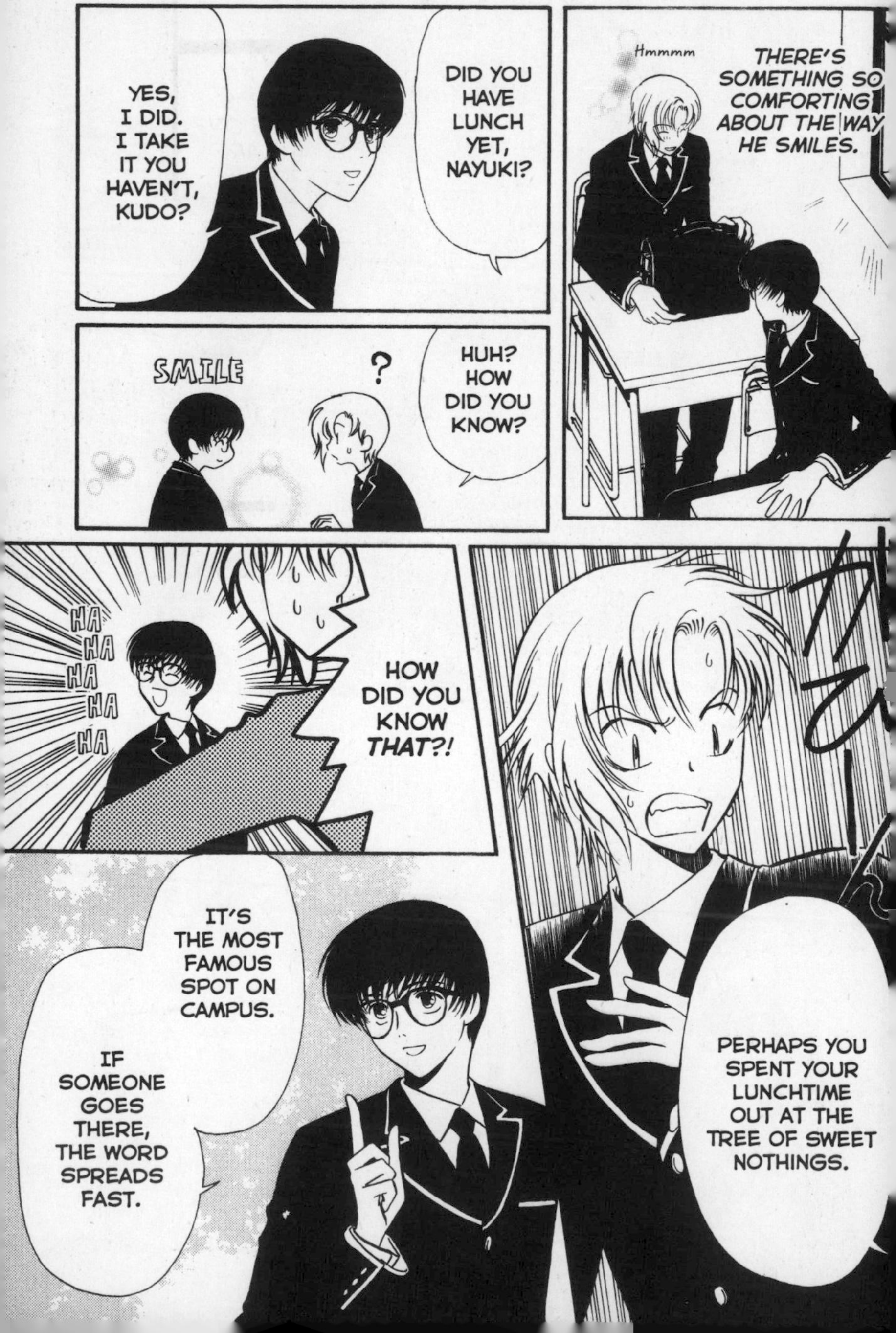
Hmmmm
THERE'S SOMETHING SO COMFORTING ABOUT THE WAY HE SMILES.
DID YOU HAVE LUNCH YET, NAYUKI?
YES, I DID. I TAKE IT YOU HAVEN'T, KUDO?
HUH? HOW DID YOU KNOW?
?
SMILE
PERHAPS YOU SPENT YOUR LUNCHTIME OUT AT THE TREE OF SWEET NOTHINGS.
HOW DID YOU KNOW *THAT?!*
HA HA HA HA HA
IT'S THE MOST FAMOUS SPOT ON CAMPUS.
IF SOMEONE GOES THERE, THE WORD SPREADS FAST.

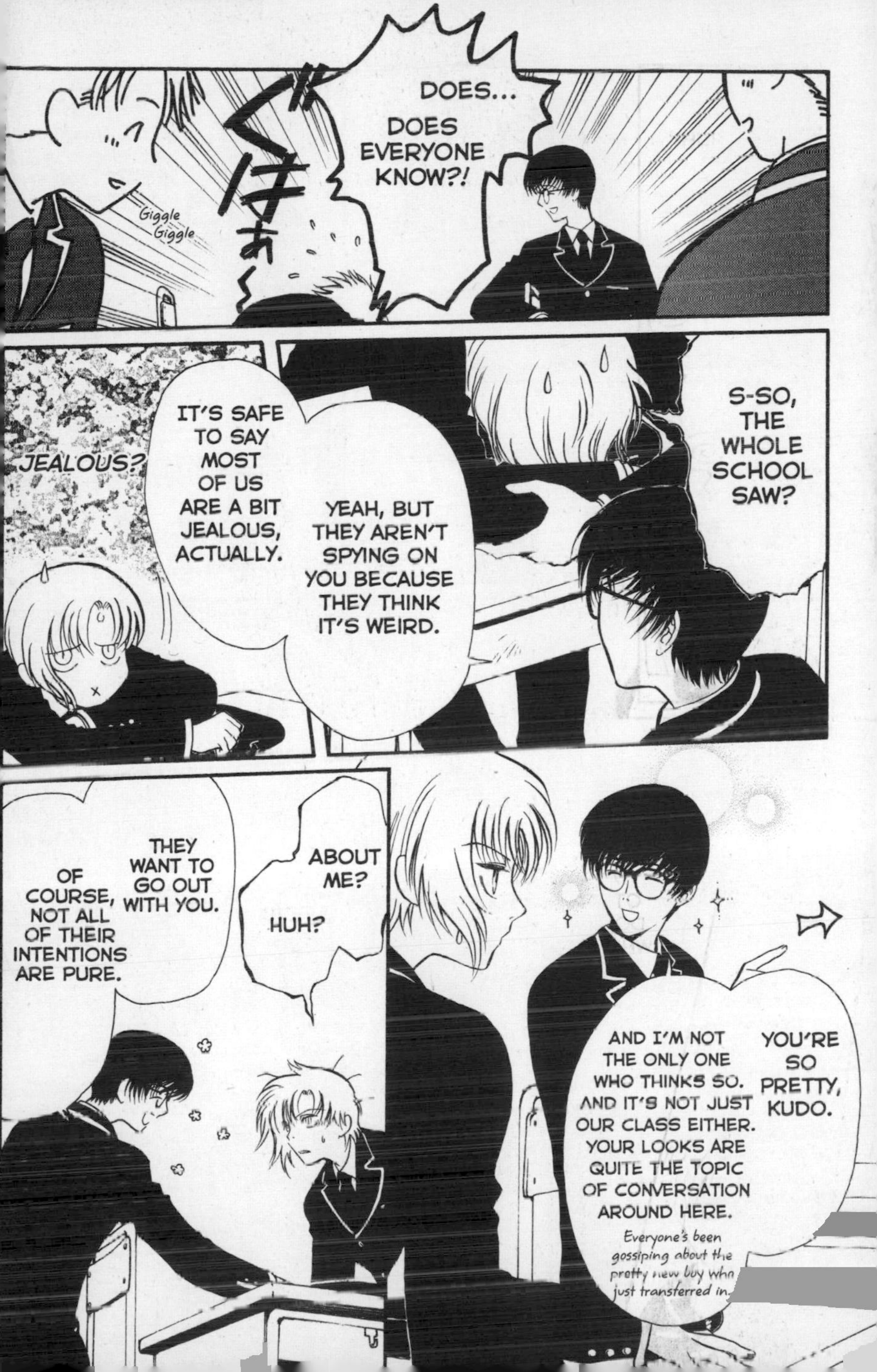

DOES...
DOES EVERYONE KNOW?!
Giggle Giggle
S-SO, THE WHOLE SCHOOL SAW?
YEAH, BUT THEY AREN'T SPYING ON YOU BECAUSE THEY THINK IT'S WEIRD.
IT'S SAFE TO SAY MOST OF US ARE A BIT JEALOUS, ACTUALLY.
JEALOUS?
YOU'RE SO PRETTY, KUDO.
AND I'M NOT THE ONLY ONE WHO THINKS SO. AND IT'S NOT JUST OUR CLASS EITHER. YOUR LOOKS ARE QUITE THE TOPIC OF CONVERSATION AROUND HERE.
Everyone's been gossiping about the pretty new boy who just transferred in.
ABOUT ME?
HUH?
THEY WANT TO GO OUT WITH YOU.
OF COURSE, NOT ALL OF THEIR INTENTIONS ARE PURE.

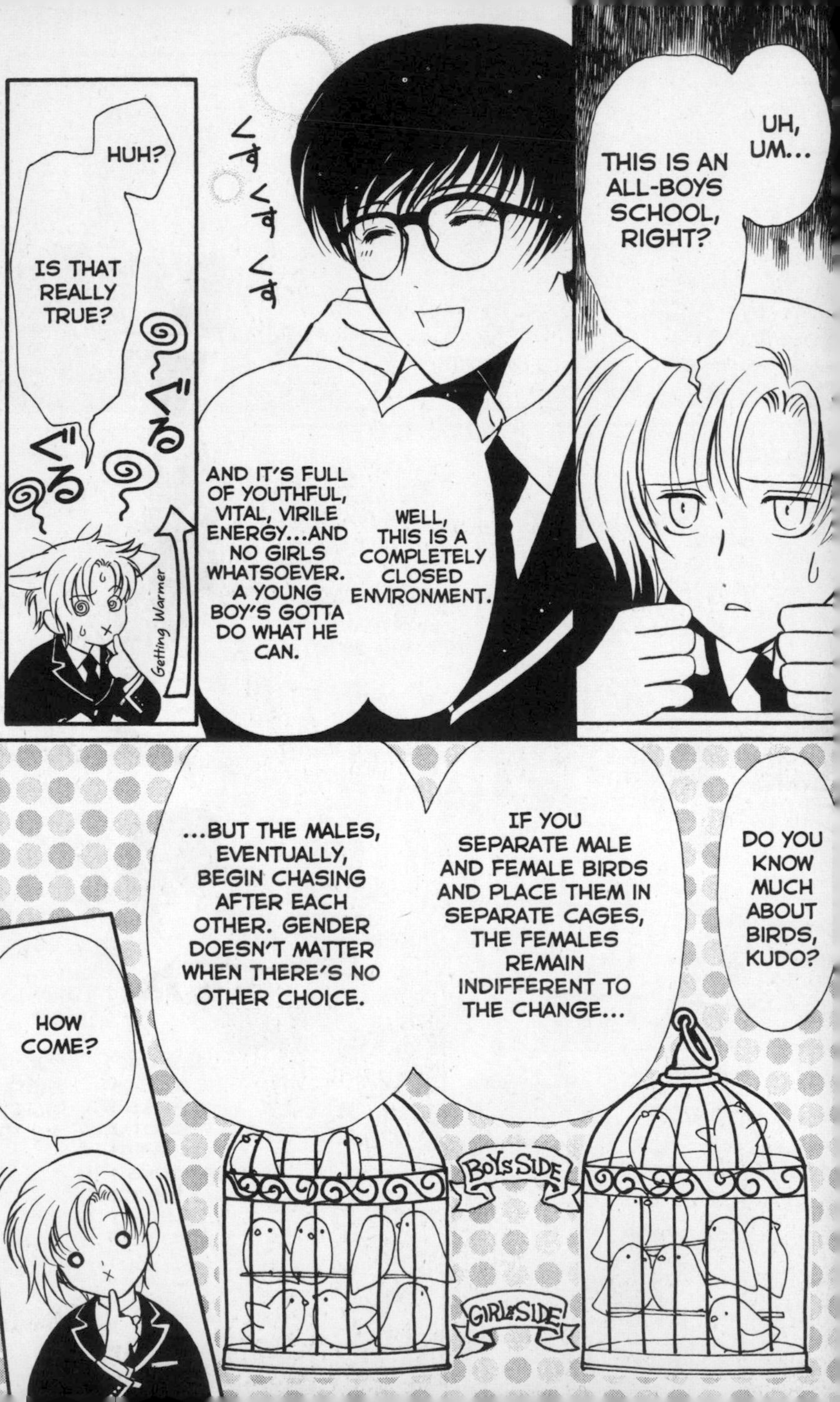
UH, UM...
THIS IS AN ALL-BOYS SCHOOL, RIGHT?
くすくすくす
WELL, THIS IS A COMPLETELY CLOSED ENVIRONMENT.
AND IT'S FULL OF YOUTHFUL, VITAL, VIRILE ENERGY...AND NO GIRLS WHATSOEVER. A YOUNG BOY'S GOTTA DO WHAT HE CAN.
HUH?
IS THAT REALLY TRUE?
ぐるぐる
Getting Warmer
DO YOU KNOW MUCH ABOUT BIRDS, KUDO?
IF YOU SEPARATE MALE AND FEMALE BIRDS AND PLACE THEM IN SEPARATE CAGES, THE FEMALES REMAIN INDIFFERENT TO THE CHANGE...
...BUT THE MALES, EVENTUALLY, BEGIN CHASING AFTER EACH OTHER. GENDER DOESN'T MATTER WHEN THERE'S NO OTHER CHOICE.
BOYS SIDE
GIRLS SIDE
HOW COME?

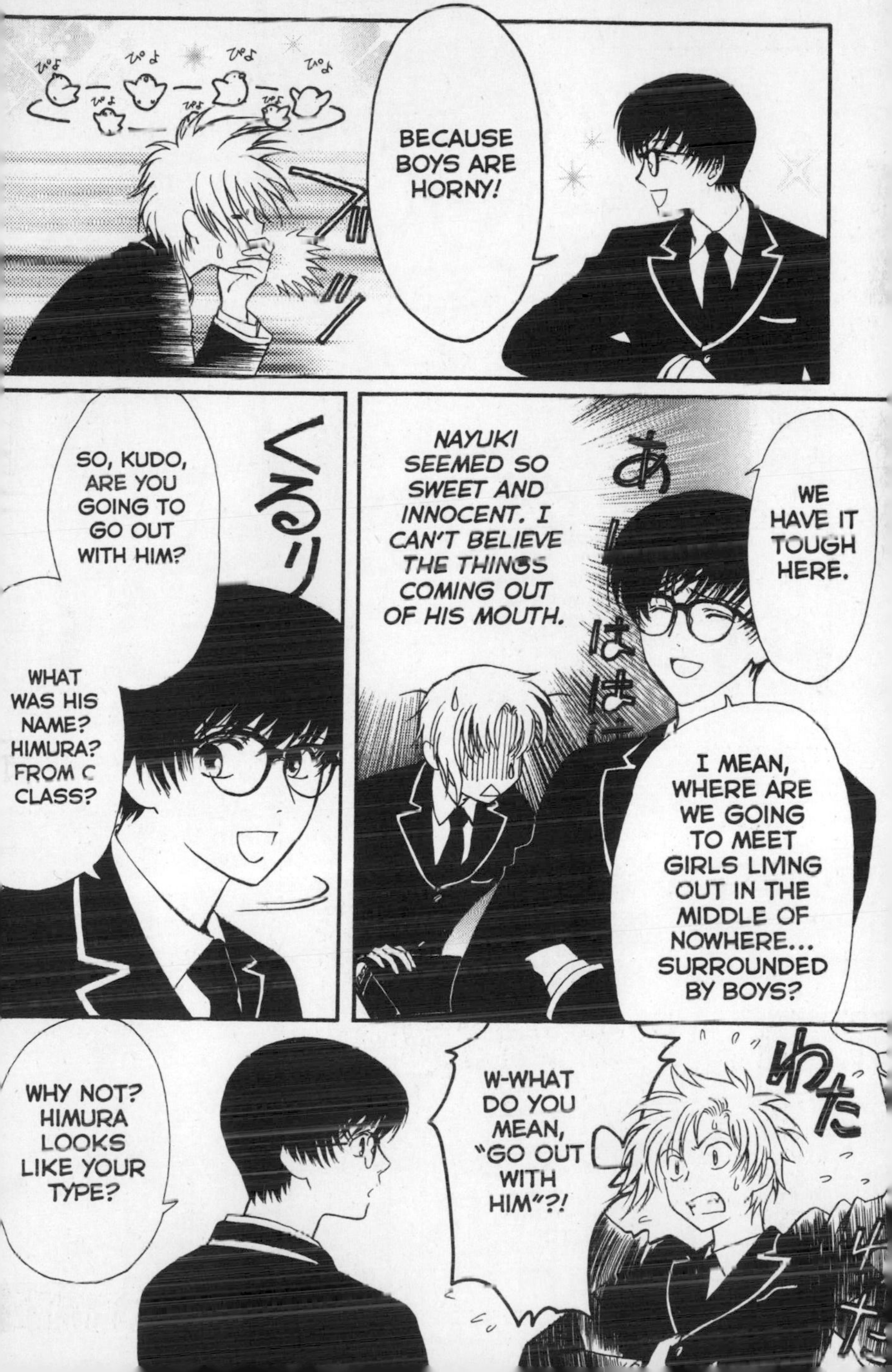
BECAUSE BOYS ARE HORNY!
WE HAVE IT TOUGH HERE.
NAYUKI SEEMED SO SWEET AND INNOCENT. I CAN'T BELIEVE THE THINGS COMING OUT OF HIS MOUTH.
I MEAN, WHERE ARE WE GOING TO MEET GIRLS LIVING OUT IN THE MIDDLE OF NOWHERE... SURROUNDED BY BOYS?
SO, KUDO, ARE YOU GOING TO GO OUT WITH HIM?
WHAT WAS HIS NAME? HIMURA? FROM C CLASS?
W-WHAT DO YOU MEAN, "GO OUT WITH HIM"?!
WHY NOT? HIMURA LOOKS LIKE YOUR TYPE?

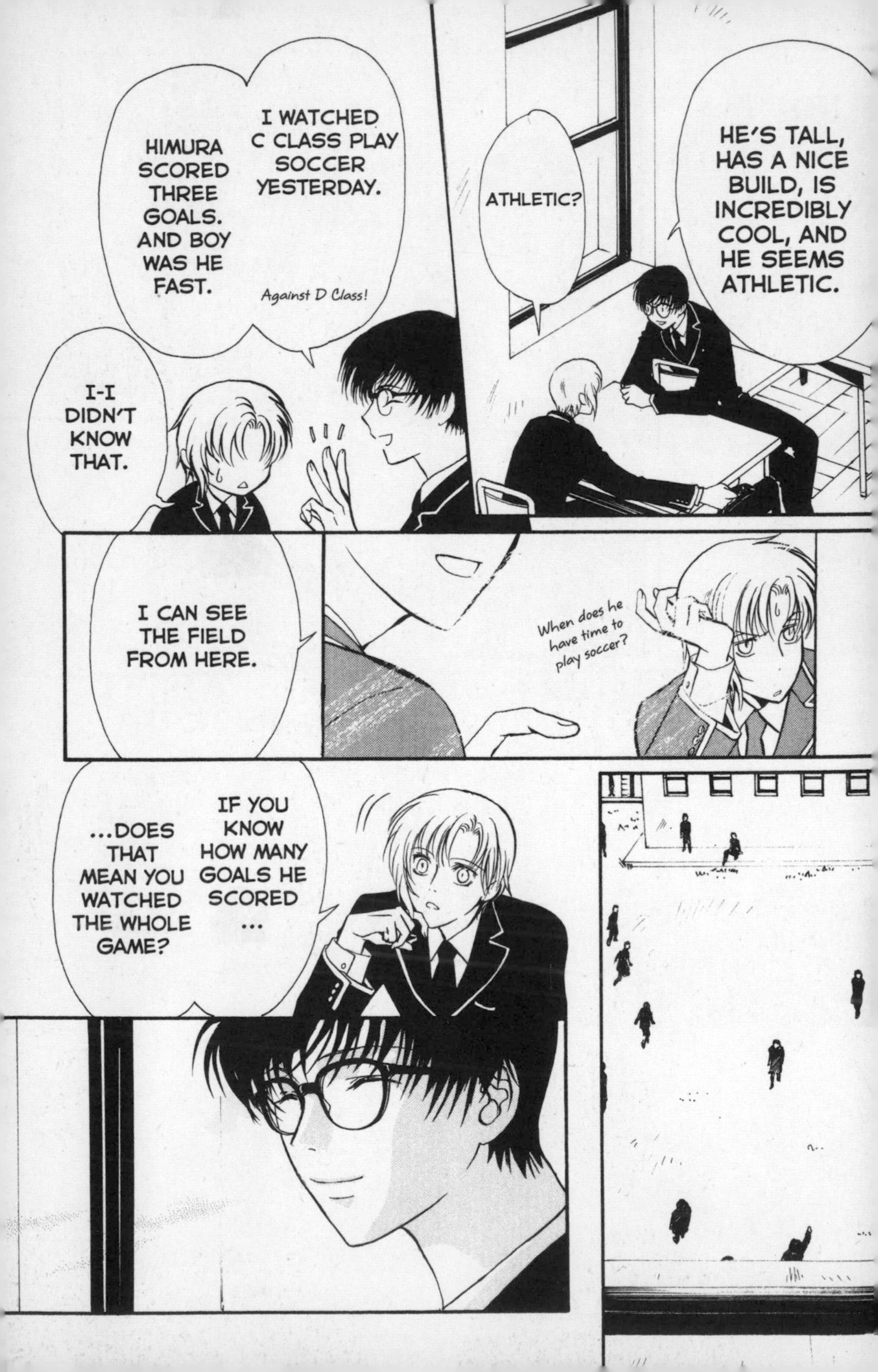
HE'S TALL, HAS A NICE BUILD, IS INCREDIBLY COOL, AND HE SEEMS ATHLETIC.
ATHLETIC?
I WATCHED C CLASS PLAY SOCCER YESTERDAY.
HIMURA SCORED THREE GOALS. AND BOY WAS HE FAST.
Against D Class!
I-I DIDN'T KNOW THAT.
When does he have time to play soccer?
I CAN SEE THE FIELD FROM HERE.
IF YOU KNOW HOW MANY GOALS HE SCORED ...
...DOES THAT MEAN YOU WATCHED THE WHOLE GAME?

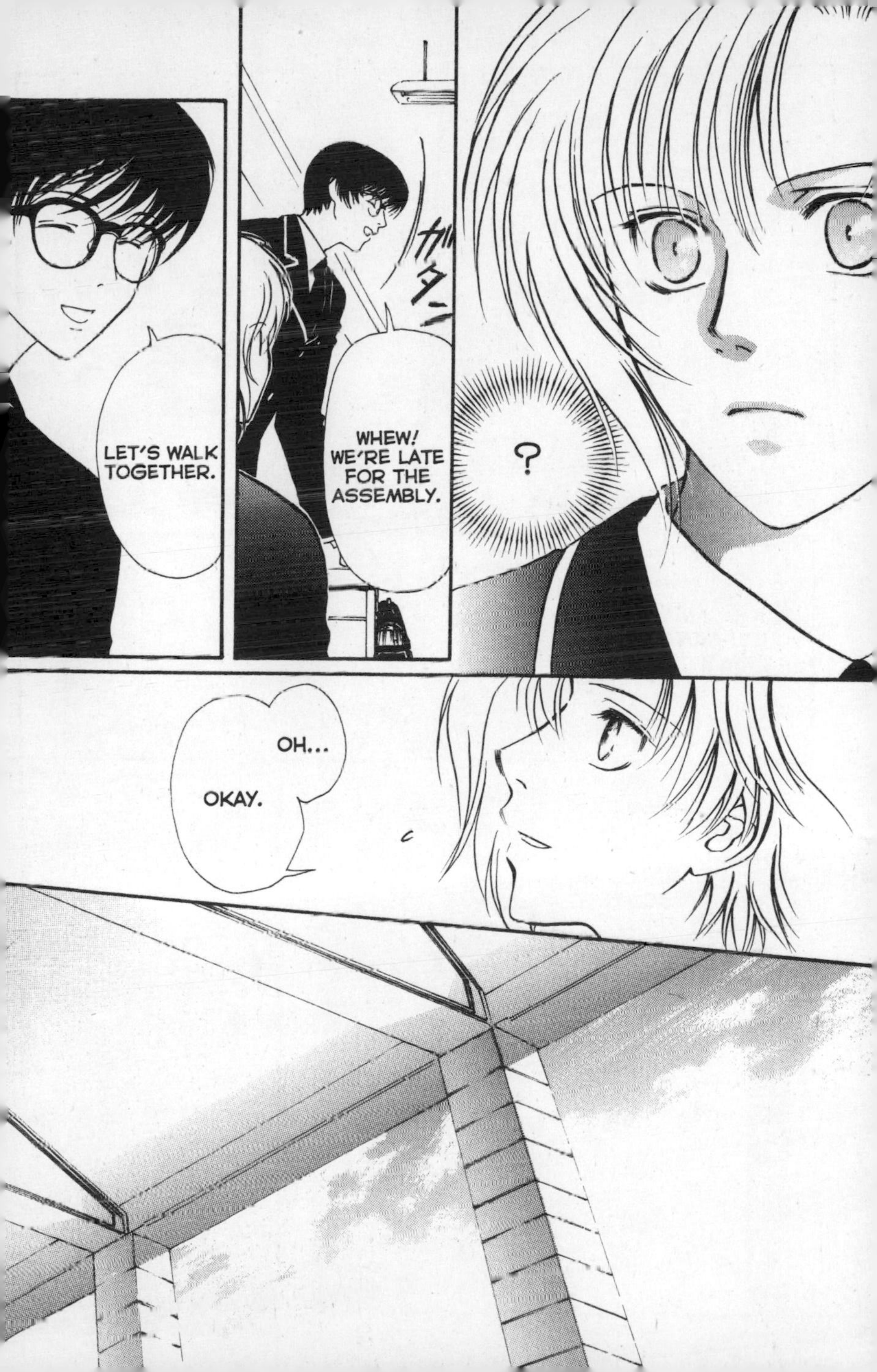
?
ガタン
WHEW! WE'RE LATE FOR THE ASSEMBLY.
LET'S WALK TOGETHER.
OH... OKAY.

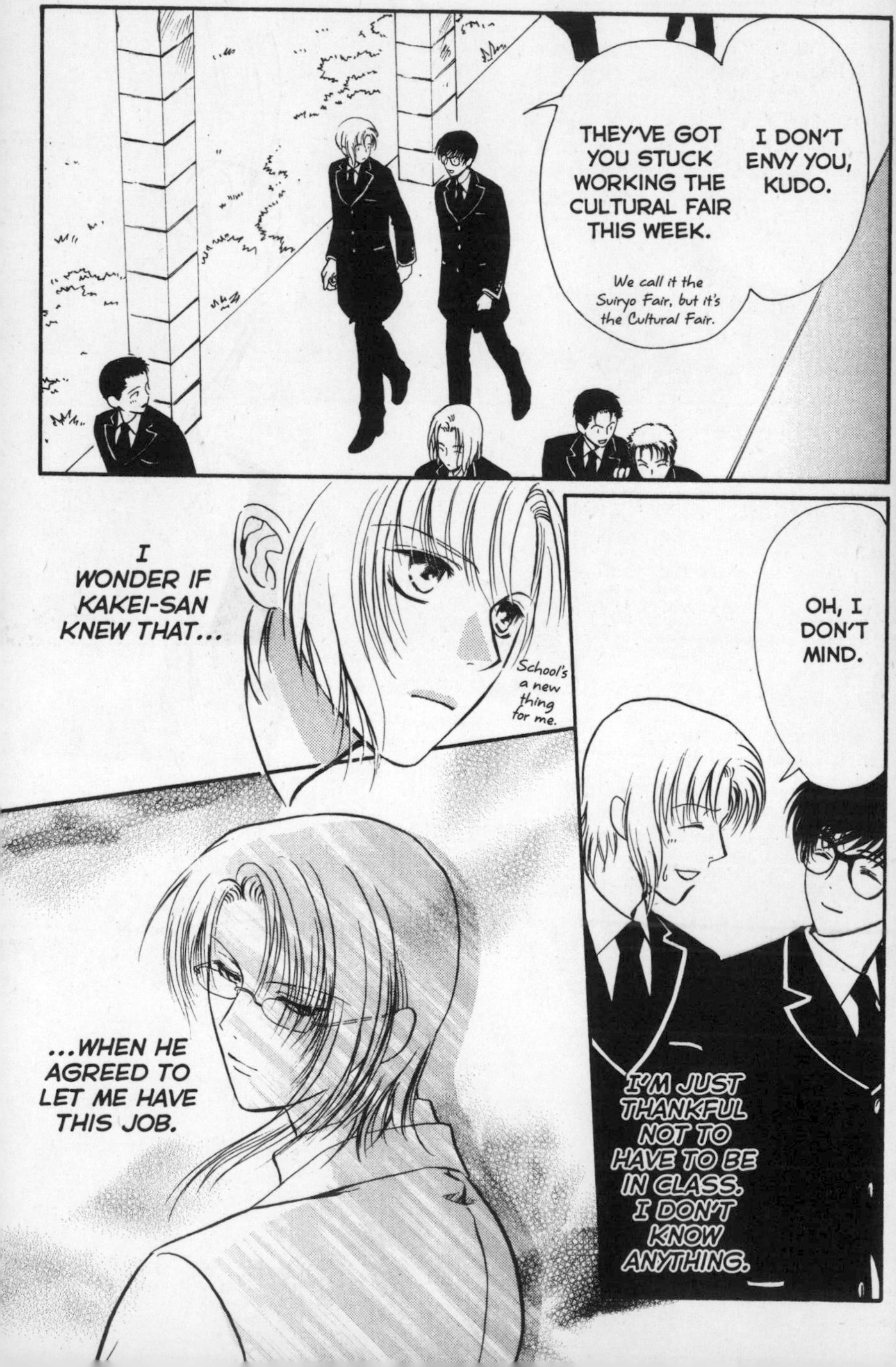
I DON'T ENVY YOU, KUDO.
THEY'VE GOT YOU STUCK WORKING THE CULTURAL FAIR THIS WEEK.
We call it the Suiryo Fair, but it's the Cultural Fair.
OH, I DON'T MIND.
School's a new thing for me.
I'M JUST THANKFUL NOT TO HAVE TO BE IN CLASS. I DON'T KNOW ANYTHING.
I WONDER IF KAKEI-SAN KNEW THAT...
...WHEN HE AGREED TO LET ME HAVE THIS JOB.

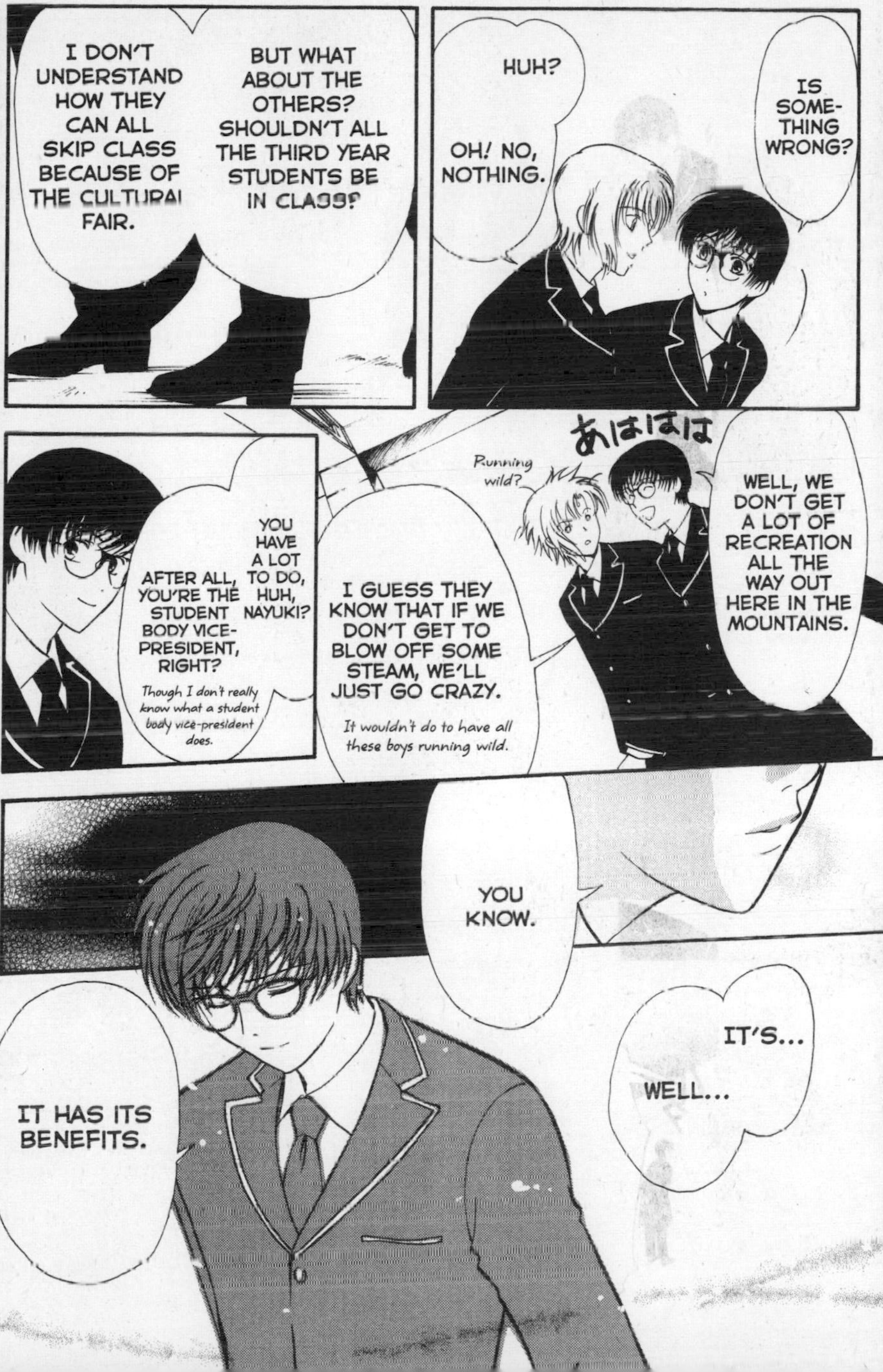
IS SOMETHING WRONG?
HUH?
OH! NO, NOTHING.
BUT WHAT ABOUT THE OTHERS? SHOULDN'T ALL THE THIRD YEAR STUDENTS BE IN CLASS?
I DON'T UNDERSTAND HOW THEY CAN ALL SKIP CLASS BECAUSE OF THE CULTURAL FAIR.
あははは
WELL, WE DON'T GET A LOT OF RECREATION ALL THE WAY OUT HERE IN THE MOUNTAINS.
Running wild?
I GUESS THEY KNOW THAT IF WE DON'T GET TO BLOW OFF SOME STEAM, WE'LL JUST GO CRAZY.
It wouldn't do to have all these boys running wild.
YOU HAVE A LOT TO DO, HUH, NAYUKI?
AFTER ALL, YOU'RE THE STUDENT BODY VICE-PRESIDENT, RIGHT?
Though I don't really know what a student body vice-president does.
YOU KNOW.
IT'S...
WELL...
IT HAS ITS BENEFITS.

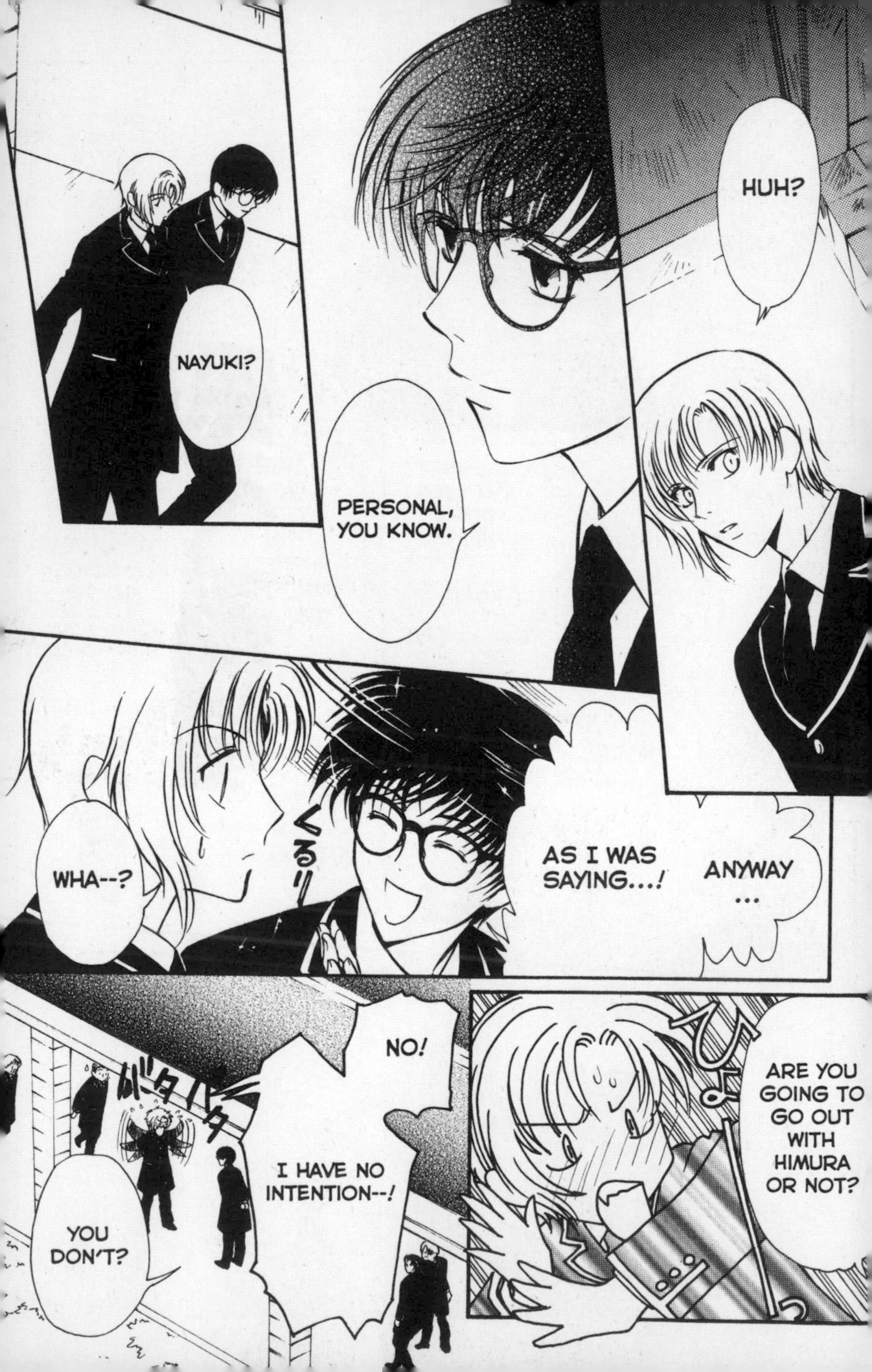
HUH?
PERSONAL, YOU KNOW.
NAYUKI?
ANYWAY ...
AS I WAS SAYING...!
WHA--?
ARE YOU GOING TO GO OUT WITH HIMURA OR NOT?
NO!
I HAVE NO INTENTION--!
バタバタ
YOU DON'T?

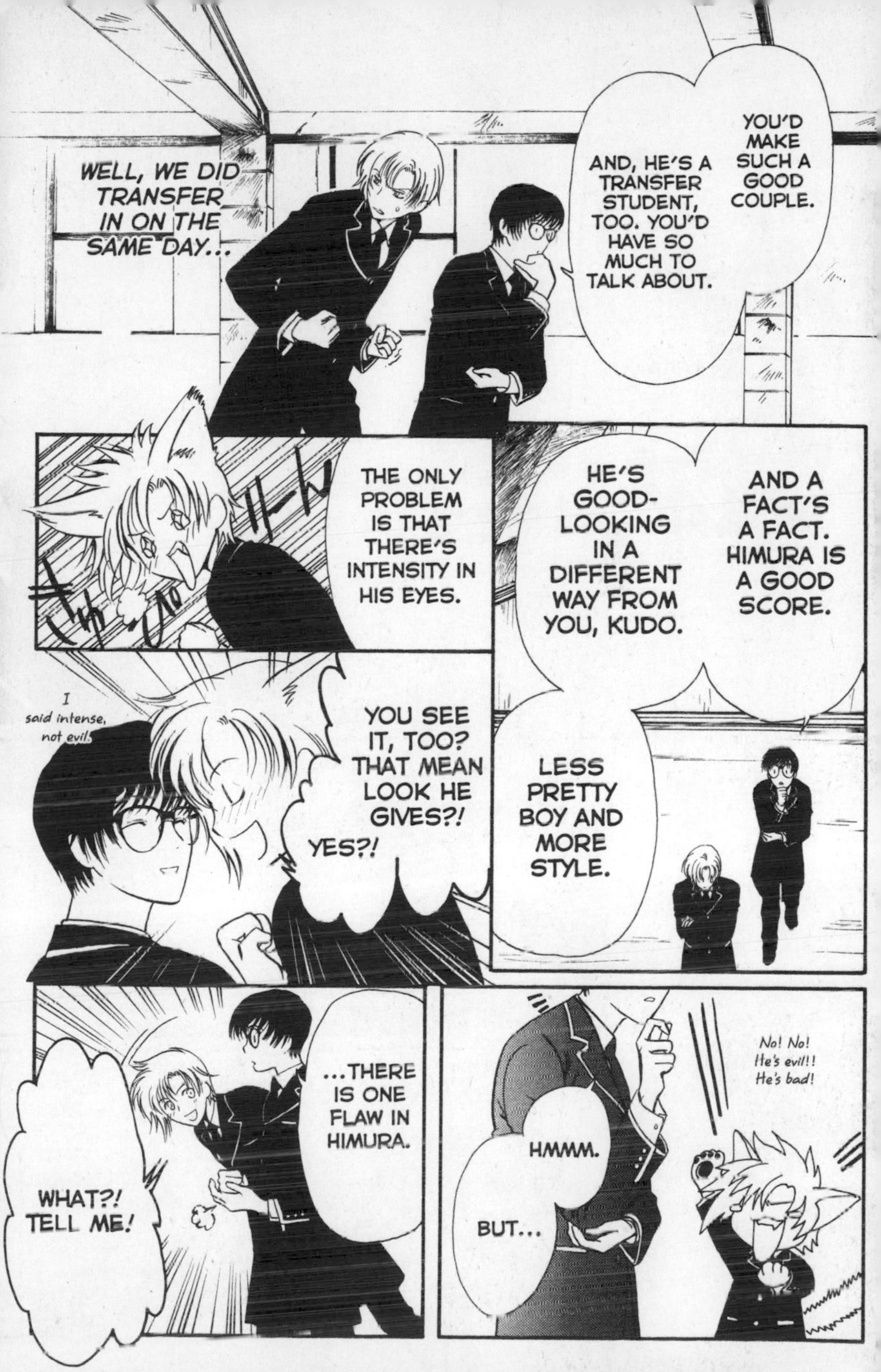
YOU'D MAKE SUCH A GOOD COUPLE.
AND, HE'S A TRANSFER STUDENT, TOO. YOU'D HAVE SO MUCH TO TALK ABOUT.
WELL, WE DID TRANSFER IN ON THE SAME DAY...
AND A FACT'S A FACT. HIMURA IS A GOOD SCORE.
HE'S GOOD-LOOKING IN A DIFFERENT WAY FROM YOU, KUDO.
LESS PRETTY BOY AND MORE STYLE.
THE ONLY PROBLEM IS THAT THERE'S INTENSITY IN HIS EYES.
YOU SEE IT, TOO? THAT MEAN LOOK HE GIVES?!
YES?!
I said intense, not evil.
HMMM.
BUT...
No! No! He's evil!! He's bad!
...THERE IS ONE FLAW IN HIMURA.
WHAT?! TELL ME!

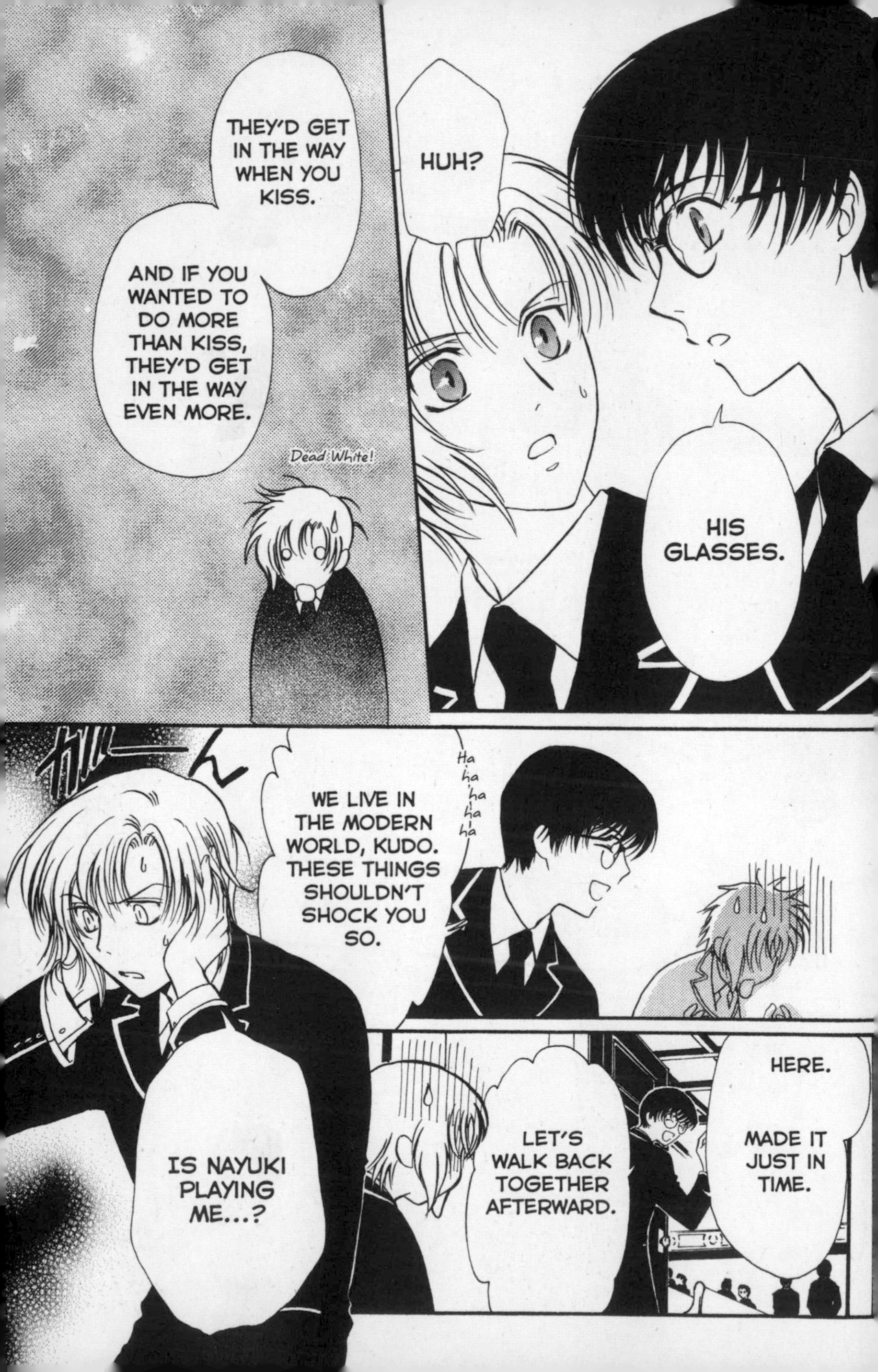
HUH?
HIS GLASSES.
THEY'D GET IN THE WAY WHEN YOU KISS.
AND IF YOU WANTED TO DO MORE THAN KISS, THEY'D GET IN THE WAY EVEN MORE.
Dead White!
Ha ha ha ha ha
WE LIVE IN THE MODERN WORLD, KUDO. THESE THINGS SHOULDN'T SHOCK YOU SO.
HERE.
MADE IT JUST IN TIME.
LET'S WALK BACK TOGETHER AFTERWARD.
IS NAYUKI PLAYING ME...?

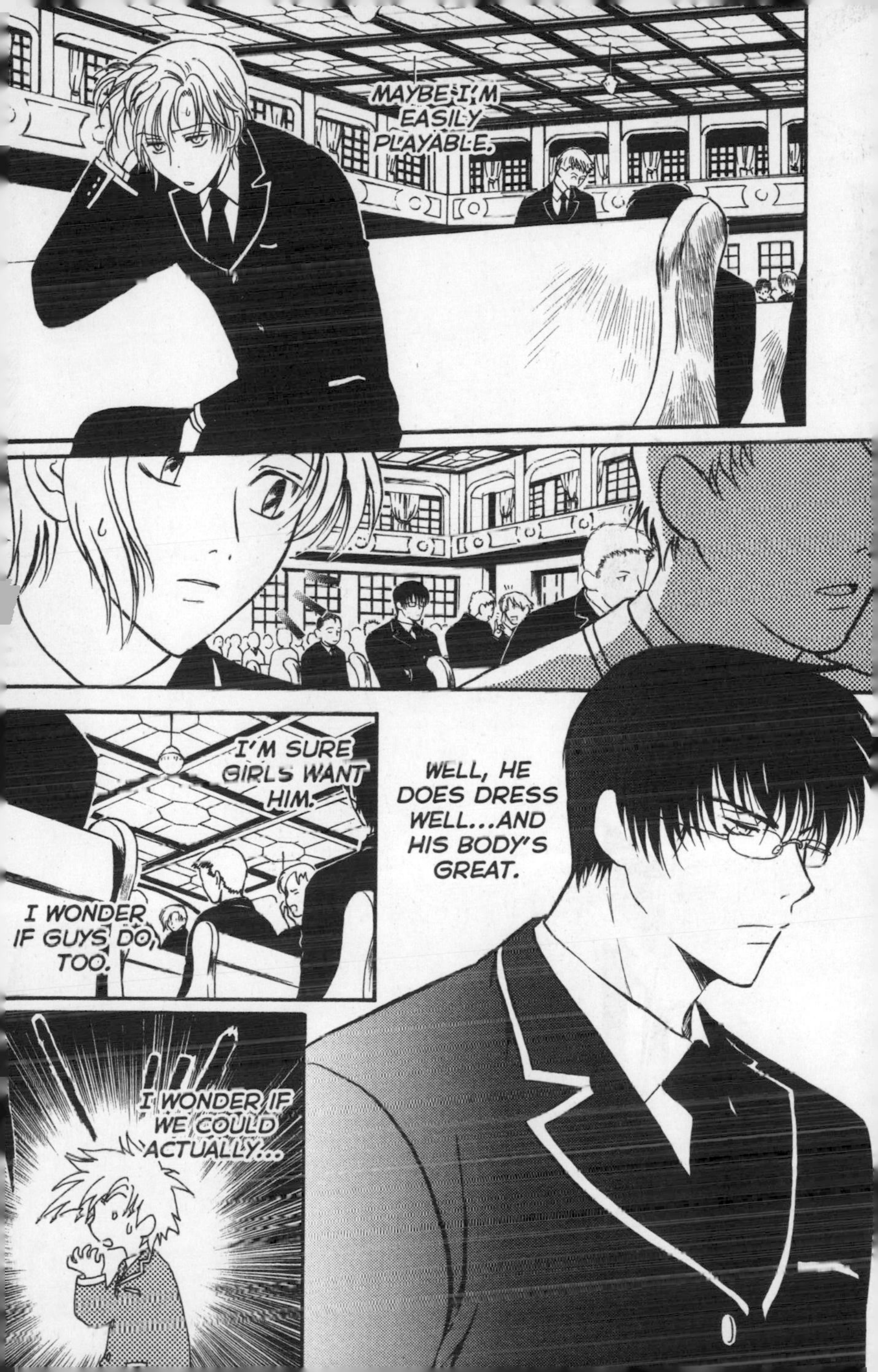
MAYBE I'M EASILY PLAYABLE.
WELL, HE DOES DRESS WELL...AND HIS BODY'S GREAT.
I'M SURE GIRLS WANT HIM.
I WONDER IF GUYS DO, TOO.
I WONDER IF WE COULD ACTUALLY...

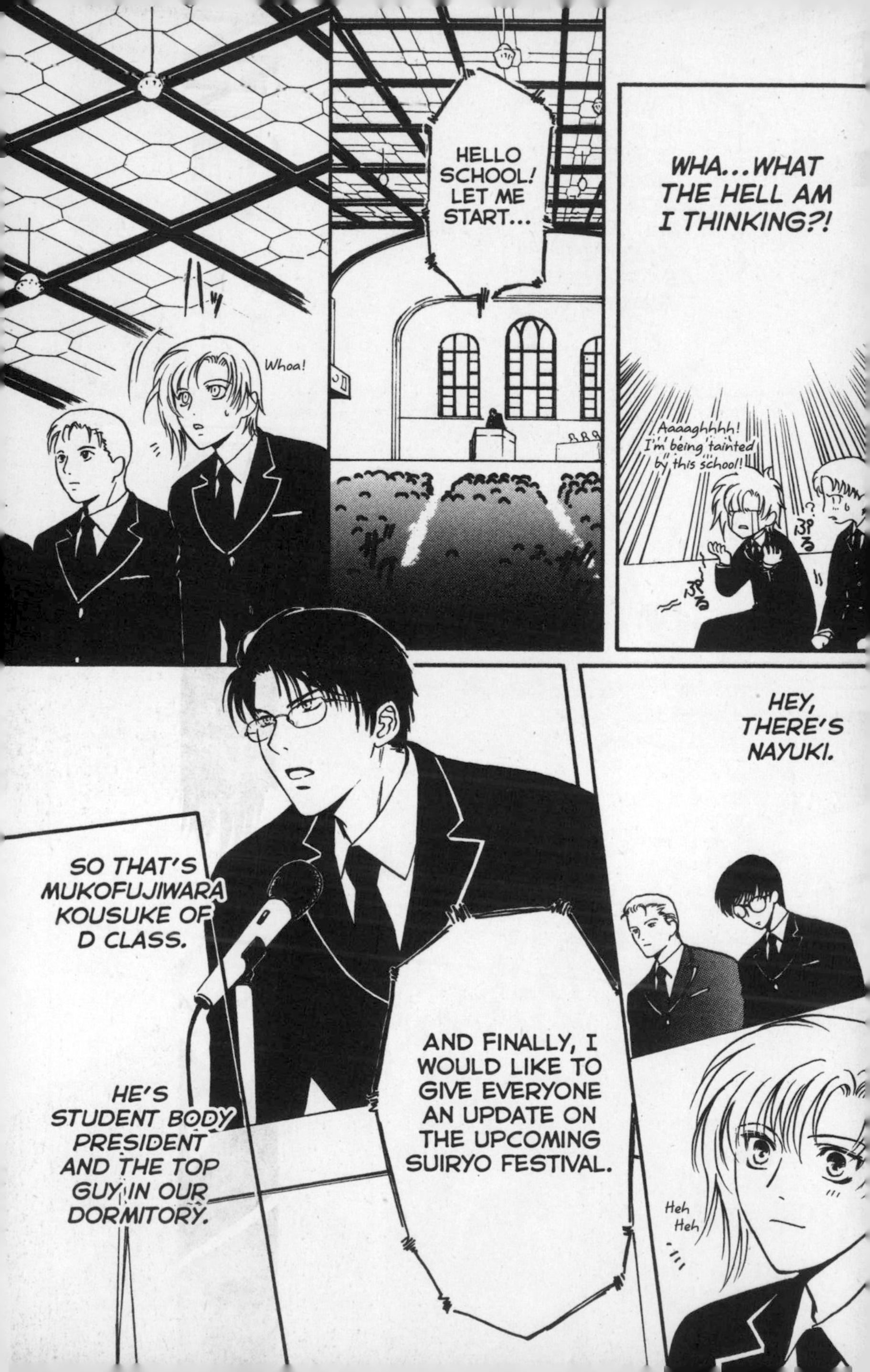
WHA...WHAT THE HELL AM I THINKING?!
Aaaaghhhh! I'm being tainted by this school!
ぷる
ぷる
HELLO SCHOOL! LET ME START...
Whoa!
HEY, THERE'S NAYUKI.
Heh Heh
AND FINALLY, I WOULD LIKE TO GIVE EVERYONE AN UPDATE ON THE UPCOMING SUIRYO FESTIVAL.
SO THAT'S MUKOFUJIWARA KOUSUKE OF D CLASS.
HE'S STUDENT BODY PRESIDENT AND THE TOP GUY IN OUR DORMITORY.

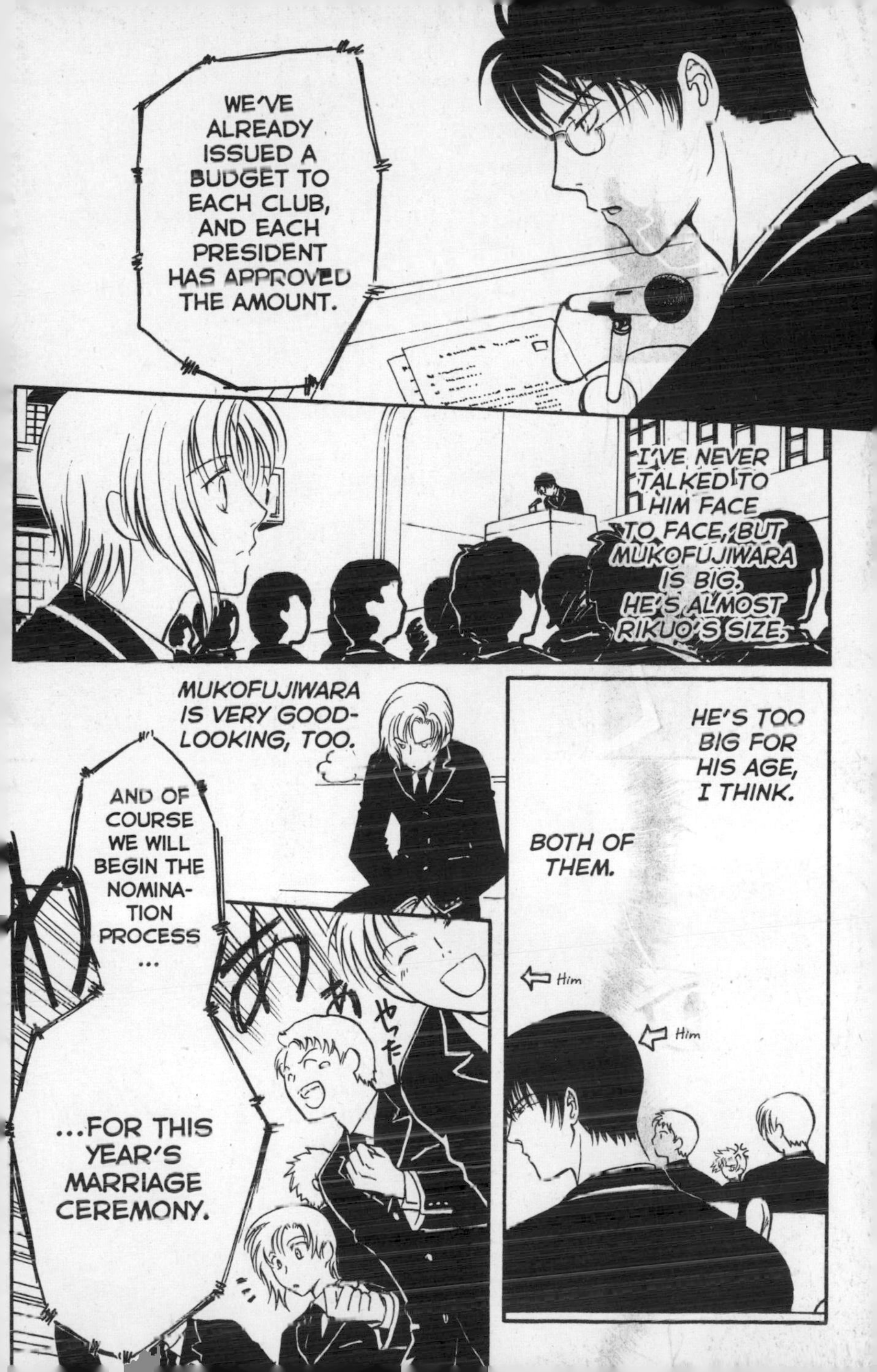
WE'VE ALREADY ISSUED A BUDGET TO EACH CLUB, AND EACH PRESIDENT HAS APPROVED THE AMOUNT.
I'VE NEVER TALKED TO HIM FACE TO FACE, BUT MUKOFUJIWARA IS BIG. HE'S ALMOST RIKUO'S SIZE.
HE'S TOO BIG FOR HIS AGE, I THINK.
BOTH OF THEM.
Him
Him
MUKOFUJIWARA IS VERY GOOD-LOOKING, TOO.
AND OF COURSE WE WILL BEGIN THE NOMINATION PROCESS ...
...FOR THIS YEAR'S MARRIAGE CEREMONY.
やった

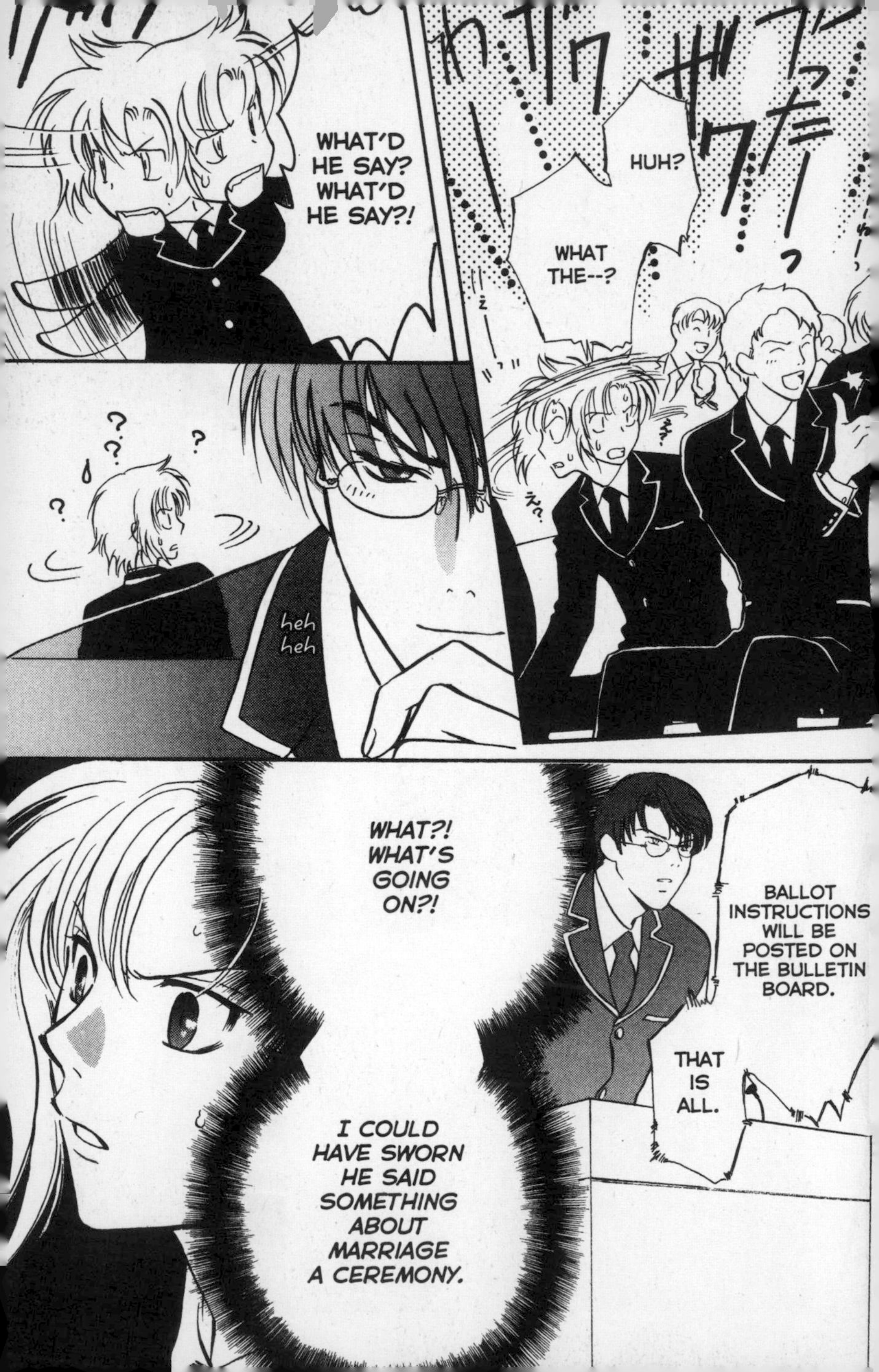
HUH?
WHAT THE--?
WHAT'D HE SAY? WHAT'D HE SAY?!
heh heh
BALLOT INSTRUCTIONS WILL BE POSTED ON THE BULLETIN BOARD.
THAT IS ALL.
WHAT?! WHAT'S GOING ON?!
I COULD HAVE SWORN HE SAID SOMETHING ABOUT MARRIAGE A CEREMONY.

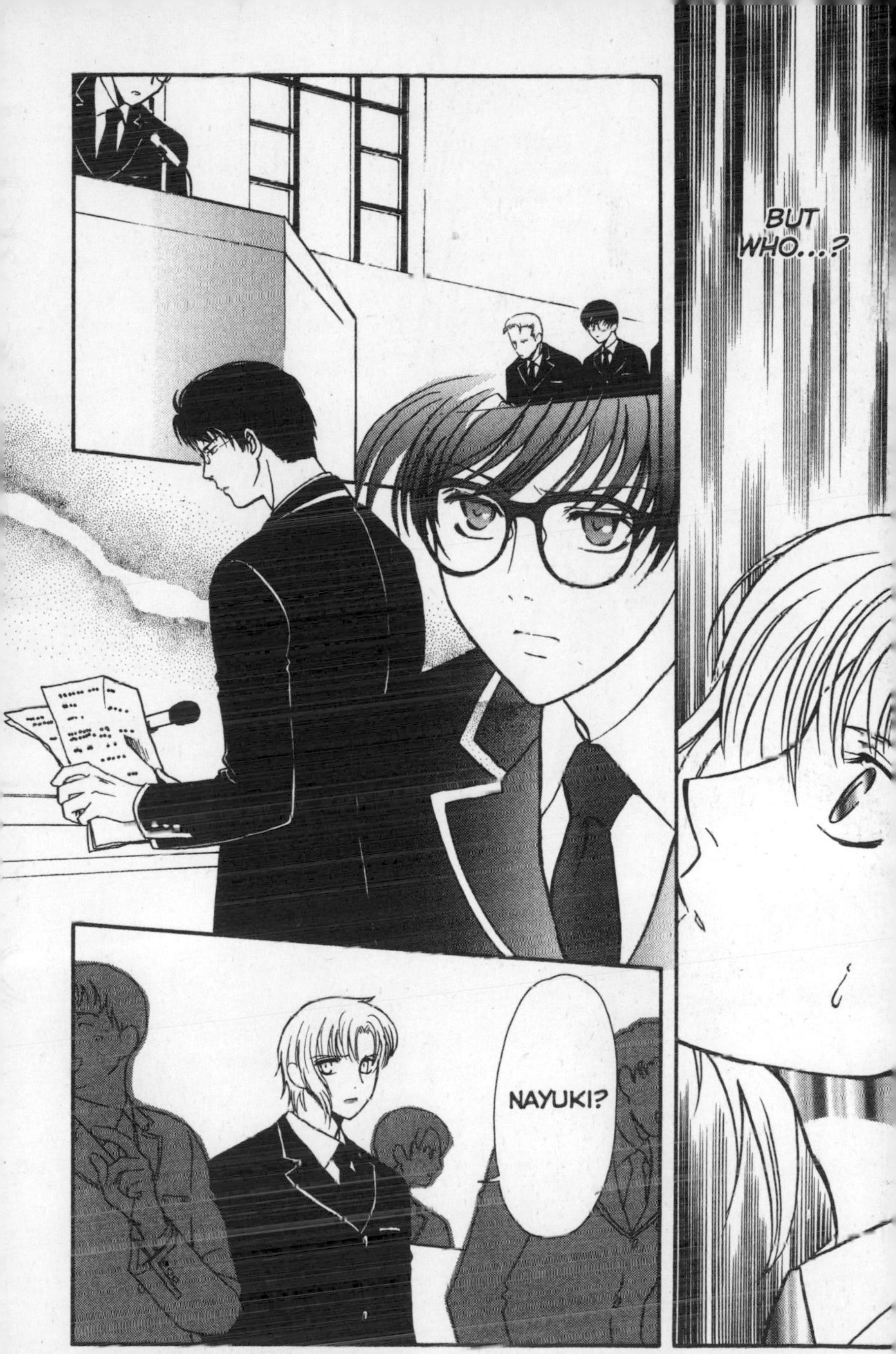
BUT WHO...?
NAYUKI?

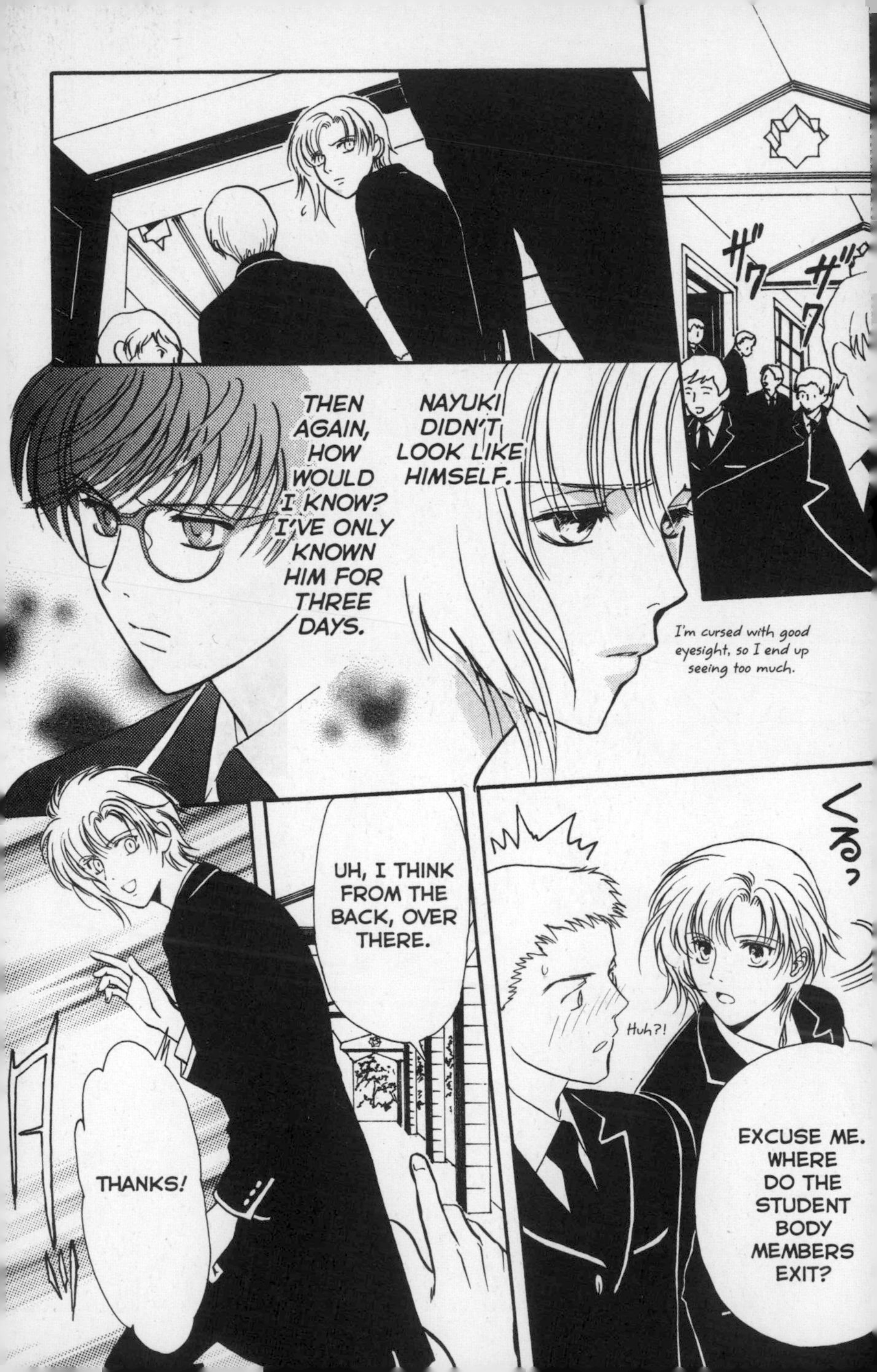
ザワ ザワ
NAYUKI DIDN'T LOOK LIKE HIMSELF.
THEN AGAIN, HOW WOULD I KNOW? I'VE ONLY KNOWN HIM FOR THREE DAYS.
I'm cursed with good eyesight, so I end up seeing too much.
くるっ
EXCUSE ME. WHERE DO THE STUDENT BODY MEMBERS EXIT?
Huh?!
UH, I THINK FROM THE BACK, OVER THERE.
THANKS!

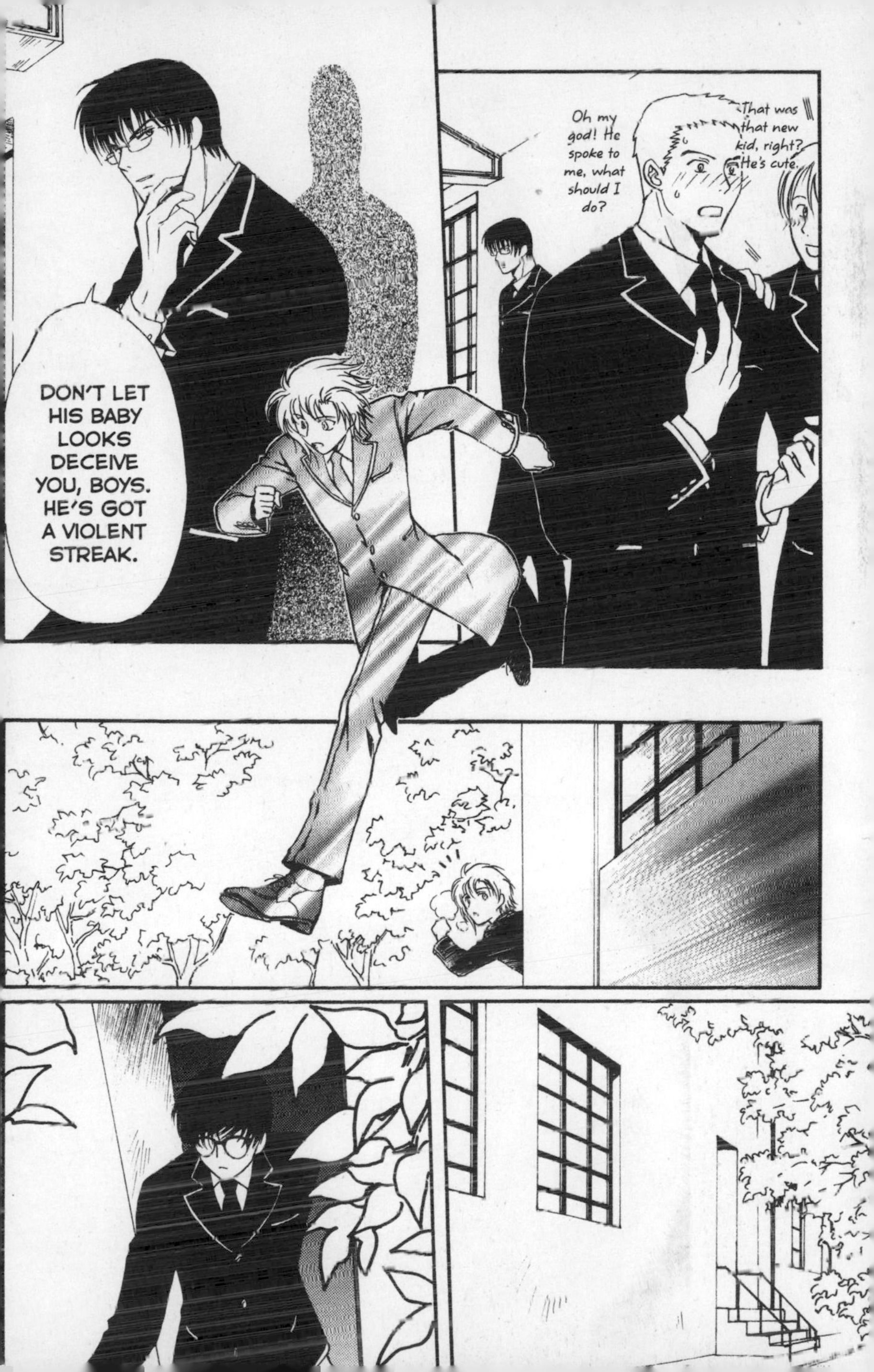
That was that new kid, right? He's cute.
Oh my god! He spoke to me, what should I do?
DON'T LET HIS BABY LOOKS DECEIVE YOU, BOYS. HE'S GOT A VIOLENT STREAK.
That was that new kid, right?

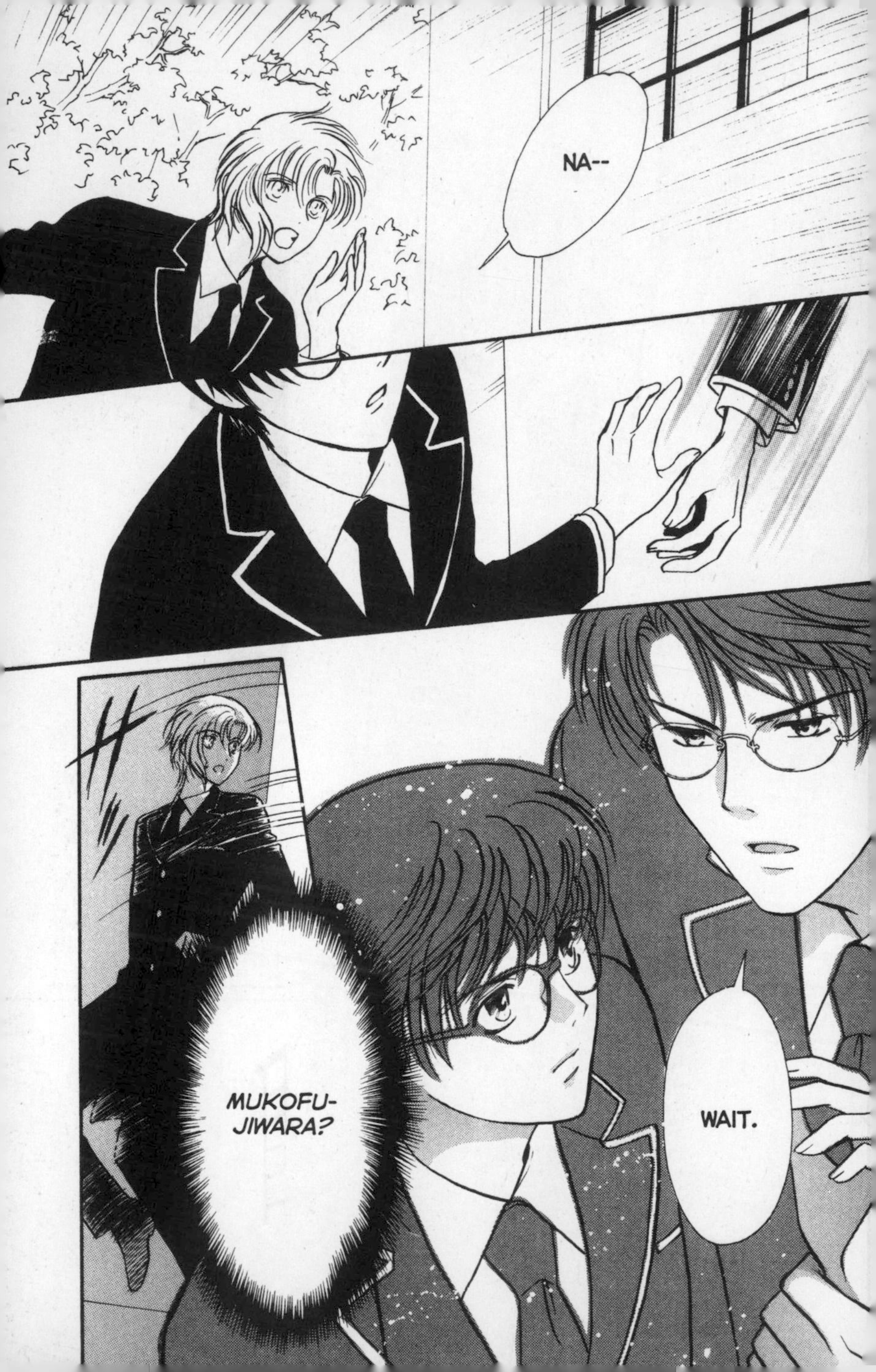
NA--
WAIT.
MUKOFU-
JIWARA?

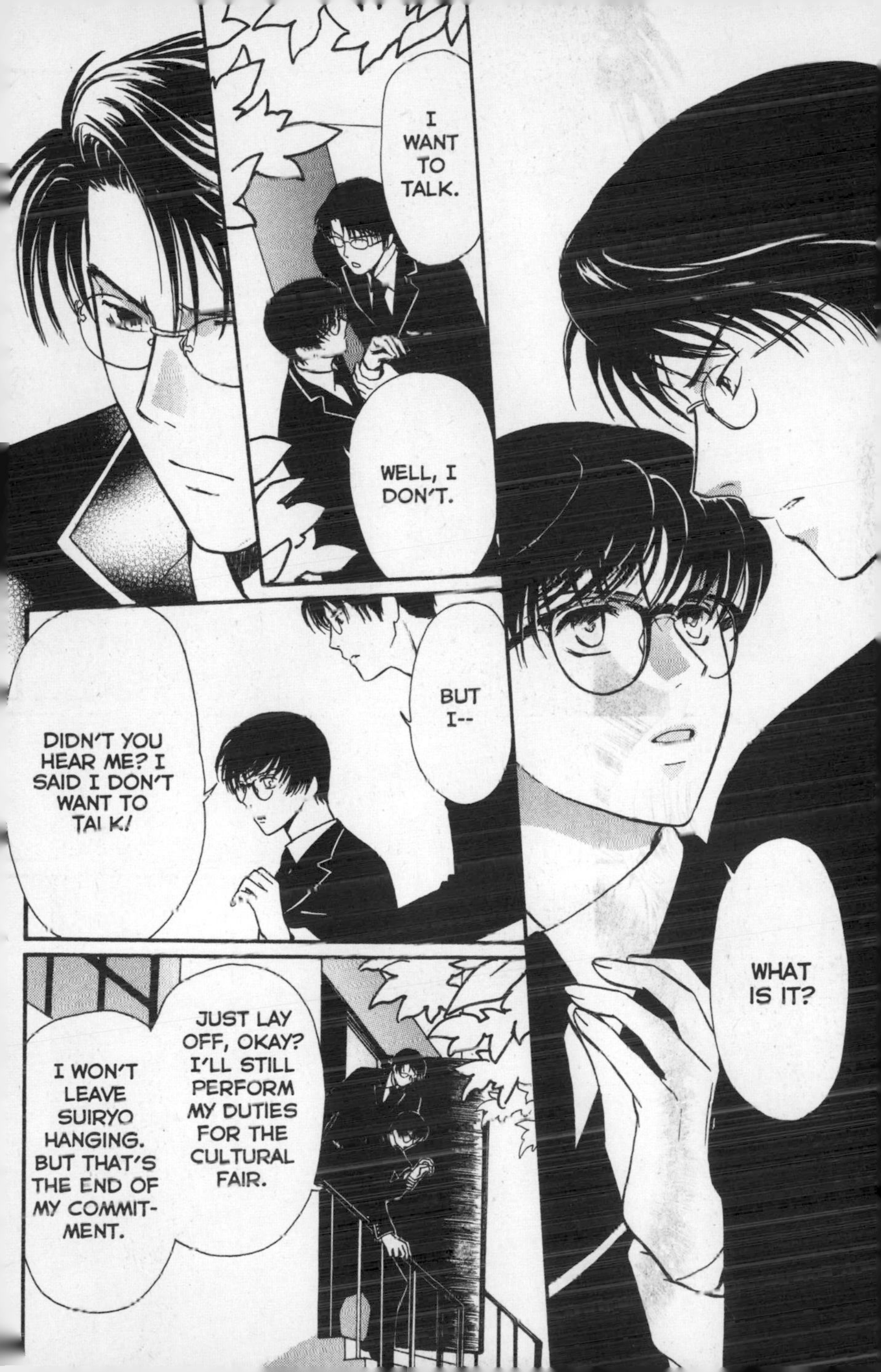
WHAT IS IT?
I WANT TO TALK.
WELL, I DON'T.
BUT I--
DIDN'T YOU HEAR ME? I SAID I DON'T WANT TO TALK!
JUST LAY OFF, OKAY? I'LL STILL PERFORM MY DUTIES FOR THE CULTURAL FAIR.
I WON'T LEAVE SUIRYO HANGING. BUT THAT'S THE END OF MY COMMIT-MENT.

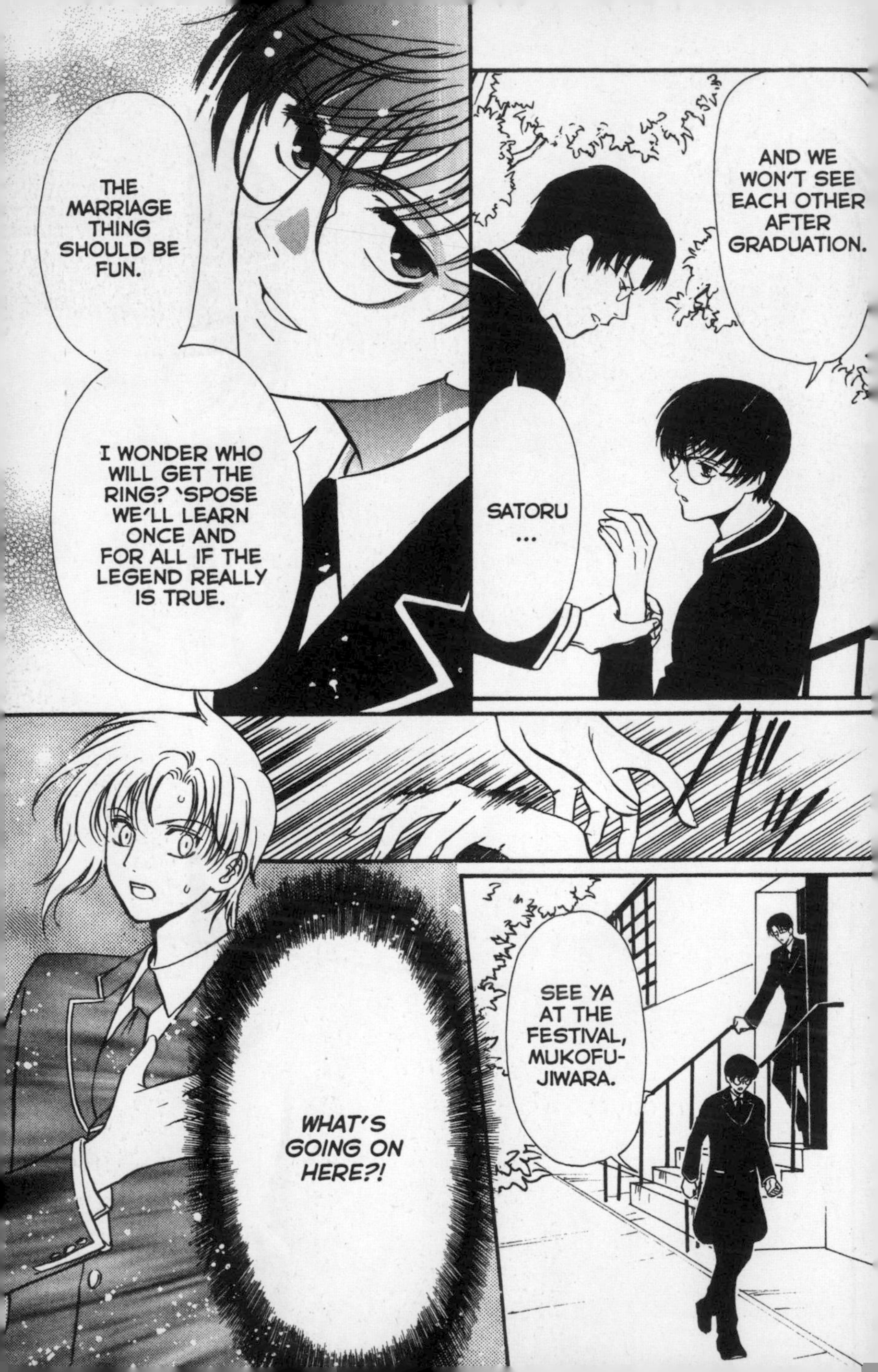
AND WE WON'T SEE EACH OTHER AFTER GRADUATION.
SATORU ...
THE MARRIAGE THING SHOULD BE FUN.
I WONDER WHO WILL GET THE RING? 'SPOSE WE'LL LEARN ONCE AND FOR ALL IF THE LEGEND REALLY IS TRUE.
SEE YA AT THE FESTIVAL, MUKOFU-JIWARA.
WHAT'S GOING ON HERE?!

合法ドラッグ
LEGAL DRUG

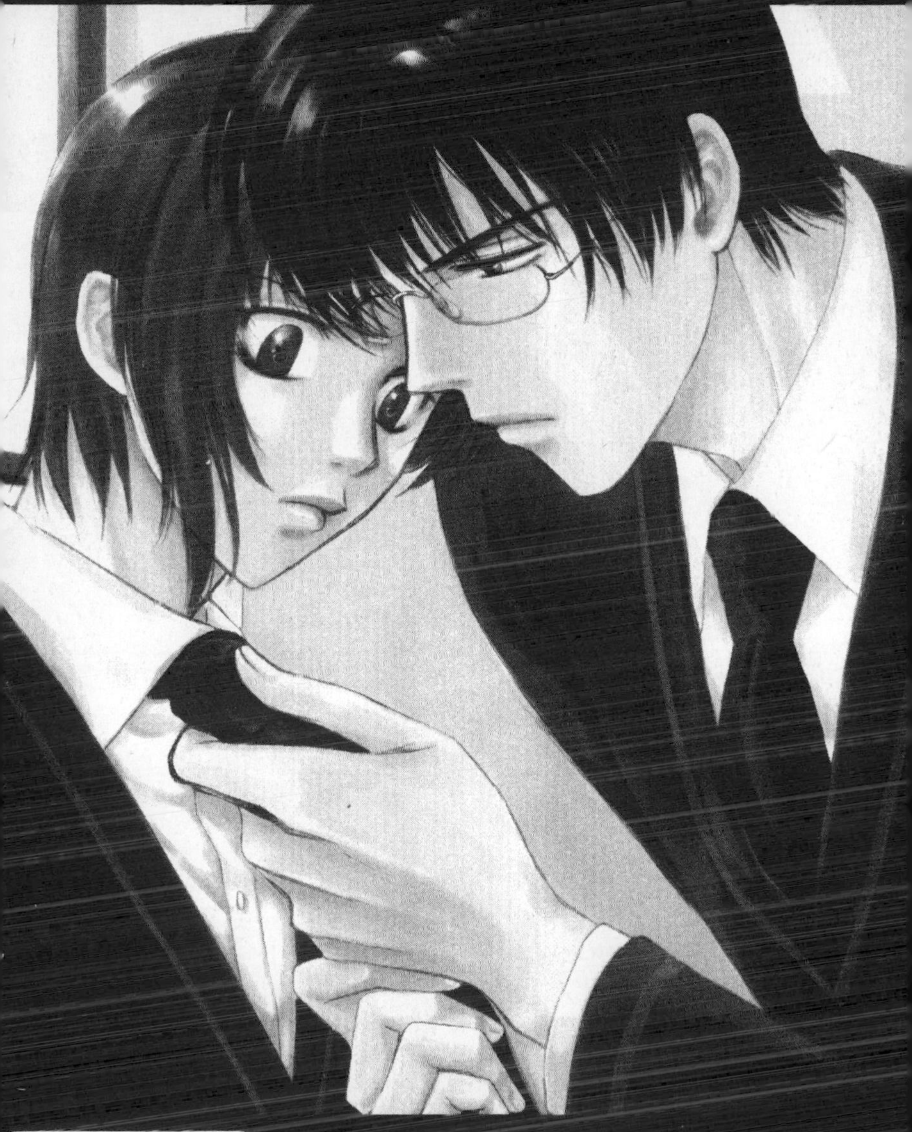

DRUG NO.13 Daily use of the drug may cause poisoning.

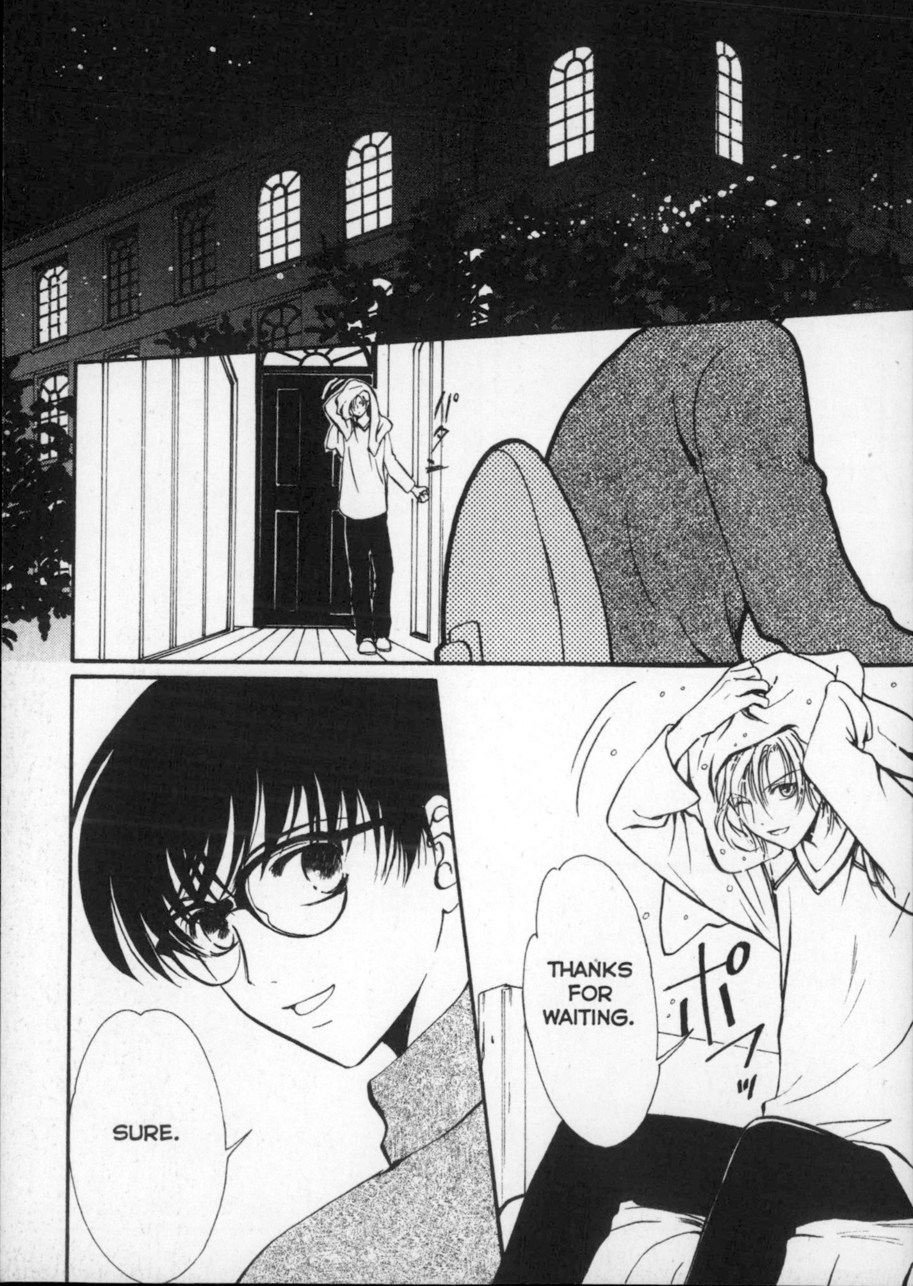
THANKS FOR WAITING.
SURE.

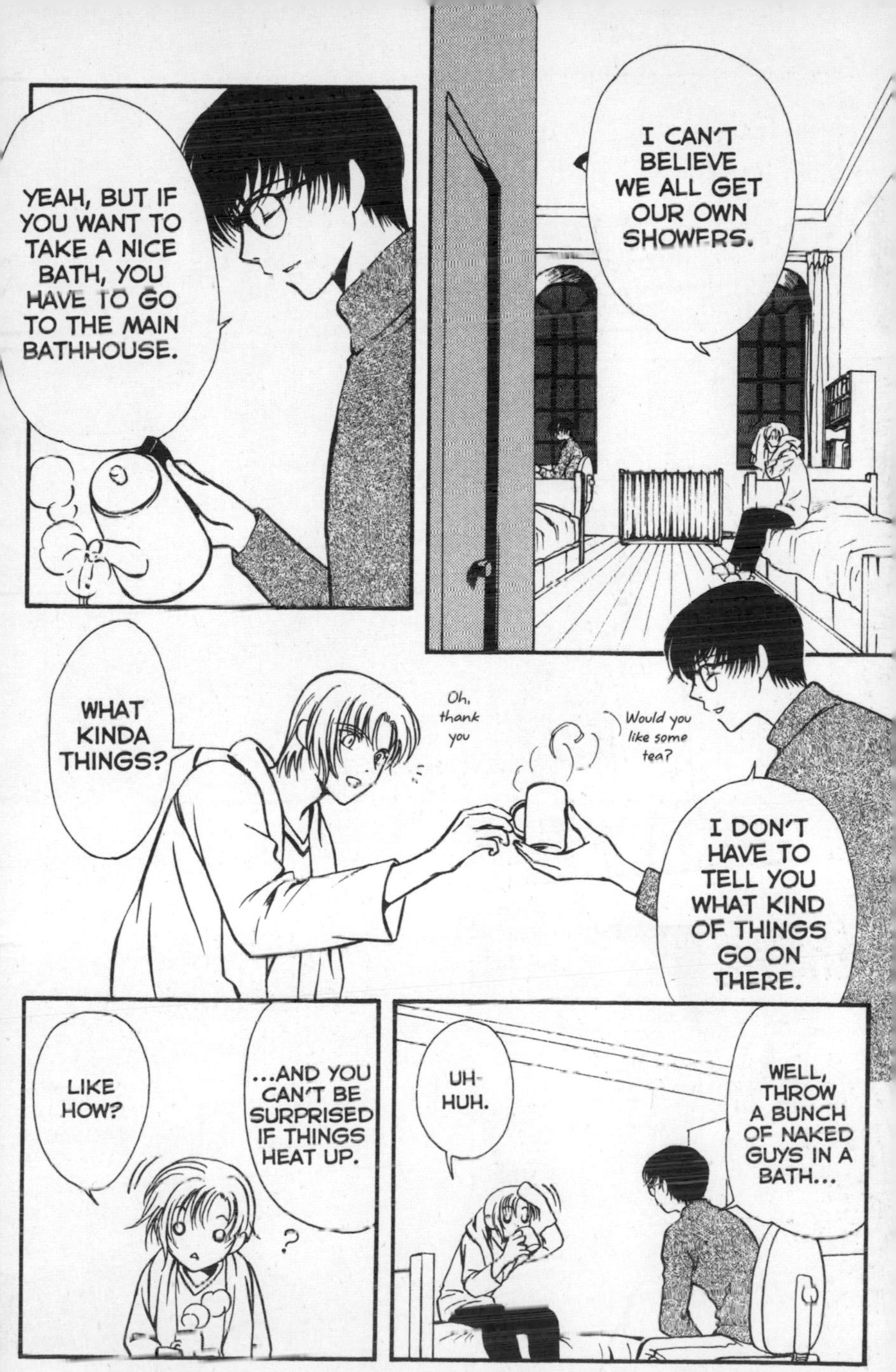
I CAN'T BELIEVE WE ALL GET OUR OWN SHOWERS.
YEAH, BUT IF YOU WANT TO TAKE A NICE BATH, YOU HAVE TO GO TO THE MAIN BATHHOUSE.
Would you like some tea?
Oh, thank you
I DON'T HAVE TO TELL YOU WHAT KIND OF THINGS GO ON THERE.
WHAT KINDA THINGS?
WELL, THROW A BUNCH OF NAKED GUYS IN A BATH...
UH-HUH.
...AND YOU CAN'T BE SURPRISED IF THINGS HEAT UP.
LIKE HOW?
?

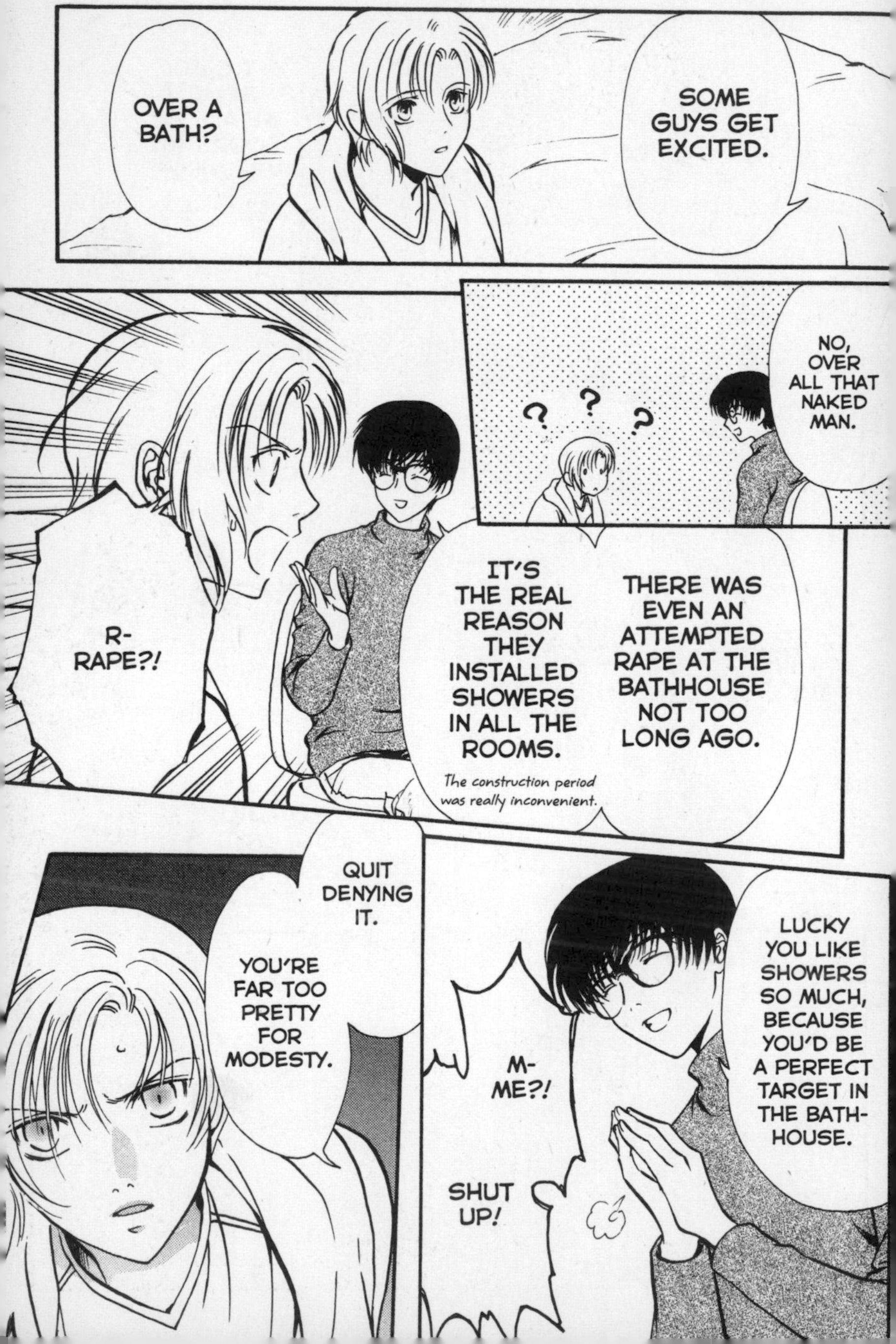
SOME GUYS GET EXCITED.
OVER A BATH?
NO, OVER ALL THAT NAKED MAN.
THERE WAS EVEN AN ATTEMPTED RAPE AT THE BATHHOUSE NOT TOO LONG AGO.
IT'S THE REAL REASON THEY INSTALLED SHOWERS IN ALL THE ROOMS.
The construction period was really inconvenient.
R- RAPE?!
LUCKY YOU LIKE SHOWERS SO MUCH, BECAUSE YOU'D BE A PERFECT TARGET IN THE BATH- HOUSE.
M- ME?!
QUIT DENYING IT.
YOU'RE FAR TOO PRETTY FOR MODESTY.
SHUT UP!

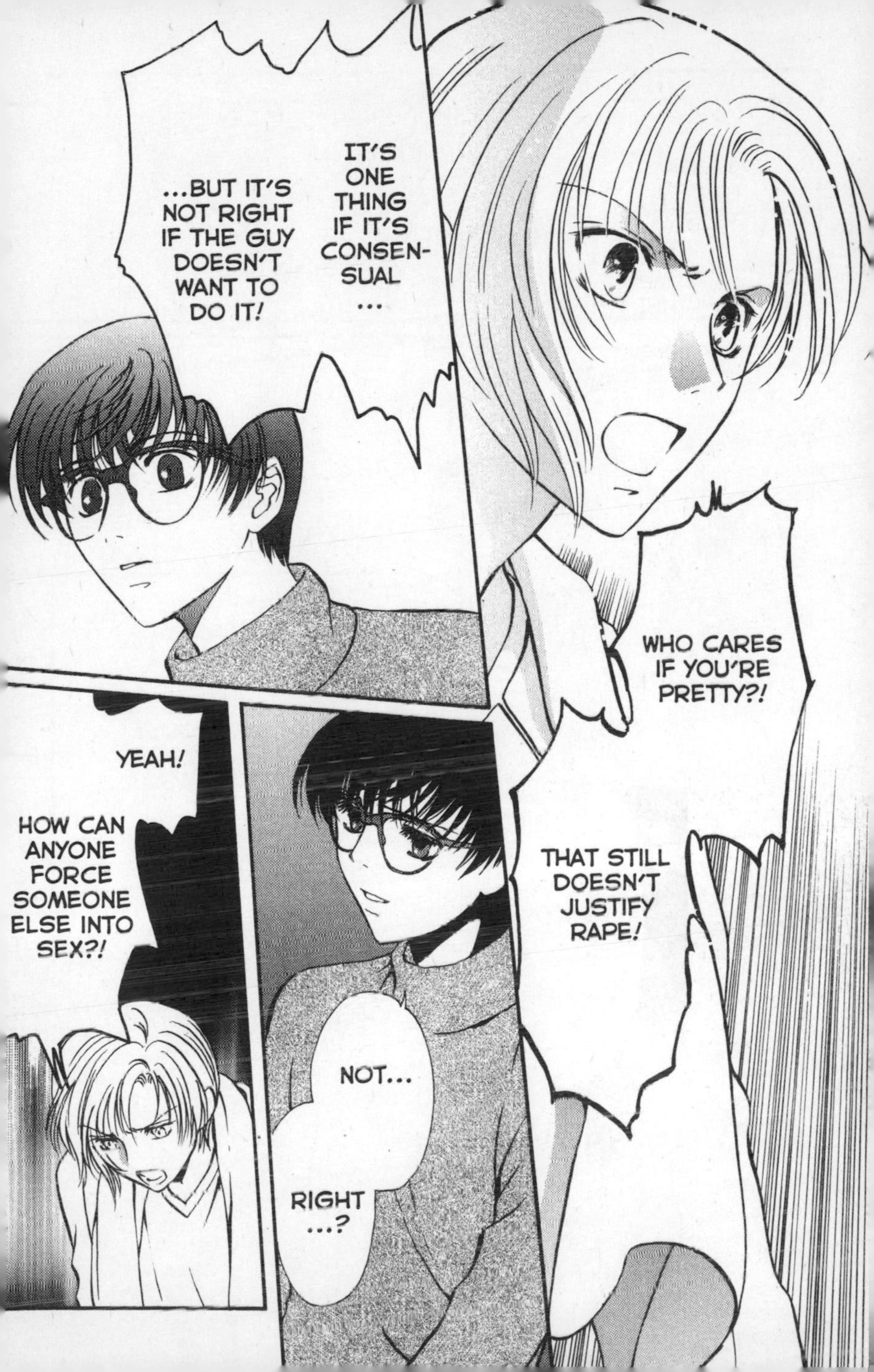
WHO CARES IF YOU'RE PRETTY?!
THAT STILL DOESN'T JUSTIFY RAPE!
IT'S ONE THING IF IT'S CONSENSUAL ...
...BUT IT'S NOT RIGHT IF THE GUY DOESN'T WANT TO DO IT!
NOT...
RIGHT ...?
YEAH!
HOW CAN ANYONE FORCE SOMEONE ELSE INTO SEX?!

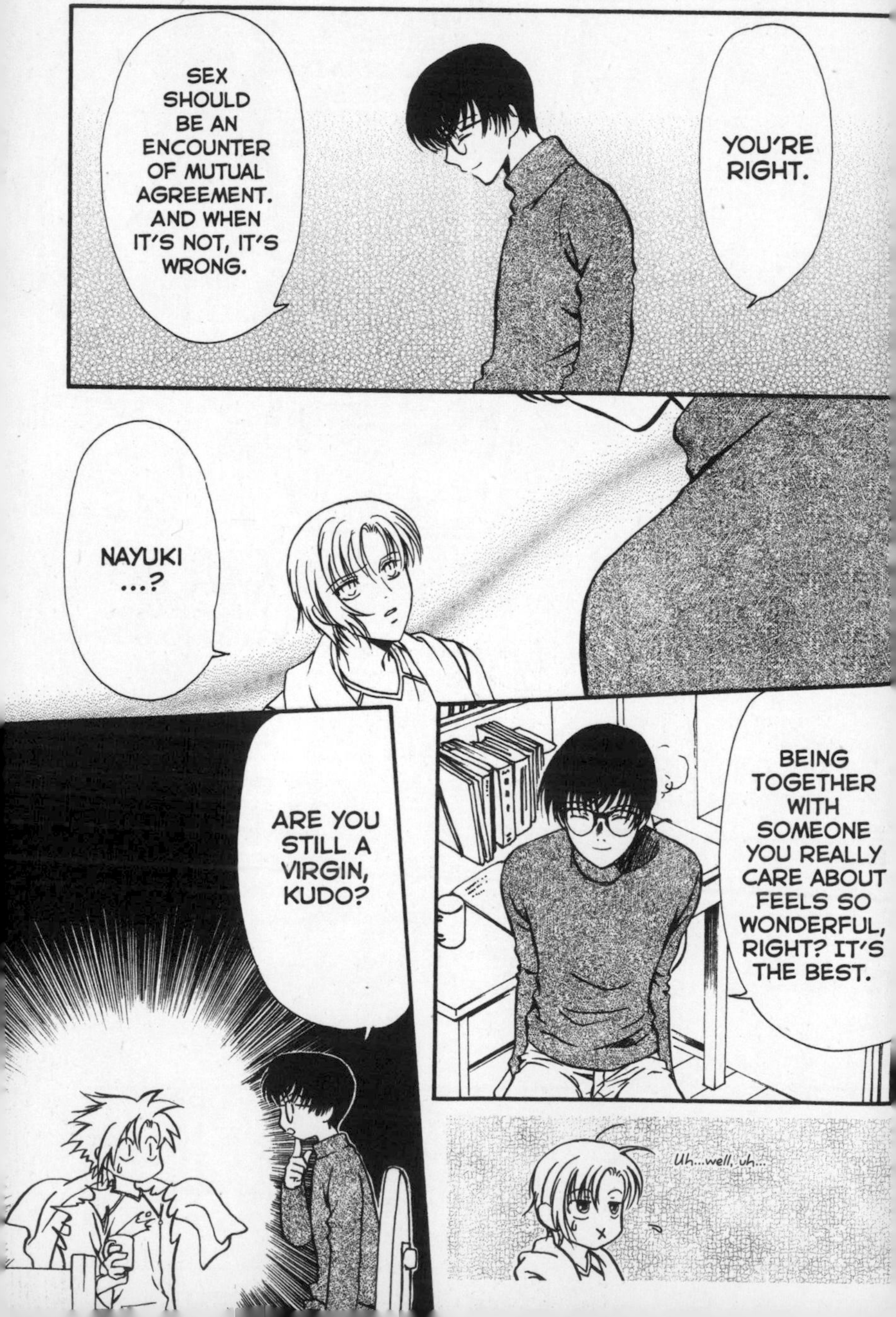
YOU'RE RIGHT.
SEX SHOULD BE AN ENCOUNTER OF MUTUAL AGREEMENT. AND WHEN IT'S NOT, IT'S WRONG.
NAYUKI ...?
BEING TOGETHER WITH SOMEONE YOU REALLY CARE ABOUT FEELS SO WONDERFUL, RIGHT? IT'S THE BEST.
ARE YOU STILL A VIRGIN, KUDO?
Uh...well, uh...

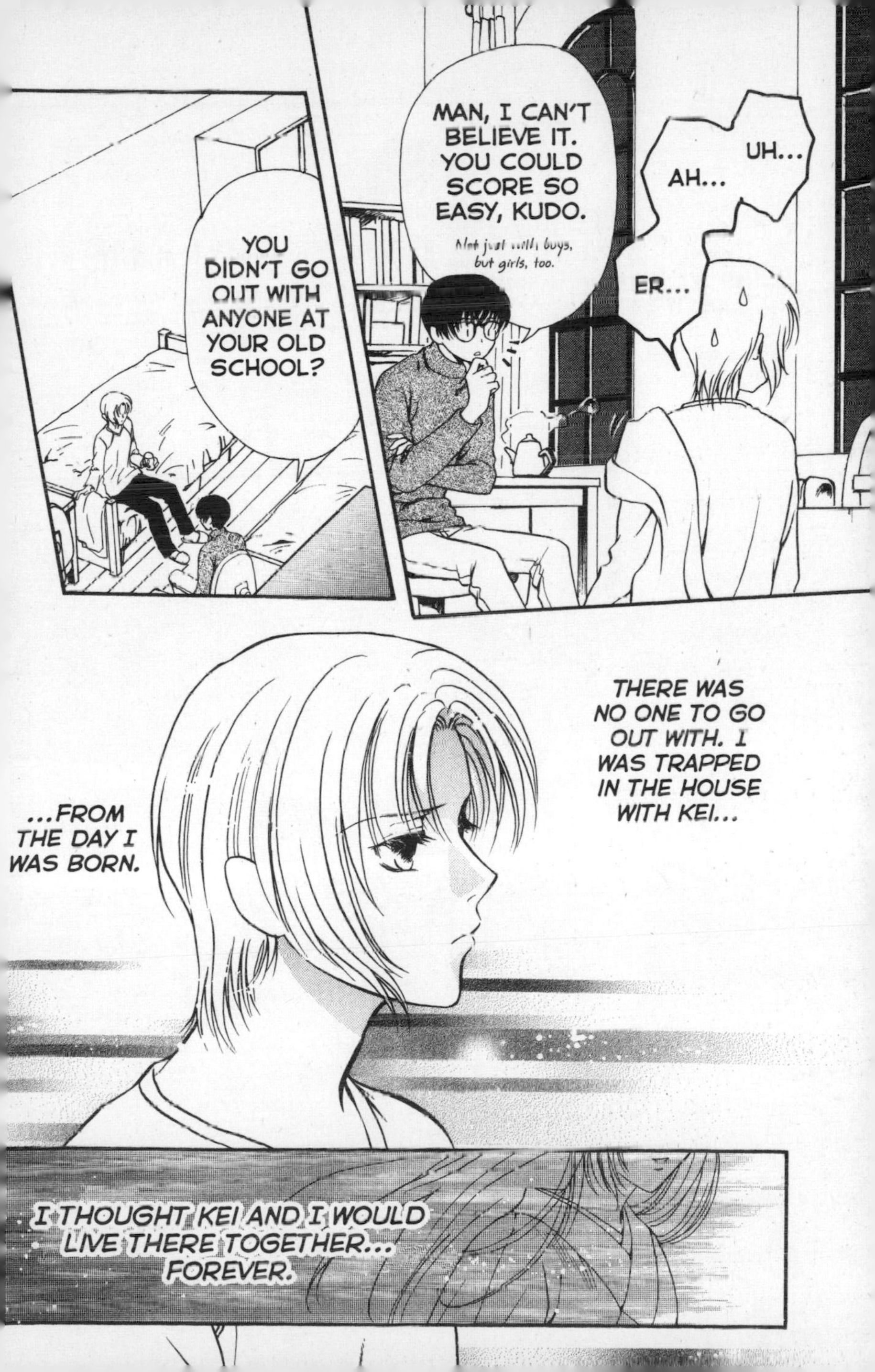
UH... AH... ER...
MAN, I CAN'T BELIEVE IT. YOU COULD SCORE SO EASY, KUDO.
Not just with boys, but girls, too.
YOU DIDN'T GO OUT WITH ANYONE AT YOUR OLD SCHOOL?
THERE WAS NO ONE TO GO OUT WITH. I WAS TRAPPED IN THE HOUSE WITH KEI...
...FROM THE DAY I WAS BORN.
I THOUGHT KEI AND I WOULD LIVE THERE TOGETHER... FOREVER.

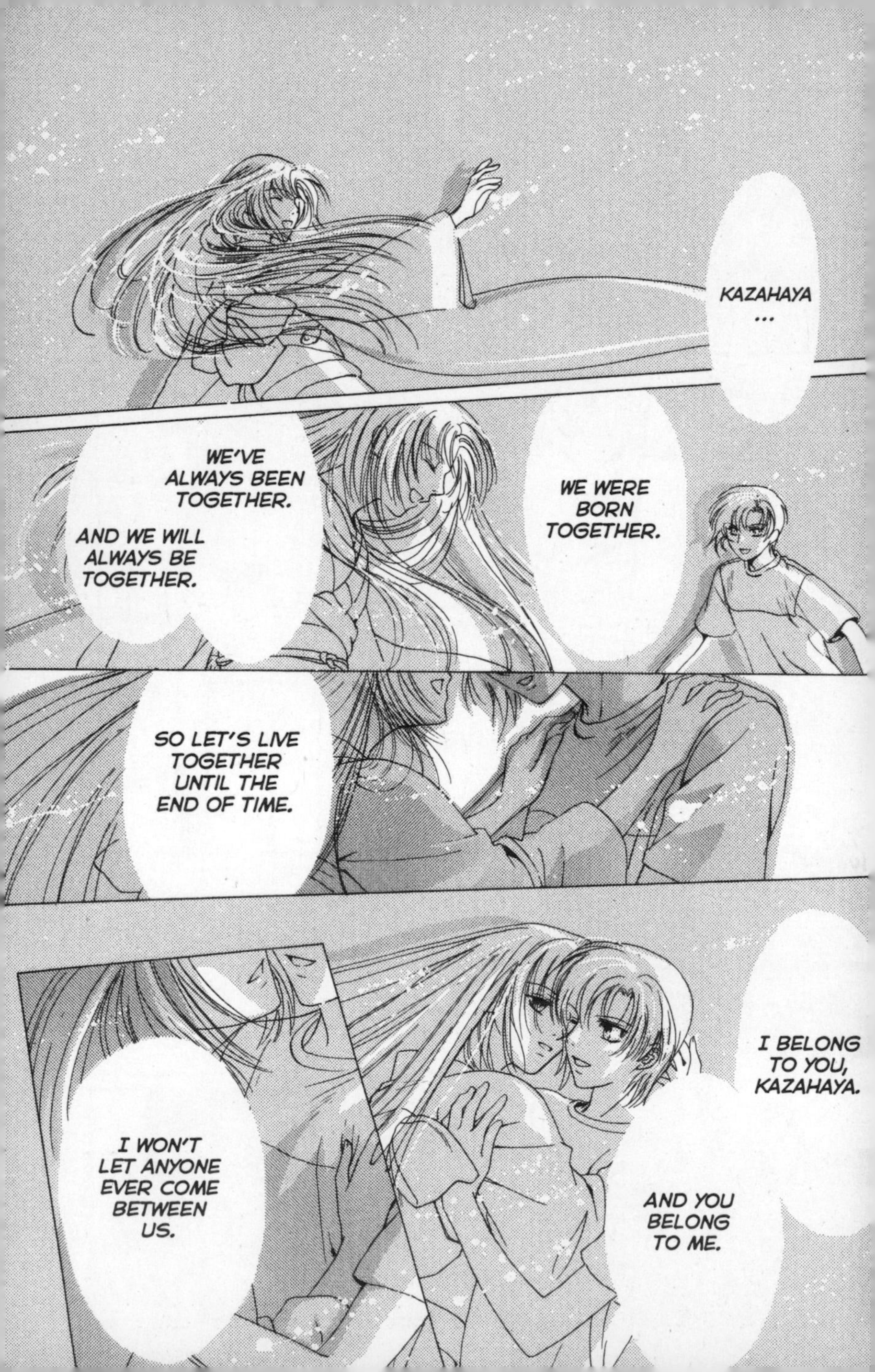
KAZAHAYA ...
WE WERE BORN TOGETHER.
WE'VE ALWAYS BEEN TOGETHER.
AND WE WILL ALWAYS BE TOGETHER.
SO LET'S LIVE TOGETHER UNTIL THE END OF TIME.
I BELONG TO YOU, KAZAHAYA.
AND YOU BELONG TO ME.
I WON'T LET ANYONE EVER COME BETWEEN US.

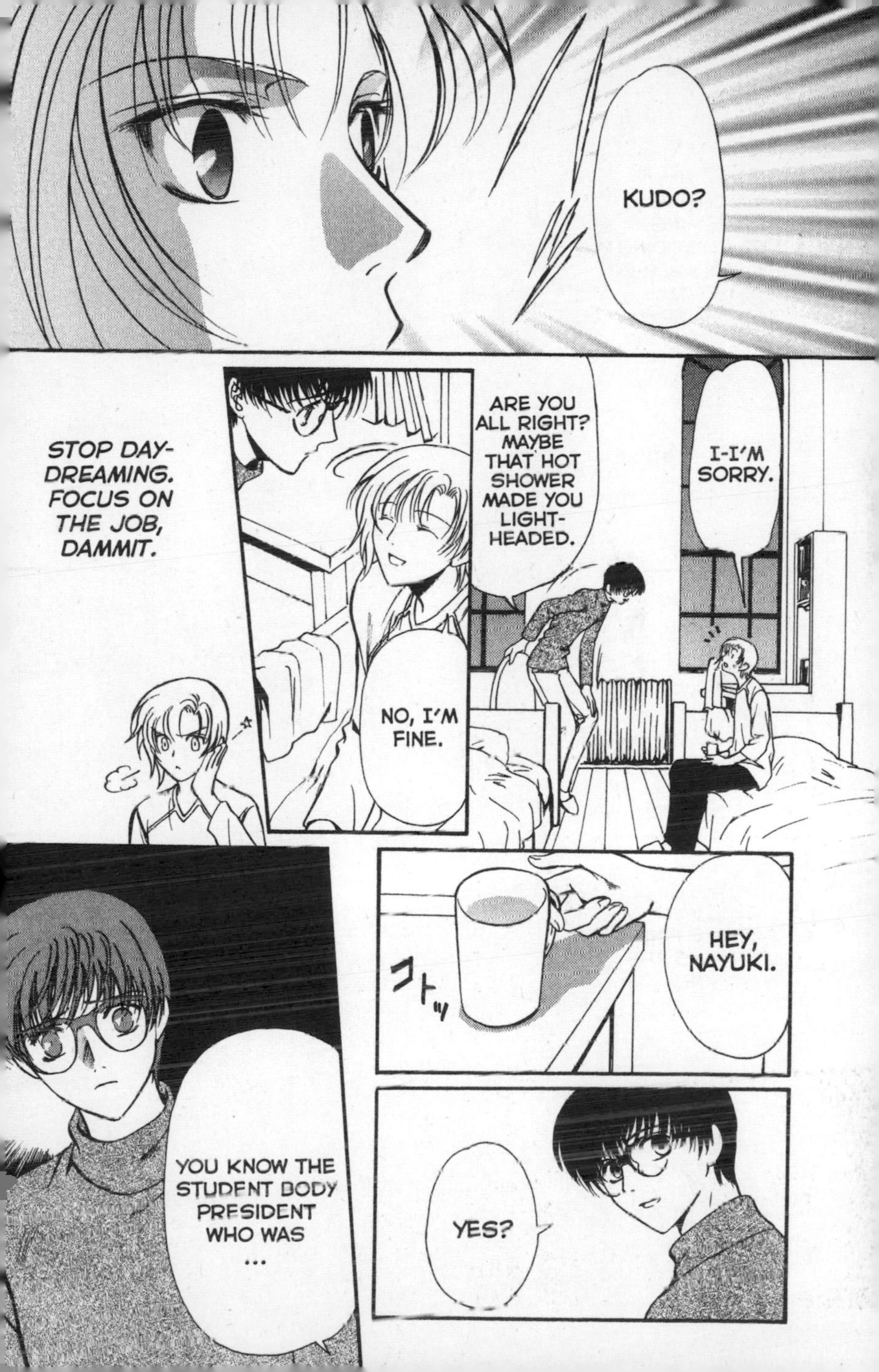
KUDO?
I-I'M SORRY.
ARE YOU ALL RIGHT? MAYBE THAT HOT SHOWER MADE YOU LIGHT-HEADED.
NO, I'M FINE.
STOP DAY-DREAMING. FOCUS ON THE JOB, DAMMIT.
HEY, NAYUKI.
コトッ
YES?
YOU KNOW THE STUDENT BODY PRESIDENT WHO WAS ...

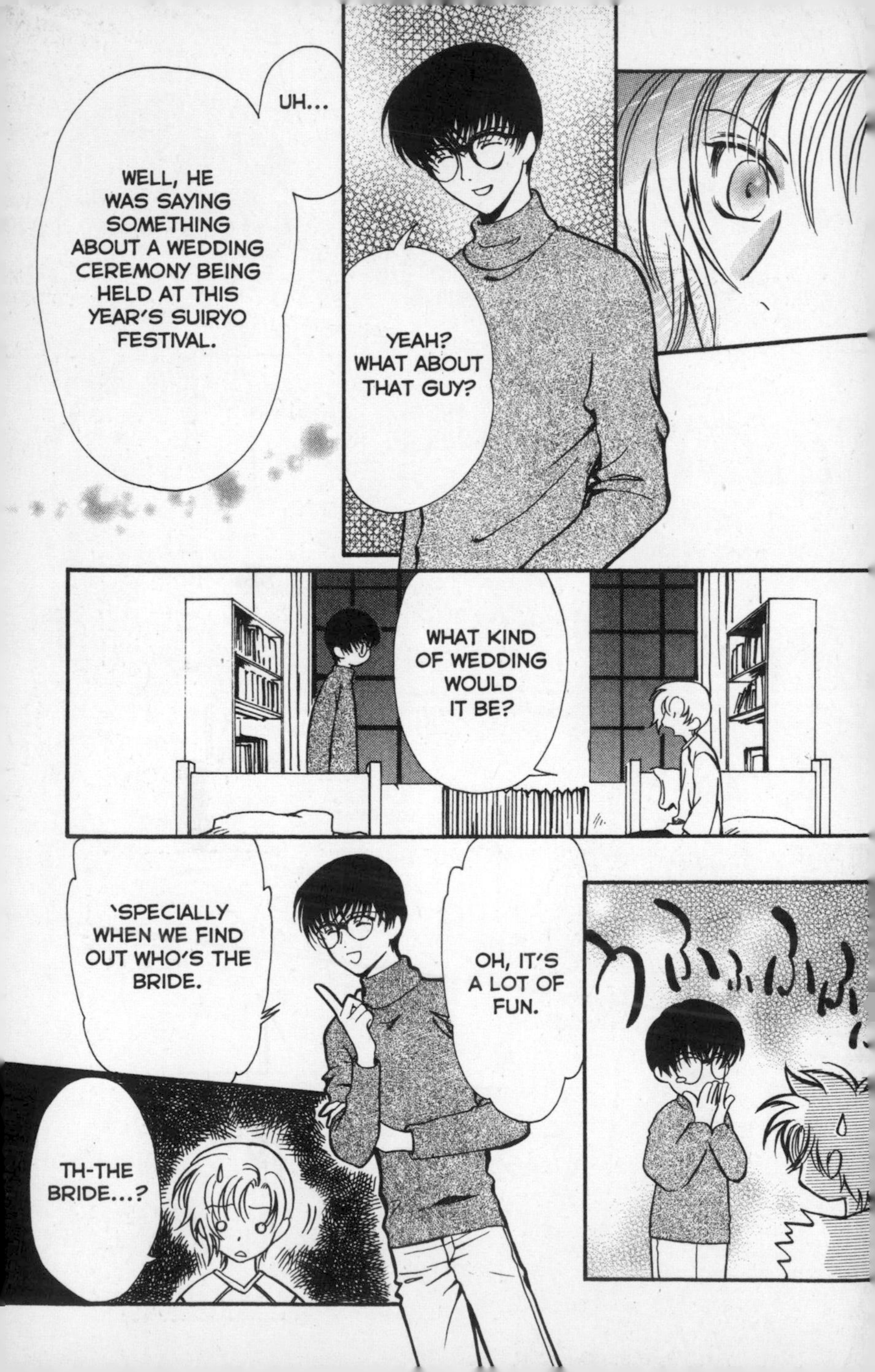
YEAH? WHAT ABOUT THAT GUY?
UH...
WELL, HE WAS SAYING SOMETHING ABOUT A WEDDING CEREMONY BEING HELD AT THIS YEAR'S SUIRYO FESTIVAL.
WHAT KIND OF WEDDING WOULD IT BE?
OH, IT'S A LOT OF FUN.
'SPECIALLY WHEN WE FIND OUT WHO'S THE BRIDE.
TH-THE BRIDE...?

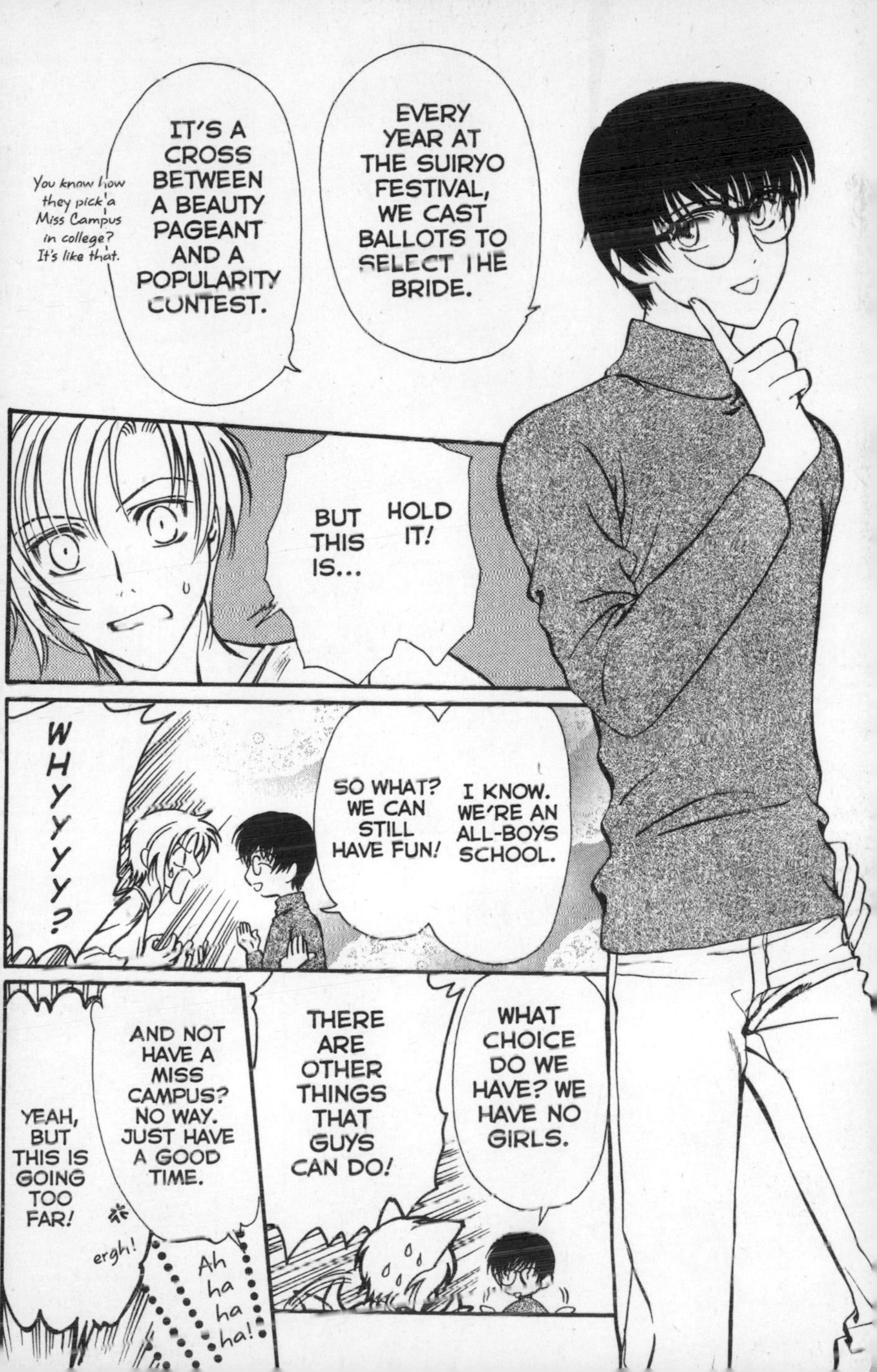
EVERY YEAR AT THE SUIRYO FESTIVAL, WE CAST BALLOTS TO SELECT THE BRIDE.
IT'S A CROSS BETWEEN A BEAUTY PAGEANT AND A POPULARITY CONTEST.
You know how they pick a Miss Campus in college? It's like that.
HOLD IT!
BUT THIS IS...
I KNOW. WE'RE AN ALL-BOYS SCHOOL.
SO WHAT? WE CAN STILL HAVE FUN!
WHYYYYY?
WHAT CHOICE DO WE HAVE? WE HAVE NO GIRLS.
THERE ARE OTHER THINGS THAT GUYS CAN DO!
AND NOT HAVE A MISS CAMPUS? NO WAY. JUST HAVE A GOOD TIME.
YEAH, BUT THIS IS GOING TOO FAR!
ergh!
Ah ha ha ha!

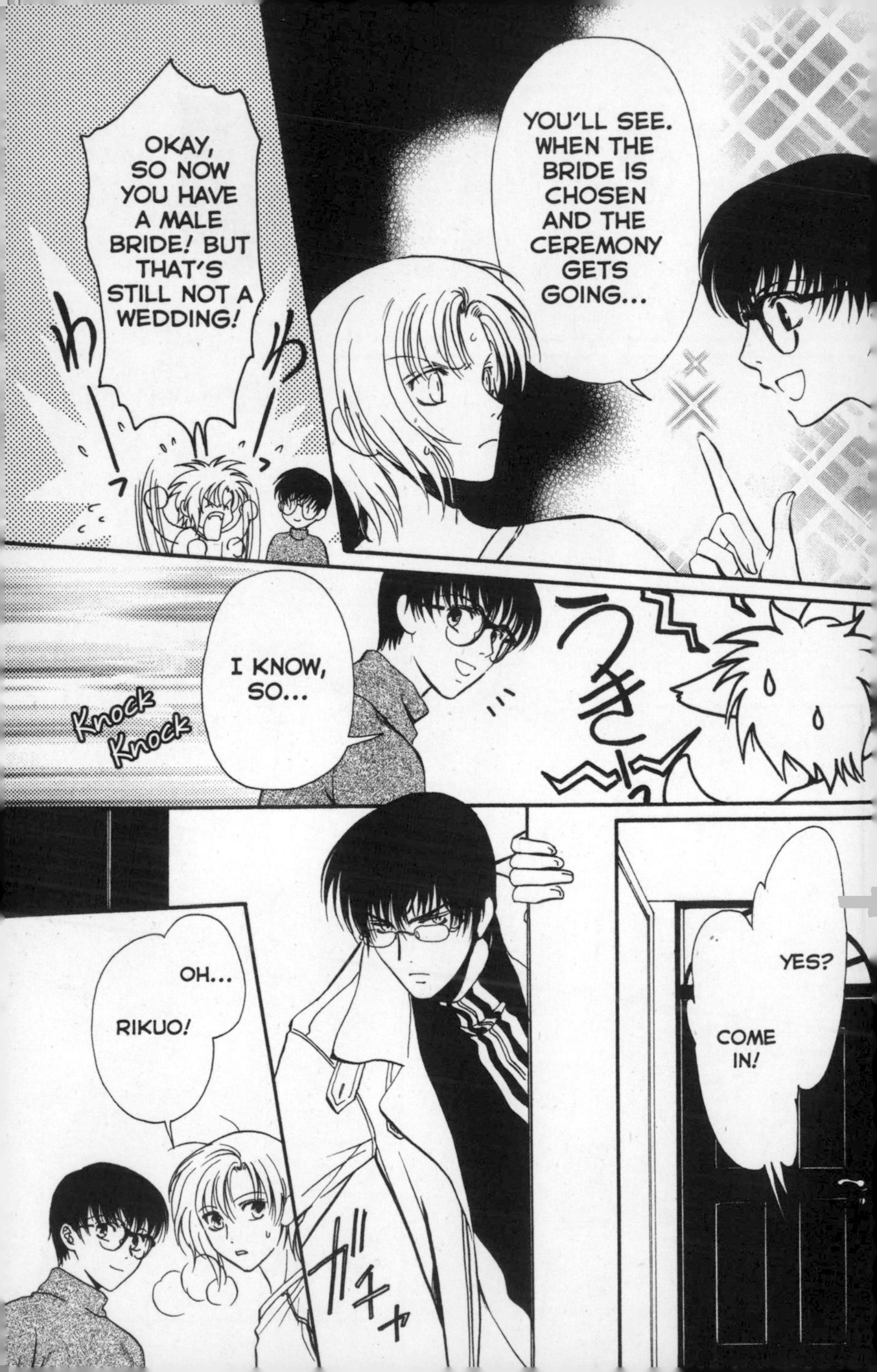
YOU'LL SEE. WHEN THE BRIDE IS CHOSEN AND THE CEREMONY GETS GOING...
OKAY, SO NOW YOU HAVE A MALE BRIDE! BUT THAT'S STILL NOT A WEDDING!
I KNOW, SO...
Knock Knock
YES?
COME IN!
OH...
RIKUO!

NO WAY!

ER?

UH...

ぶん
ぶん

あはははは

OH, YOU GUYS ARE ALREADY FRIENDLY ENOUGH TO CALL EACH OTHER BY YOUR FIRST NAMES?

きゃっ

CAN I TALK TO YOU?

OKAY. SURE.

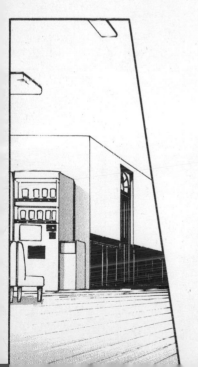

Go on! Stay out late! I'll sign you in at curfew!

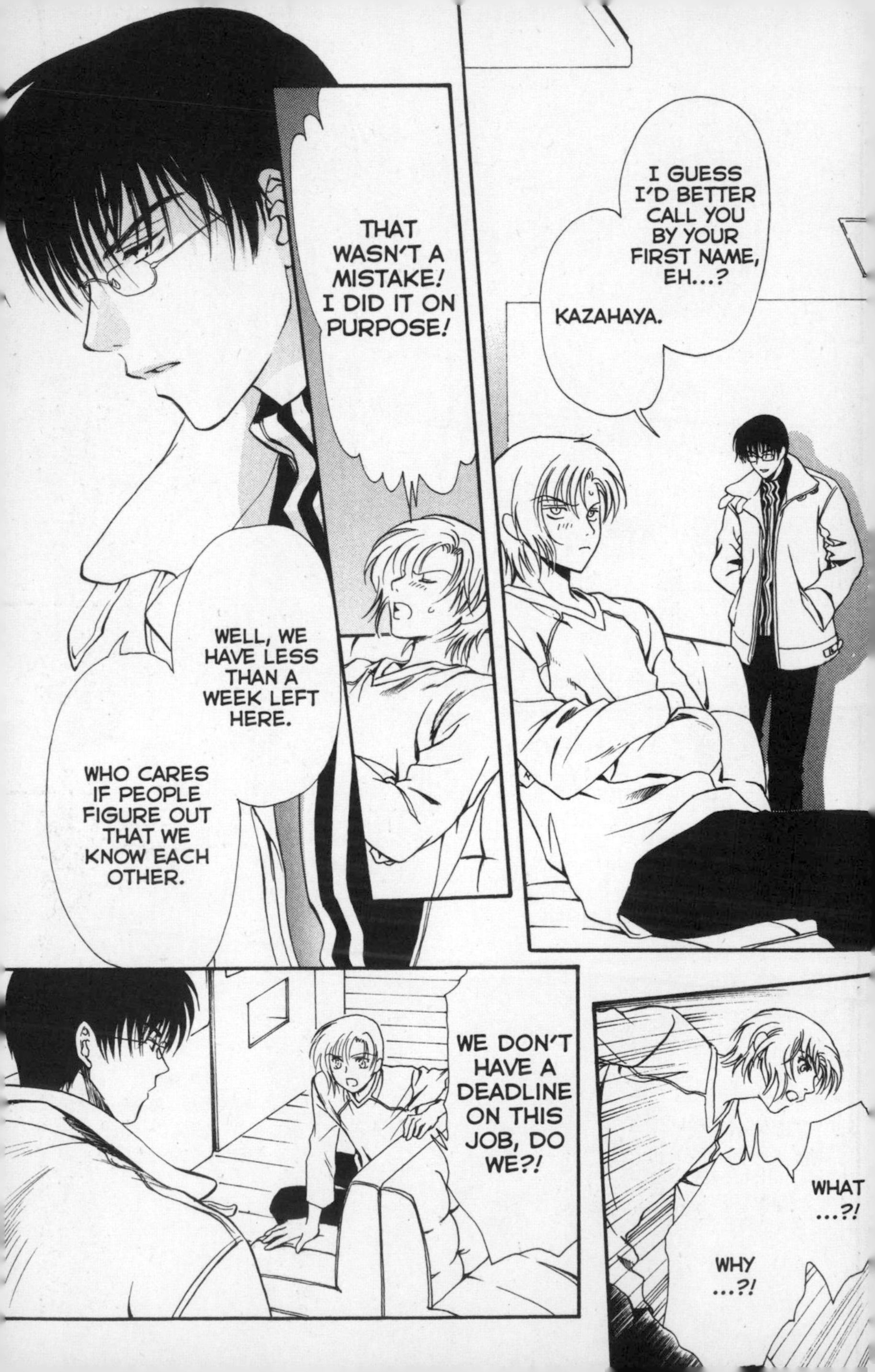
I GUESS I'D BETTER CALL YOU BY YOUR FIRST NAME, EH...?
KAZAHAYA.
THAT WASN'T A MISTAKE! I DID IT ON PURPOSE!
WELL, WE HAVE LESS THAN A WEEK LEFT HERE.
WHO CARES IF PEOPLE FIGURE OUT THAT WE KNOW EACH OTHER.
WHAT...?!
WHY...?!
WE DON'T HAVE A DEADLINE ON THIS JOB, DO WE?!

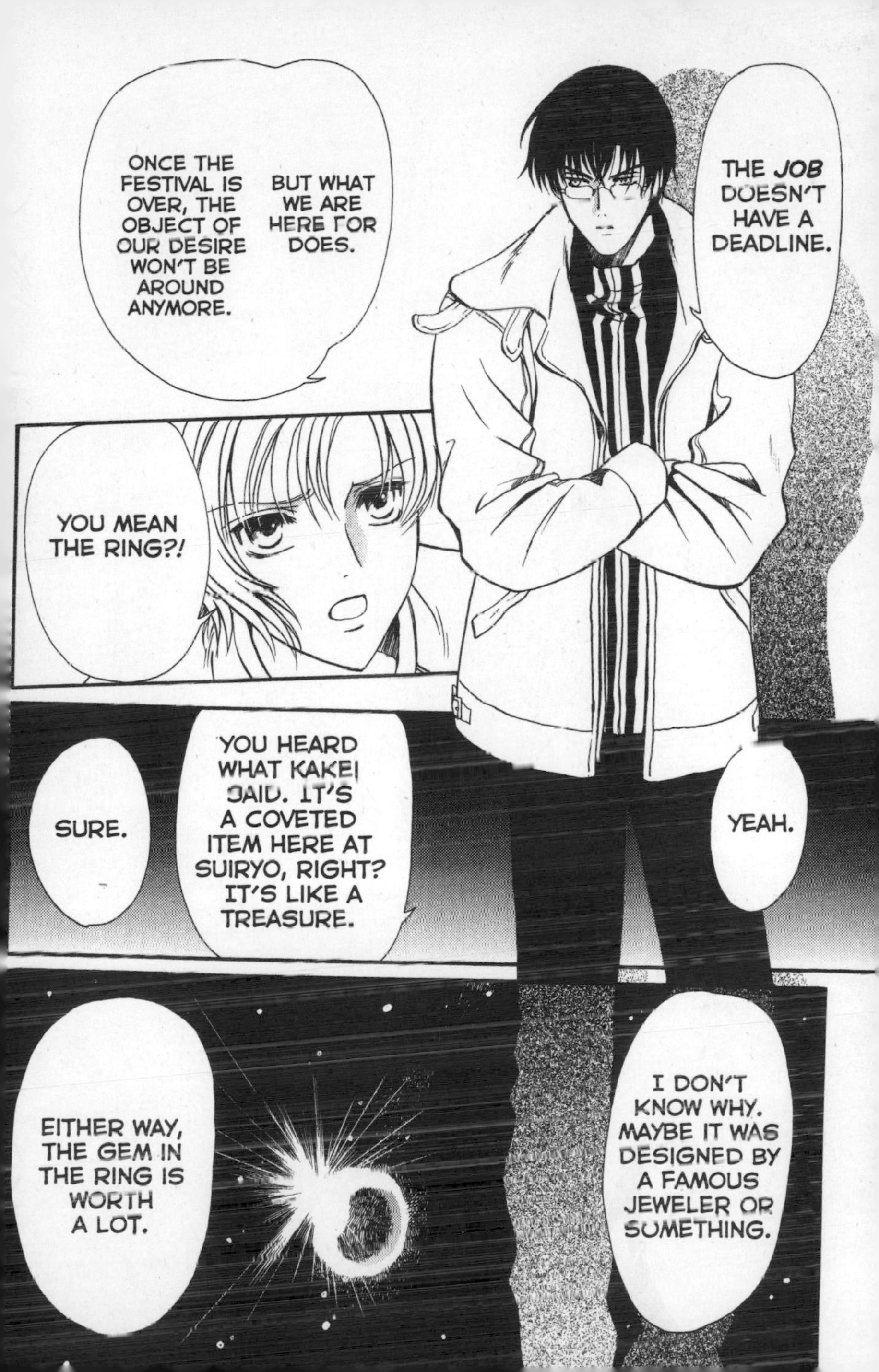
THE *JOB* DOESN'T HAVE A DEADLINE.
BUT WHAT WE ARE HERE FOR DOES.
ONCE THE FESTIVAL IS OVER, THE OBJECT OF OUR DESIRE WON'T BE AROUND ANYMORE.
YOU MEAN THE RING?!
YEAH.
YOU HEARD WHAT KAKEI SAID. IT'S A COVETED ITEM HERE AT SUIRYO, RIGHT? IT'S LIKE A TREASURE.
SURE.
I DON'T KNOW WHY. MAYBE IT WAS DESIGNED BY A FAMOUS JEWELER OR SOMETHING.
EITHER WAY, THE GEM IN THE RING IS WORTH A LOT.

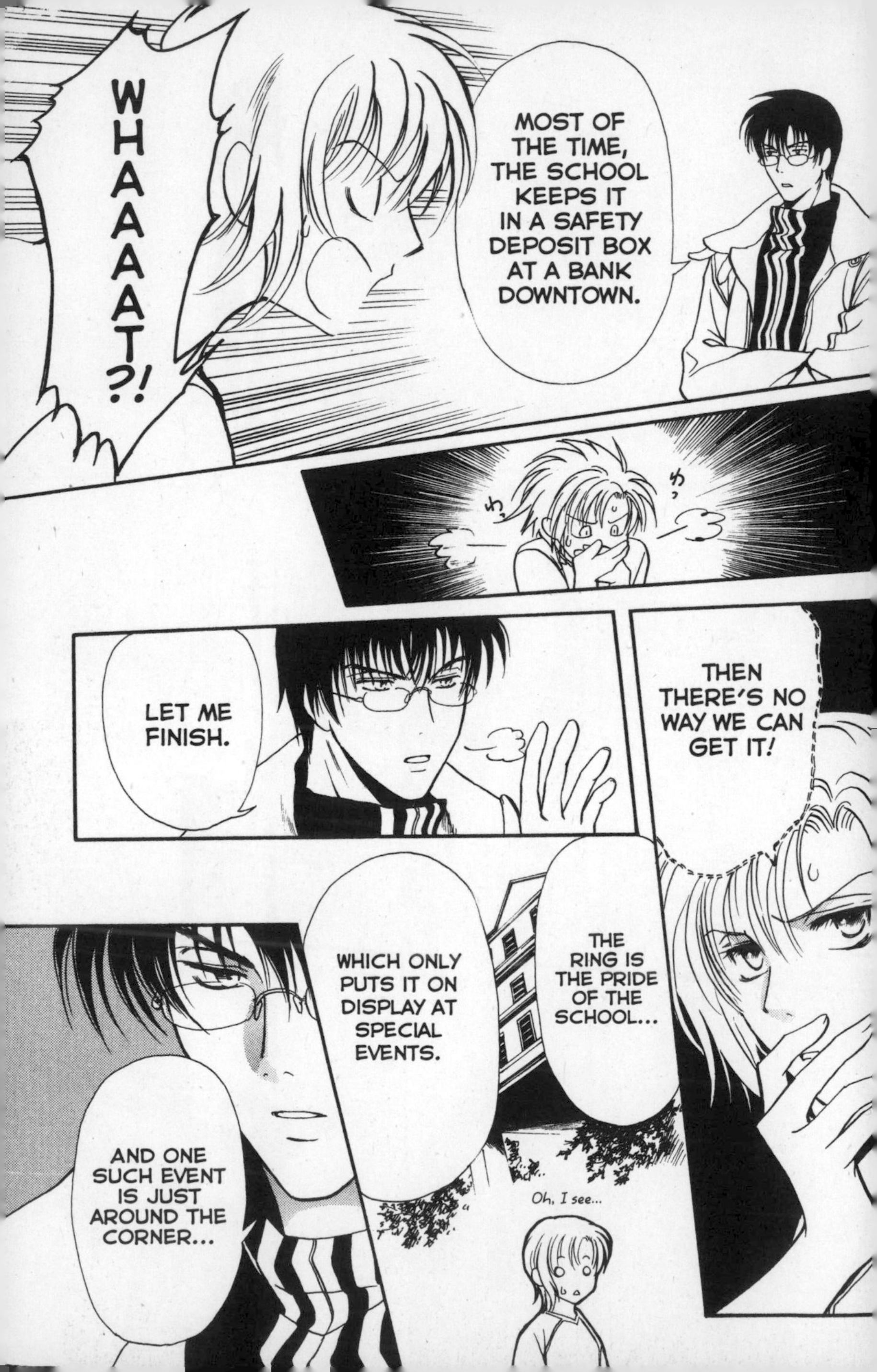
MOST OF THE TIME, THE SCHOOL KEEPS IT IN A SAFETY DEPOSIT BOX AT A BANK DOWNTOWN.
WHAAAAAT?!
THEN THERE'S NO WAY WE CAN GET IT!
LET ME FINISH.
THE RING IS THE PRIDE OF THE SCHOOL...
WHICH ONLY PUTS IT ON DISPLAY AT SPECIAL EVENTS.
Oh, I see...
AND ONE SUCH EVENT IS JUST AROUND THE CORNER...

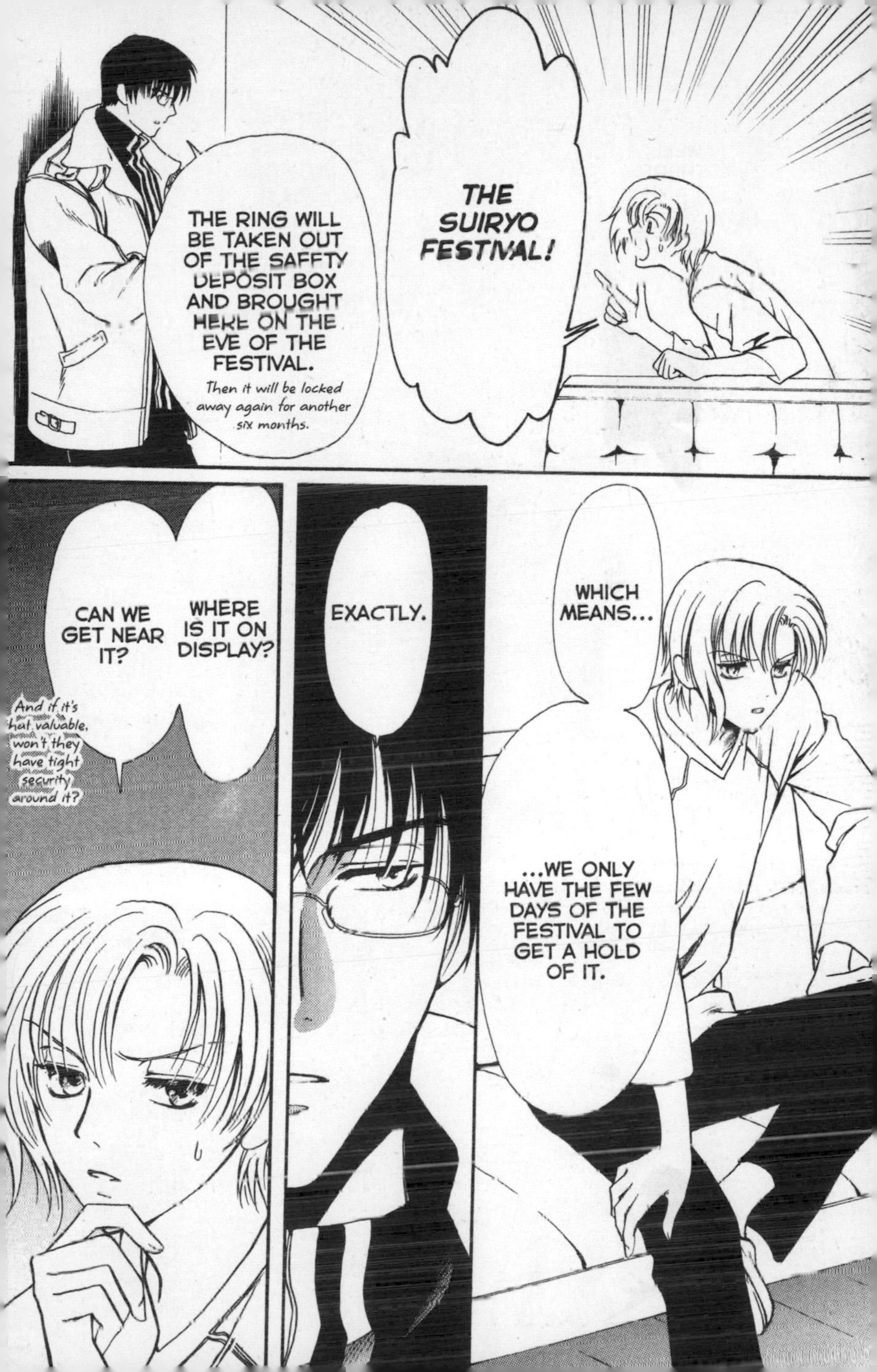
THE SUIRYO FESTIVAL!
THE RING WILL BE TAKEN OUT OF THE SAFETY DEPOSIT BOX AND BROUGHT HERE ON THE EVE OF THE FESTIVAL.
Then it will be locked away again for another six months.
WHICH MEANS...
...WE ONLY HAVE THE FEW DAYS OF THE FESTIVAL TO GET A HOLD OF IT.
EXACTLY.
WHERE IS IT ON DISPLAY?
CAN WE GET NEAR IT?
And if it's hat valuable, won't they have tight security around it?

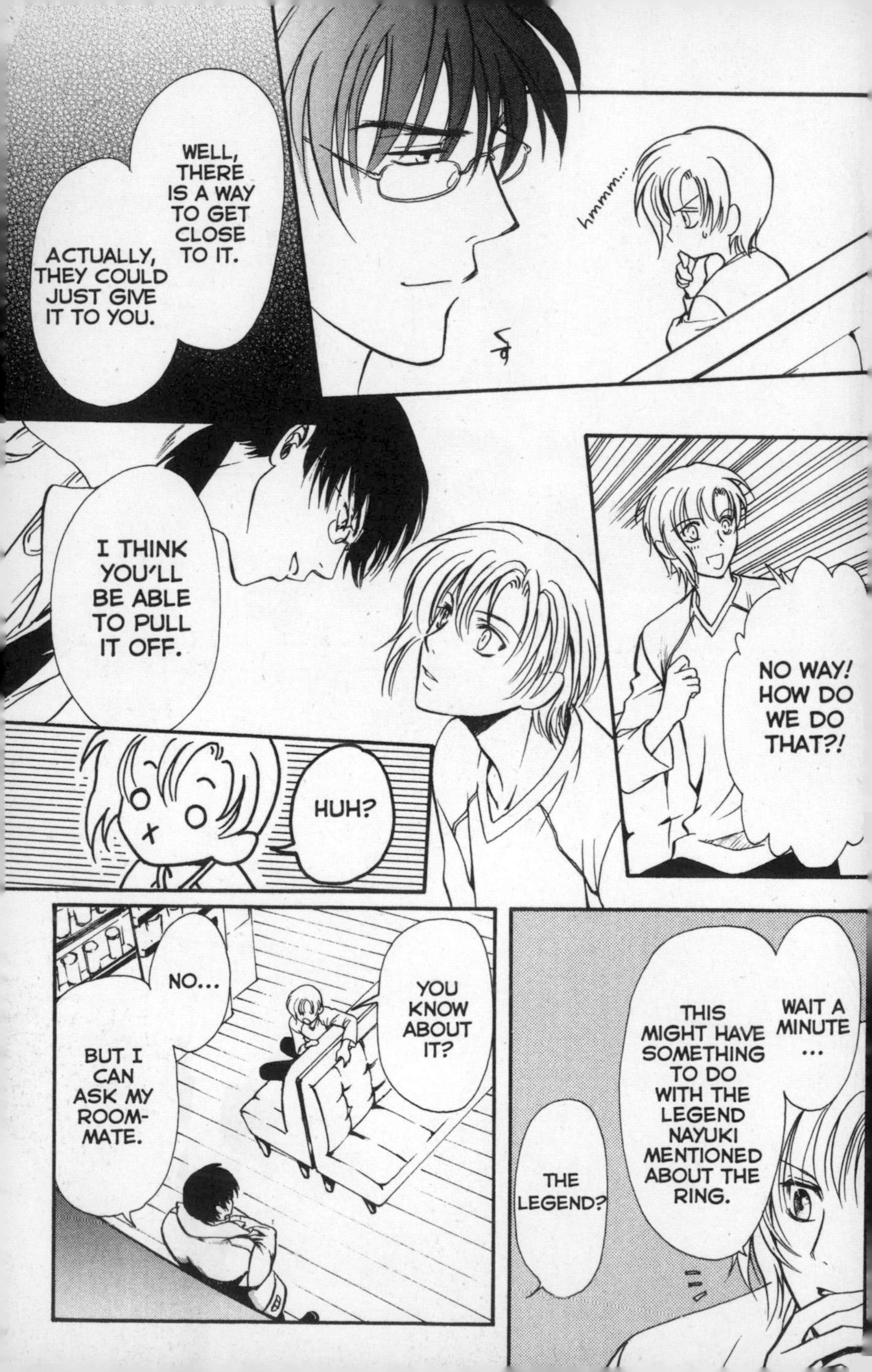
hmmm...
WELL, THERE IS A WAY TO GET CLOSE TO IT.
ACTUALLY, THEY COULD JUST GIVE IT TO YOU.
NO WAY! HOW DO WE DO THAT?!
I THINK YOU'LL BE ABLE TO PULL IT OFF.
HUH?
WAIT A MINUTE ...
THIS MIGHT HAVE SOMETHING TO DO WITH THE LEGEND NAYUKI MENTIONED ABOUT THE RING.
THE LEGEND?
YOU KNOW ABOUT IT?
NO...
BUT I CAN ASK MY ROOM-MATE.

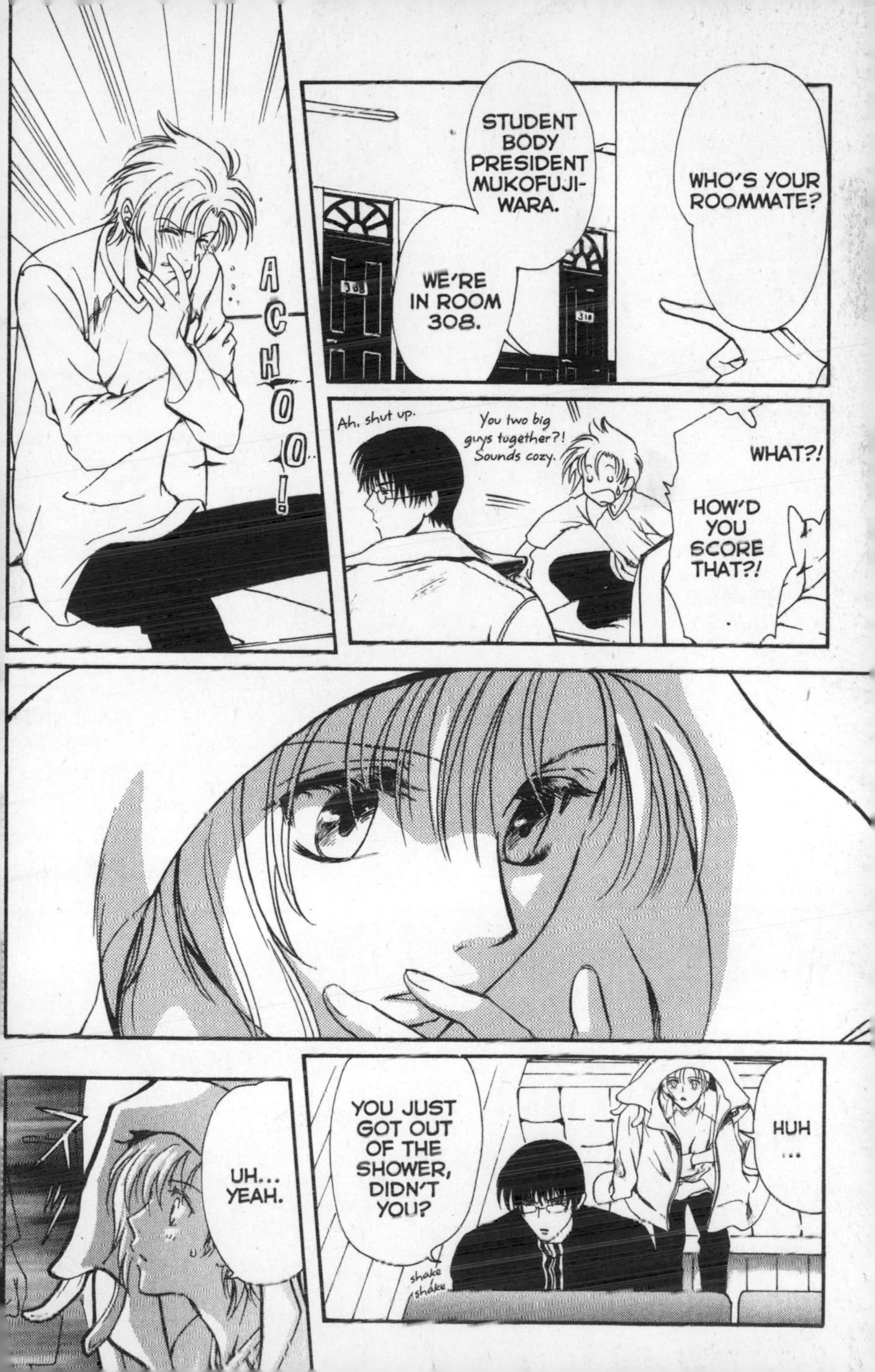
WHO'S YOUR ROOMMATE?
STUDENT BODY PRESIDENT MUKOFUJI-WARA.
WE'RE IN ROOM 308.
WHAT?!
HOW'D YOU SCORE THAT?!
You two big guys together?! Sounds cozy.
Ah, shut up.
ACHOO!..
HUH...
YOU JUST GOT OUT OF THE SHOWER, DIDN'T YOU?
shake shake
UH... YEAH.

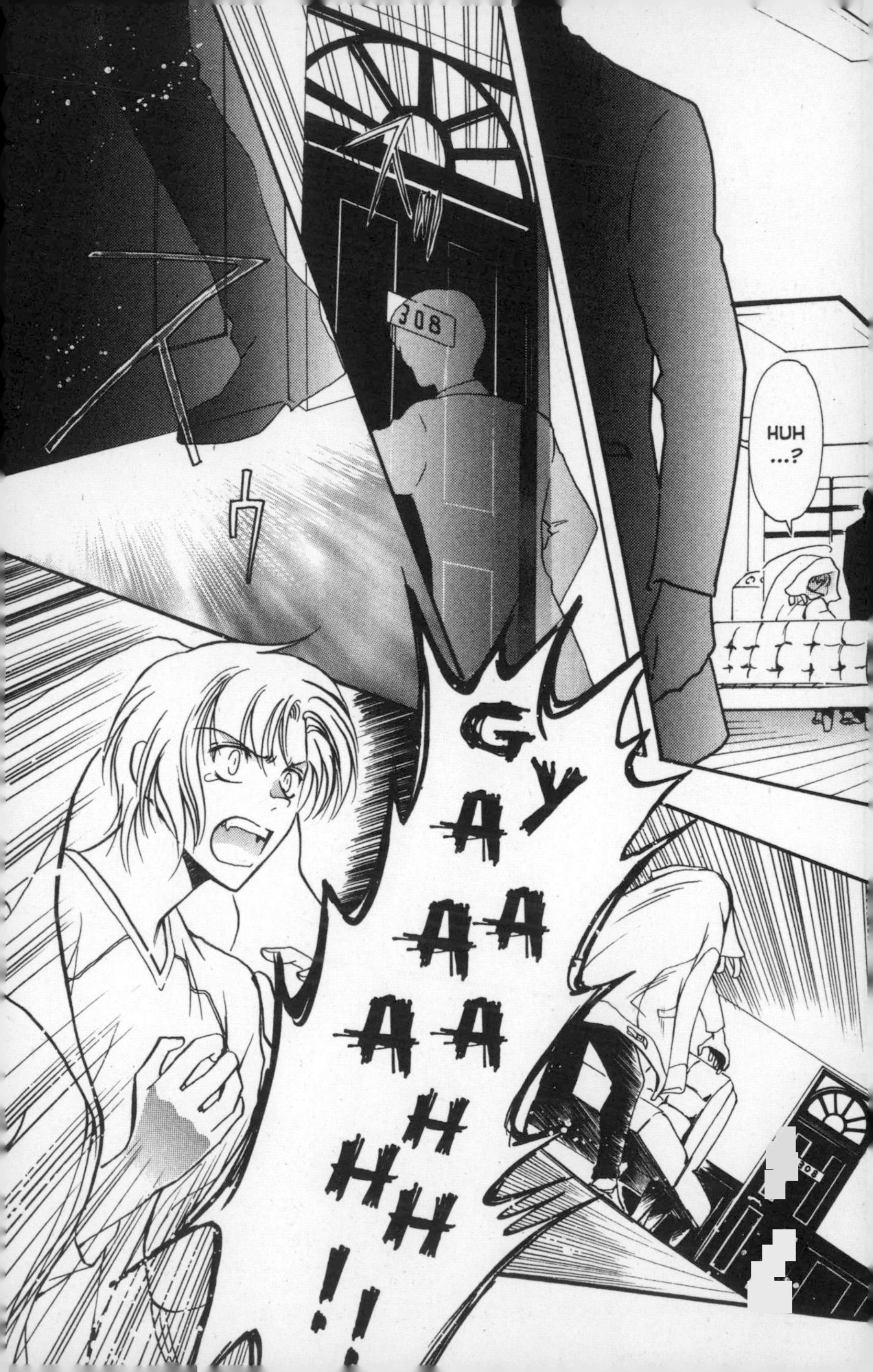
HUH ...?
GYAAAAAHHHH!!

合法ドラッグ

LEGAL DRUG

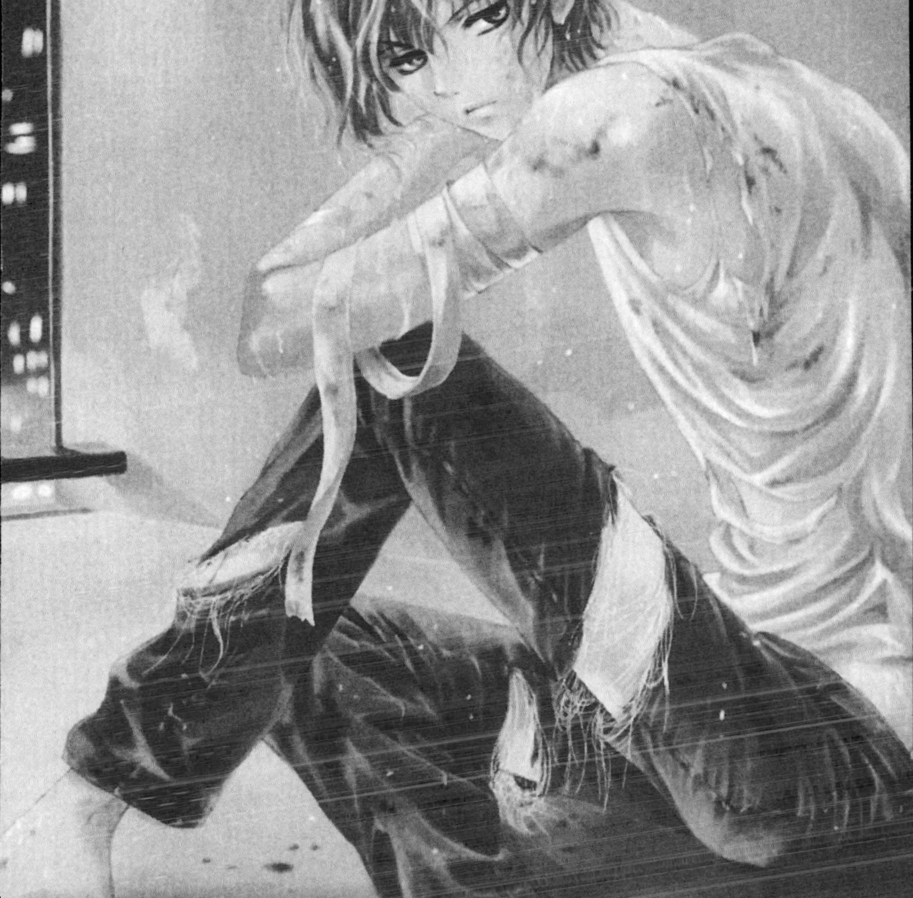

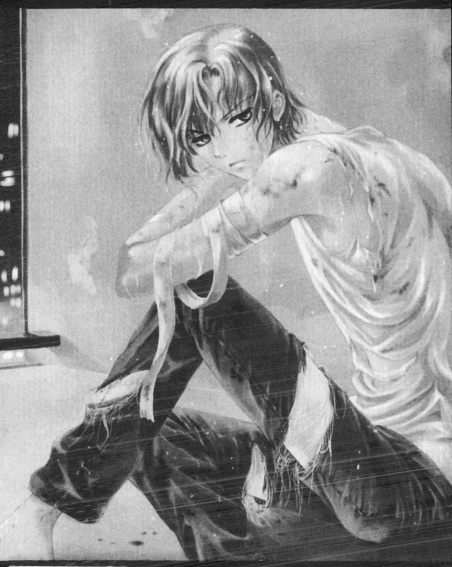

DRUG NO.14 Daily use of the drug may cause poisoning.

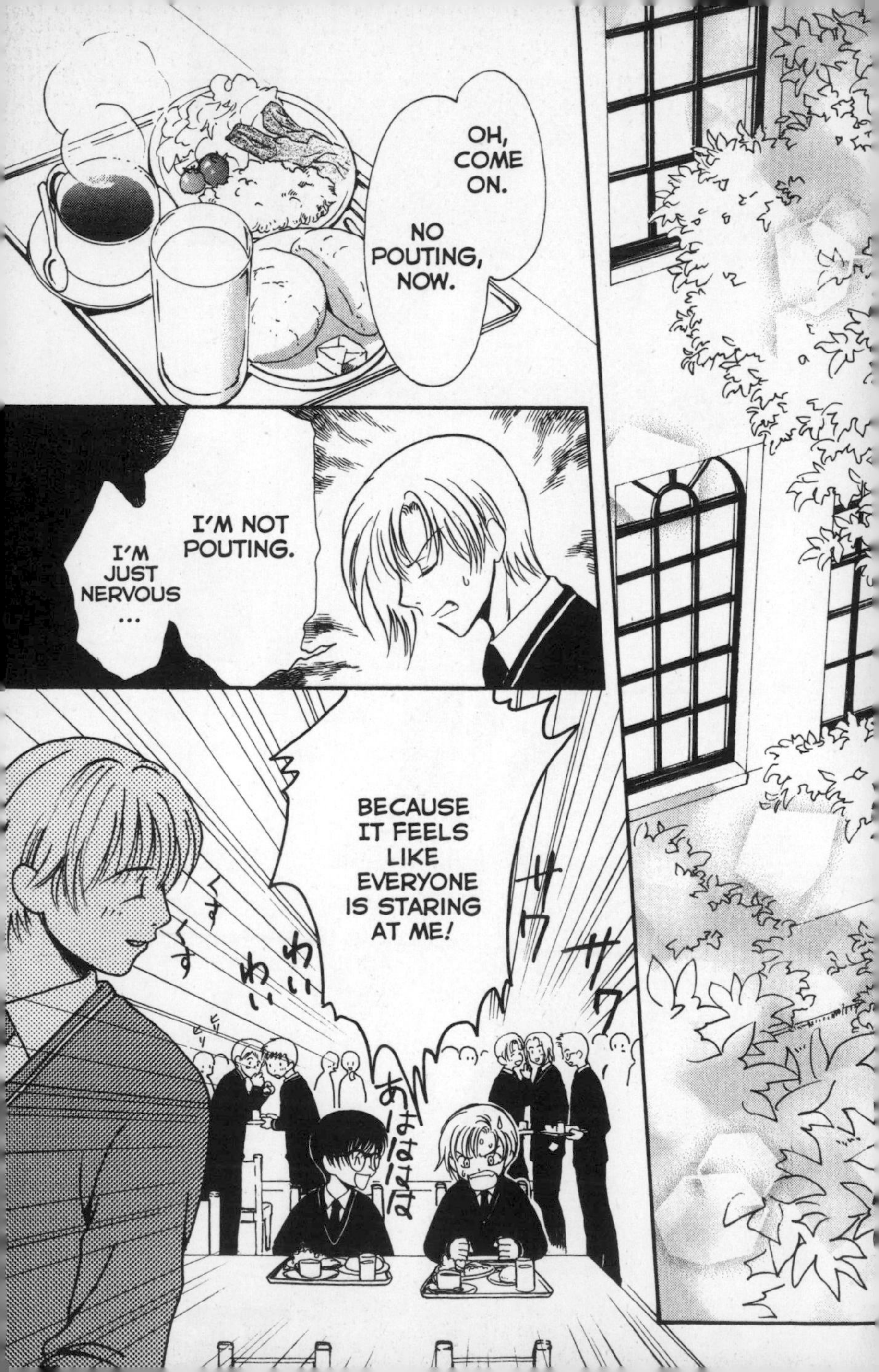
OH, COME ON.
NO POUTING, NOW.
I'M NOT POUTING.
I'M JUST NERVOUS ...
サワサワ
BECAUSE IT FEELS LIKE EVERYONE IS STARING AT ME!
わいわい
くすくす
あははは

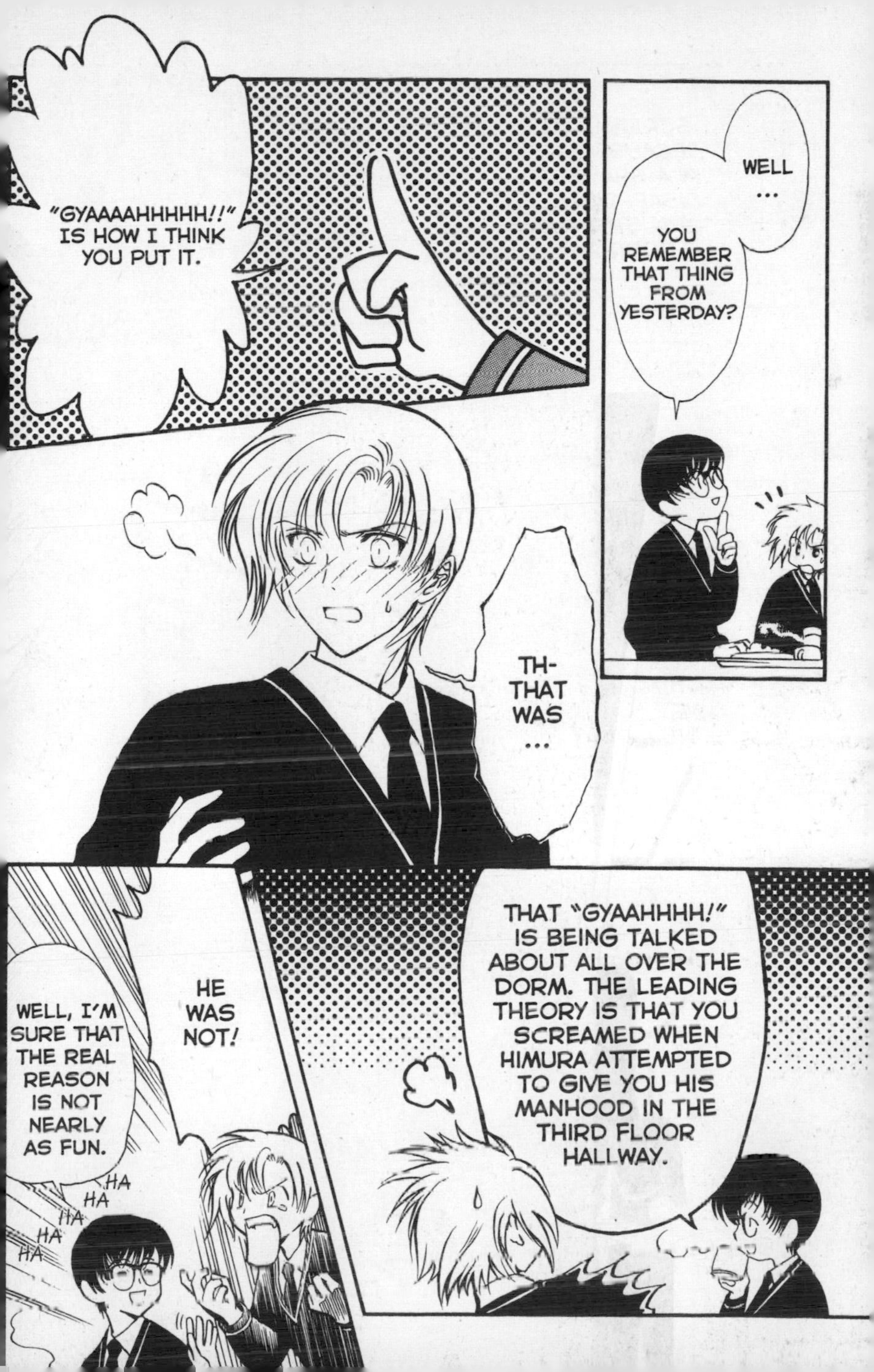
WELL ... YOU REMEMBER THAT THING FROM YESTERDAY?
"GYAAAAHHHHH!!" IS HOW I THINK YOU PUT IT.
TH-THAT WAS ...
THAT "GYAAHHHH!" IS BEING TALKED ABOUT ALL OVER THE DORM. THE LEADING THEORY IS THAT YOU SCREAMED WHEN HIMURA ATTEMPTED TO GIVE YOU HIS MANHOOD IN THE THIRD FLOOR HALLWAY.
HE WAS NOT!
WELL, I'M SURE THAT THE REAL REASON IS NOT NEARLY AS FUN.
HA HA HA HA HA

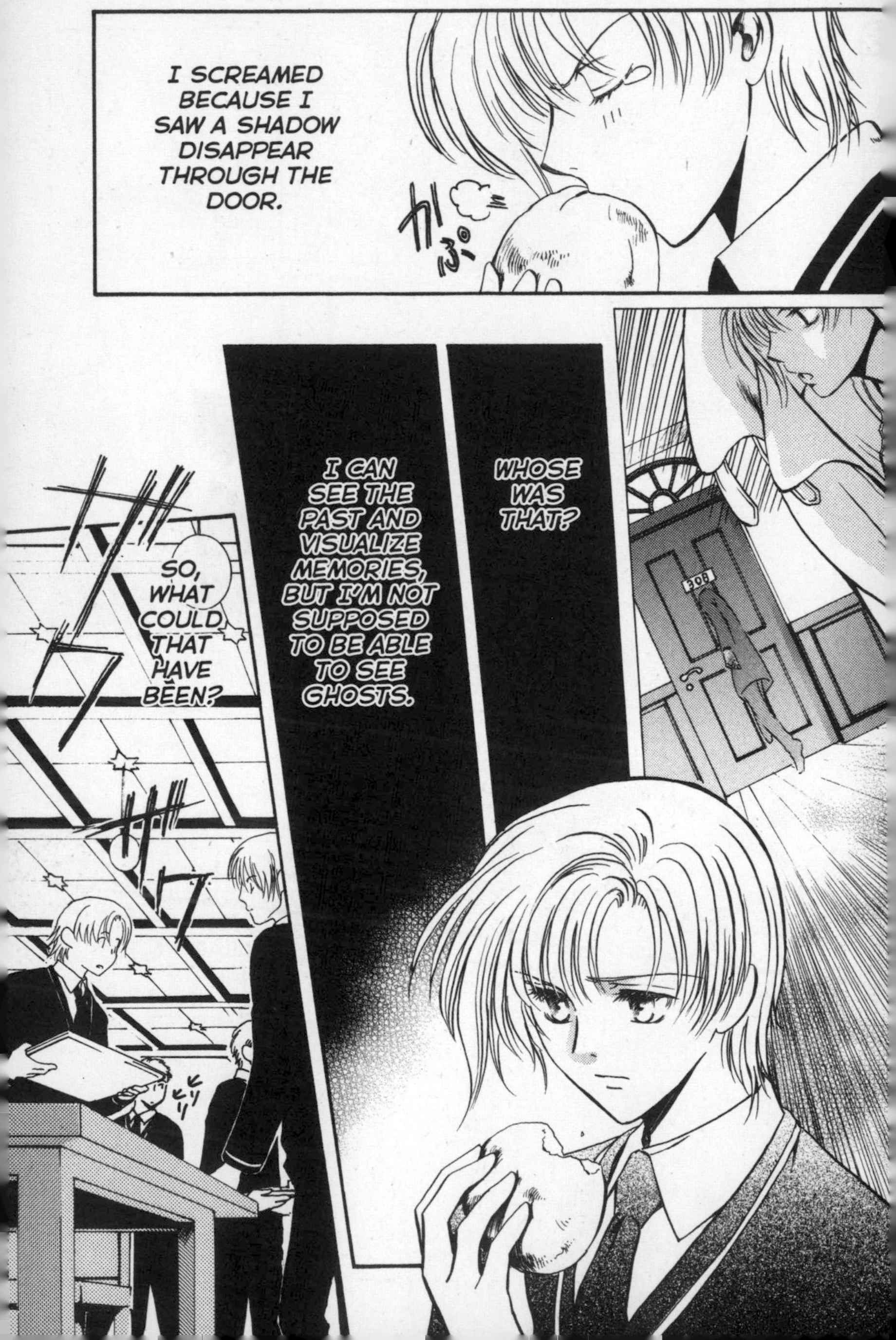
I SCREAMED BECAUSE I SAW A SHADOW DISAPPEAR THROUGH THE DOOR.
WHOSE WAS THAT?
I CAN SEE THE PAST AND VISUALIZE MEMORIES, BUT I'M NOT SUPPOSED TO BE ABLE TO SEE GHOSTS.
SO, WHAT COULD THAT HAVE BEEN?
308

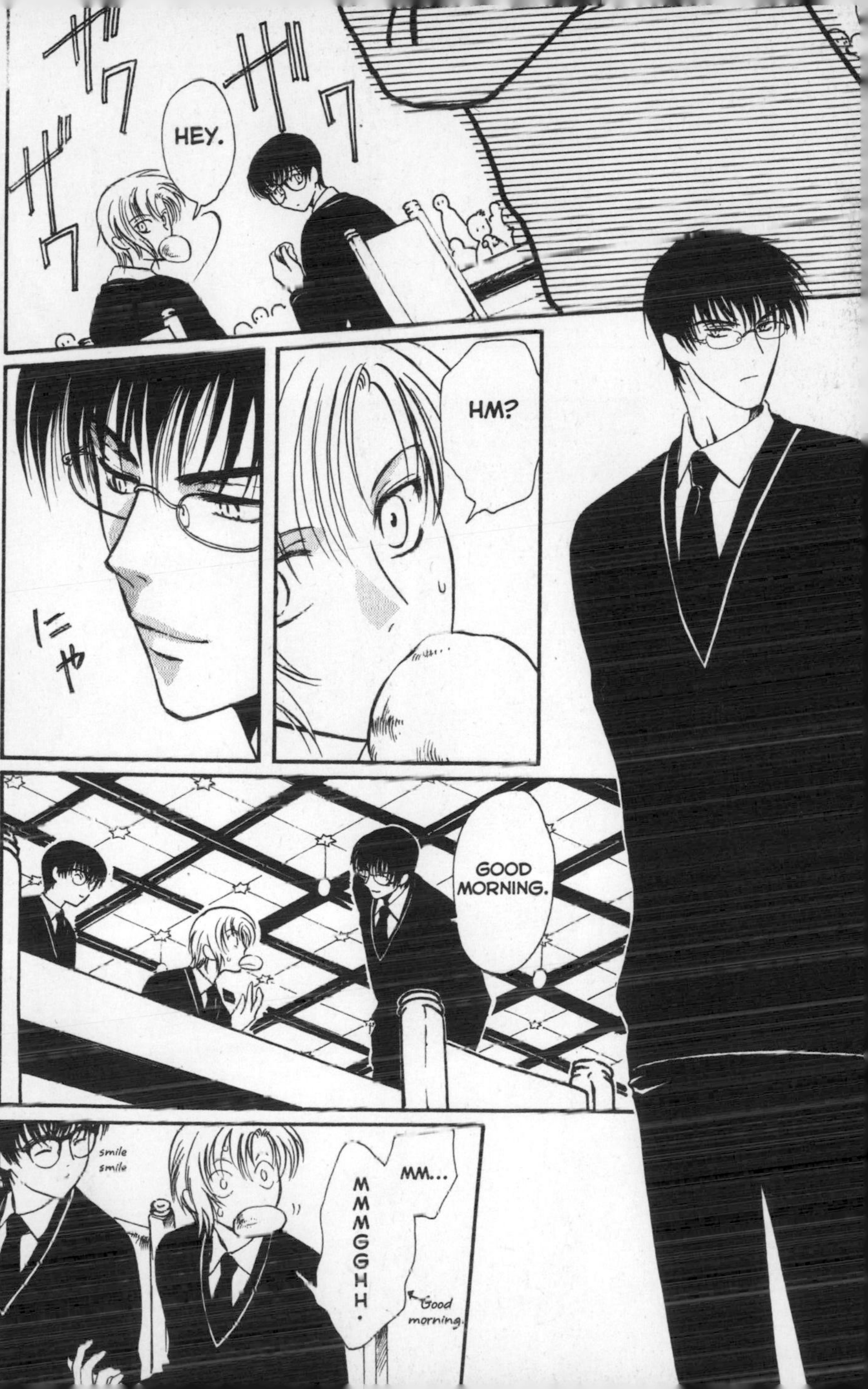
ザワ
ザワ
ザワ
HEY.
HM?
にや
GOOD MORNING.
MM...
MMMGGHH.
Good morning.
smile smile

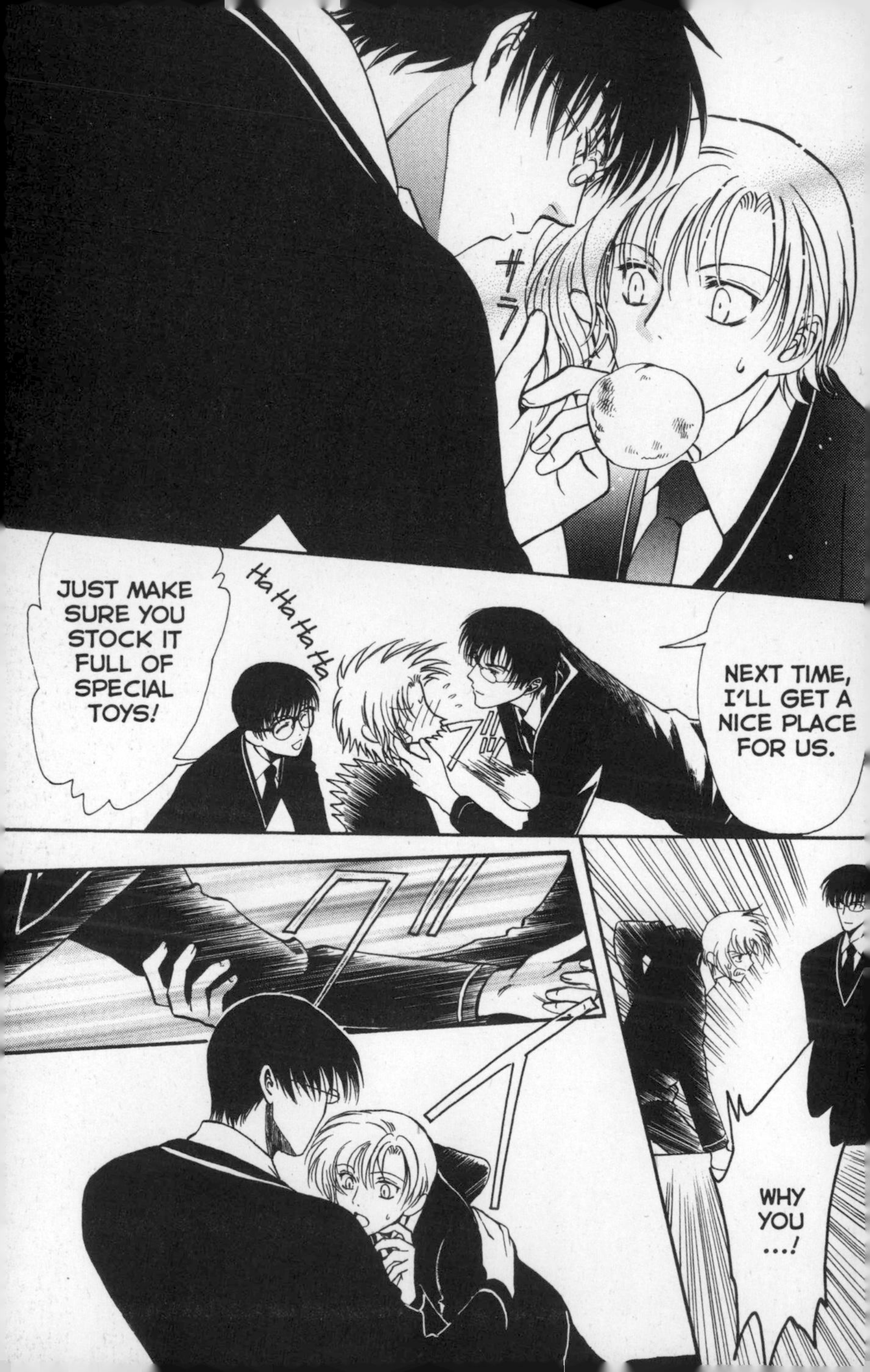
サラ
NEXT TIME, I'LL GET A NICE PLACE FOR US.
Ha Ha Ha Ha
JUST MAKE SURE YOU STOCK IT FULL OF SPECIAL TOYS!
WHY YOU ...!

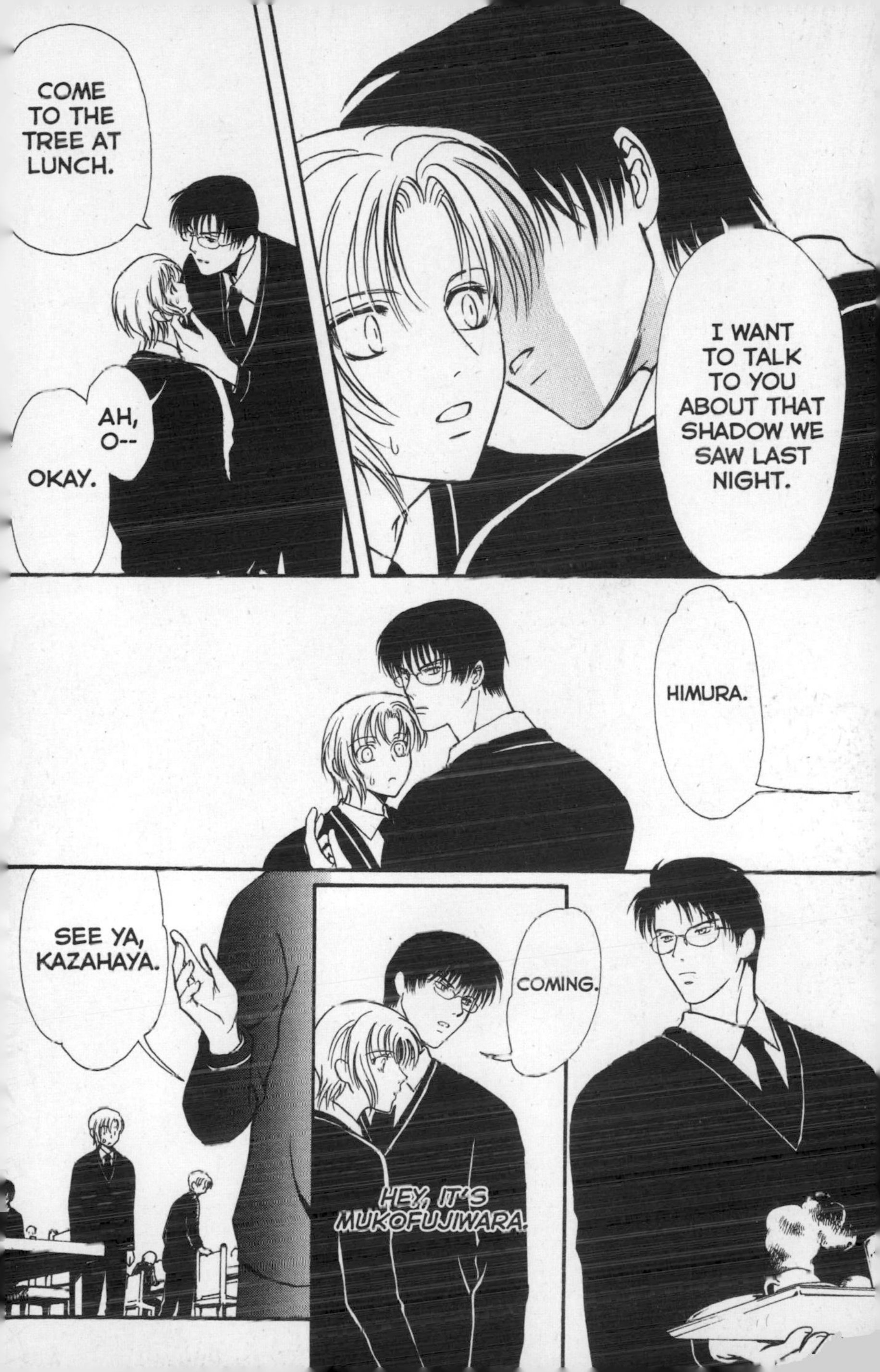
I WANT TO TALK TO YOU ABOUT THAT SHADOW WE SAW LAST NIGHT.
COME TO THE TREE AT LUNCH.
AH, O-- OKAY.
HIMURA.
COMING.
HEY, IT'S MUKOFUJIWARA.
SEE YA, KAZAHAYA.

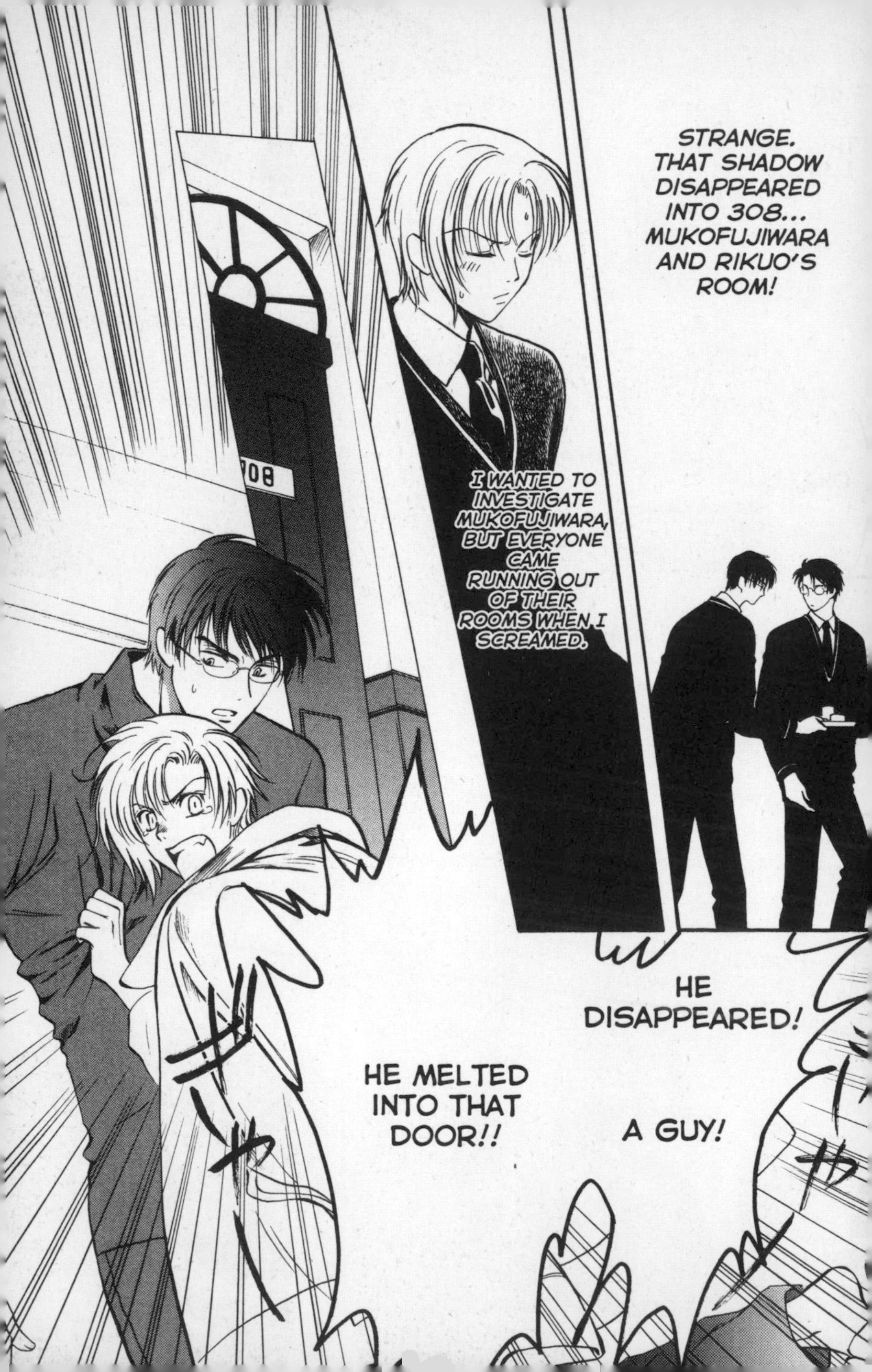
STRANGE. THAT SHADOW DISAPPEARED INTO 308... MUKOFUJIWARA AND RIKUO'S ROOM!
I WANTED TO INVESTIGATE MUKOFUJIWARA, BUT EVERYONE CAME RUNNING OUT OF THEIR ROOMS WHEN I SCREAMED.
HE DISAPPEARED!
A GUY!
HE MELTED INTO THAT DOOR!!

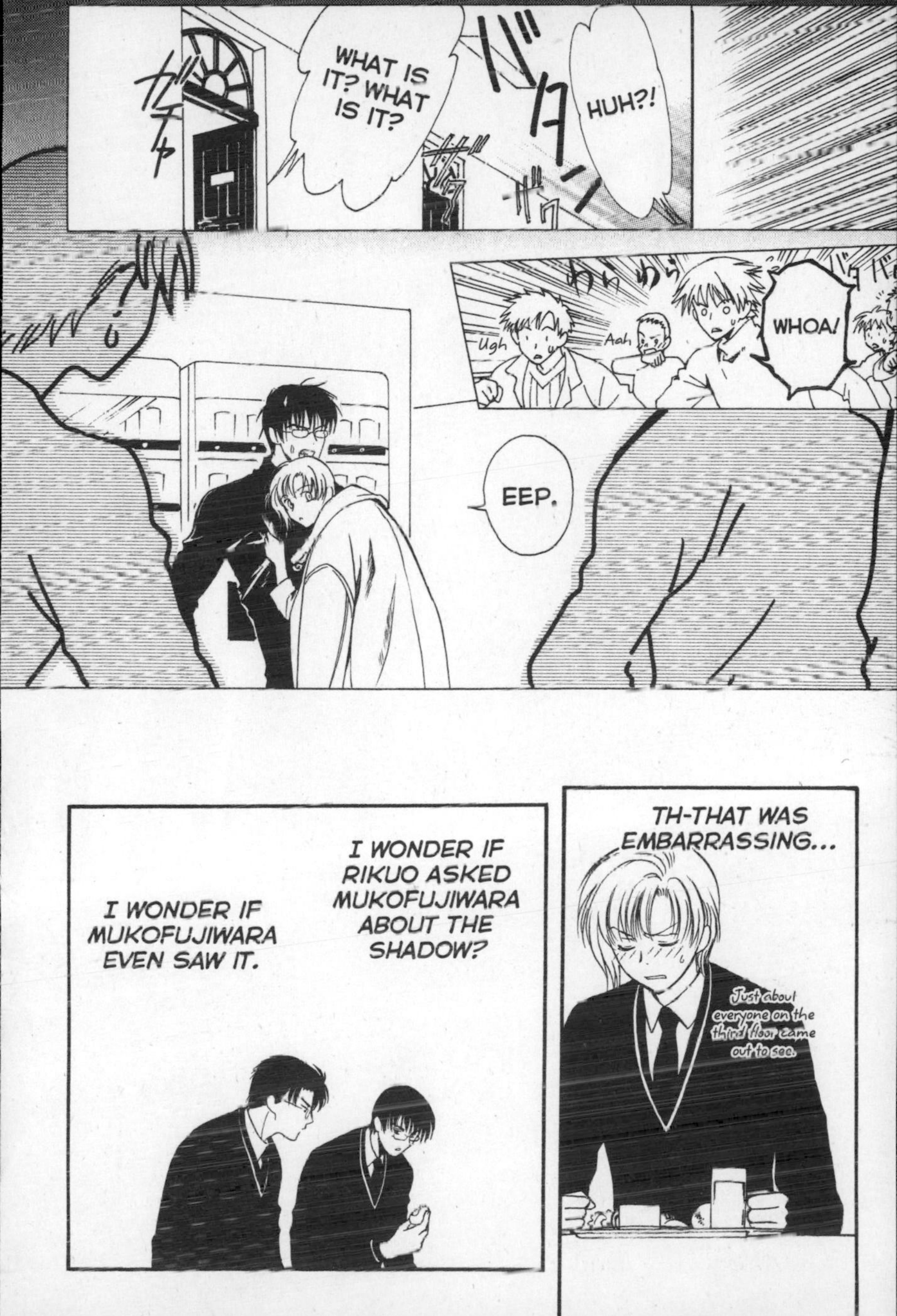
HUH?!
WHAT IS IT? WHAT IS IT?
WHOA!
Aah
Ugh
EEP.
TH-THAT WAS EMBARRASSING...
Just about everyone on the third floor came out to see.
I WONDER IF RIKUO ASKED MUKOFUJIWARA ABOUT THE SHADOW?
I WONDER IF MUKOFUJIWARA EVEN SAW IT.

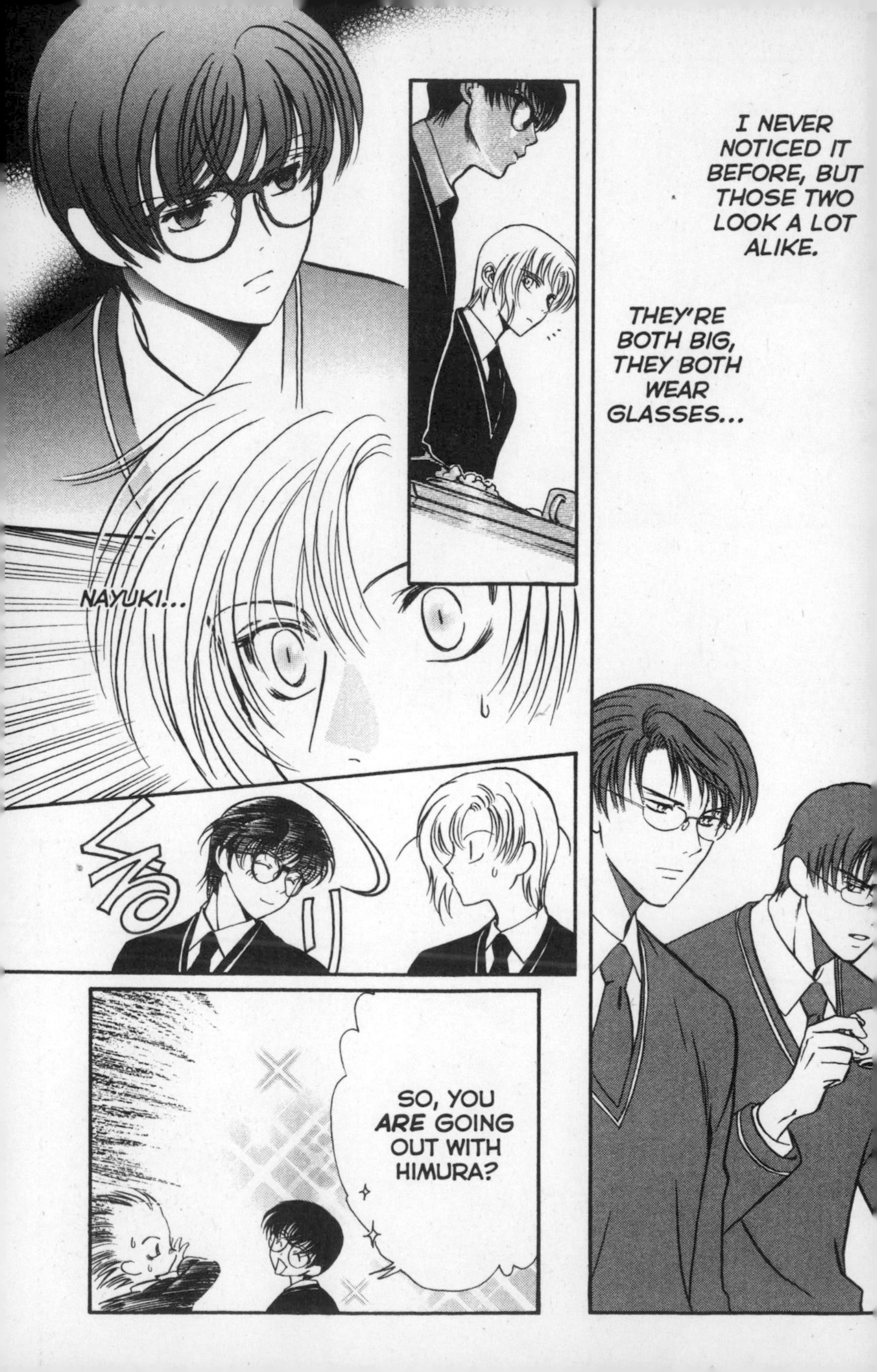
I NEVER NOTICED IT BEFORE, BUT THOSE TWO LOOK A LOT ALIKE.
THEY'RE BOTH BIG, THEY BOTH WEAR GLASSES...
NAYUKI...
SO, YOU *ARE* GOING OUT WITH HIMURA?

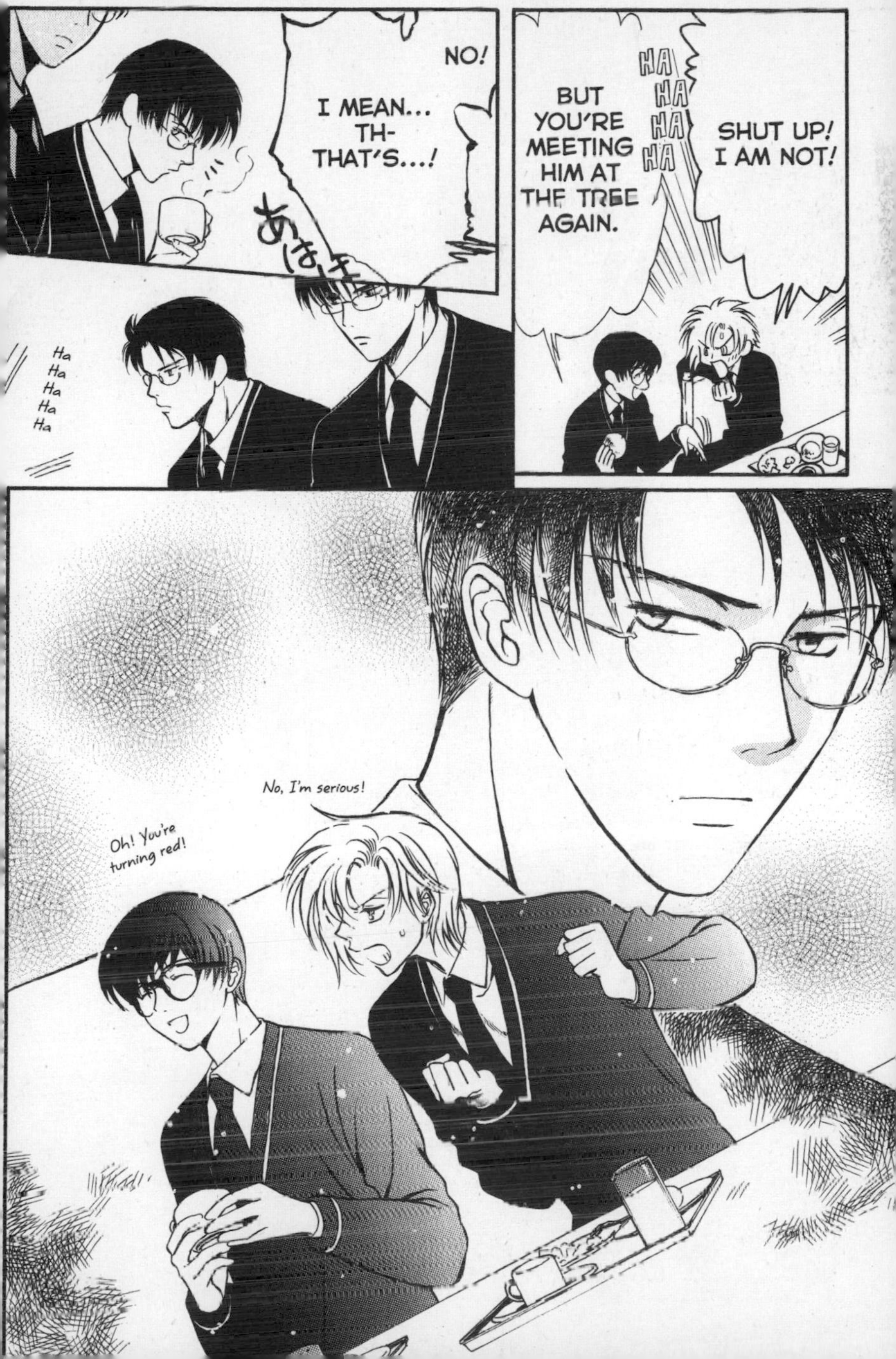
SHUT UP! I AM NOT!
HA HA HA HA
BUT YOU'RE MEETING HIM AT THE TREE AGAIN.
NO!
I MEAN... TH- THAT'S...!
あは
Ha Ha Ha Ha Ha
No, I'm serious!
Oh! You're turning red!

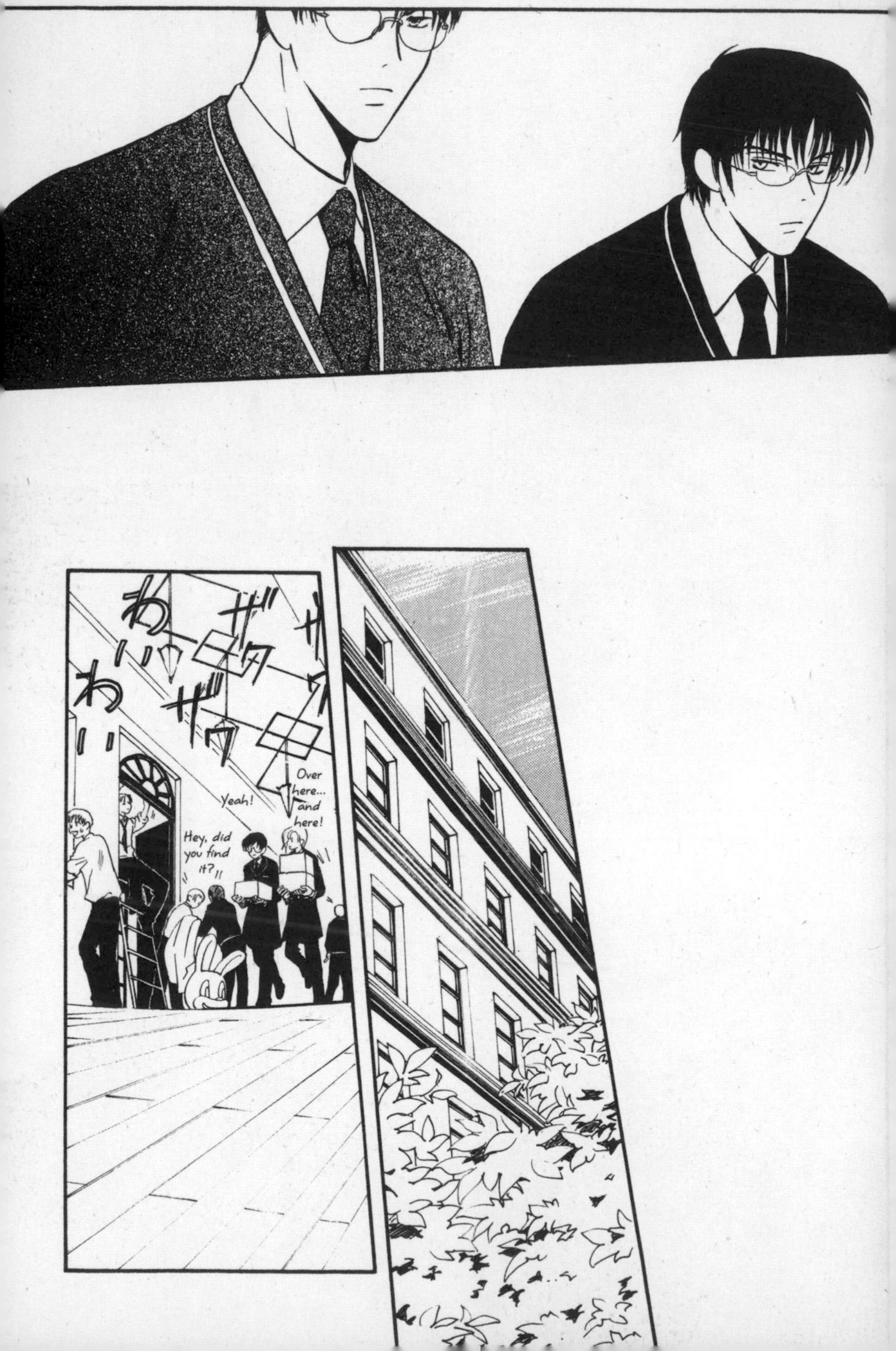
ザワザワ
わーわー
Over here... and here!
Yeah!
Hey, did you find it??

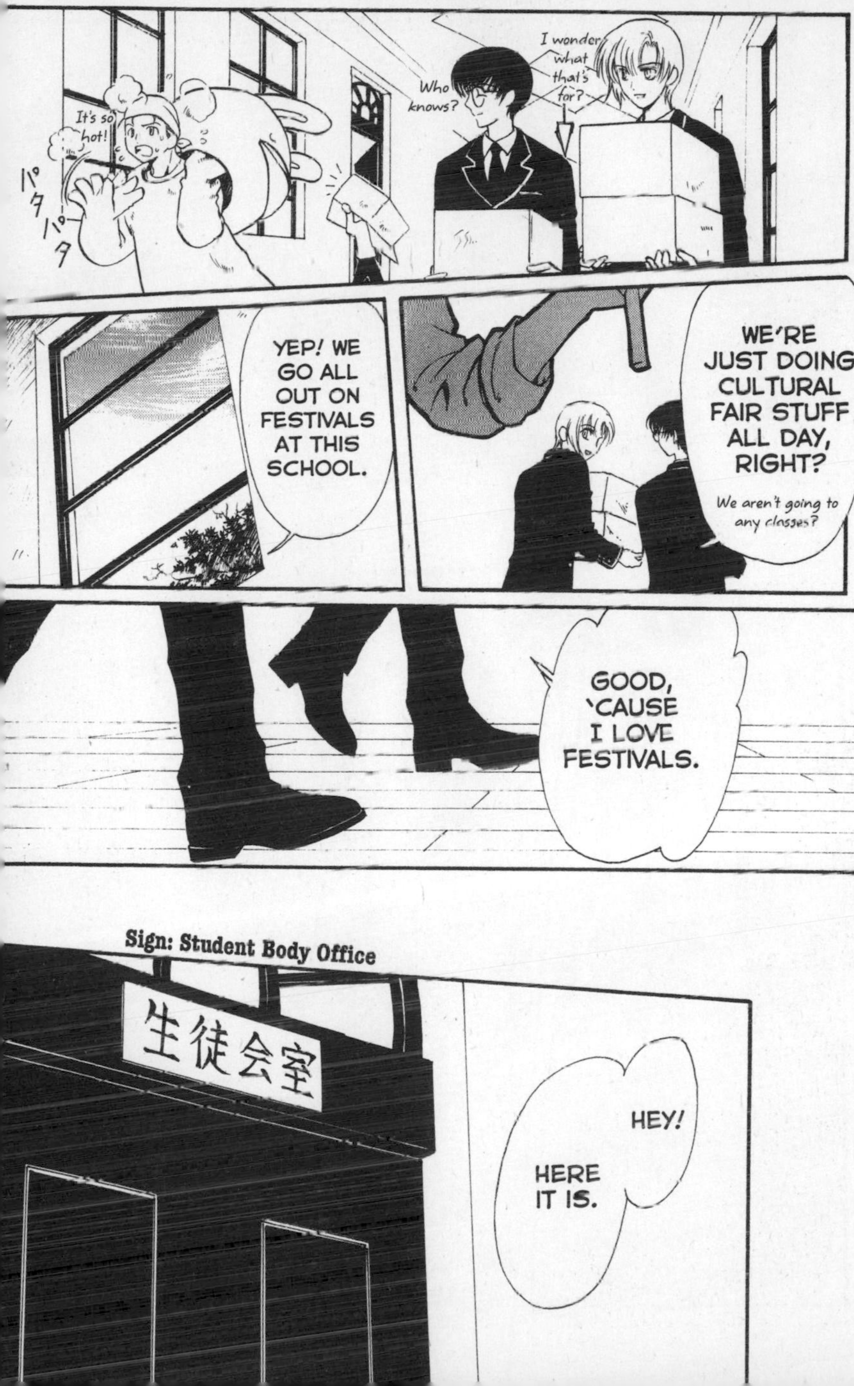
I wonder what that's for?
Who knows?
It's so hot!
パタパタ
WE'RE JUST DOING CULTURAL FAIR STUFF ALL DAY, RIGHT?
We aren't going to any classes?
YEP! WE GO ALL OUT ON FESTIVALS AT THIS SCHOOL.
GOOD, 'CAUSE I LOVE FESTIVALS.
Sign: Student Body Office
生徒会室
HEY!
HERE IT IS.

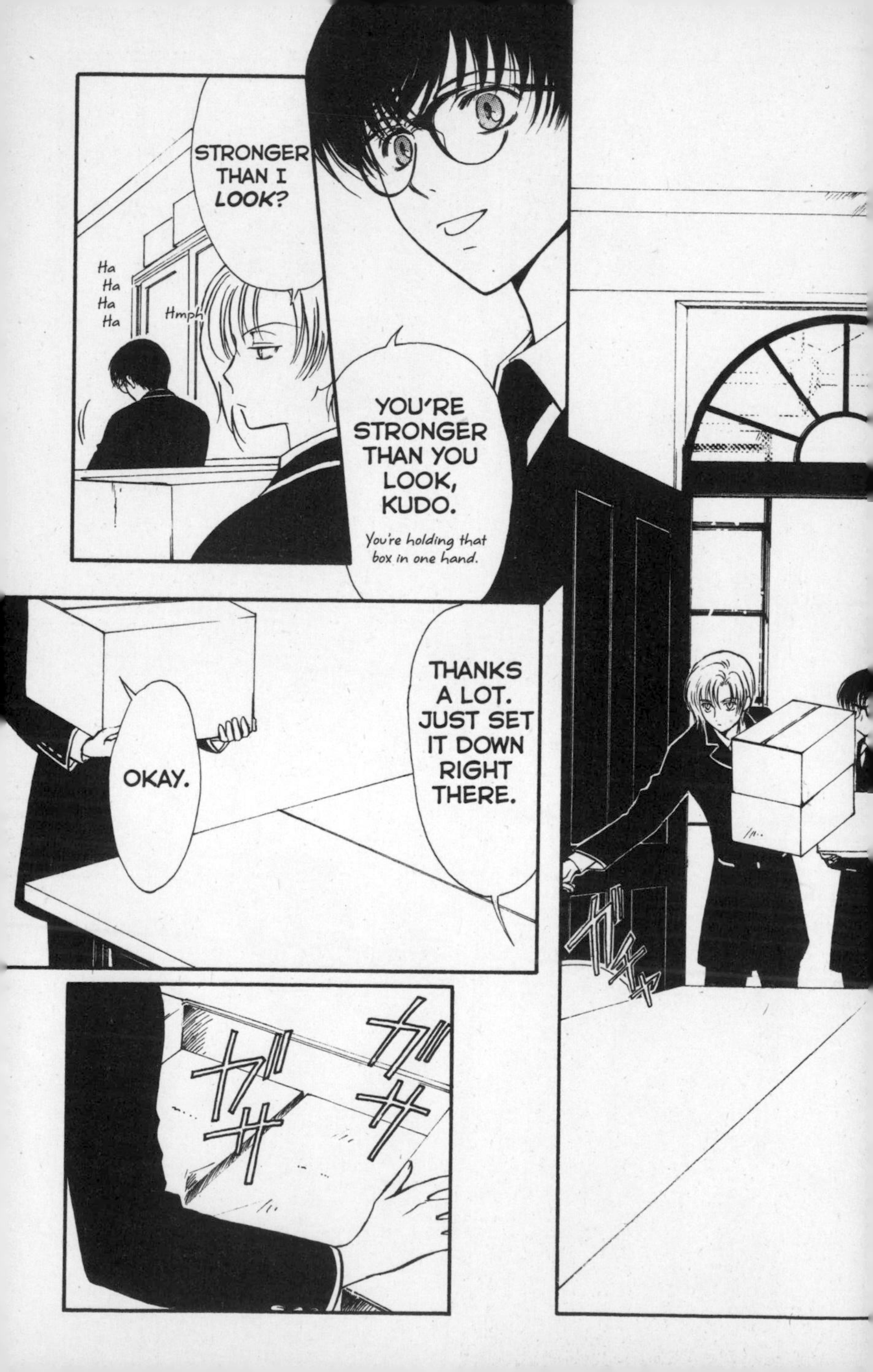

YOU'RE STRONGER THAN YOU LOOK, KUDO.
You're holding that box in one hand.
STRONGER THAN I *LOOK?*
Hmph
Ha Ha Ha Ha
ガチャ
THANKS A LOT. JUST SET IT DOWN RIGHT THERE.
OKAY.
ガサ
ガサ

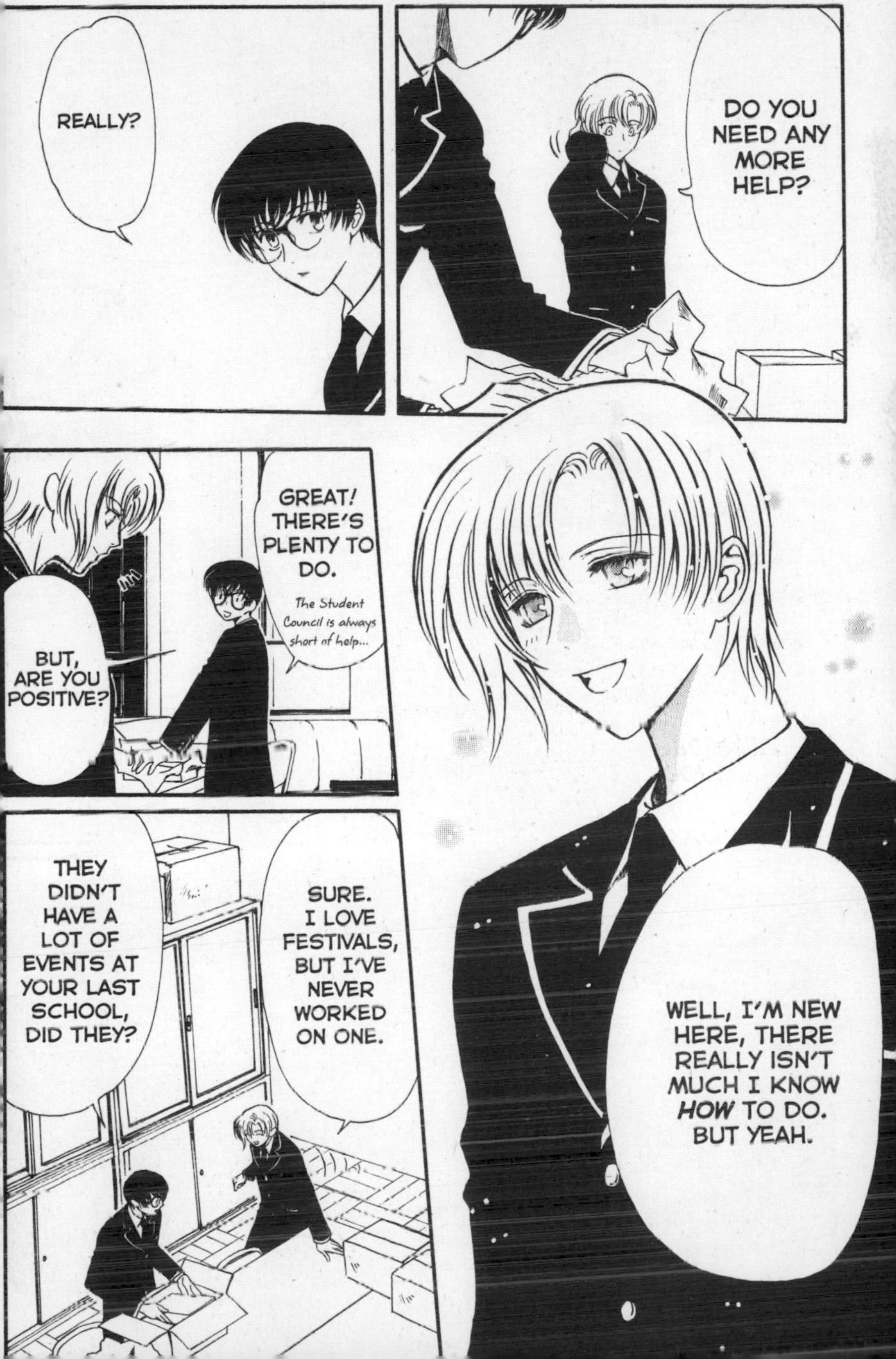
DO YOU NEED ANY MORE HELP?
REALLY?
WELL, I'M NEW HERE, THERE REALLY ISN'T MUCH I KNOW *HOW* TO DO. BUT YEAH.
GREAT! THERE'S PLENTY TO DO.
The Student Council is always short of help...
BUT, ARE YOU POSITIVE?
SURE. I LOVE FESTIVALS, BUT I'VE NEVER WORKED ON ONE.
THEY DIDN'T HAVE A LOT OF EVENTS AT YOUR LAST SCHOOL, DID THEY?

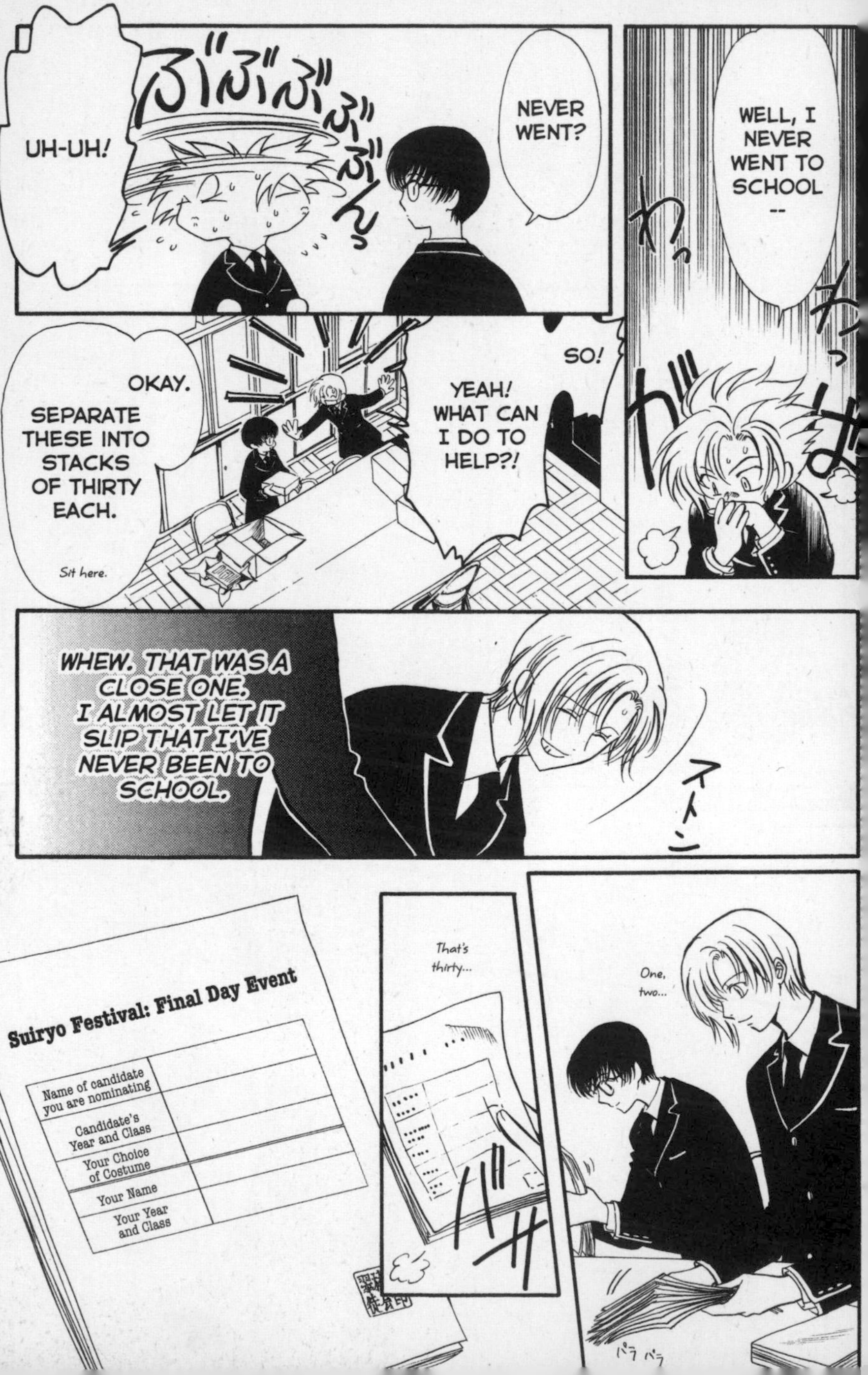

WELL, I NEVER WENT TO SCHOOL --
NEVER WENT?
UH-UH!
SO!
YEAH! WHAT CAN I DO TO HELP?!
OKAY. SEPARATE THESE INTO STACKS OF THIRTY EACH.
Sit here.
WHEW. THAT WAS A CLOSE ONE. I ALMOST LET IT SLIP THAT I'VE NEVER BEEN TO SCHOOL.
One, two...
That's thirty...
Suiryo Festival: Final Day Event
Name of candidate you are nominating
Candidate's Year and Class
Your Choice of Costume
Your Name
Your Year and Class

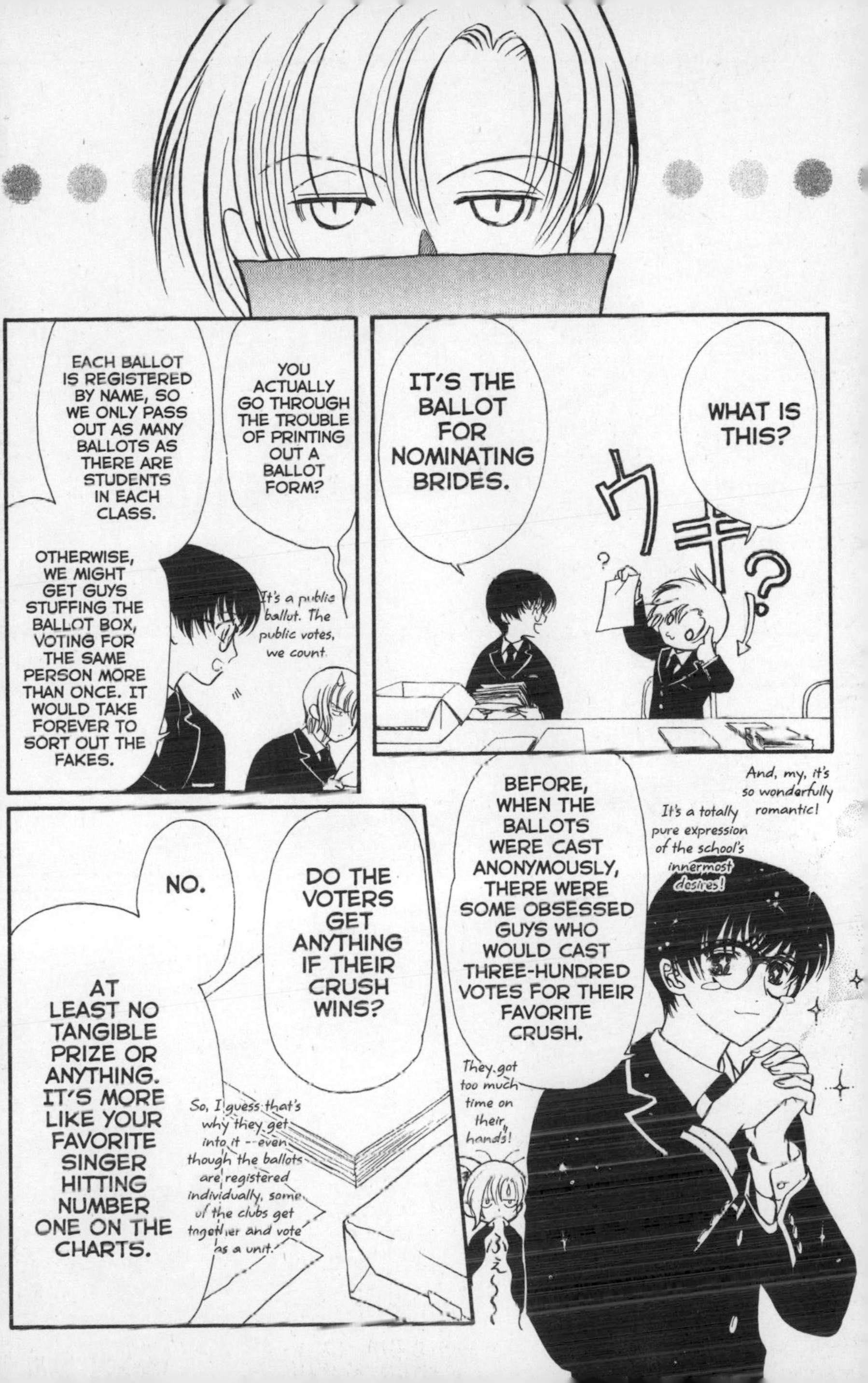
WHAT IS THIS?
ウキ
IT'S THE BALLOT FOR NOMINATING BRIDES.
YOU ACTUALLY GO THROUGH THE TROUBLE OF PRINTING OUT A BALLOT FORM?
EACH BALLOT IS REGISTERED BY NAME, SO WE ONLY PASS OUT AS MANY BALLOTS AS THERE ARE STUDENTS IN EACH CLASS.
OTHERWISE, WE MIGHT GET GUYS STUFFING THE BALLOT BOX, VOTING FOR THE SAME PERSON MORE THAN ONCE. IT WOULD TAKE FOREVER TO SORT OUT THE FAKES.
It's a public ballot. The public votes, we count.
And, my, it's so wonderfully romantic!
It's a totally pure expression of the school's innermost desires!
BEFORE, WHEN THE BALLOTS WERE CAST ANONYMOUSLY, THERE WERE SOME OBSESSED GUYS WHO WOULD CAST THREE-HUNDRED VOTES FOR THEIR FAVORITE CRUSH.
They got too much time on their hands!
ふえ〜
DO THE VOTERS GET ANYTHING IF THEIR CRUSH WINS?
NO.
AT LEAST NO TANGIBLE PRIZE OR ANYTHING. IT'S MORE LIKE YOUR FAVORITE SINGER HITTING NUMBER ONE ON THE CHARTS.
So, I guess that's why they get into it --even though the ballots are registered individually, some of the clubs get together and vote as a unit.

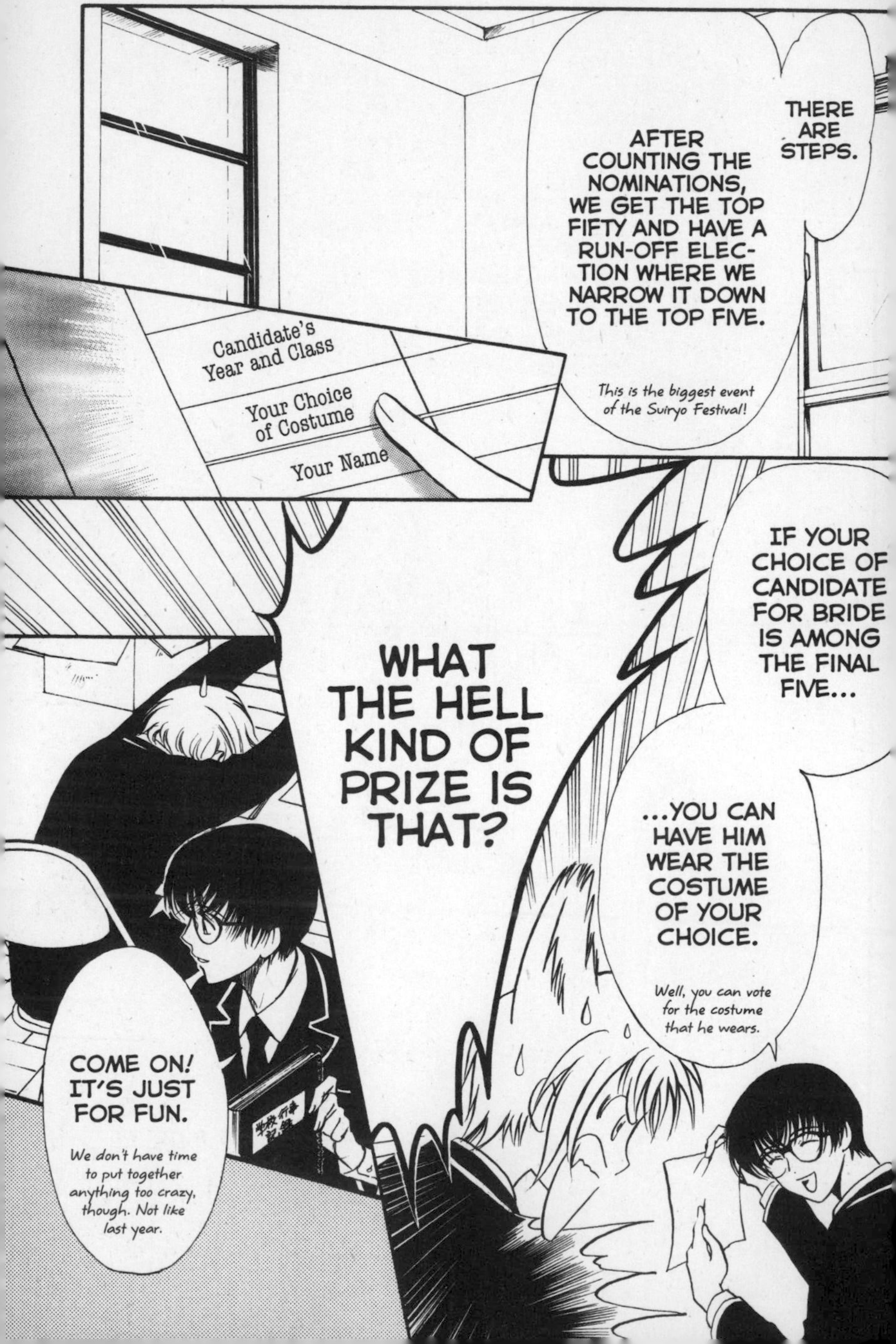
THERE ARE STEPS.
AFTER COUNTING THE NOMINATIONS, WE GET THE TOP FIFTY AND HAVE A RUN-OFF ELECTION WHERE WE NARROW IT DOWN TO THE TOP FIVE.
This is the biggest event of the Suiryo Festival!
Candidate's Year and Class
Your Choice of Costume
Your Name
IF YOUR CHOICE OF CANDIDATE FOR BRIDE IS AMONG THE FINAL FIVE...
...YOU CAN HAVE HIM WEAR THE COSTUME OF YOUR CHOICE.
Well, you can vote for the costume that he wears.
WHAT THE HELL KIND OF PRIZE IS THAT?
COME ON! IT'S JUST FOR FUN.
We don't have time to put together anything too crazy, though. Not like last year.

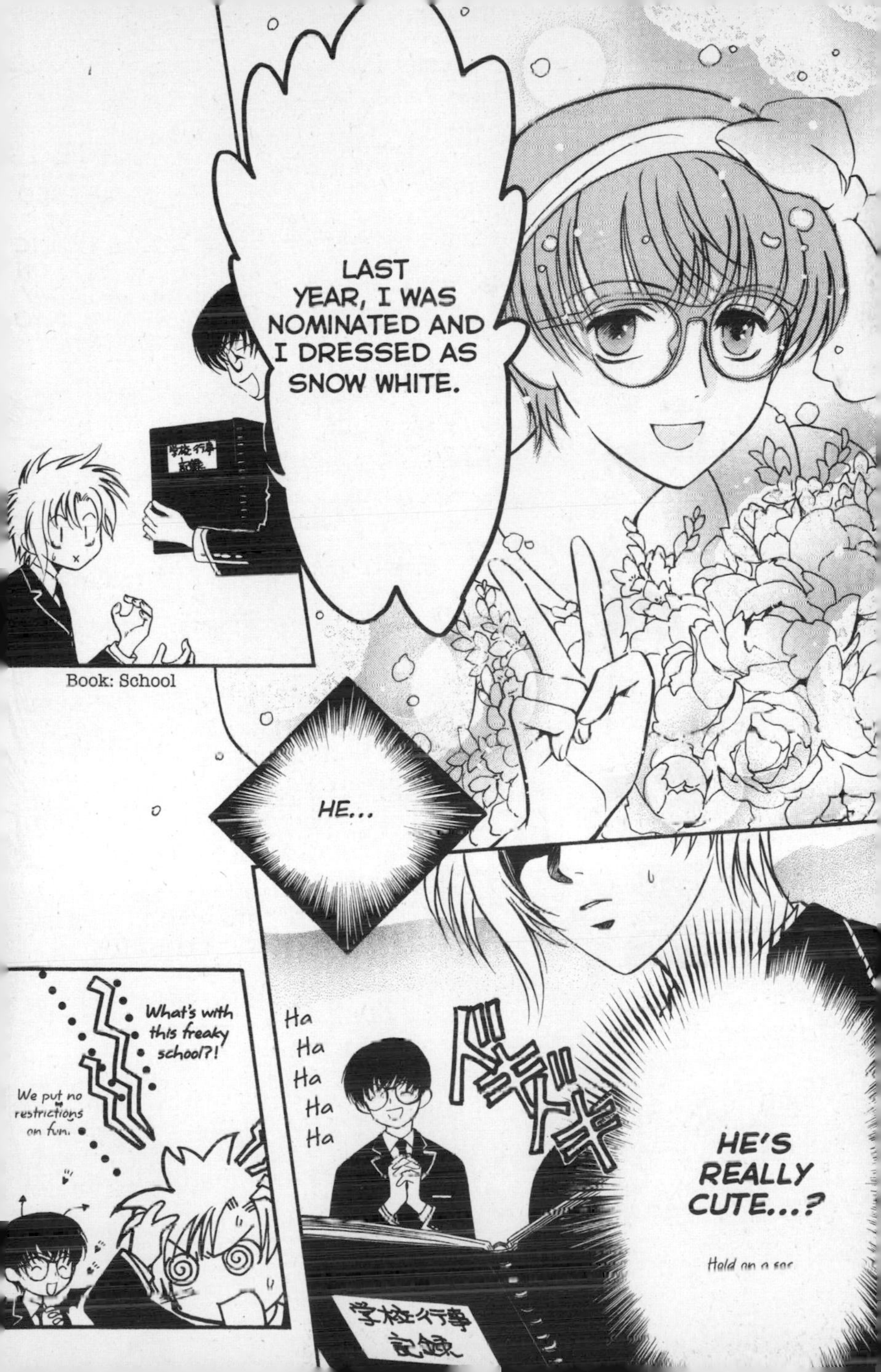
LAST YEAR, I WAS NOMINATED AND I DRESSED AS SNOW WHITE.
Book: School
HE...
Ha Ha Ha Ha Ha
HE'S REALLY CUTE...?
Hold on a sec
What's with this freaky school?!
We put no restrictions on fun.

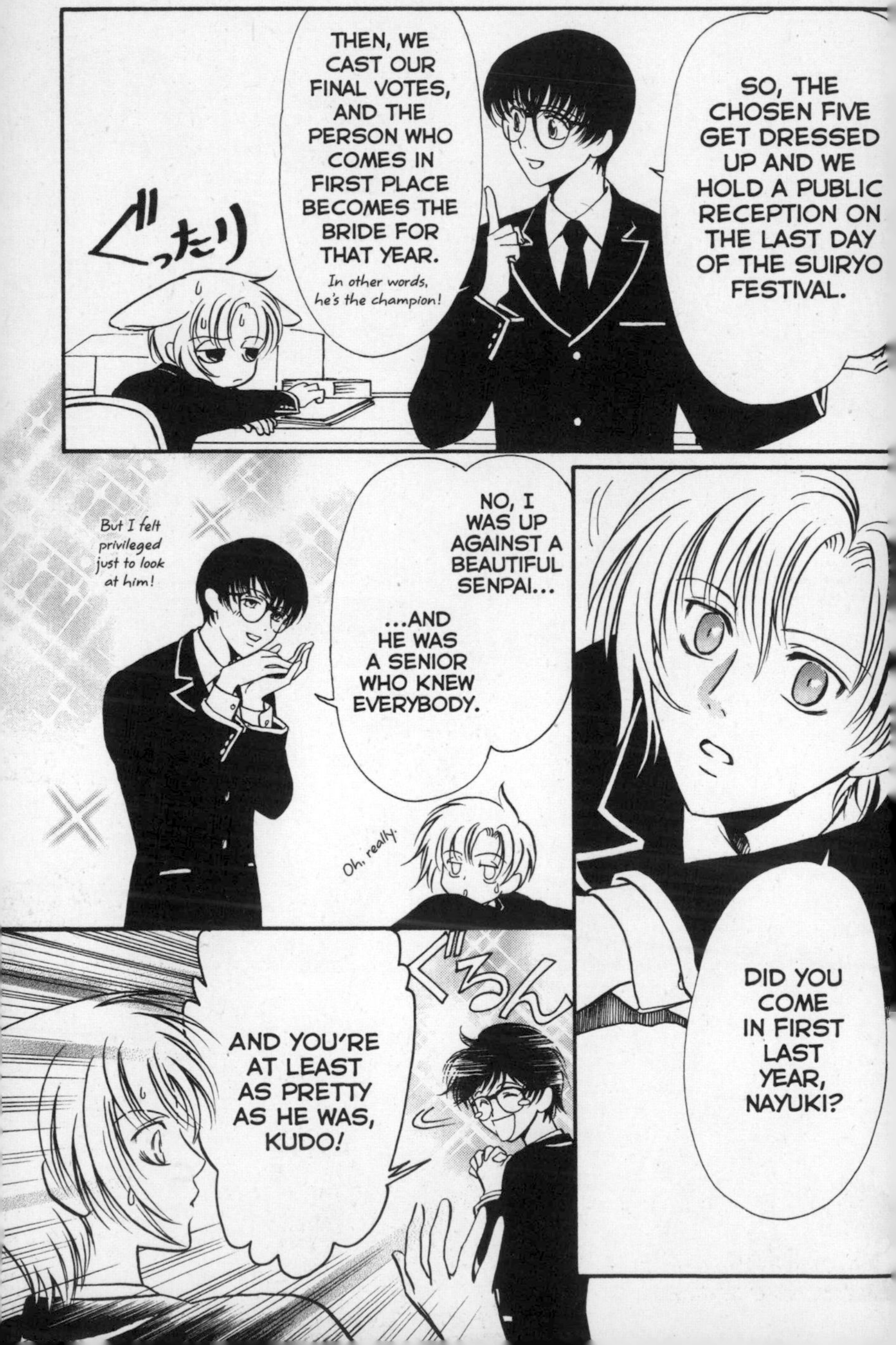
SO, THE CHOSEN FIVE GET DRESSED UP AND WE HOLD A PUBLIC RECEPTION ON THE LAST DAY OF THE SUIRYO FESTIVAL.
THEN, WE CAST OUR FINAL VOTES, AND THE PERSON WHO COMES IN FIRST PLACE BECOMES THE BRIDE FOR THAT YEAR.
In other words, he's the champion!
ぐったり
DID YOU COME IN FIRST LAST YEAR, NAYUKI?
NO, I WAS UP AGAINST A BEAUTIFUL SENPAI...
...AND HE WAS A SENIOR WHO KNEW EVERYBODY.
But I felt privileged just to look at him!
Oh, really.
ぐろん
AND YOU'RE AT LEAST AS PRETTY AS HE WAS, KUDO!

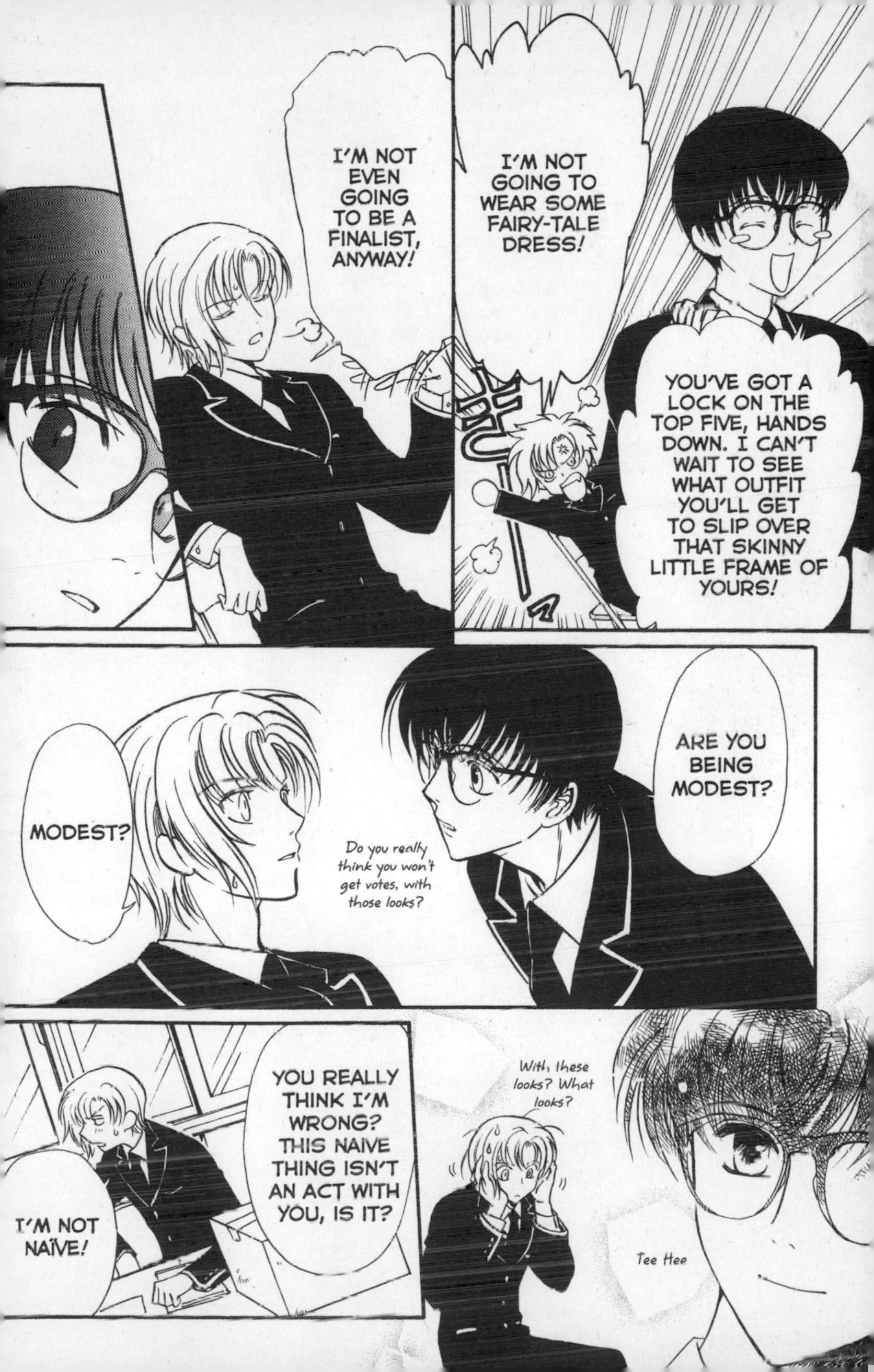
YOU'VE GOT A LOCK ON THE TOP FIVE, HANDS DOWN. I CAN'T WAIT TO SEE WHAT OUTFIT YOU'LL GET TO SLIP OVER THAT SKINNY LITTLE FRAME OF YOURS!
I'M NOT GOING TO WEAR SOME FAIRY-TALE DRESS!
I'M NOT EVEN GOING TO BE A FINALIST, ANYWAY!
ARE YOU BEING MODEST?
Do you really think you won't get votes, with those looks?
MODEST?
With these looks? What looks?
Tee Hee
YOU REALLY THINK I'M WRONG? THIS NAIVE THING ISN'T AN ACT WITH YOU, IS IT?
I'M NOT NAÏVE!

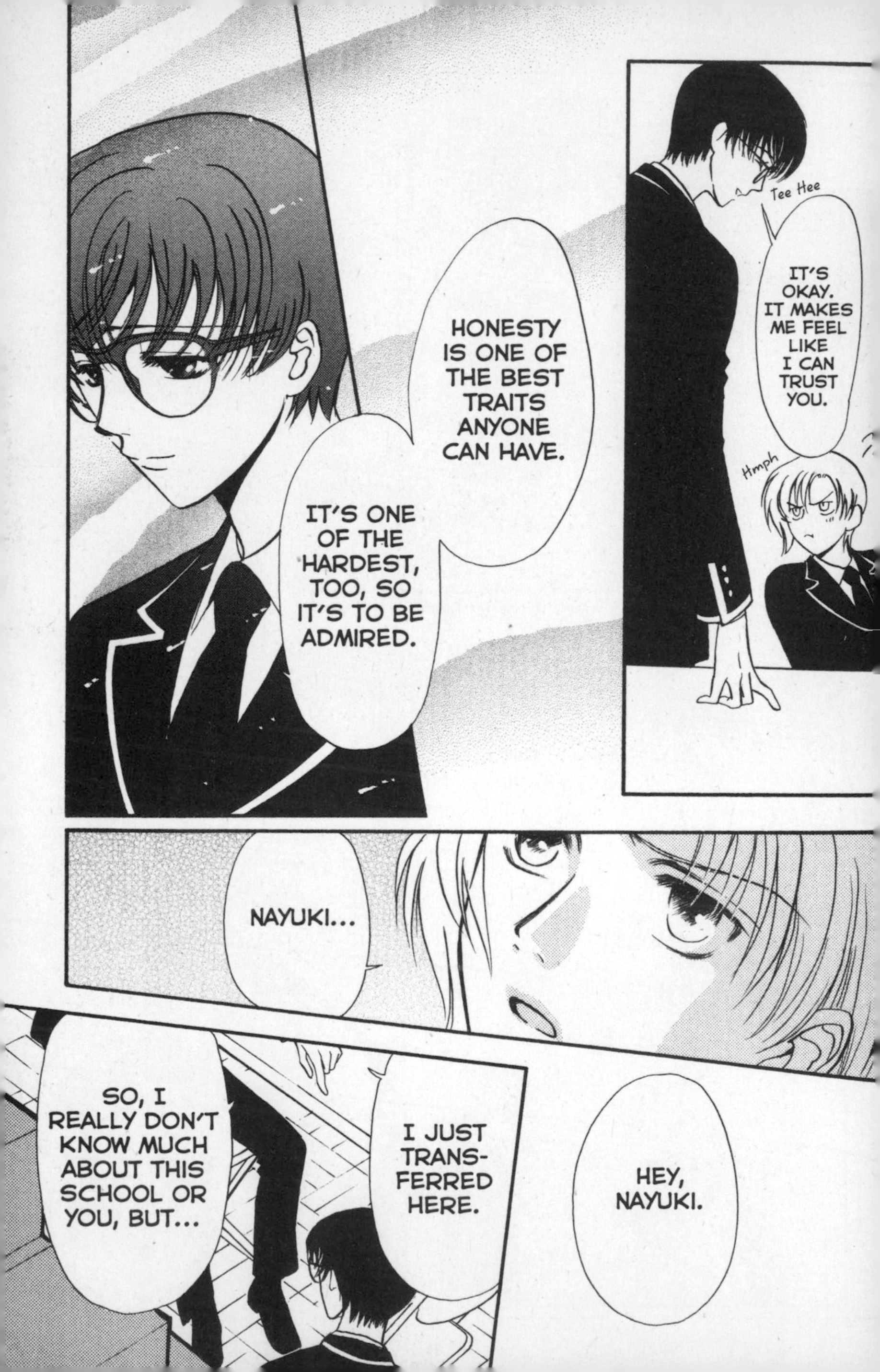
Tee Hee
IT'S OKAY. IT MAKES ME FEEL LIKE I CAN TRUST YOU.
Hmph
HONESTY IS ONE OF THE BEST TRAITS ANYONE CAN HAVE.
IT'S ONE OF THE HARDEST, TOO, SO IT'S TO BE ADMIRED.
NAYUKI...
HEY, NAYUKI.
I JUST TRANS-FERRED HERE.
SO, I REALLY DON'T KNOW MUCH ABOUT THIS SCHOOL OR YOU, BUT...

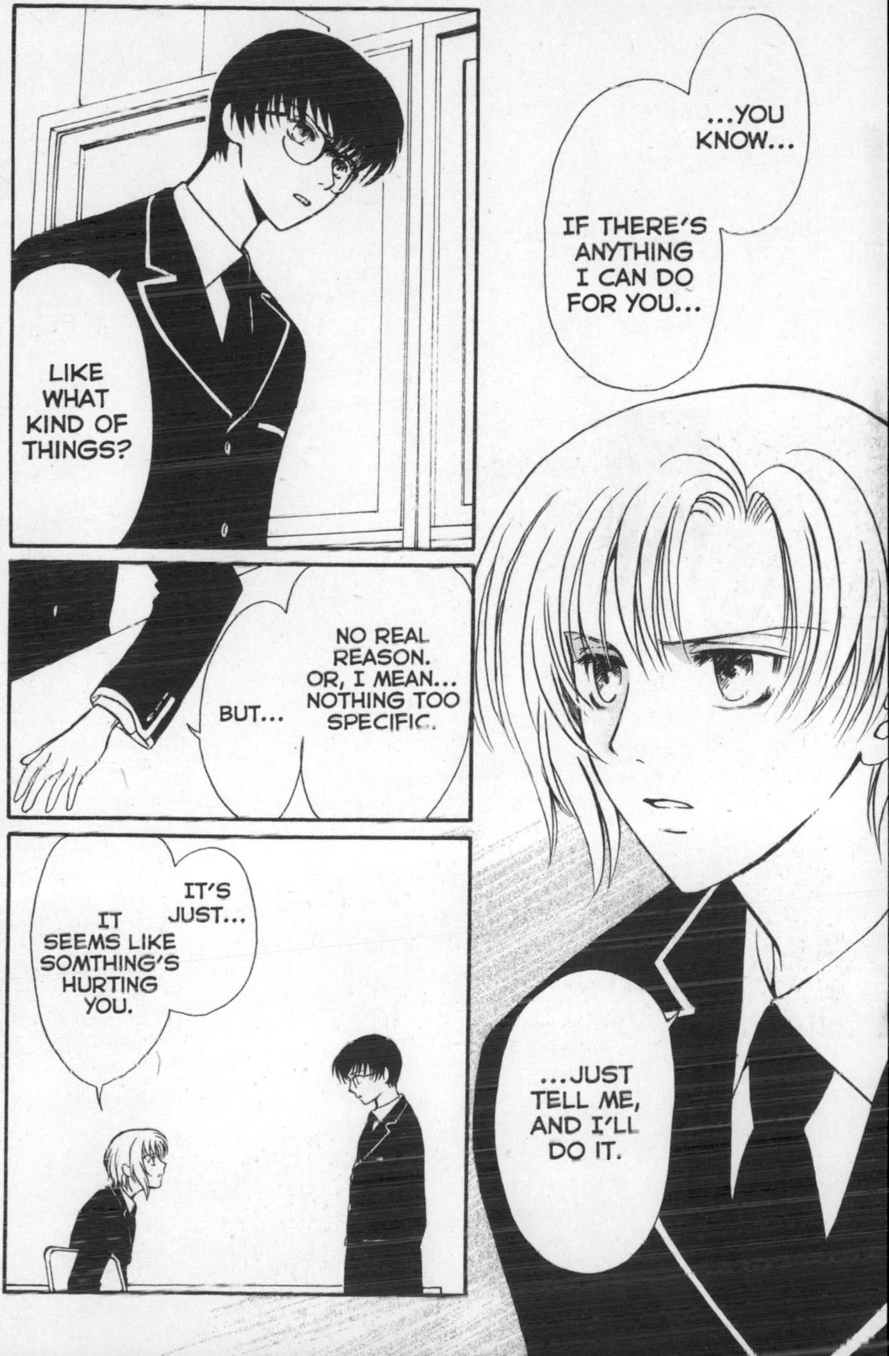
...YOU KNOW...
IF THERE'S ANYTHING I CAN DO FOR YOU...
...JUST TELL ME, AND I'LL DO IT.
LIKE WHAT KIND OF THINGS?
NO REAL REASON. OR, I MEAN... NOTHING TOO SPECIFIC.
BUT...
IT'S JUST...
IT SEEMS LIKE SOMTHING'S HURTING YOU.

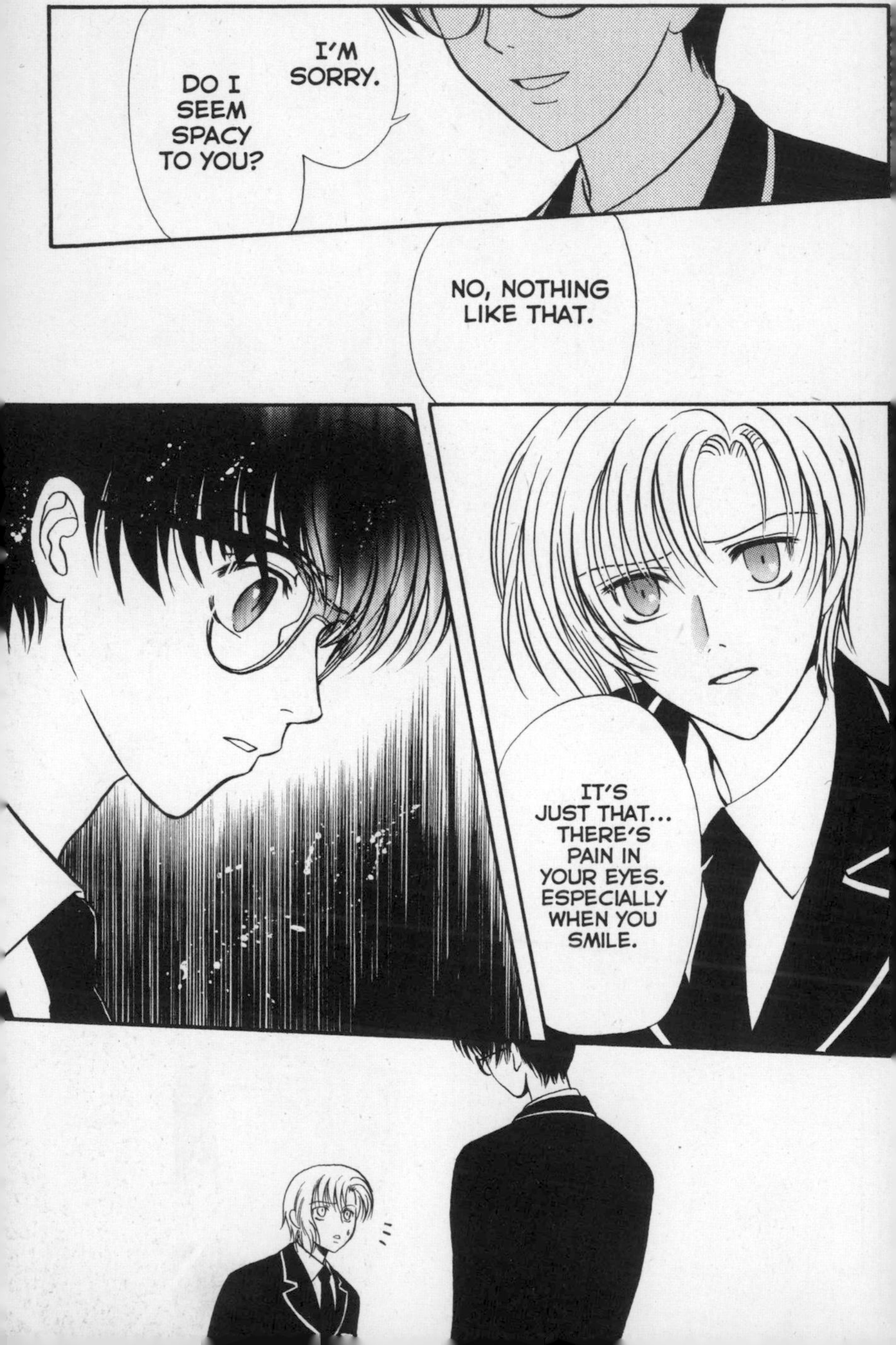
I'M SORRY.
DO I SEEM SPACY TO YOU?
NO, NOTHING LIKE THAT.
IT'S JUST THAT... THERE'S PAIN IN YOUR EYES. ESPECIALLY WHEN YOU SMILE.

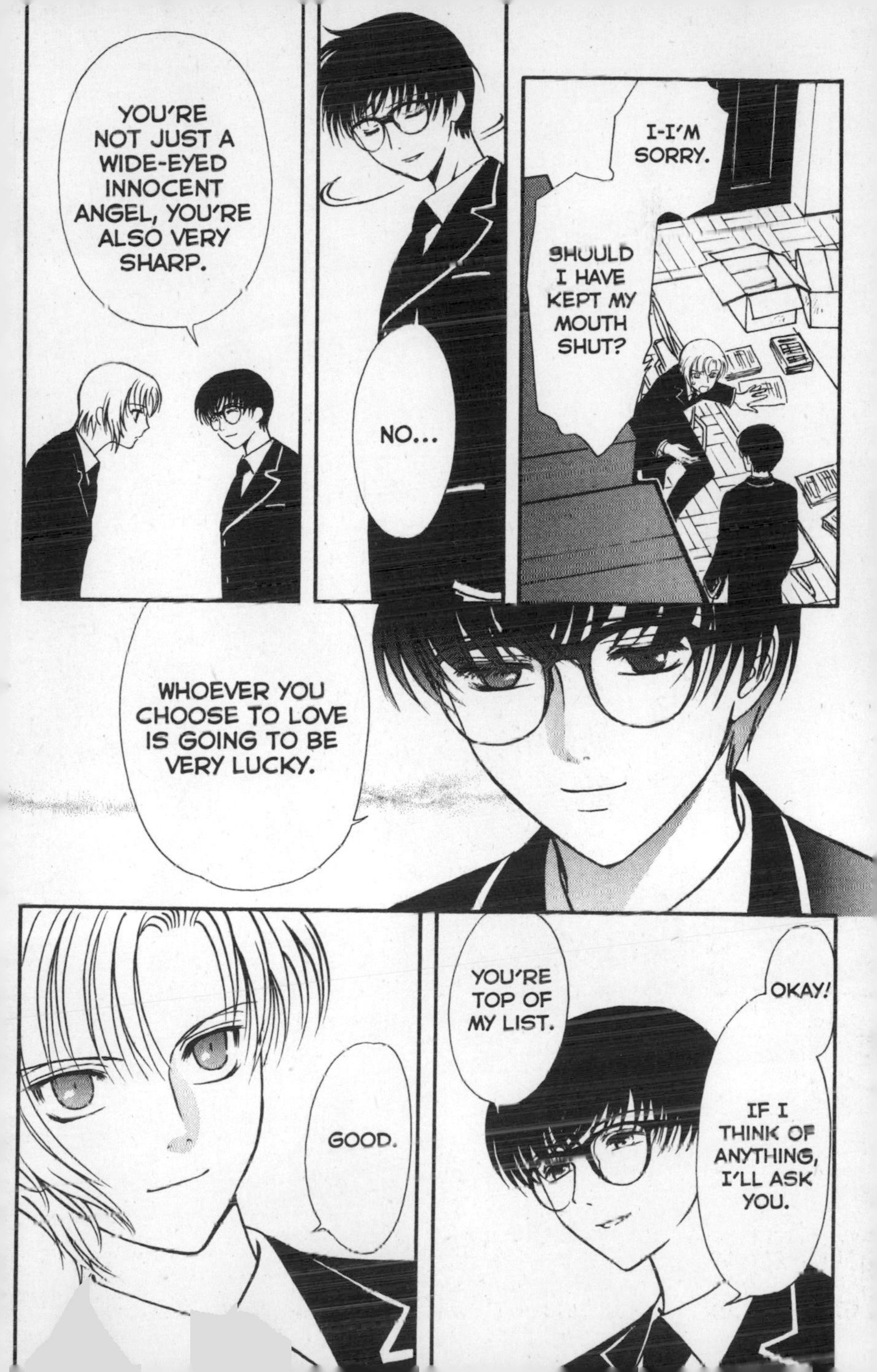
I-I'M SORRY.
SHOULD I HAVE KEPT MY MOUTH SHUT?
NO...
YOU'RE NOT JUST A WIDE-EYED INNOCENT ANGEL, YOU'RE ALSO VERY SHARP.
WHOEVER YOU CHOOSE TO LOVE IS GOING TO BE VERY LUCKY.
OKAY!
IF I THINK OF ANYTHING, I'LL ASK YOU.
YOU'RE TOP OF MY LIST.
GOOD.

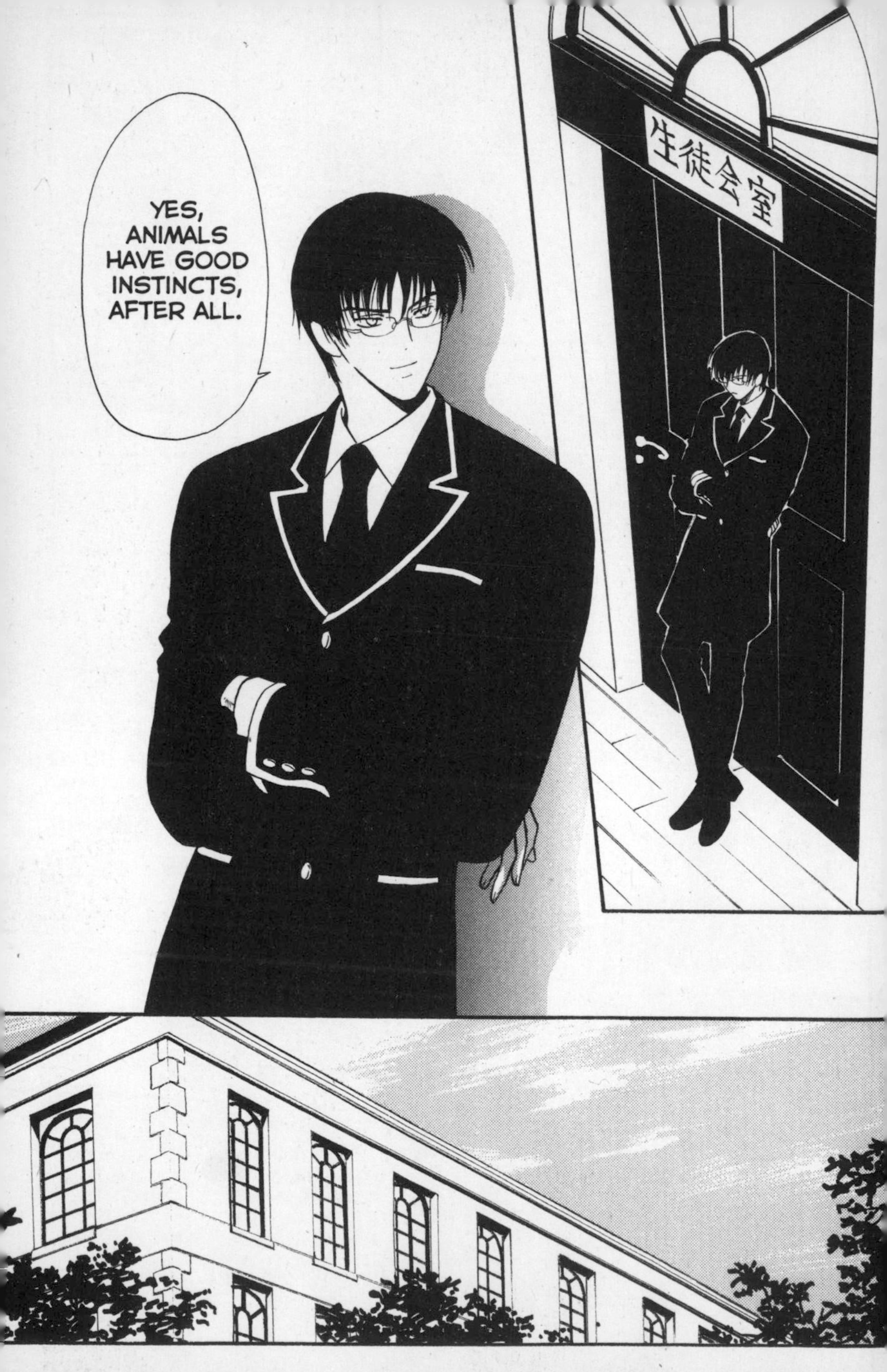
生徒会室
YES, ANIMALS HAVE GOOD INSTINCTS, AFTER ALL.

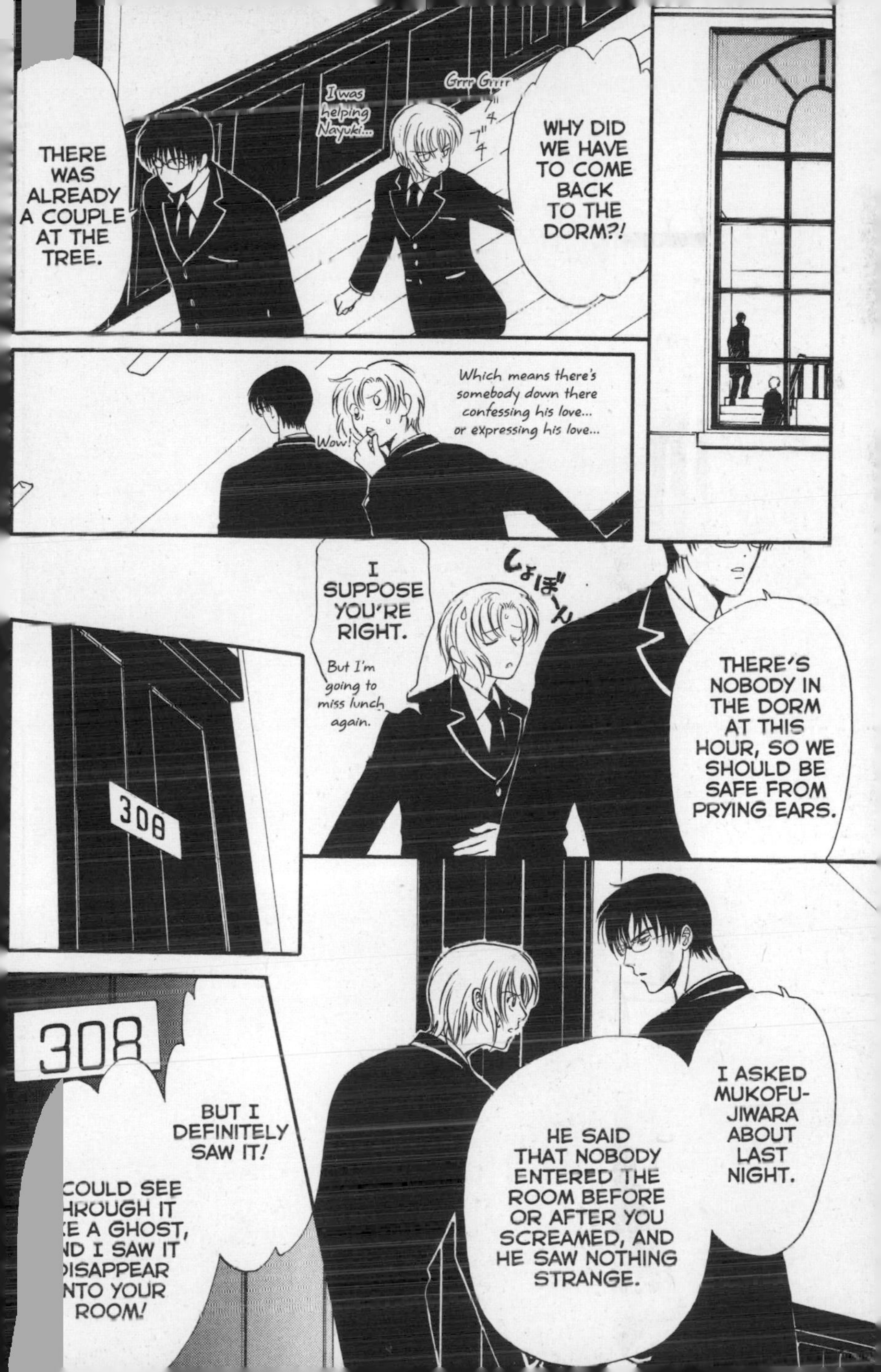
WHY DID WE HAVE TO COME BACK TO THE DORM?!
Grrr Grrr
ブチ ブチ
I was helping Nayuki...
THERE WAS ALREADY A COUPLE AT THE TREE.
Which means there's somebody down there confessing his love... or expressing his love...
Wow!
THERE'S NOBODY IN THE DORM AT THIS HOUR, SO WE SHOULD BE SAFE FROM PRYING EARS.
しょぼーん
I SUPPOSE YOU'RE RIGHT.
But I'm going to miss lunch again.
308
I ASKED MUKOFU-JIWARA ABOUT LAST NIGHT.
HE SAID THAT NOBODY ENTERED THE ROOM BEFORE OR AFTER YOU SCREAMED, AND HE SAW NOTHING STRANGE.
308
BUT I DEFINITELY SAW IT!
COULD SEE HROUGH IT KE A GHOST, ND I SAW IT DISAPPEAR NTO YOUR ROOM!

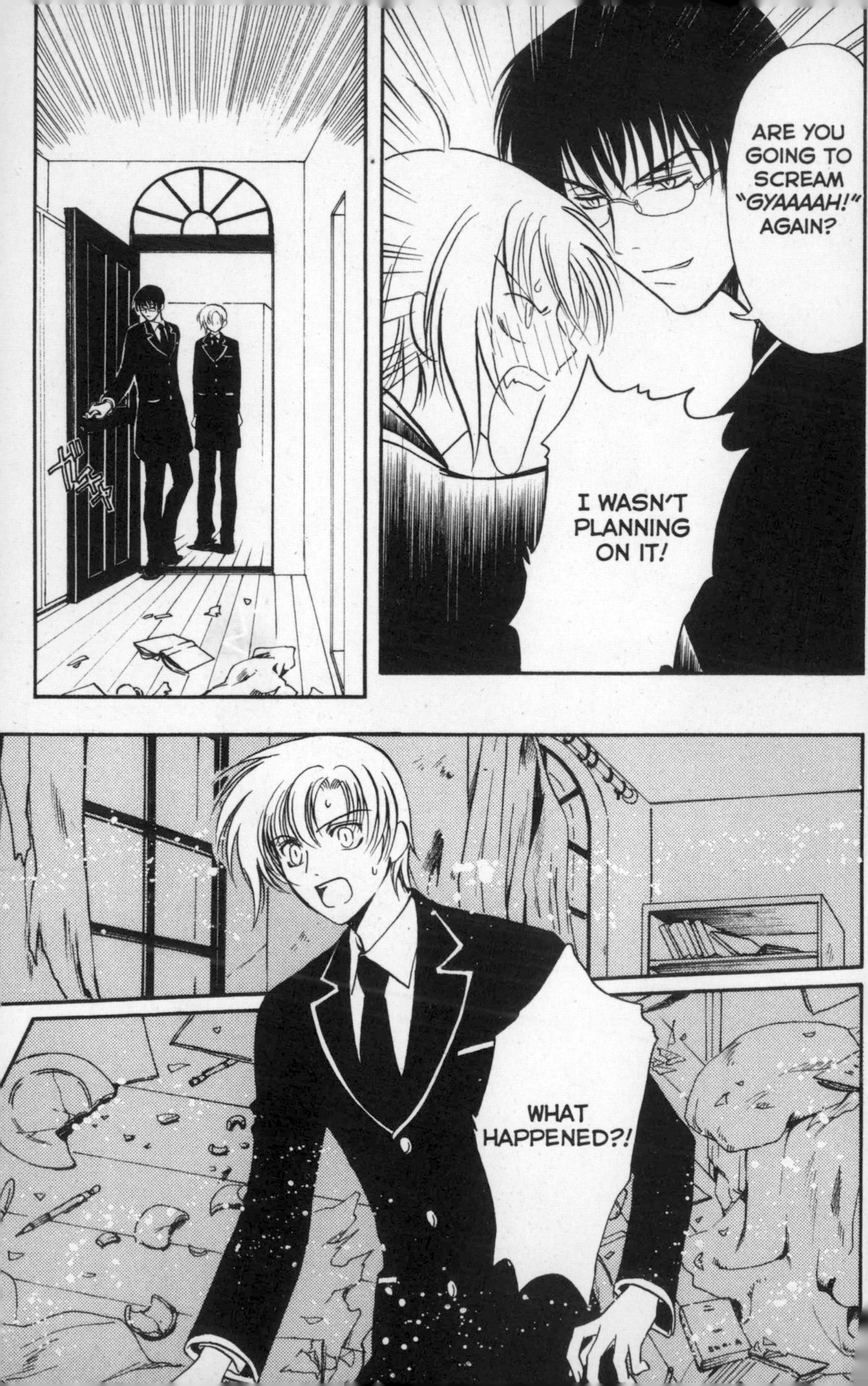
ARE YOU GOING TO SCREAM "GYAAAAH!" AGAIN?
I WASN'T PLANNING ON IT!
WHAT HAPPENED?!

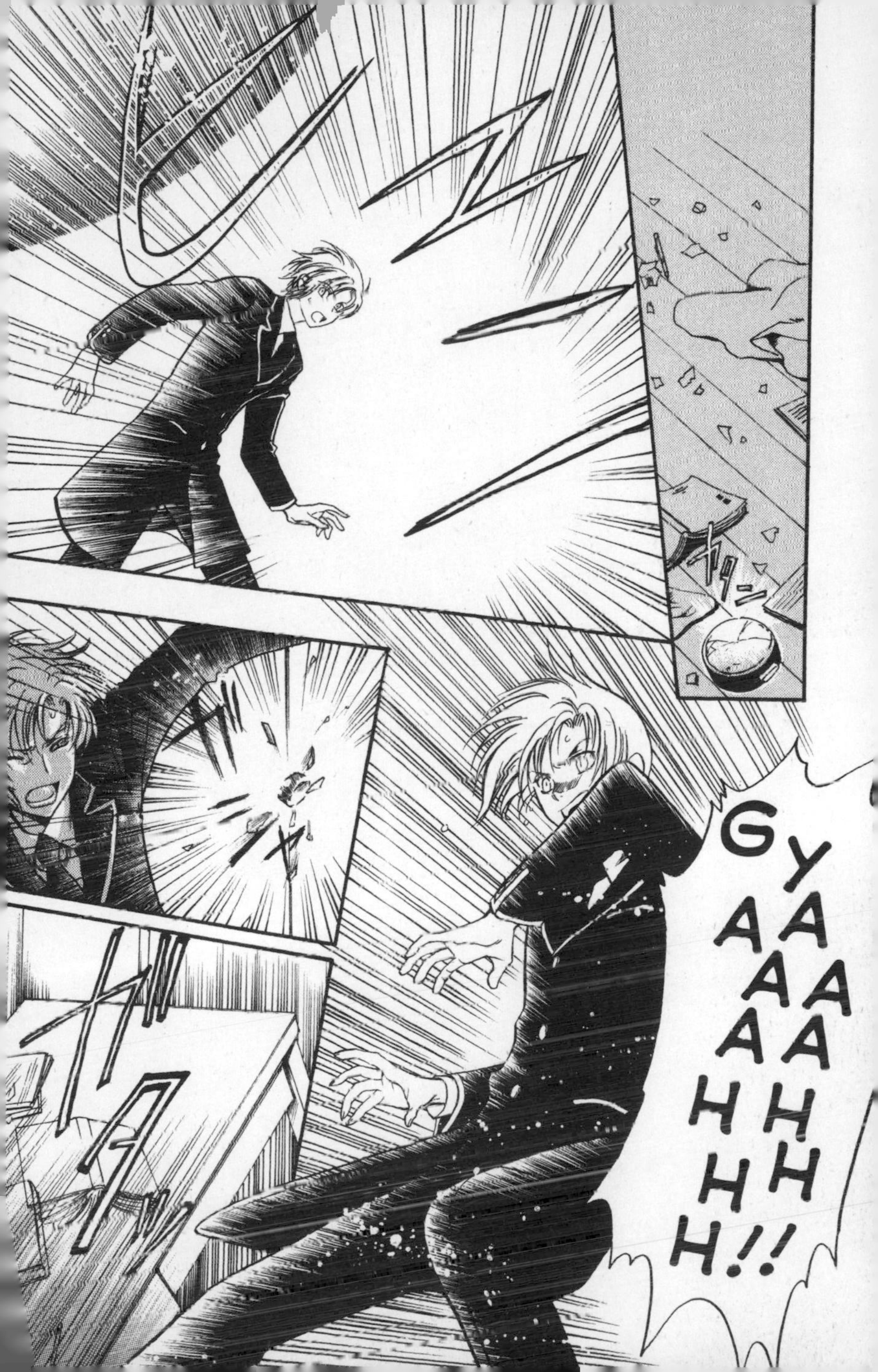
GYAAAAAAHHHHH!!

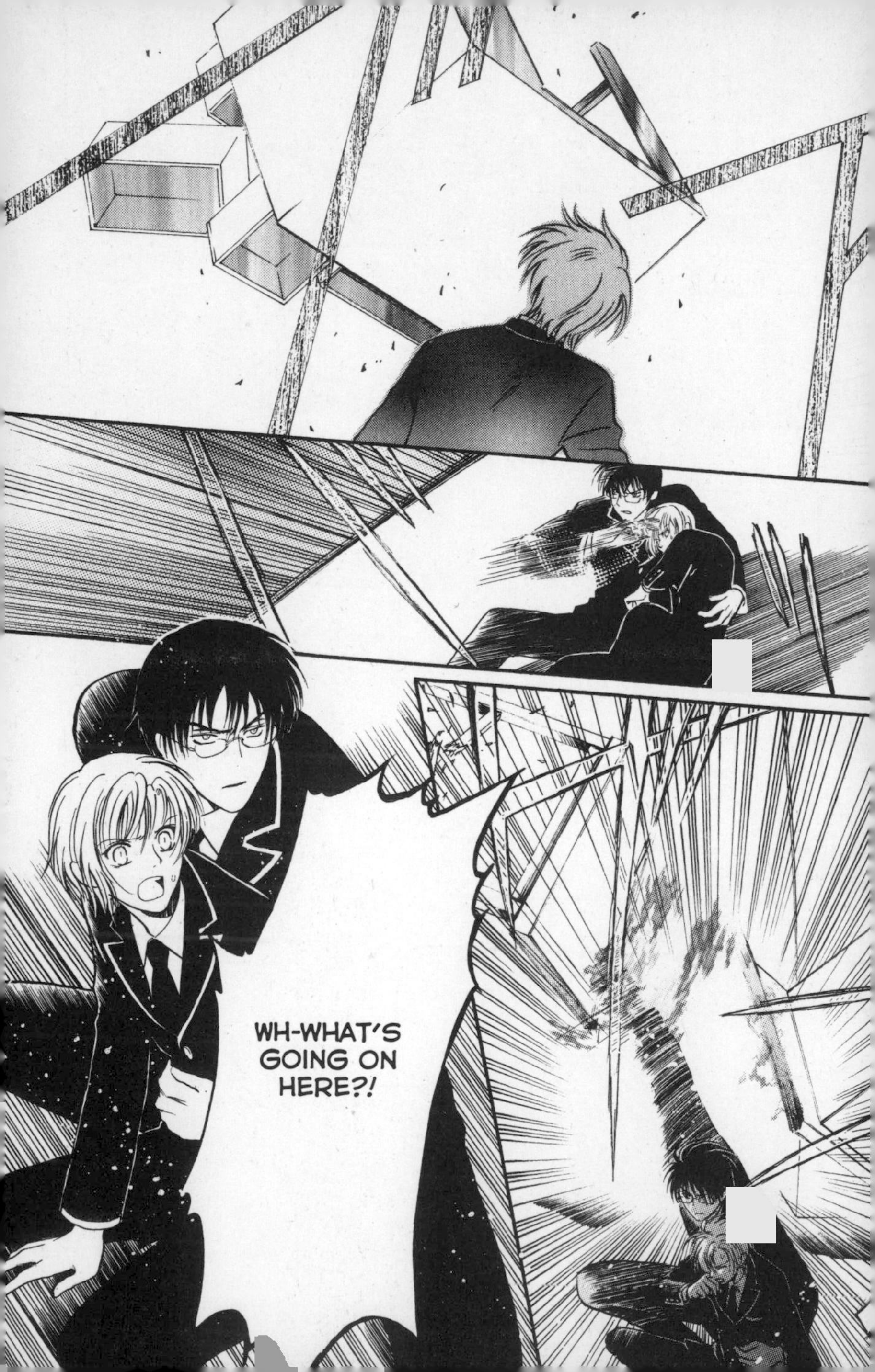
WH-WHAT'S
GOING ON
HERE?!

合法ドラッグ
LEGAL DRUG

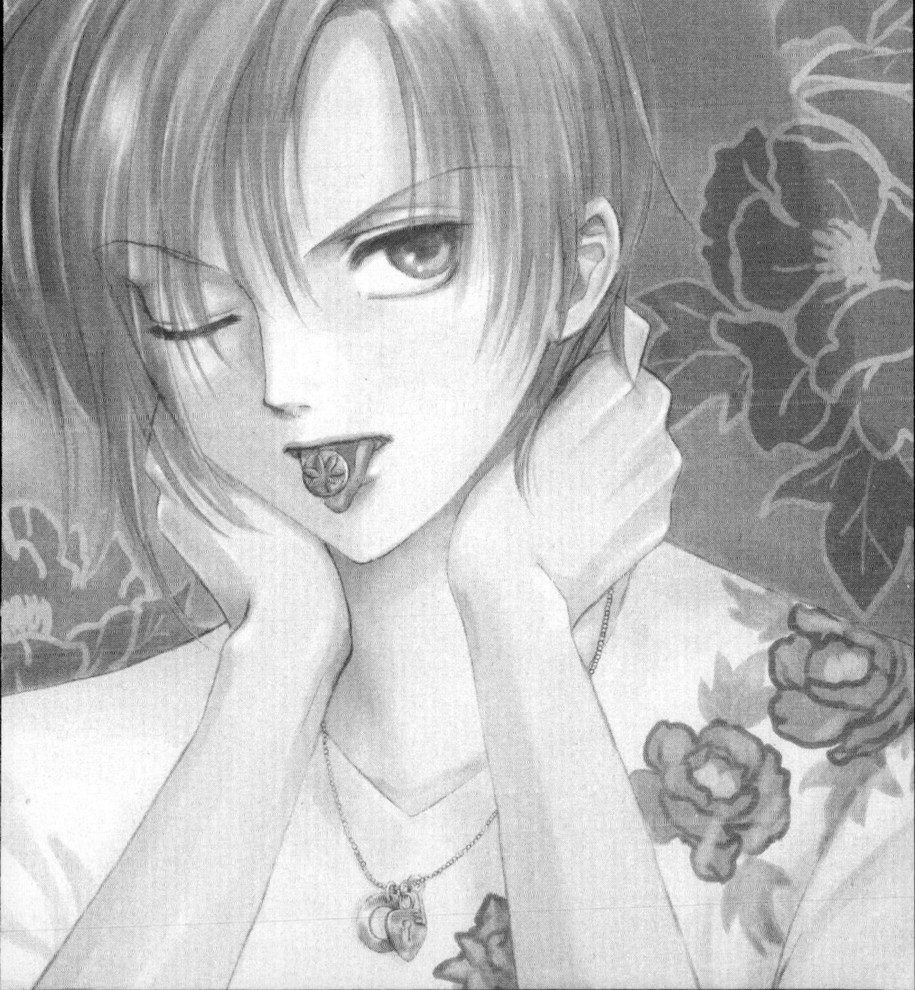

DRUG NO.15 Daily use of the drug may cause poisoning.

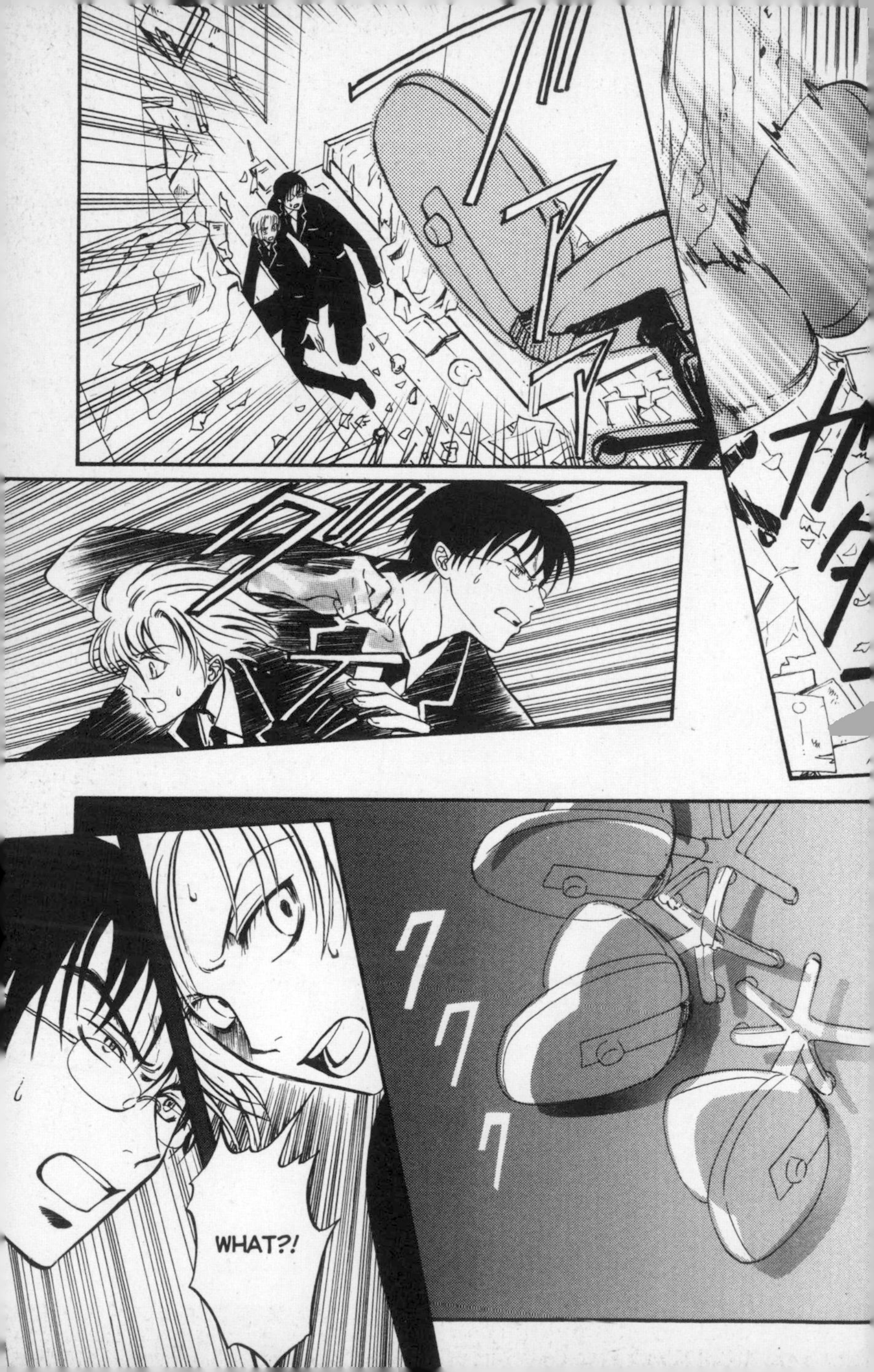
WHAT?!

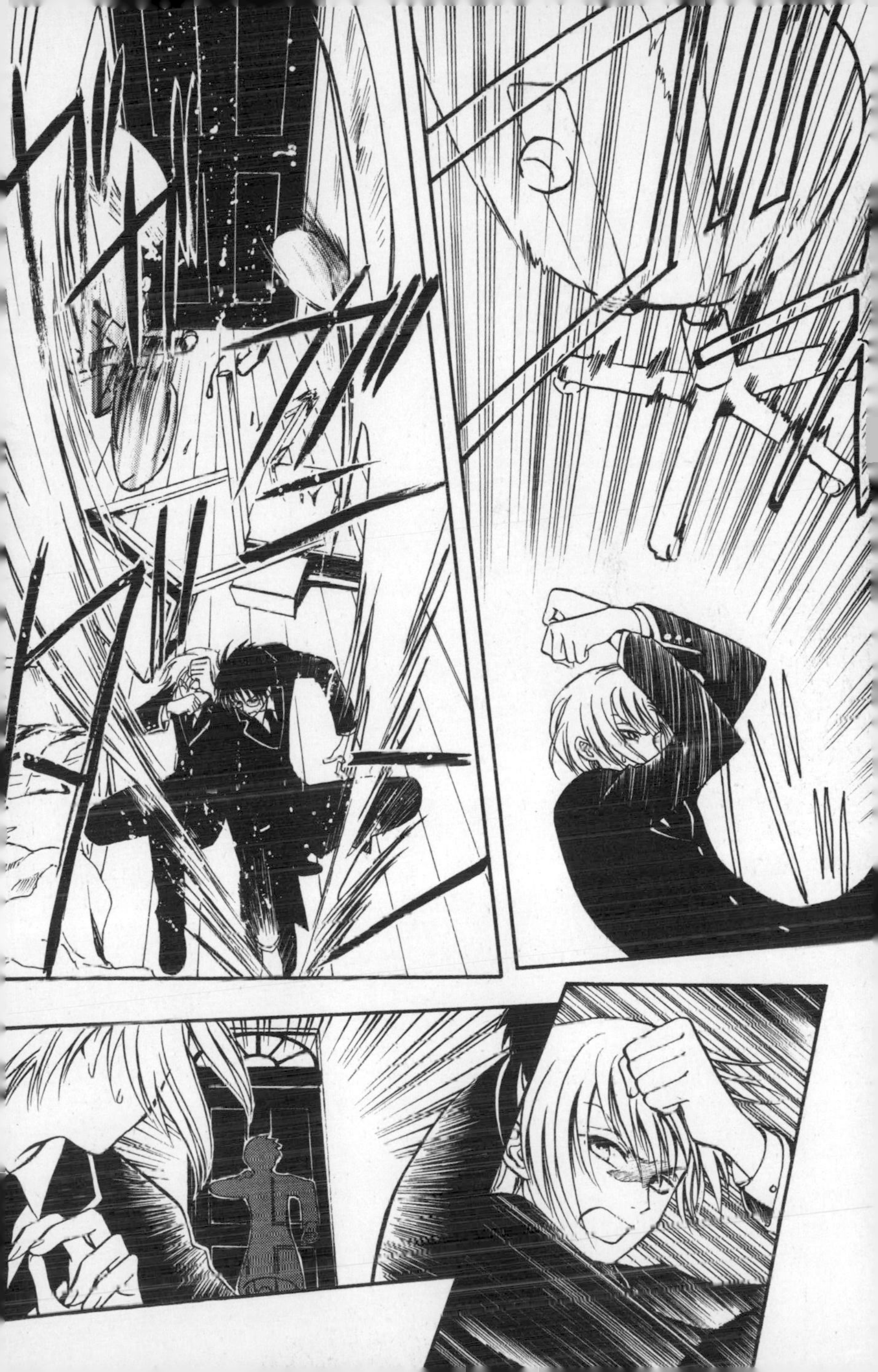

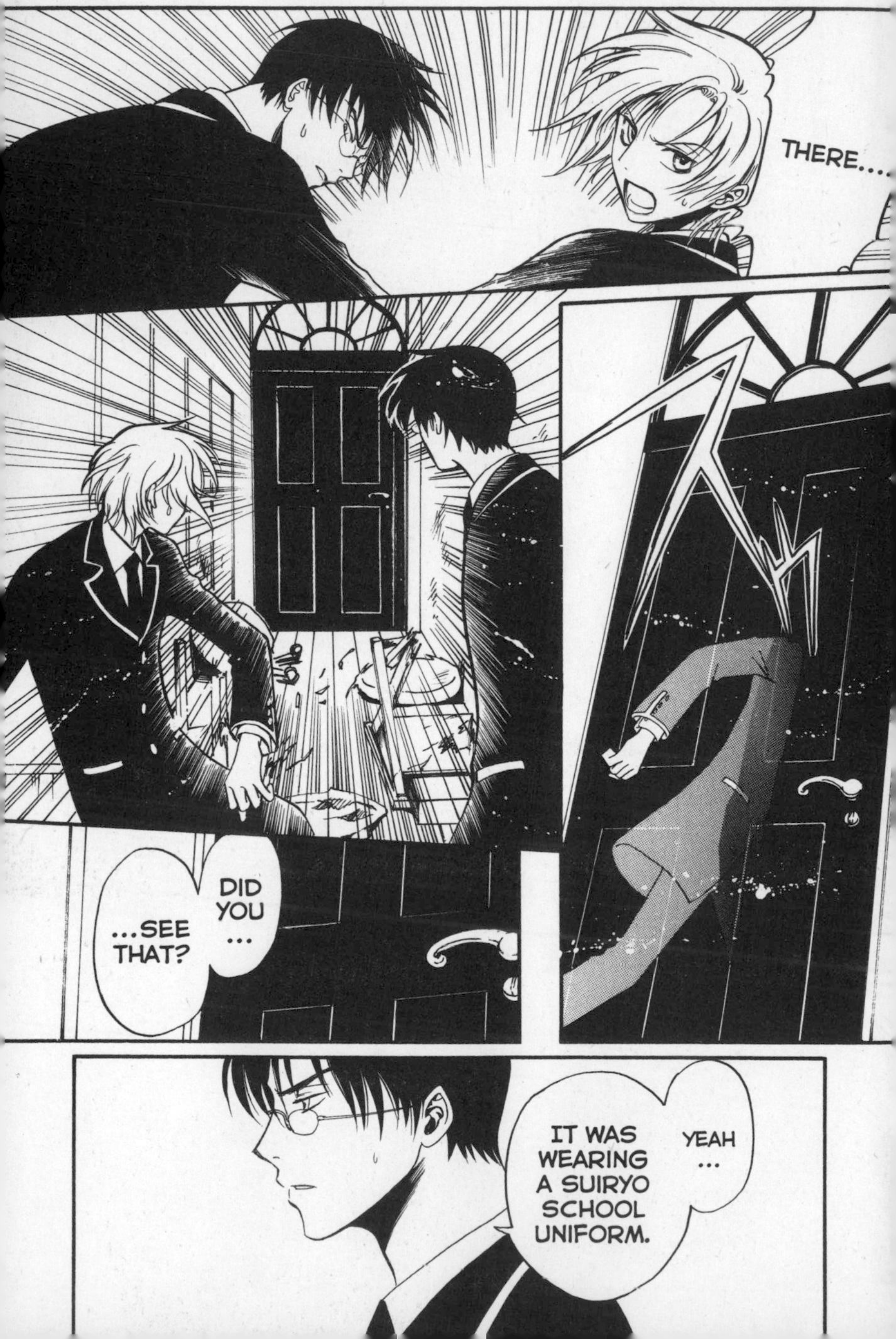
THERE....
DID YOU ... ...SEE THAT?
YEAH ...
IT WAS WEARING A SUIRYO SCHOOL UNIFORM.

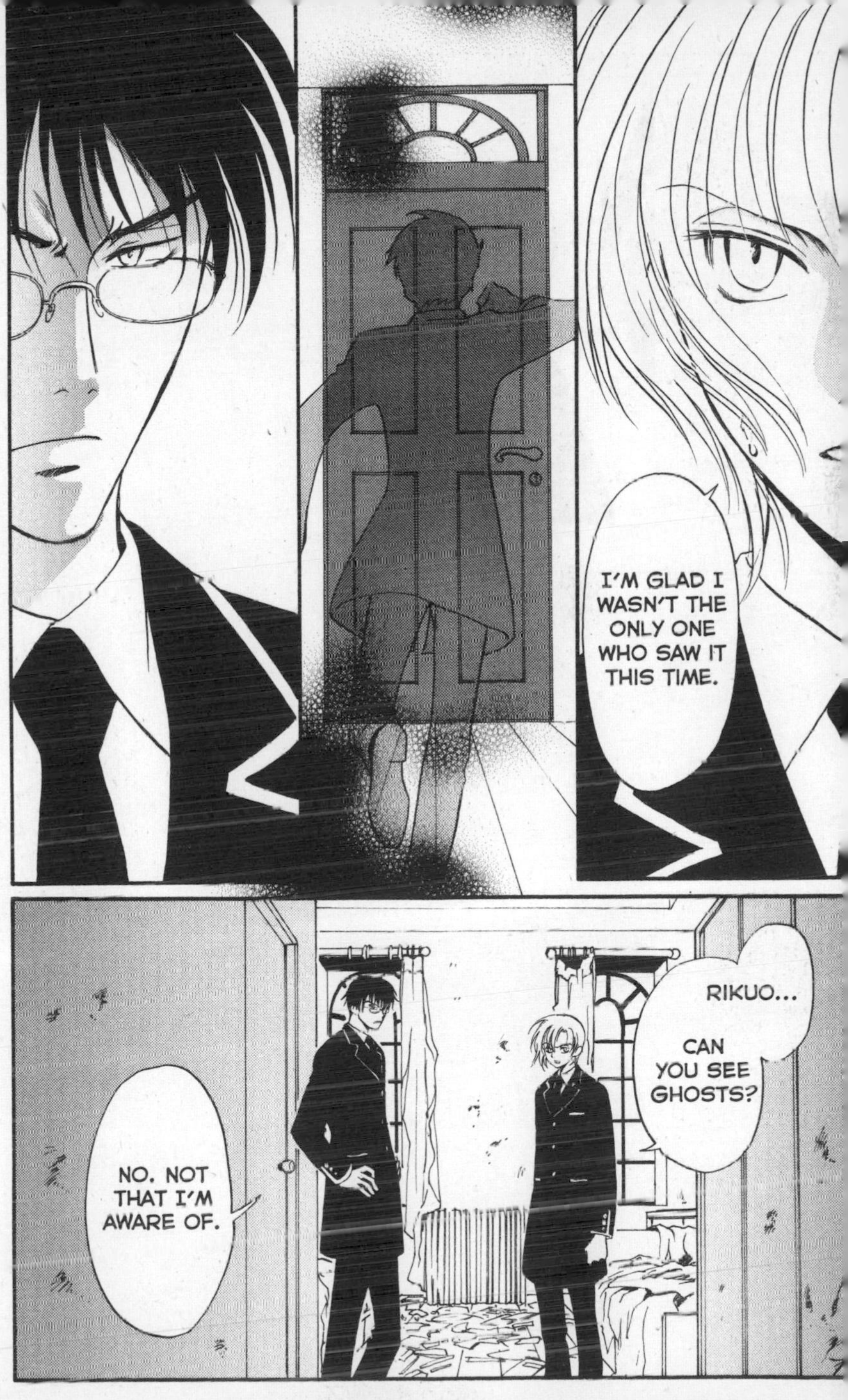
I'M GLAD I WASN'T THE ONLY ONE WHO SAW IT THIS TIME.
RIKUO...
CAN YOU SEE GHOSTS?
NO. NOT THAT I'M AWARE OF.

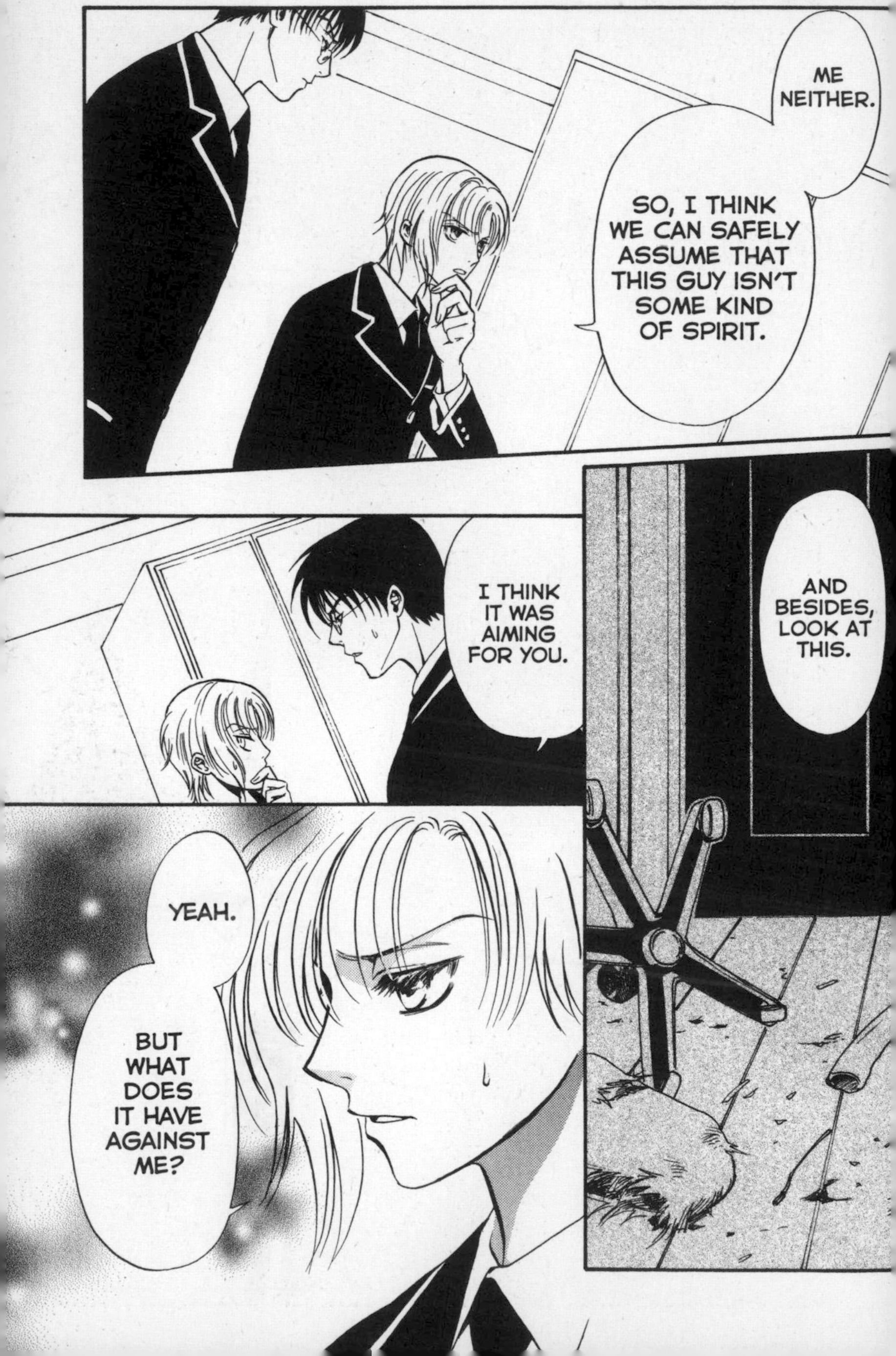
ME NEITHER.
SO, I THINK WE CAN SAFELY ASSUME THAT THIS GUY ISN'T SOME KIND OF SPIRIT.
AND BESIDES, LOOK AT THIS.
I THINK IT WAS AIMING FOR YOU.
YEAH.
BUT WHAT DOES IT HAVE AGAINST ME?

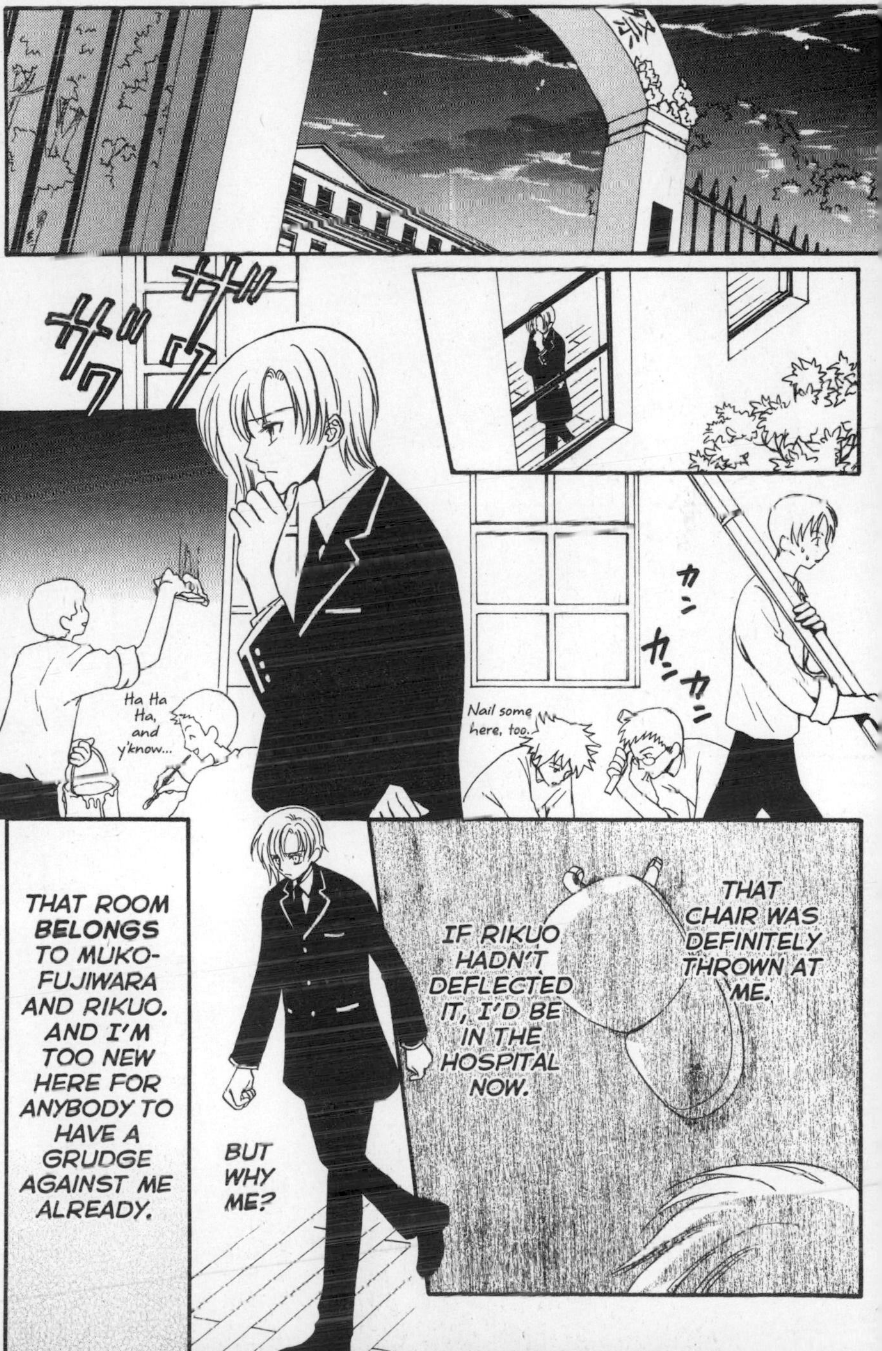
ザッ
ザッ
カン
カンカン
Nail some here, too.
Ha Ha Ha, and y'know...
THAT CHAIR WAS DEFINITELY THROWN AT ME.
IF RIKUO HADN'T DEFLECTED IT, I'D BE IN THE HOSPITAL NOW.
THAT ROOM BELONGS TO MUKO-FUJIWARA AND RIKUO. AND I'M TOO NEW HERE FOR ANYBODY TO HAVE A GRUDGE AGAINST ME ALREADY.
BUT WHY ME?

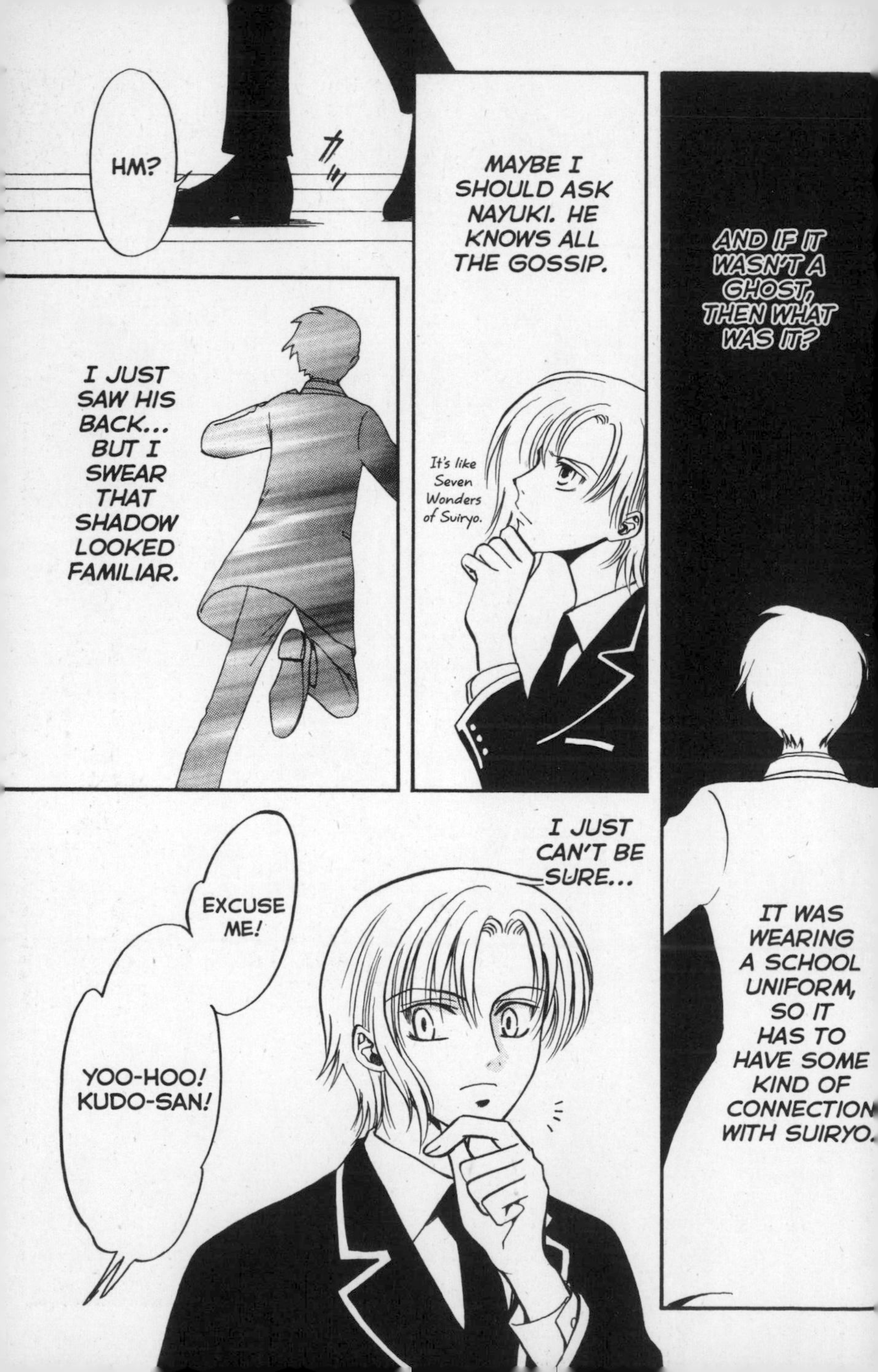
AND IF IT WASN'T A GHOST, THEN WHAT WAS IT?
IT WAS WEARING A SCHOOL UNIFORM, SO IT HAS TO HAVE SOME KIND OF CONNECTION WITH SUIRYO.
MAYBE I SHOULD ASK NAYUKI. HE KNOWS ALL THE GOSSIP.
It's like Seven Wonders of Suiryo.
HM?
I JUST SAW HIS BACK... BUT I SWEAR THAT SHADOW LOOKED FAMILIAR.
I JUST CAN'T BE SURE...
EXCUSE ME!
YOO-HOO! KUDO-SAN!

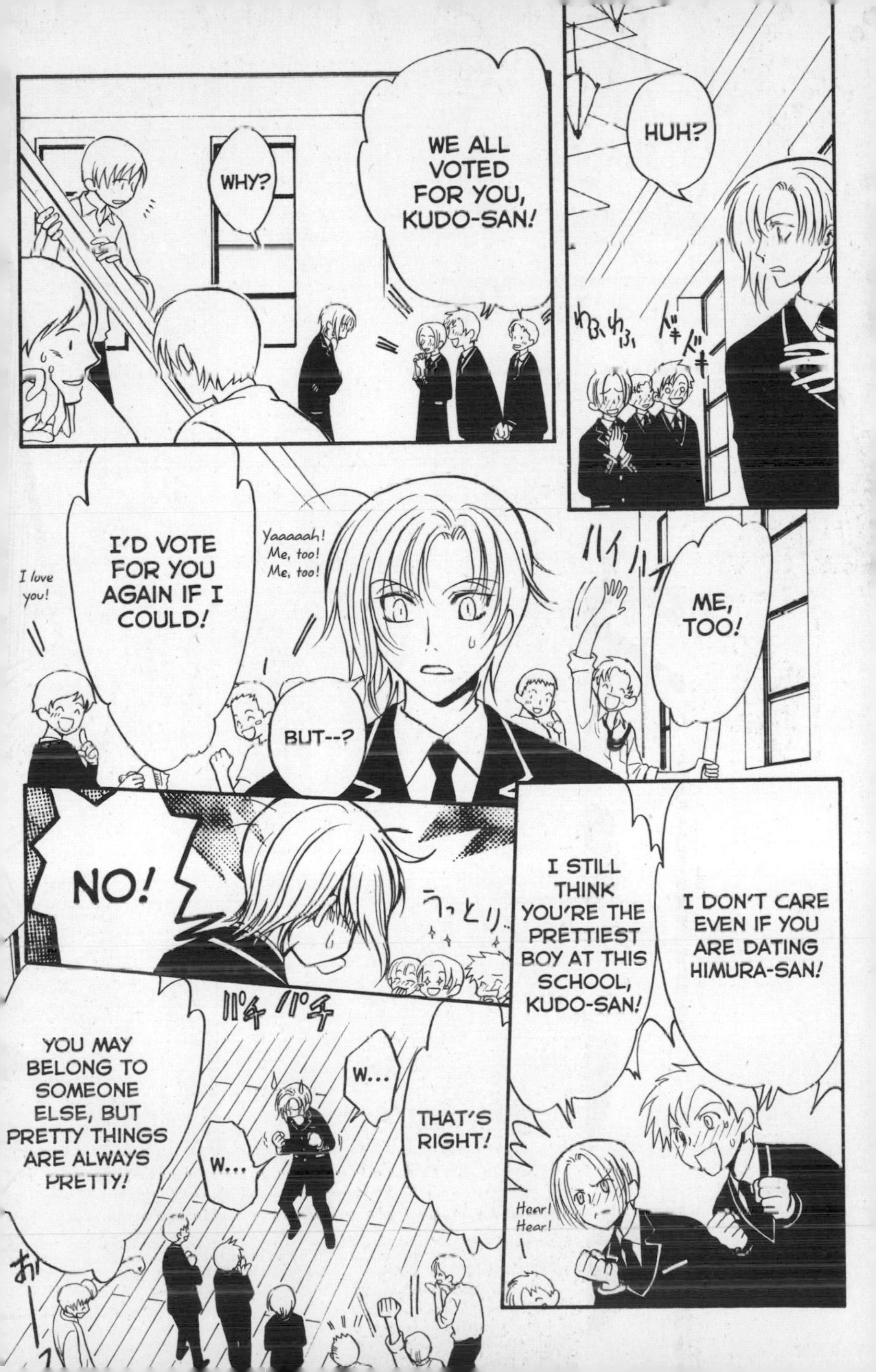
HUH?
WE ALL VOTED FOR YOU, KUDO-SAN!
WHY?
ME, TOO!
Yaaaaah! Me, too! Me, too!
I'D VOTE FOR YOU AGAIN IF I COULD!
I love you!
BUT--?
I DON'T CARE EVEN IF YOU ARE DATING HIMURA-SAN!
I STILL THINK YOU'RE THE PRETTIEST BOY AT THIS SCHOOL, KUDO-SAN!
Hear! Hear!
NO!
うっとり
パチパチ
W...
THAT'S RIGHT!
YOU MAY BELONG TO SOMEONE ELSE, BUT PRETTY THINGS ARE ALWAYS PRETTY!
W...

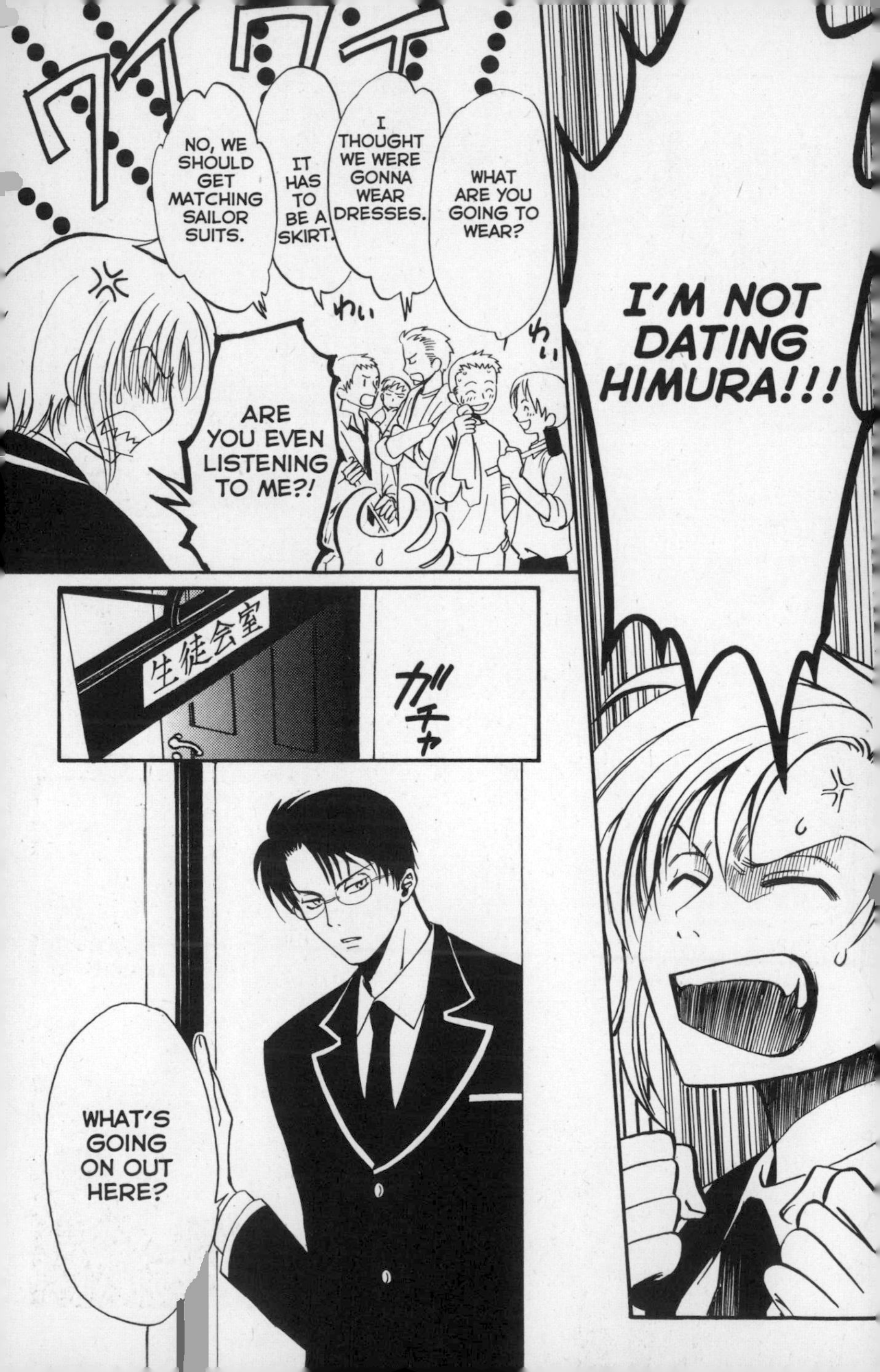
I'M NOT DATING HIMURA!!!
ワイワイ
WHAT ARE YOU GOING TO WEAR?
I THOUGHT WE WERE GONNA WEAR DRESSES.
IT HAS TO BE A SKIRT.
NO, WE SHOULD GET MATCHING SAILOR SUITS.
わい
わい
ARE YOU EVEN LISTENING TO ME?!
生徒会室
ガチャ
WHAT'S GOING ON OUT HERE?

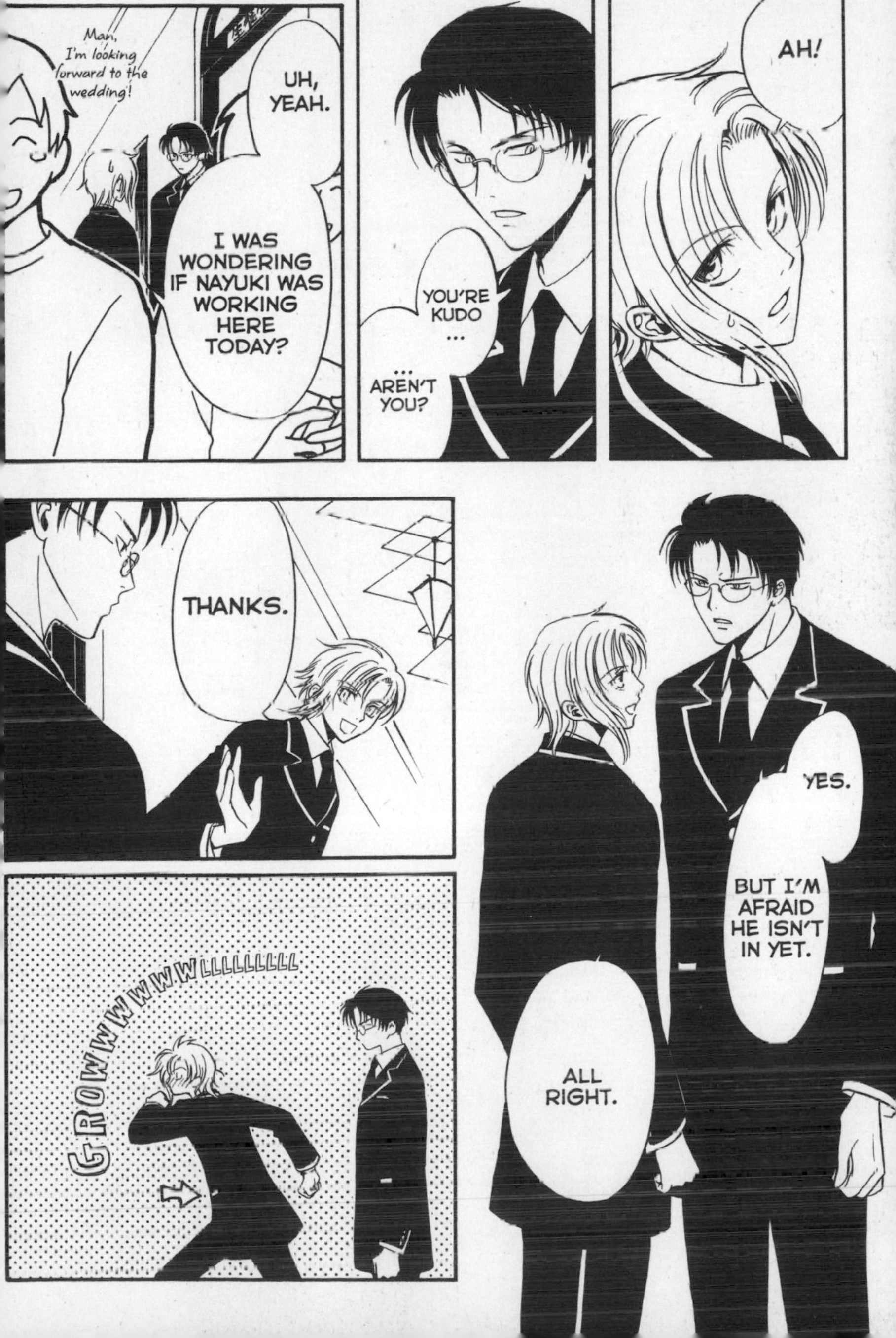
AH!
YOU'RE KUDO ...
... AREN'T YOU?
UH, YEAH.
I WAS WONDERING IF NAYUKI WAS WORKING HERE TODAY?
Man, I'm looking forward to the wedding!
YES.
BUT I'M AFRAID HE ISN'T IN YET.
ALL RIGHT.
THANKS.
GROWWWWWWWLLLLLLLLL

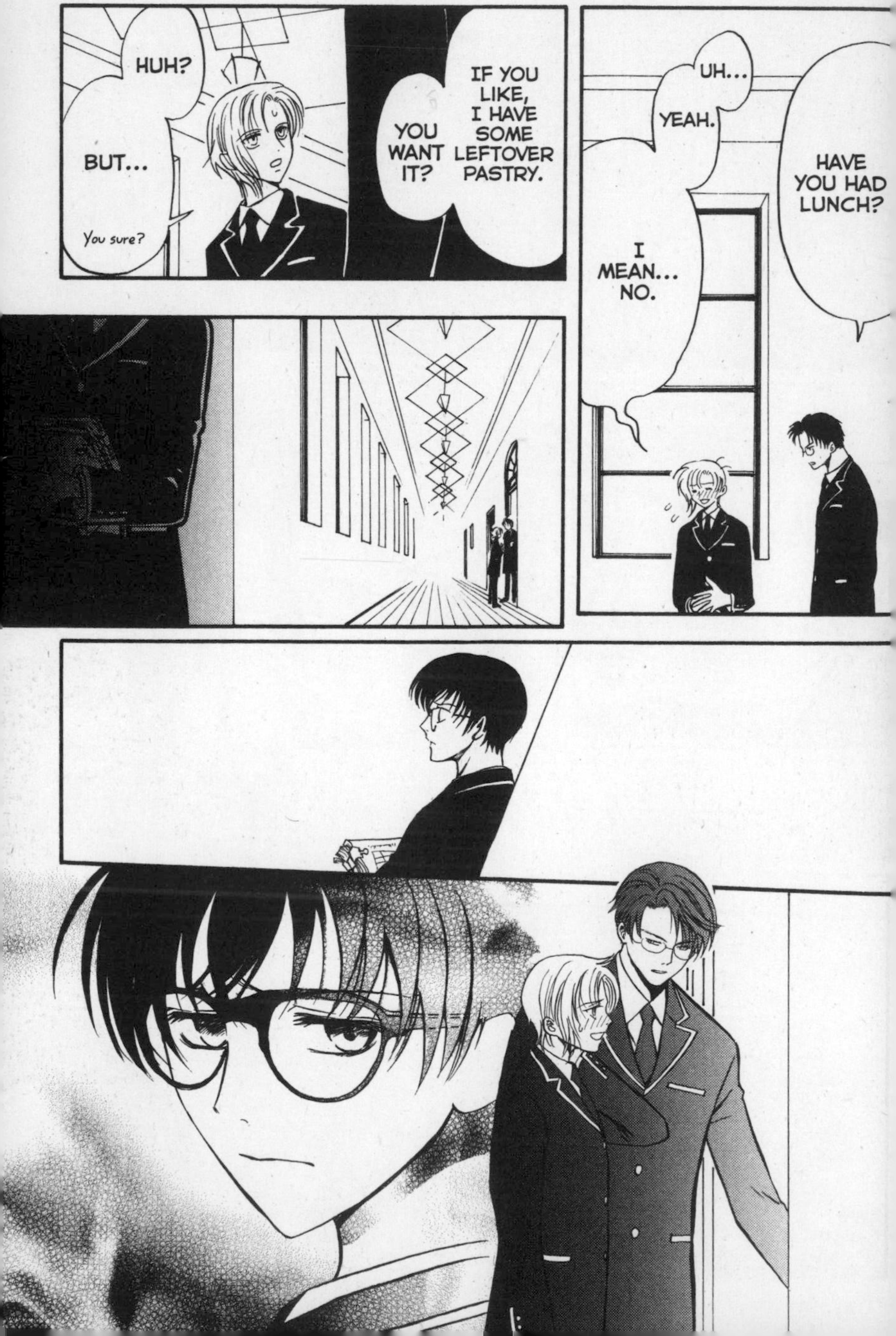
HAVE YOU HAD LUNCH?
UH... YEAH.
I MEAN... NO.
IF YOU LIKE, I HAVE SOME LEFTOVER PASTRY.
YOU WANT IT?
HUH?
BUT...
You sure?

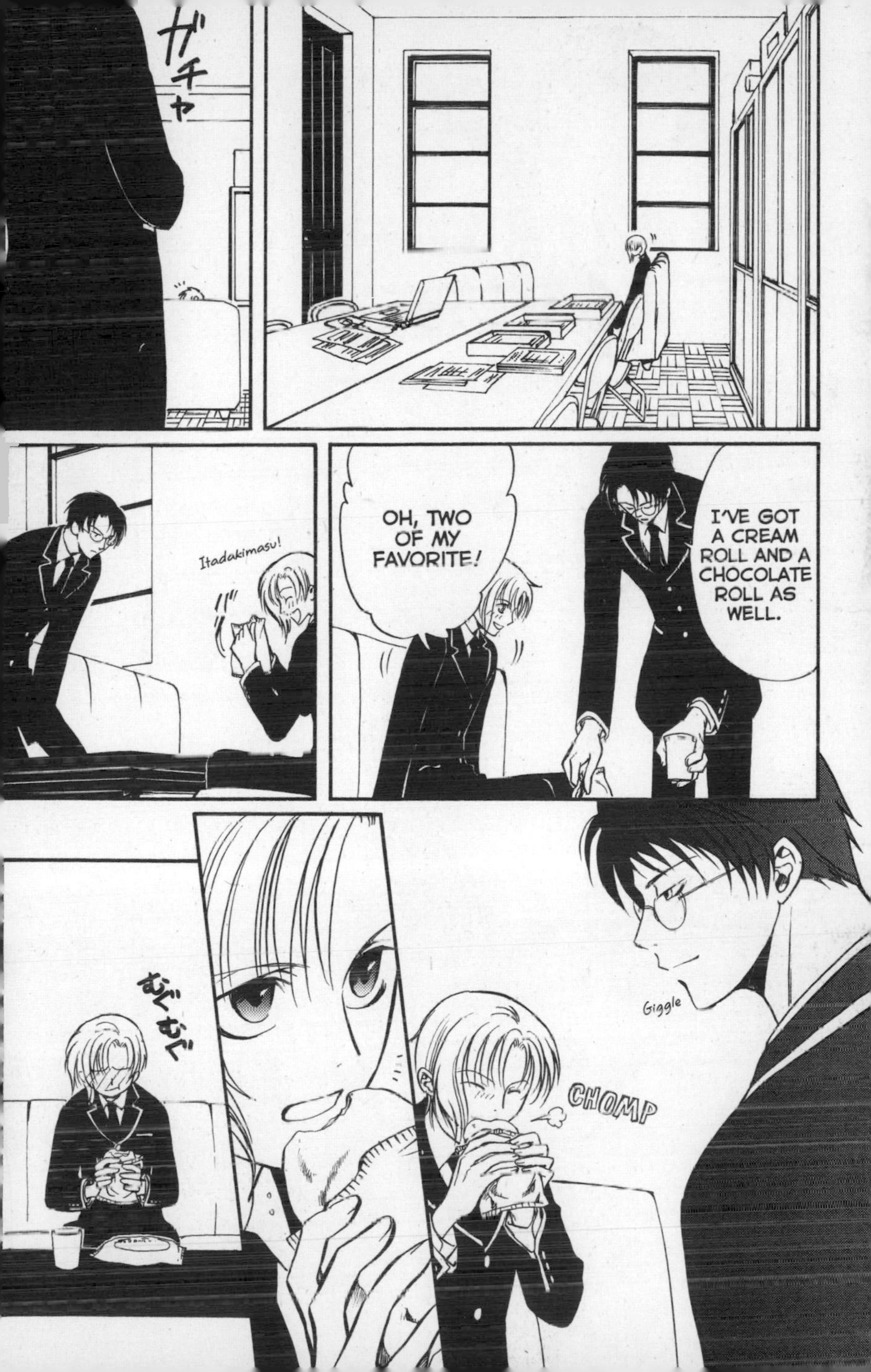
ガチャ
I'VE GOT A CREAM ROLL AND A CHOCOLATE ROLL AS WELL.
OH, TWO OF MY FAVORITE!
Itadakimasu!
Giggle
CHOMP
むぐむぐ

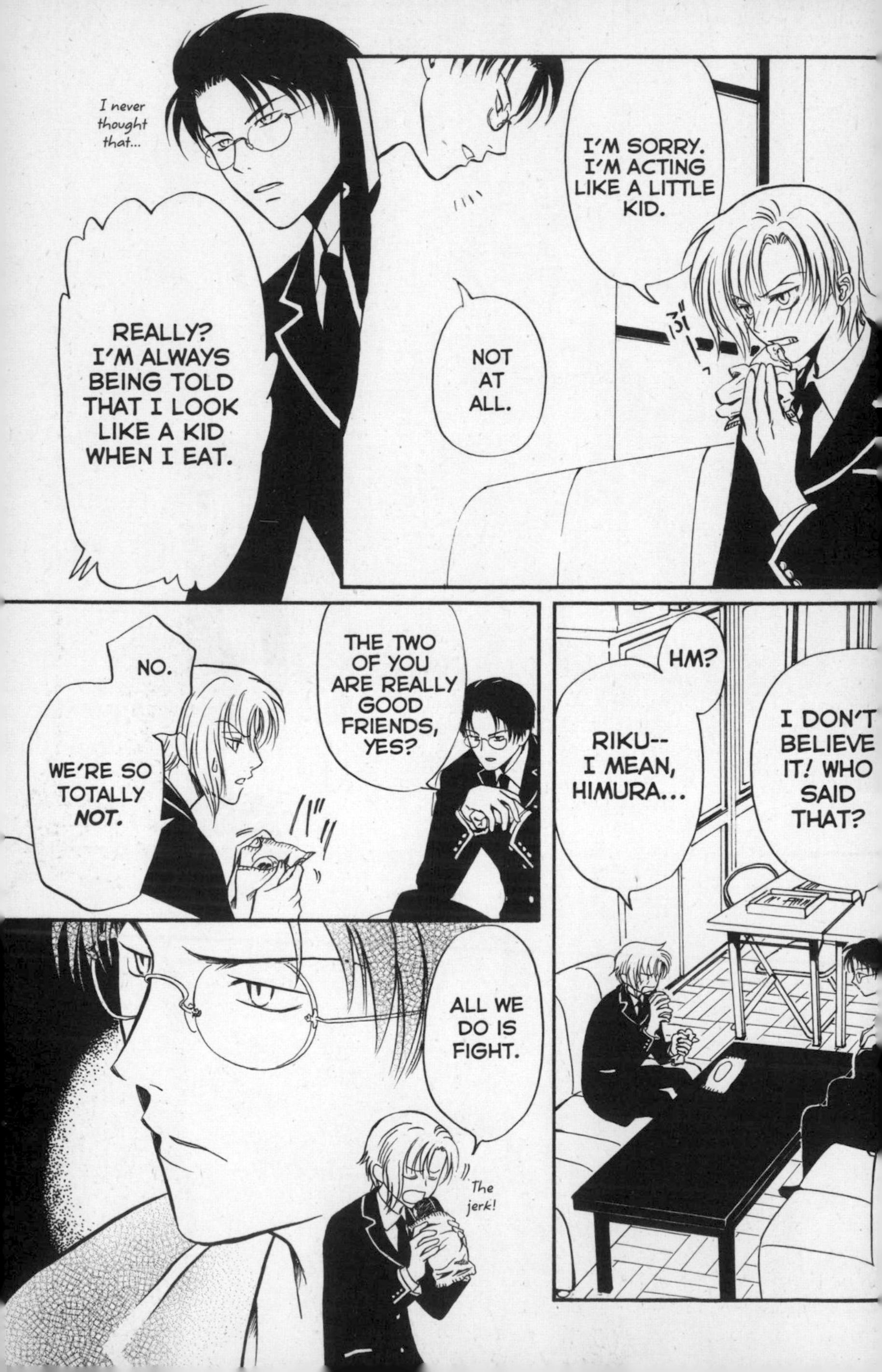

I'M SORRY. I'M ACTING LIKE A LITTLE KID.
NOT AT ALL.
I never thought that...
REALLY? I'M ALWAYS BEING TOLD THAT I LOOK LIKE A KID WHEN I EAT.
I DON'T BELIEVE IT! WHO SAID THAT?
HM?
RIKU-- I MEAN, HIMURA...
THE TWO OF YOU ARE REALLY GOOD FRIENDS, YES?
NO.
WE'RE SO TOTALLY ***NOT.***
ALL WE DO IS FIGHT.
The jerk!

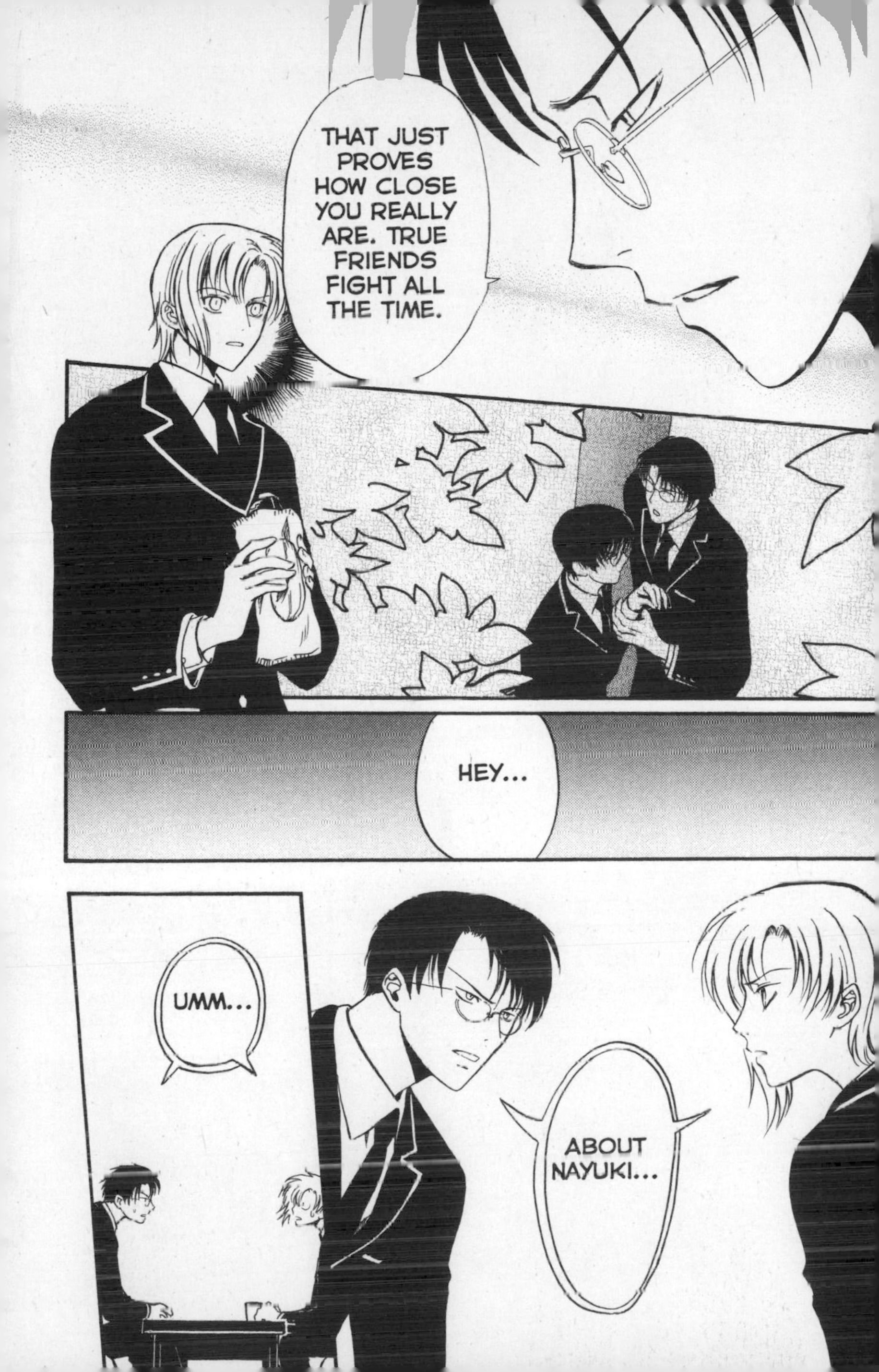
THAT JUST PROVES HOW CLOSE YOU REALLY ARE. TRUE FRIENDS FIGHT ALL THE TIME.
HEY...
ABOUT NAYUKI...
UMM...

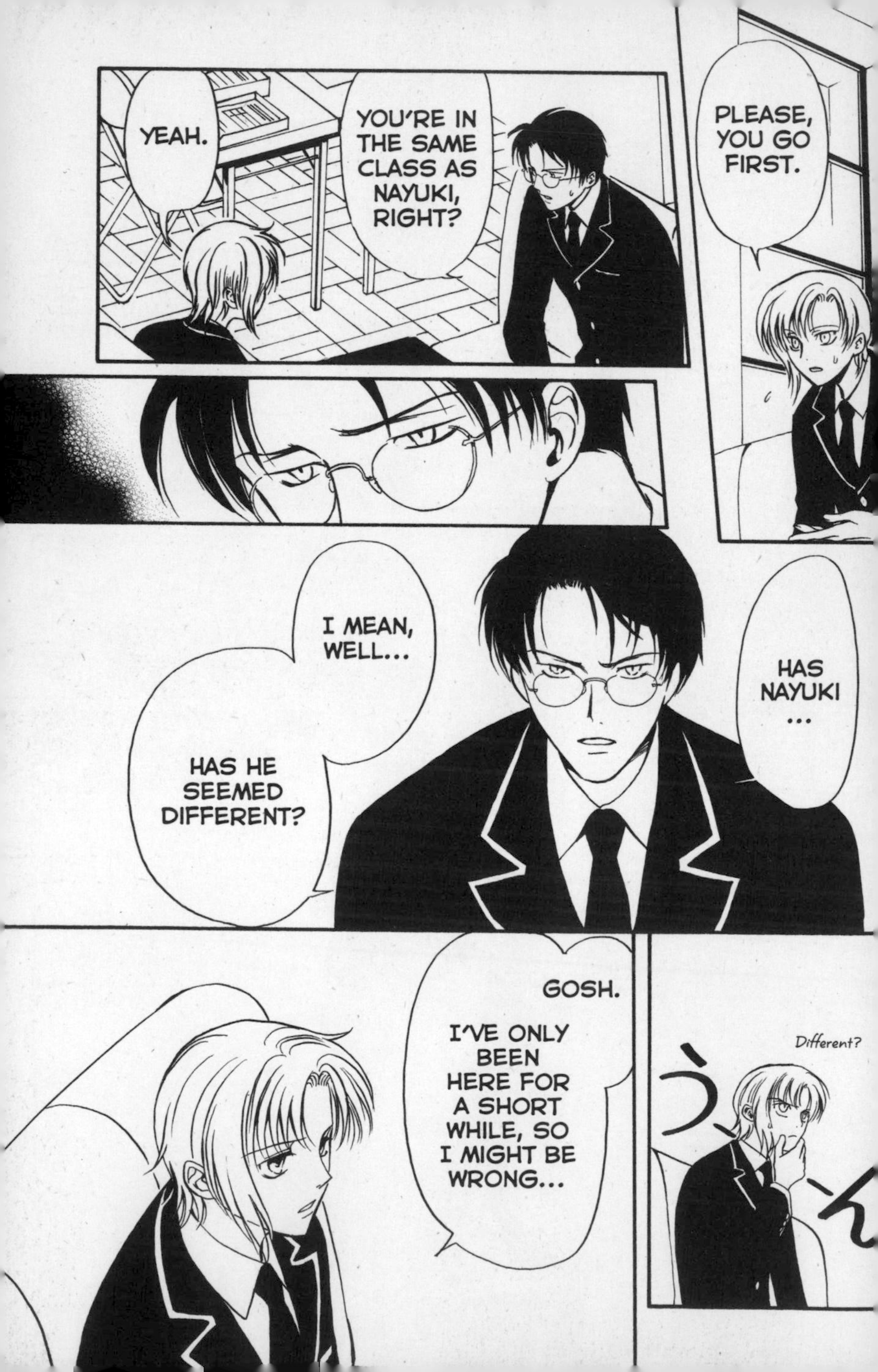
PLEASE, YOU GO FIRST.
YOU'RE IN THE SAME CLASS AS NAYUKI, RIGHT?
YEAH.
HAS NAYUKI ...
I MEAN, WELL...
HAS HE SEEMED DIFFERENT?
う～ん
Different?
GOSH.
I'VE ONLY BEEN HERE FOR A SHORT WHILE, SO I MIGHT BE WRONG...

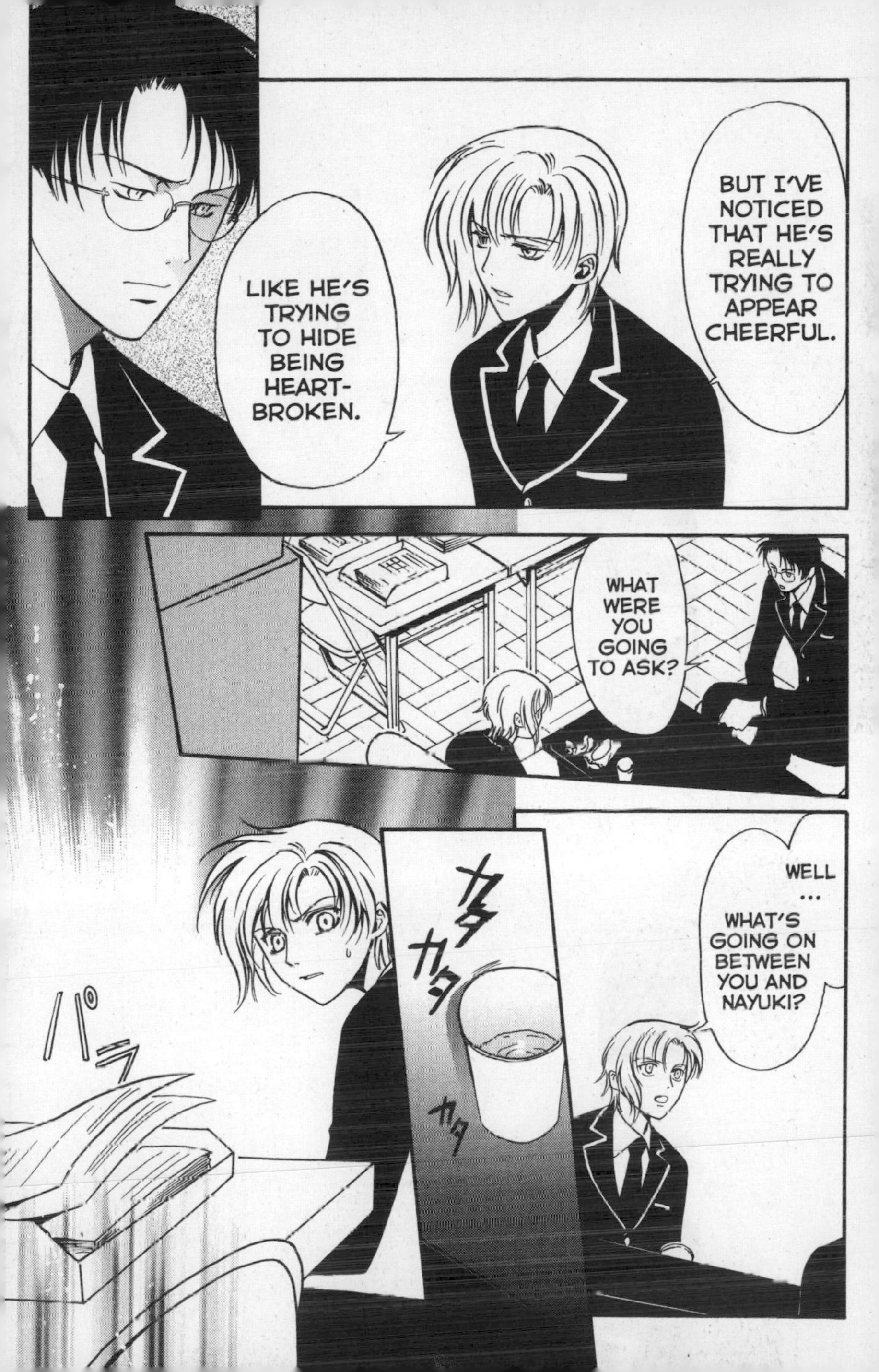
BUT I'VE NOTICED THAT HE'S REALLY TRYING TO APPEAR CHEERFUL.
LIKE HE'S TRYING TO HIDE BEING HEART-BROKEN.
WHAT WERE YOU GOING TO ASK?
WELL ... WHAT'S GOING ON BETWEEN YOU AND NAYUKI?
カタカタ
カタ
パラ

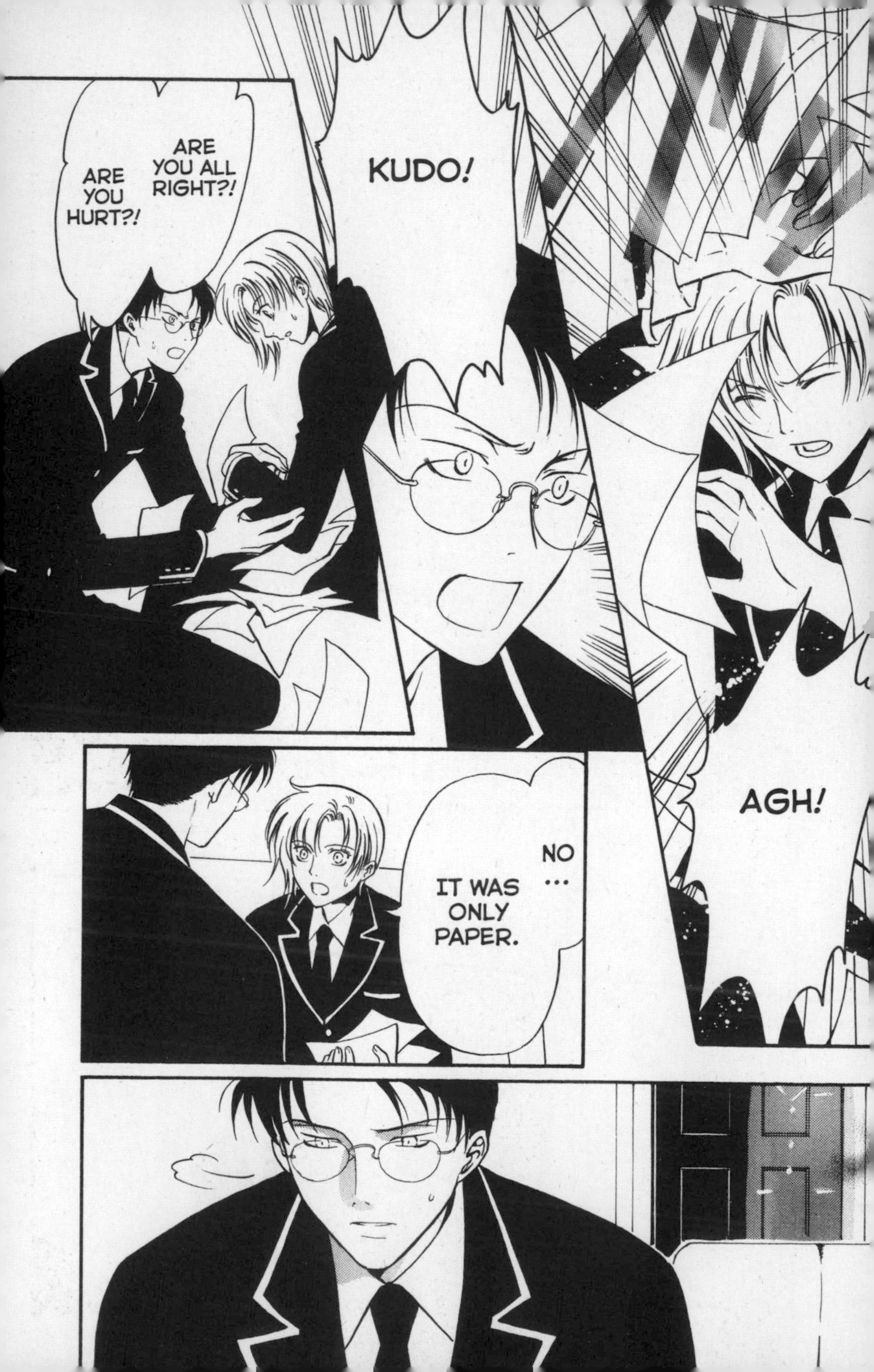
AGH!
KUDO!
ARE YOU ALL RIGHT?! ARE YOU HURT?!
NO ... IT WAS ONLY PAPER.

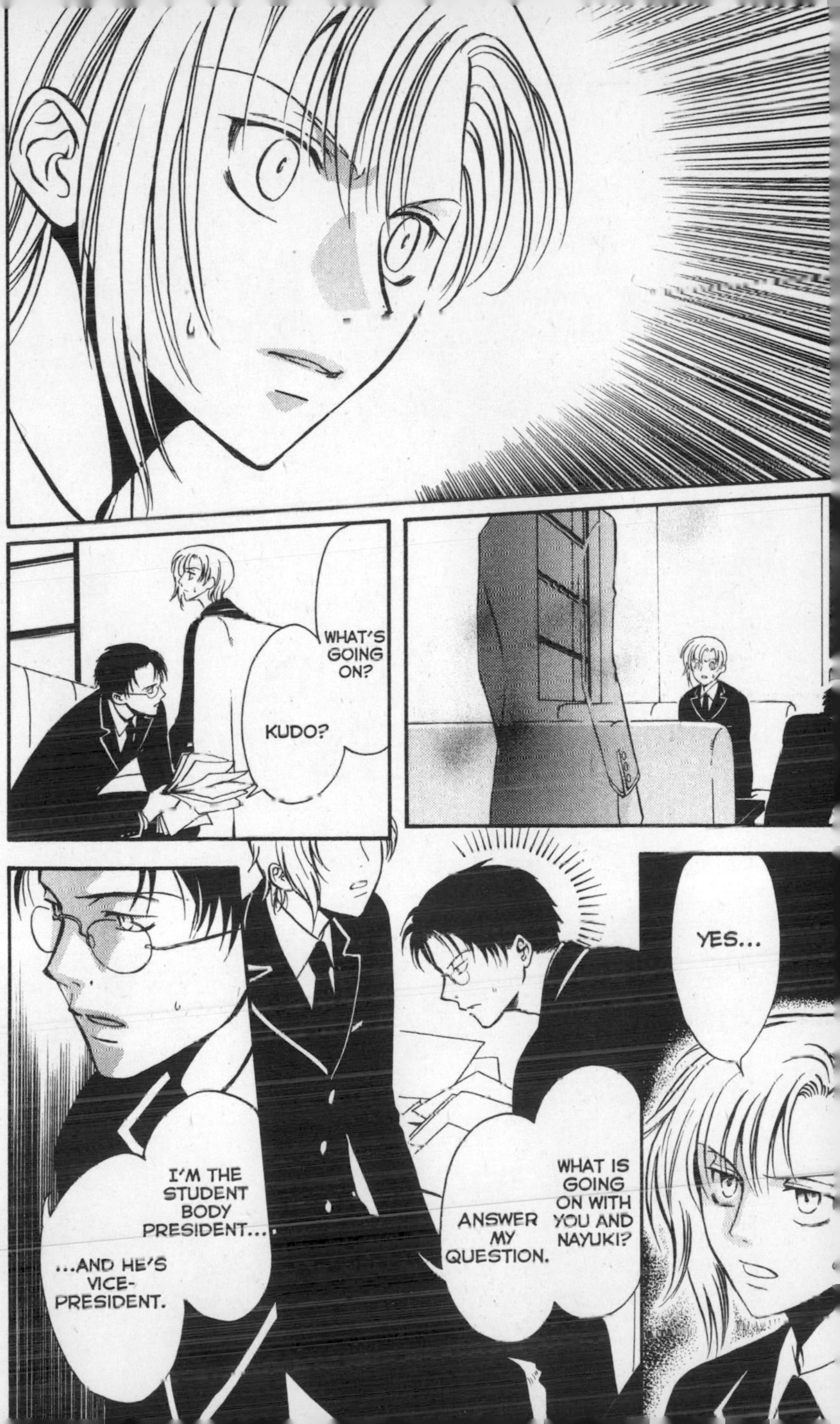
WHAT'S GOING ON?
KUDO?
YES...
WHAT IS GOING ON WITH YOU AND NAYUKI?
ANSWER MY QUESTION.
I'M THE STUDENT BODY PRESIDENT...
...AND HE'S VICE-PRESIDENT.

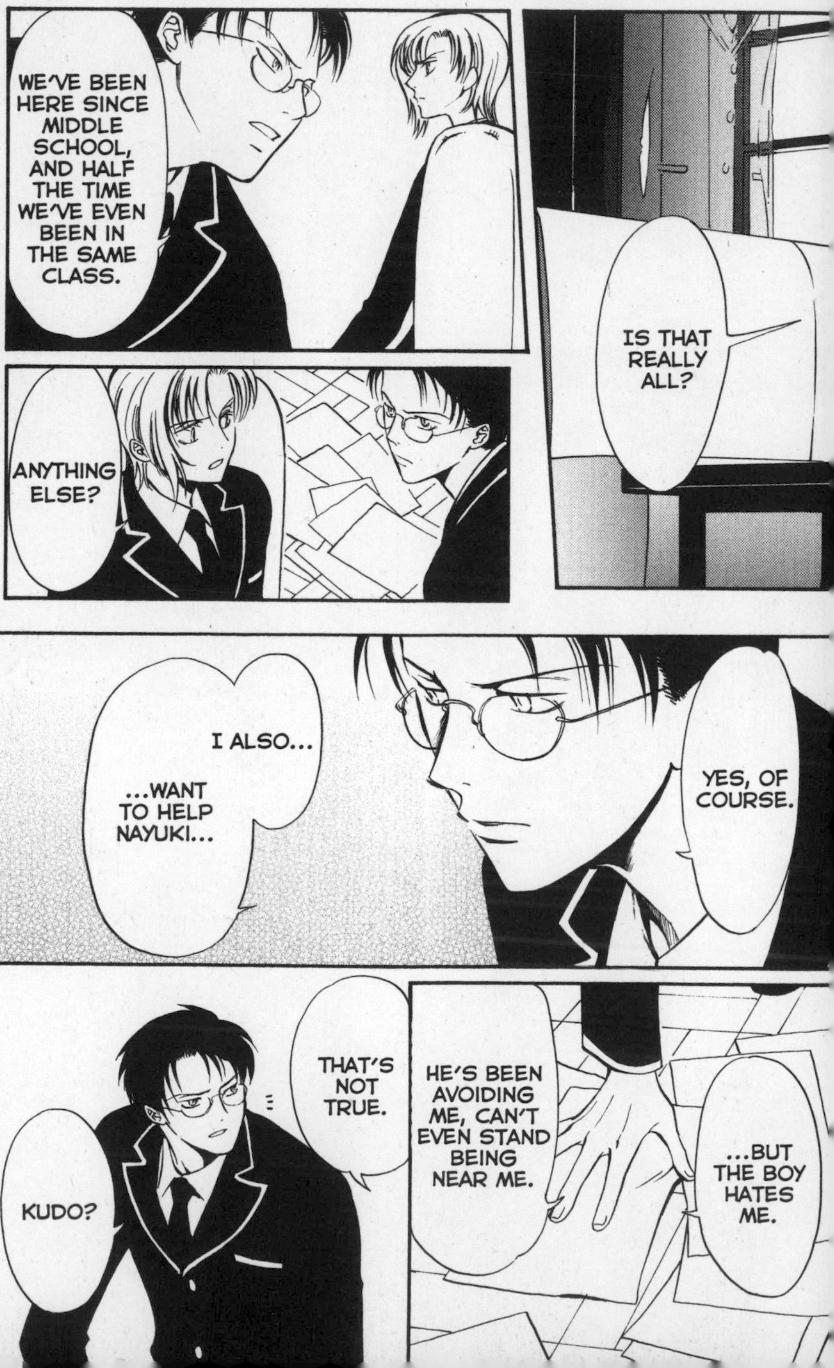
IS THAT REALLY ALL?
WE'VE BEEN HERE SINCE MIDDLE SCHOOL, AND HALF THE TIME WE'VE EVEN BEEN IN THE SAME CLASS.
ANYTHING ELSE?
YES, OF COURSE.
I ALSO...
...WANT TO HELP NAYUKI...
...BUT THE BOY HATES ME.
HE'S BEEN AVOIDING ME, CAN'T EVEN STAND BEING NEAR ME.
THAT'S NOT TRUE.
KUDO?

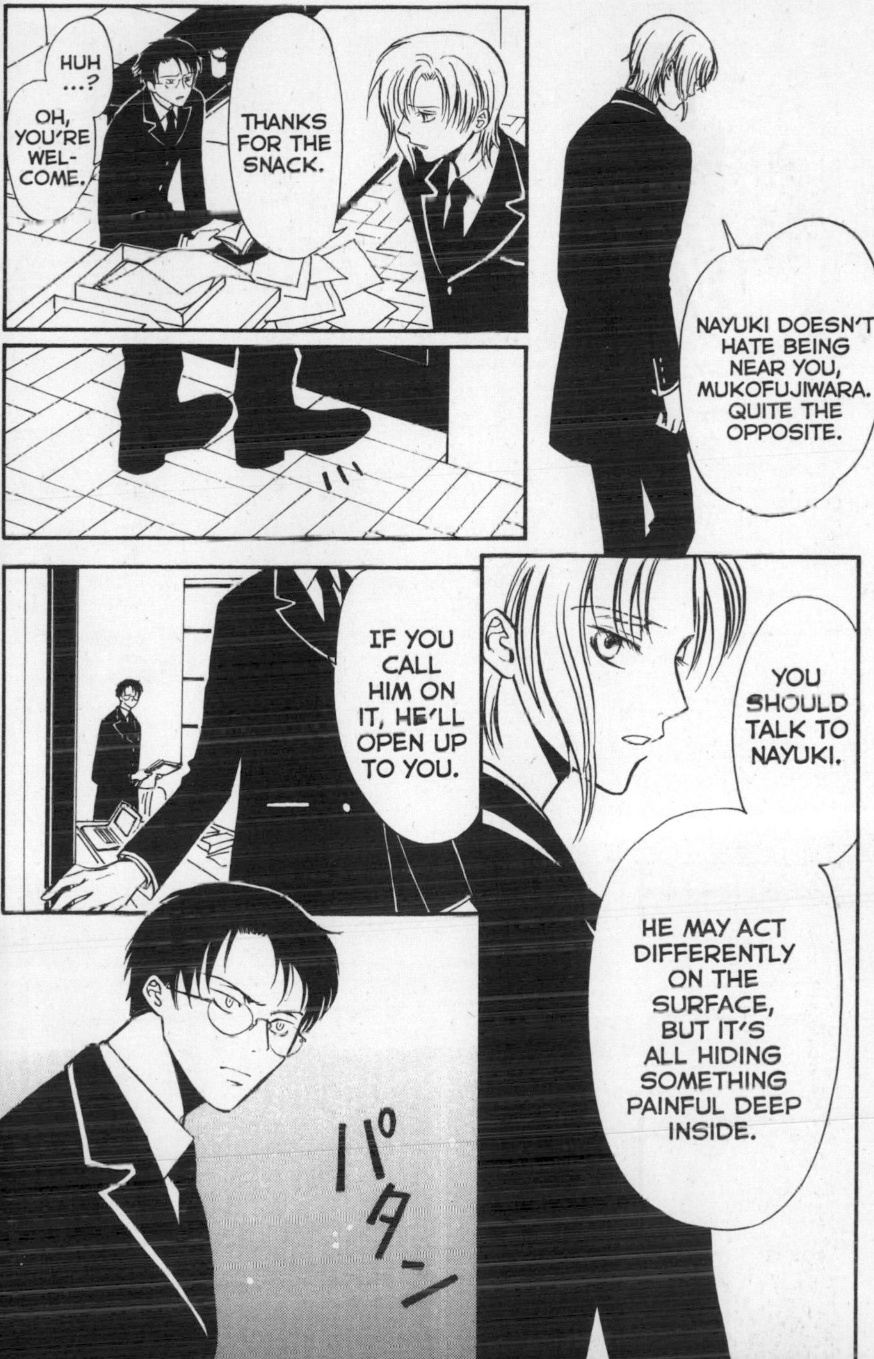
NAYUKI DOESN'T HATE BEING NEAR YOU, MUKOFUJIWARA. QUITE THE OPPOSITE.
THANKS FOR THE SNACK.
HUH ...?
OH, YOU'RE WEL-COME.
YOU SHOULD TALK TO NAYUKI.
HE MAY ACT DIFFERENTLY ON THE SURFACE, BUT IT'S ALL HIDING SOMETHING PAINFUL DEEP INSIDE.
IF YOU CALL HIM ON IT, HE'LL OPEN UP TO YOU.
パターン

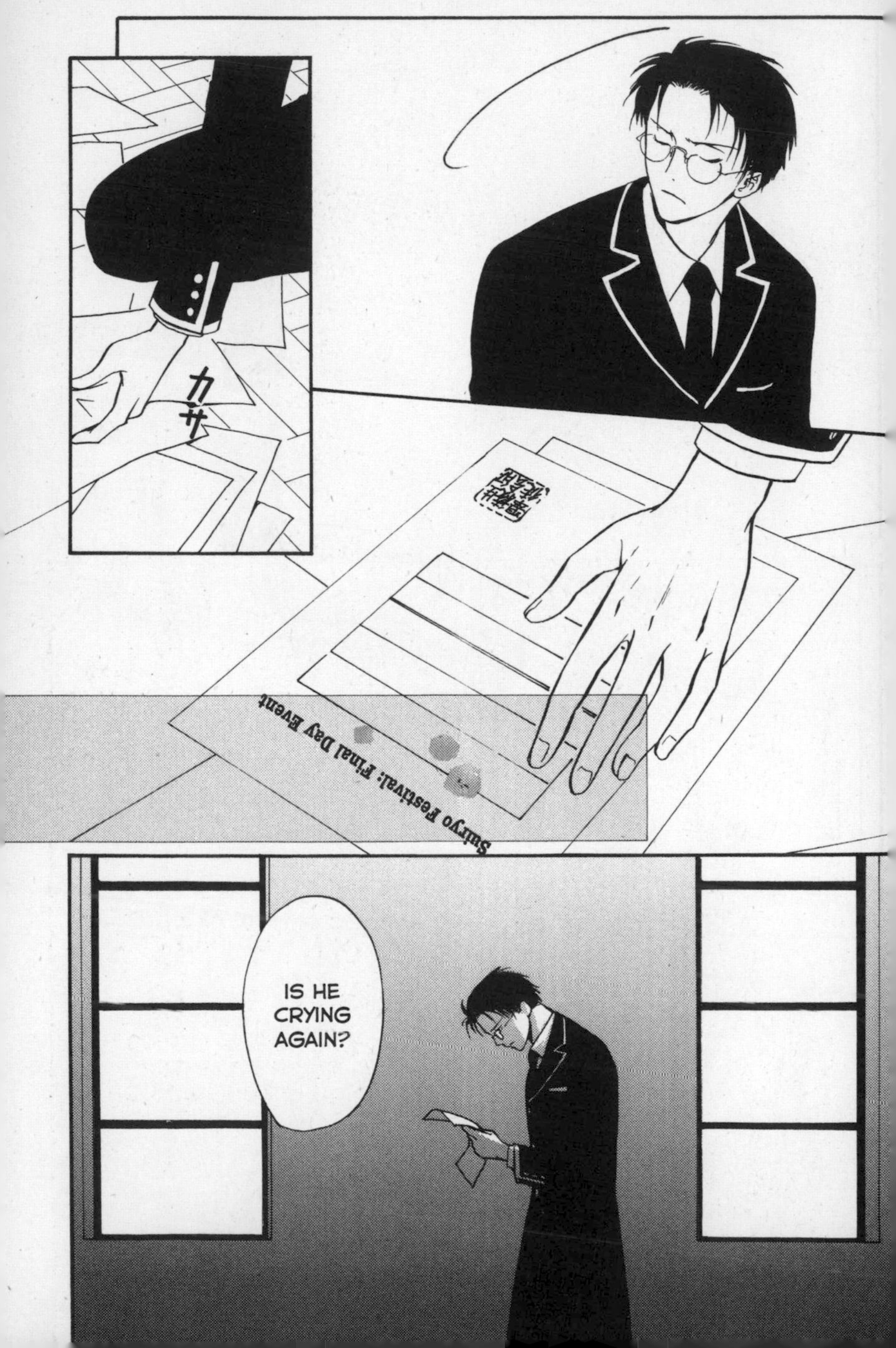
カサ
Suiryo Festival: Final Day Event
IS HE CRYING AGAIN?

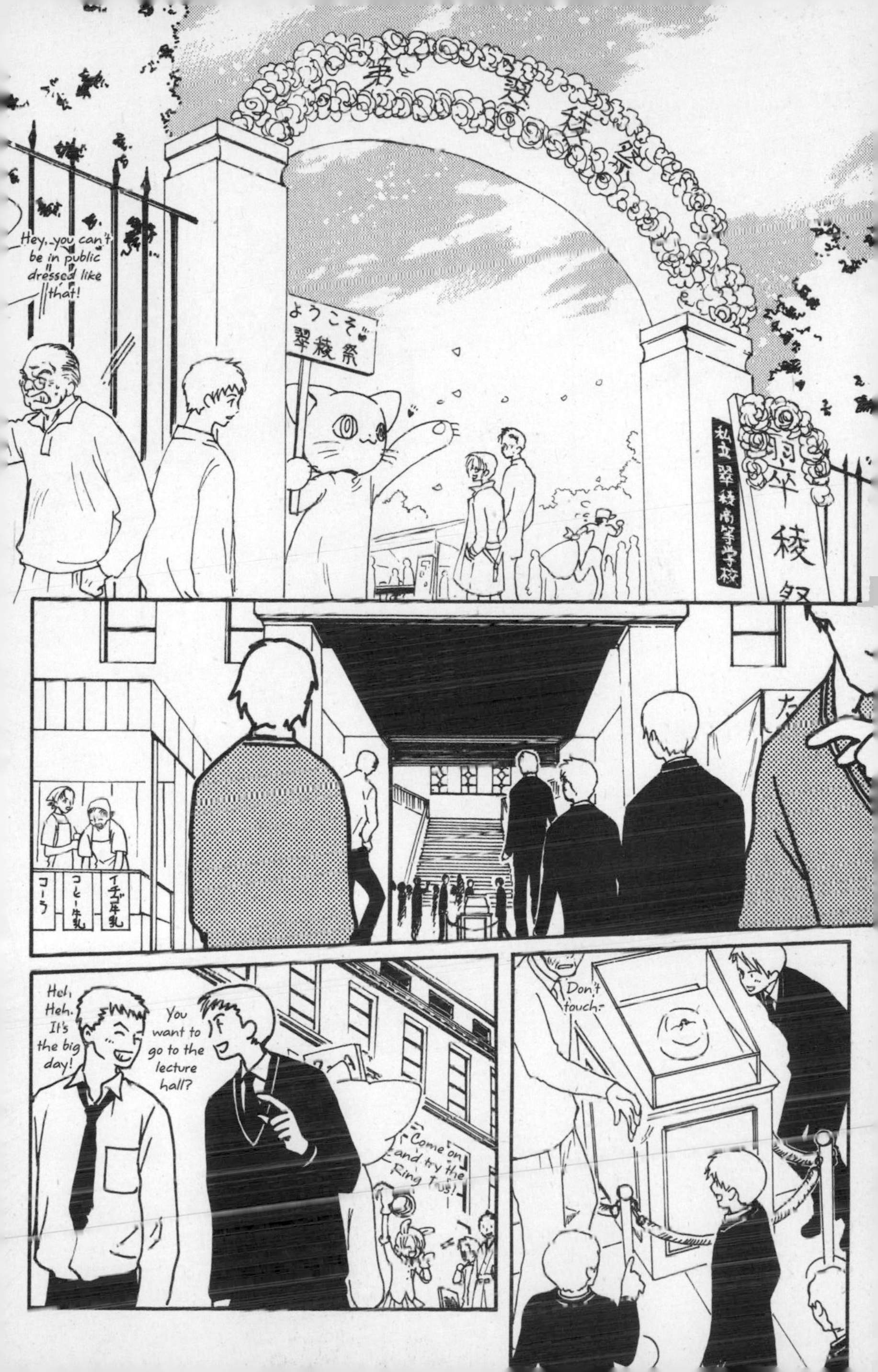
Hey, you can't be in public dressed like that!
ようこそ翠稜祭
私立翠稜高等学校
イチゴ牛乳
コーヒー牛乳
コーラ
Don't touch.
You want to go to the lecture hall?
Heh, Heh. It's the big day!
Come on and try the Ring Toss!

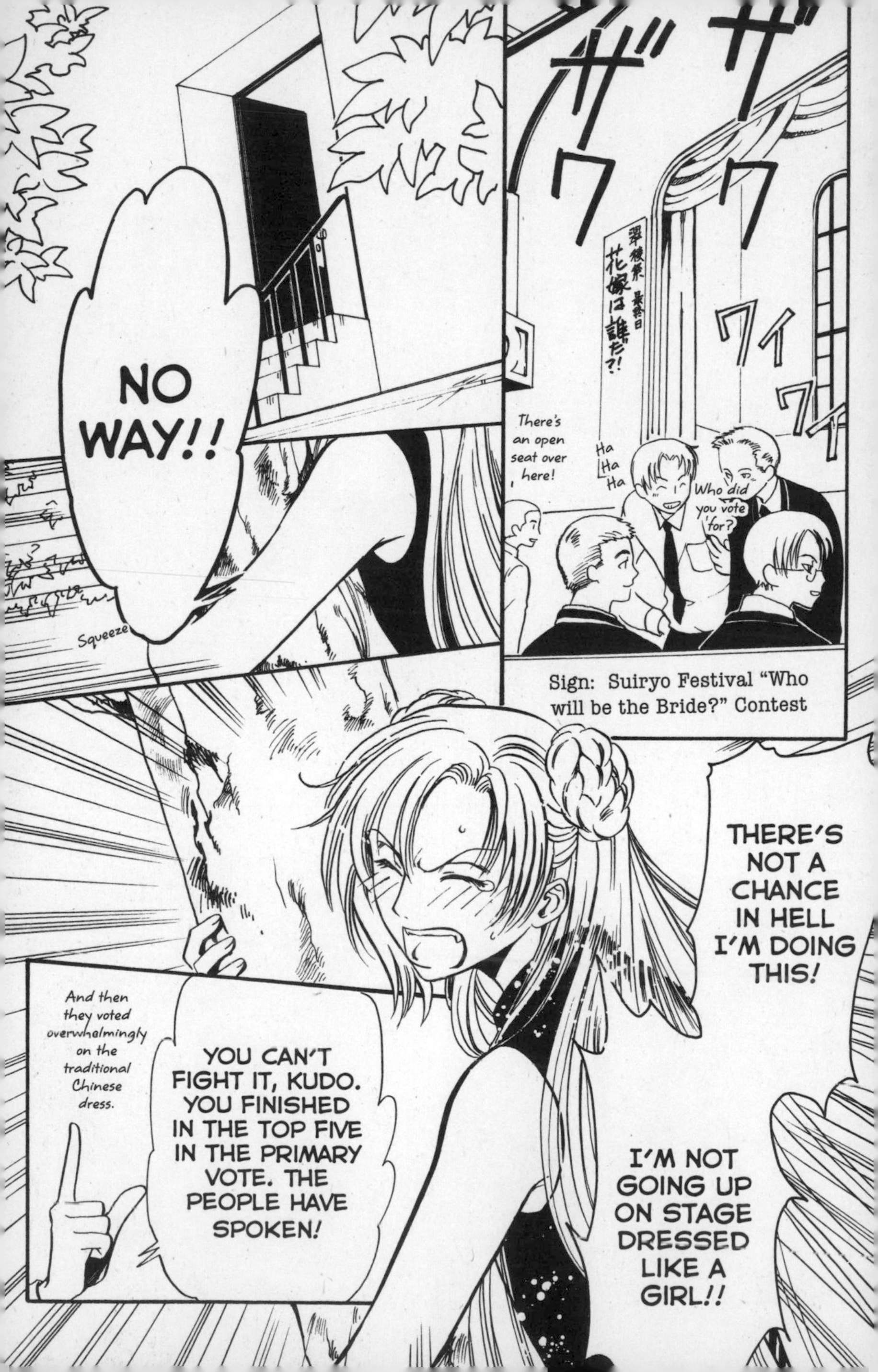
ザワザワ
翠稜祭 最終日
花嫁は誰だ?!
ワイワイ
There's an open seat over here!
Ha Ha Ha
Who did you vote for?
Sign: Suiryo Festival "Who will be the Bride?" Contest
NO WAY!!
Squeeze
THERE'S NOT A CHANCE IN HELL I'M DOING THIS!
I'M NOT GOING UP ON STAGE DRESSED LIKE A GIRL!!
And then they voted overwhelmingly on the traditional Chinese dress.
YOU CAN'T FIGHT IT, KUDO. YOU FINISHED IN THE TOP FIVE IN THE PRIMARY VOTE. THE PEOPLE HAVE SPOKEN!

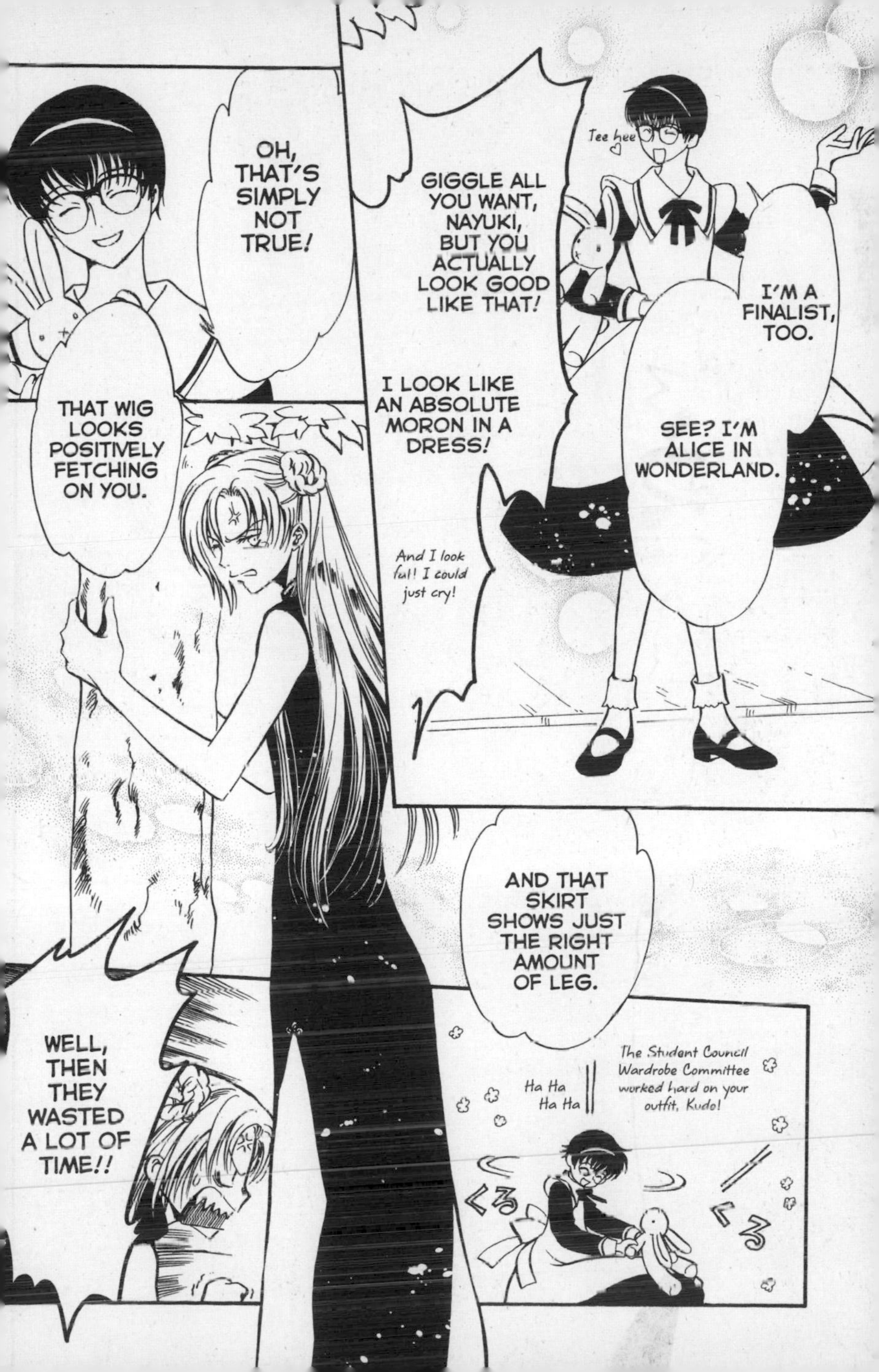
Tee hee
I'M A FINALIST, TOO.
SEE? I'M ALICE IN WONDERLAND.
GIGGLE ALL YOU WANT, NAYUKI, BUT YOU ACTUALLY LOOK GOOD LIKE THAT!
I LOOK LIKE AN ABSOLUTE MORON IN A DRESS!
And I look fat! I could just cry!
OH, THAT'S SIMPLY NOT TRUE!
THAT WIG LOOKS POSITIVELY FETCHING ON YOU.
AND THAT SKIRT SHOWS JUST THE RIGHT AMOUNT OF LEG.
The Student Council Wardrobe Committee worked hard on your outfit, Kudo!
Ha Ha Ha Ha
くる くる
WELL, THEN THEY WASTED A LOT OF TIME!!

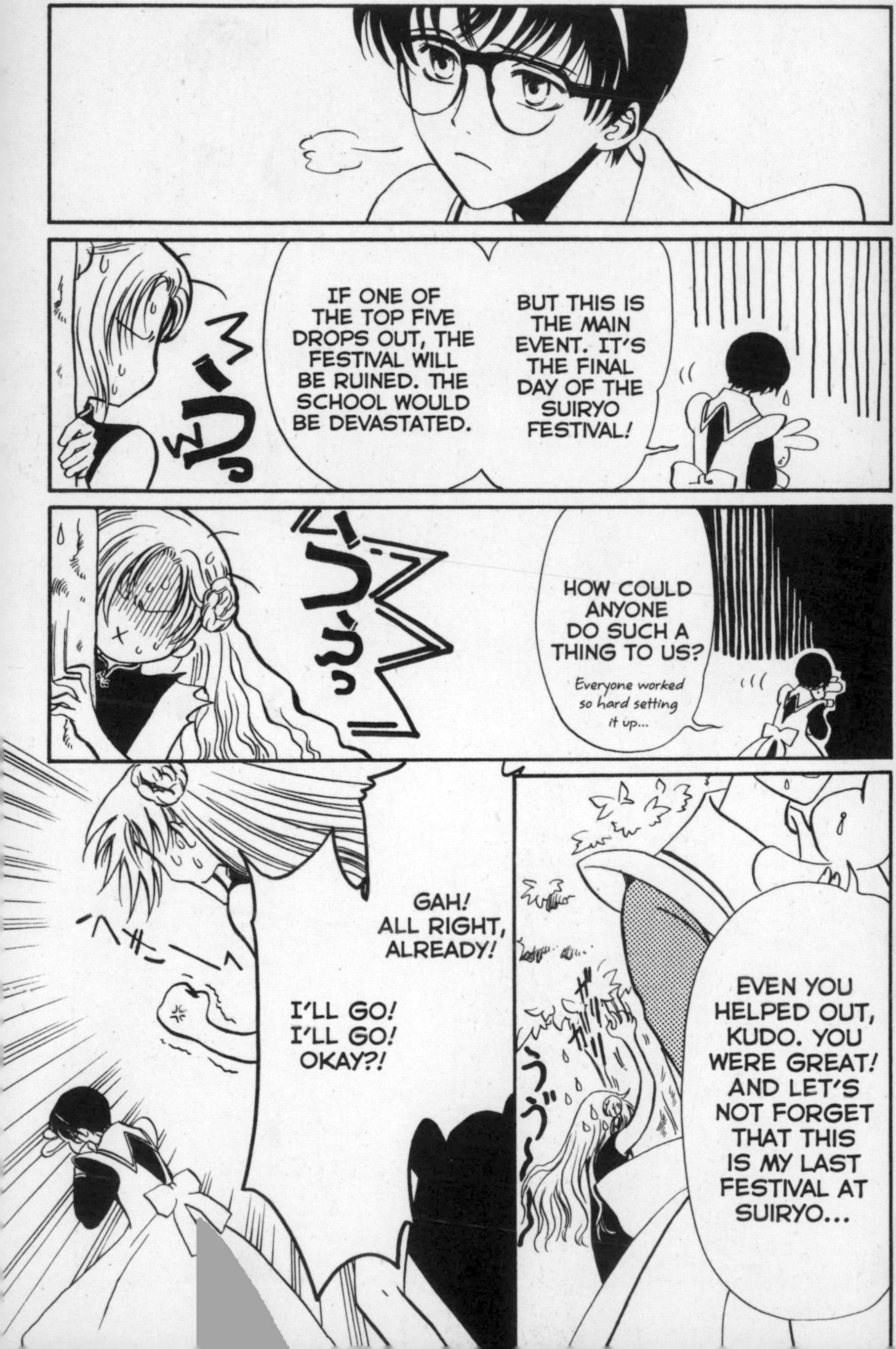
BUT THIS IS THE MAIN EVENT. IT'S THE FINAL DAY OF THE SUIRYO FESTIVAL!
IF ONE OF THE TOP FIVE DROPS OUT, THE FESTIVAL WILL BE RUINED. THE SCHOOL WOULD BE DEVASTATED.
HOW COULD ANYONE DO SUCH A THING TO US?
Everyone worked so hard setting it up...
EVEN YOU HELPED OUT, KUDO. YOU WERE GREAT! AND LET'S NOT FORGET THAT THIS IS MY LAST FESTIVAL AT SUIRYO...
GAH! ALL RIGHT, ALREADY!
I'LL GO! I'LL GO! OKAY?!

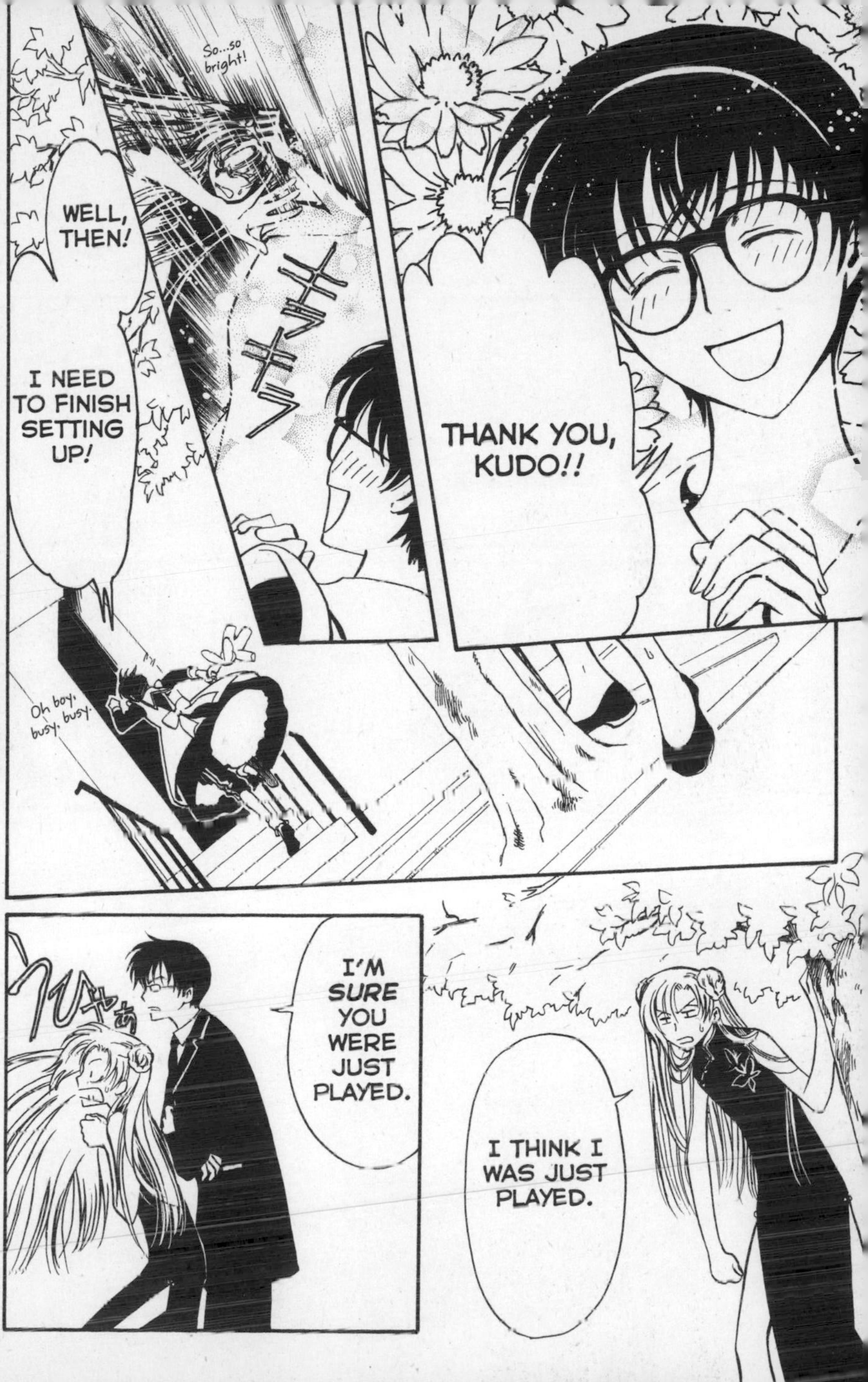
THANK YOU, KUDO!!
So...so bright!
キラキラ
WELL, THEN!
I NEED TO FINISH SETTING UP!
Oh boy, busy, busy.
I THINK I WAS JUST PLAYED.
I'M SURE YOU WERE JUST PLAYED.

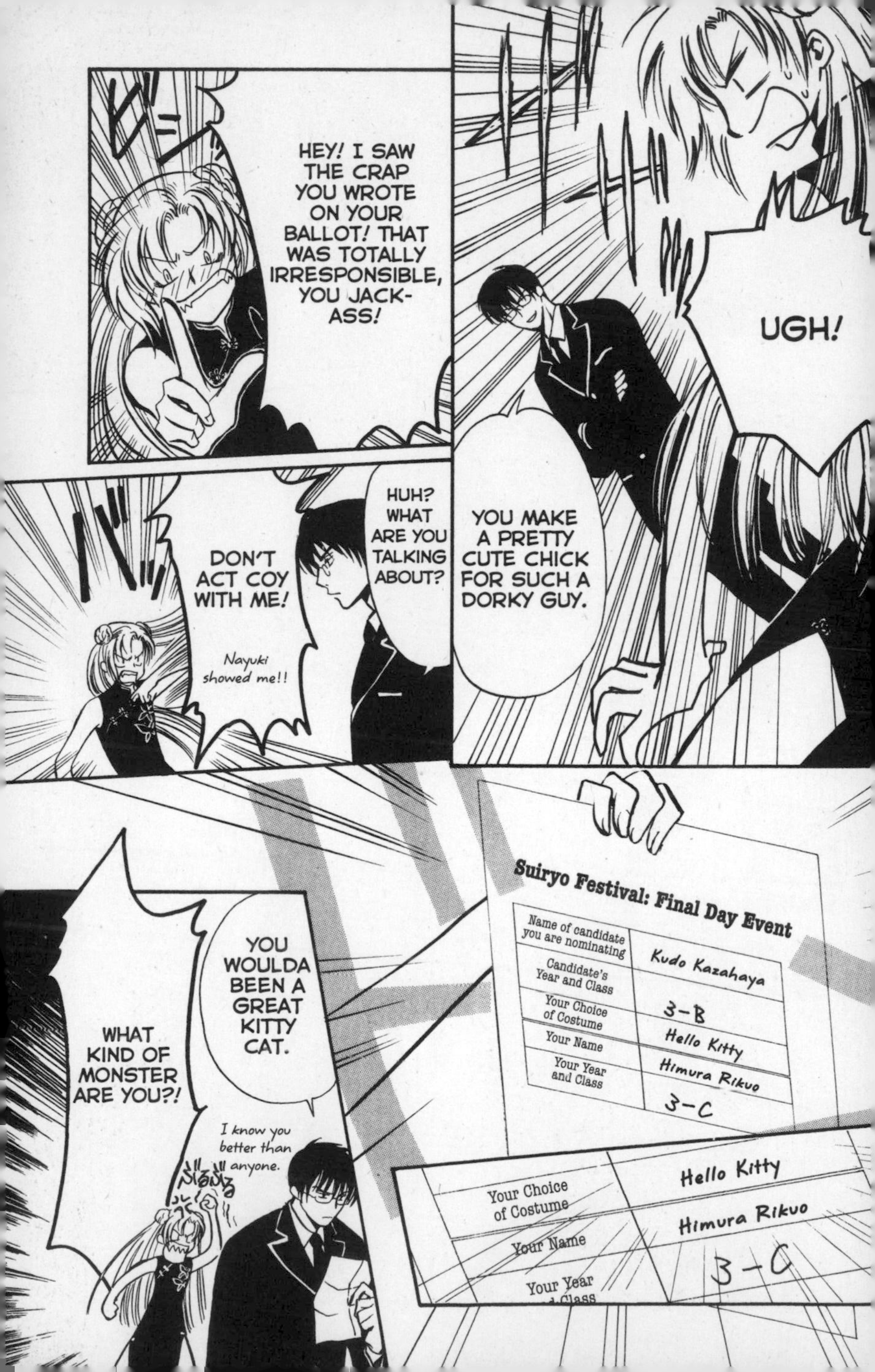
UGH!
YOU MAKE A PRETTY CUTE CHICK FOR SUCH A DORKY GUY.
HEY! I SAW THE CRAP YOU WROTE ON YOUR BALLOT! THAT WAS TOTALLY IRRESPONSIBLE, YOU JACK-ASS!
HUH? WHAT ARE YOU TALKING ABOUT?
DON'T ACT COY WITH ME!
Nayuki showed me!!
Suiryo Festival: Final Day Event
Name of candidate you are nominating
Kudo Kazahaya
Candidate's Year and Class
3-B
Your Choice of Costume
Hello Kitty
Your Name
Himura Rikuo
Your Year and Class
3-C
Your Choice of Costume
Hello Kitty
Your Name
Himura Rikuo
Your Year
3-C
YOU WOULDA BEEN A GREAT KITTY CAT.
WHAT KIND OF MONSTER ARE YOU?!
I know you better than anyone.

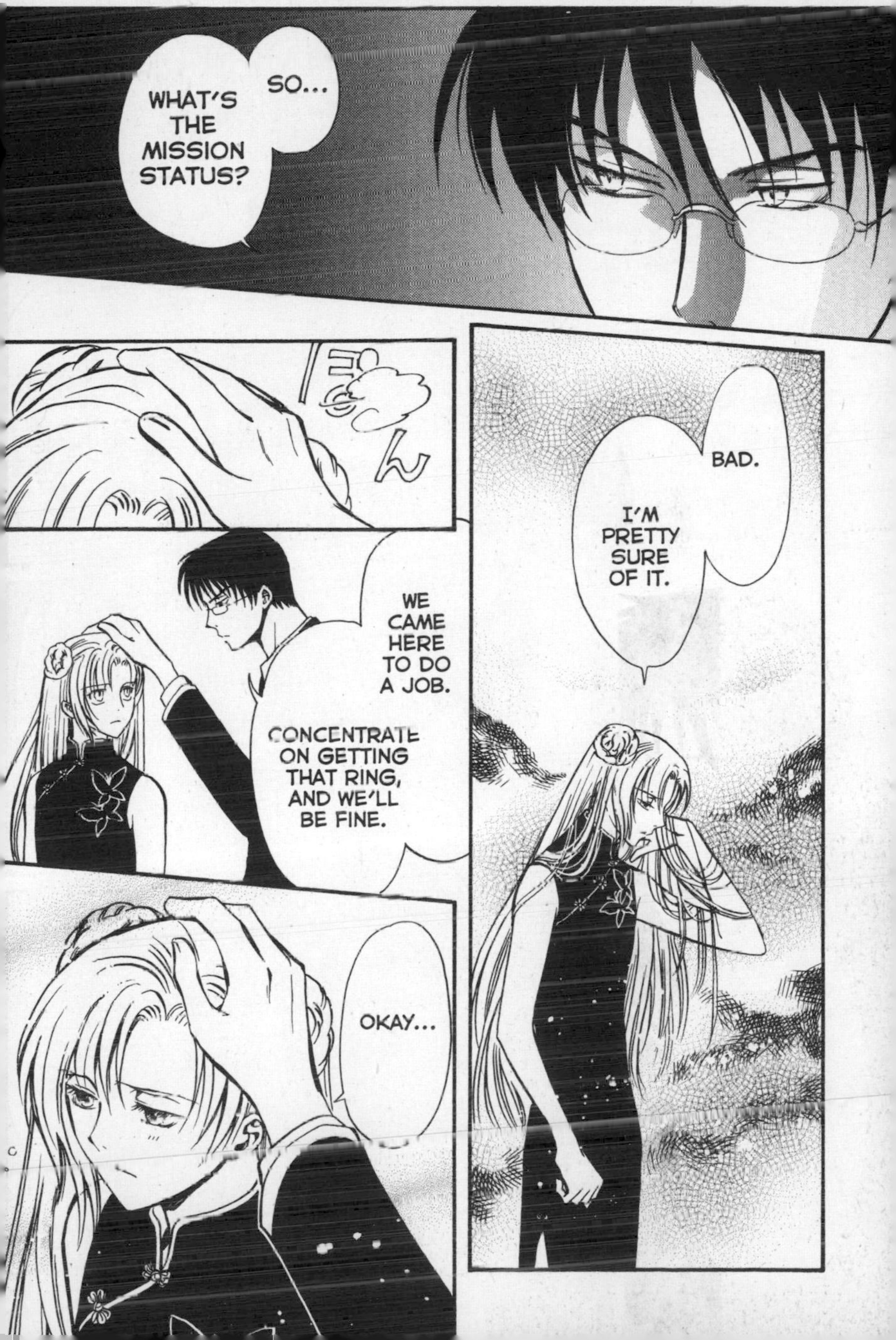
SO...
WHAT'S THE MISSION STATUS?
BAD.
I'M PRETTY SURE OF IT.
WE CAME HERE TO DO A JOB.
CONCENTRATE ON GETTING THAT RING, AND WE'LL BE FINE.
OKAY...

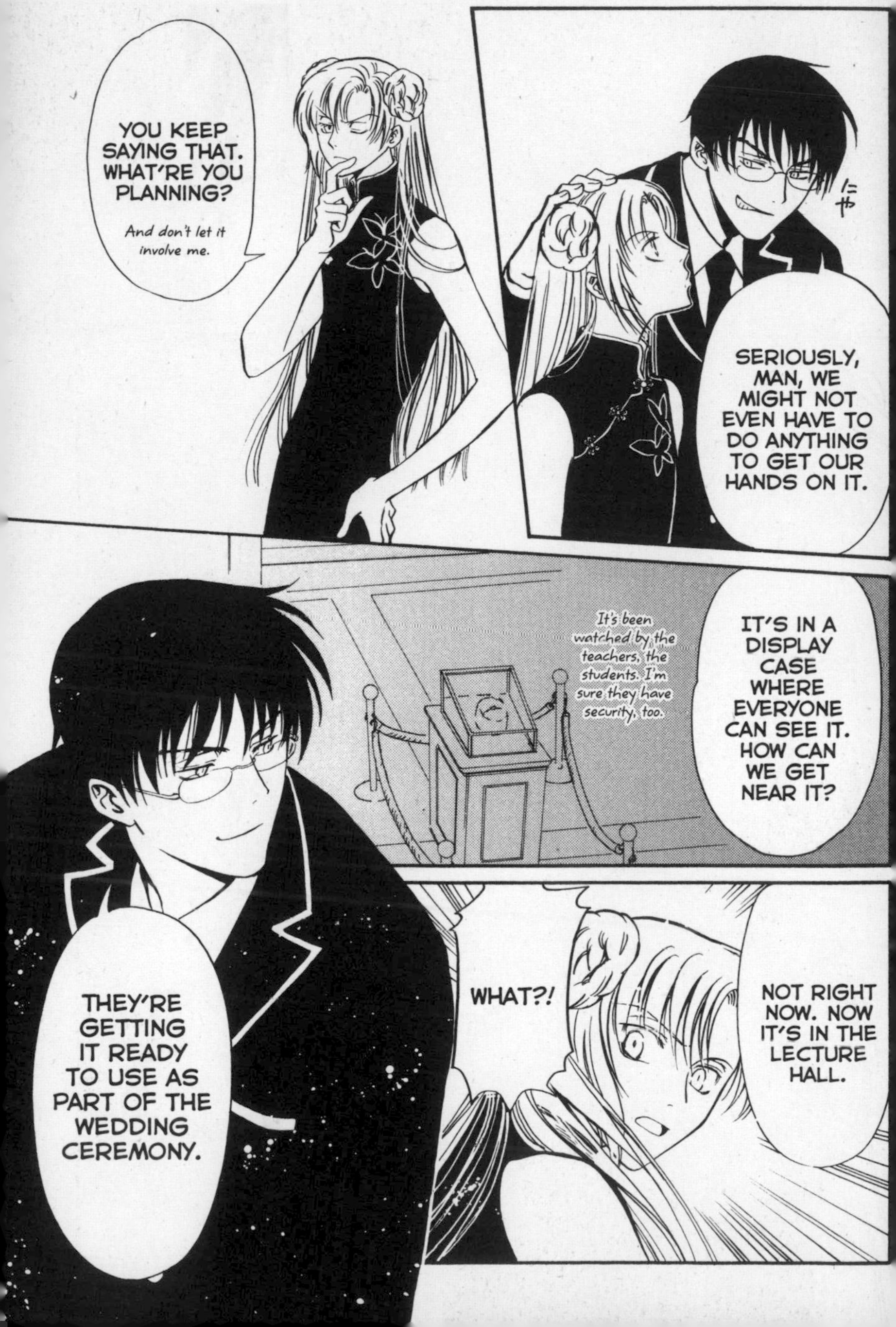
にゃ
SERIOUSLY, MAN, WE MIGHT NOT EVEN HAVE TO DO ANYTHING TO GET OUR HANDS ON IT.
YOU KEEP SAYING THAT. WHAT'RE YOU PLANNING?
And don't let it involve me.
IT'S IN A DISPLAY CASE WHERE EVERYONE CAN SEE IT. HOW CAN WE GET NEAR IT?
It's been watched by the teachers, the students. I'm sure they have security, too.
NOT RIGHT NOW. NOW IT'S IN THE LECTURE HALL.
WHAT?!
THEY'RE GETTING IT READY TO USE AS PART OF THE WEDDING CEREMONY.

合法ドラッグ
LEGAL DRUG

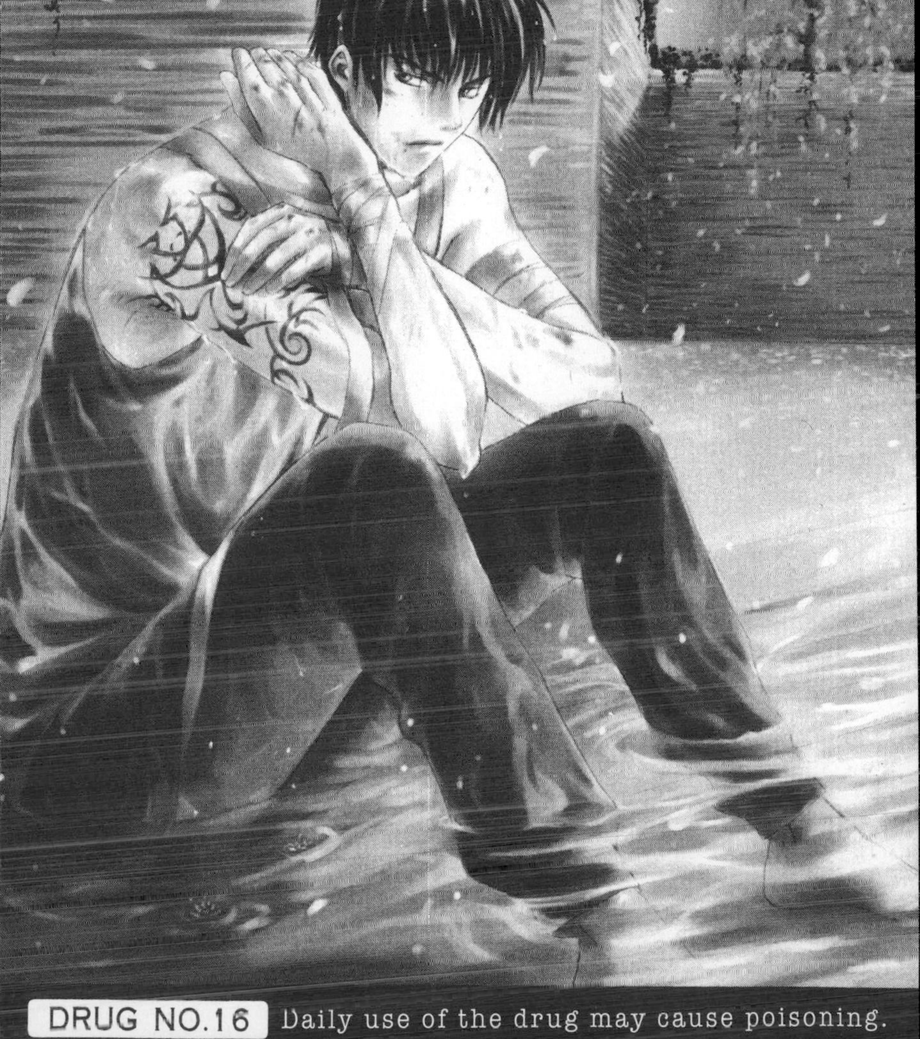

DRUG NO.16 Daily use of the drug may cause poisoning.

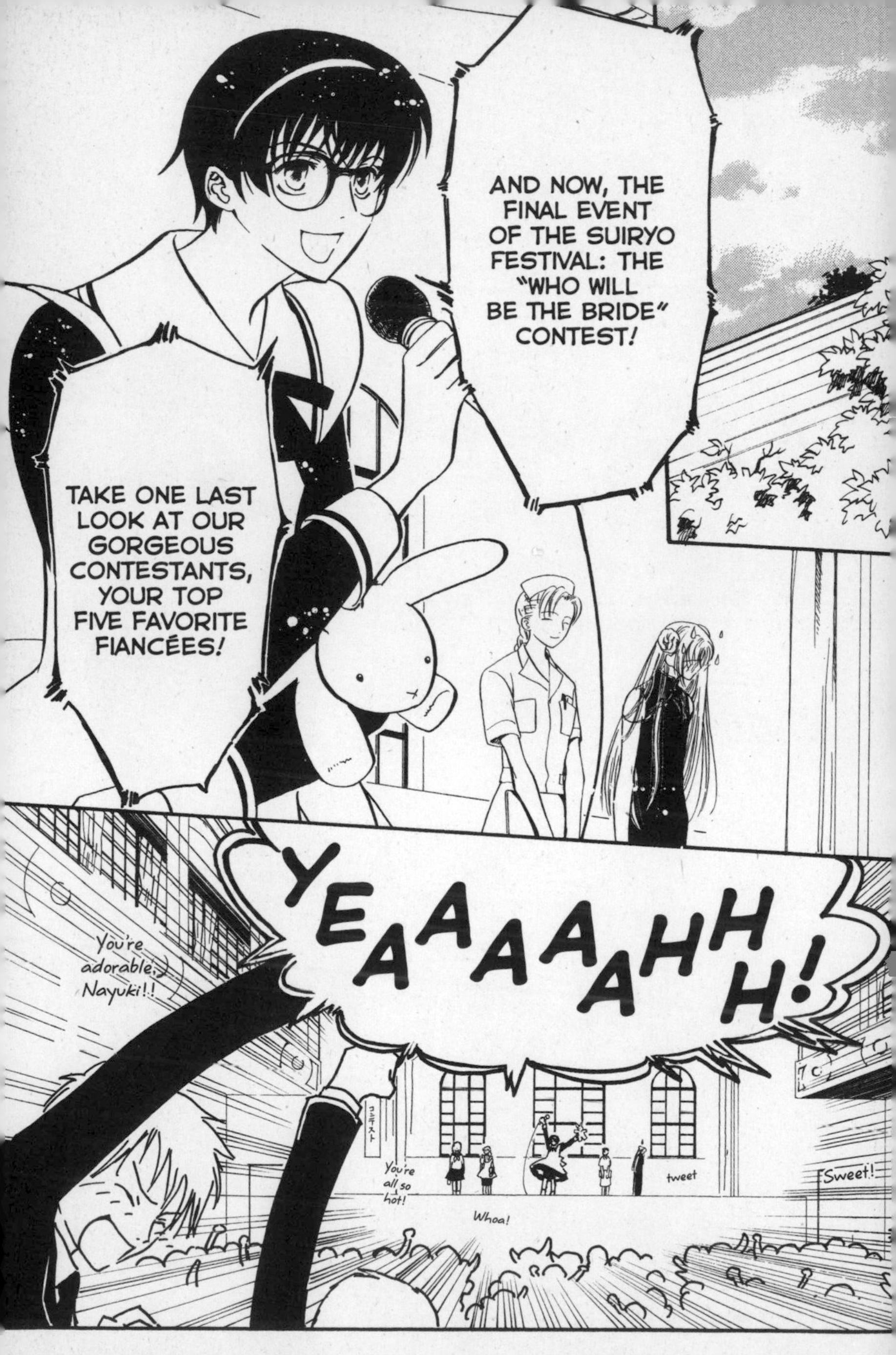
AND NOW, THE FINAL EVENT OF THE SUIRYO FESTIVAL: THE "WHO WILL BE THE BRIDE" CONTEST!
TAKE ONE LAST LOOK AT OUR GORGEOUS CONTESTANTS, YOUR TOP FIVE FAVORITE FIANCÉES!
YEAAAAAHHH!
Sweet!
tweet
Whoa!
You're all so hot!
You're adorable, Nayuki!!

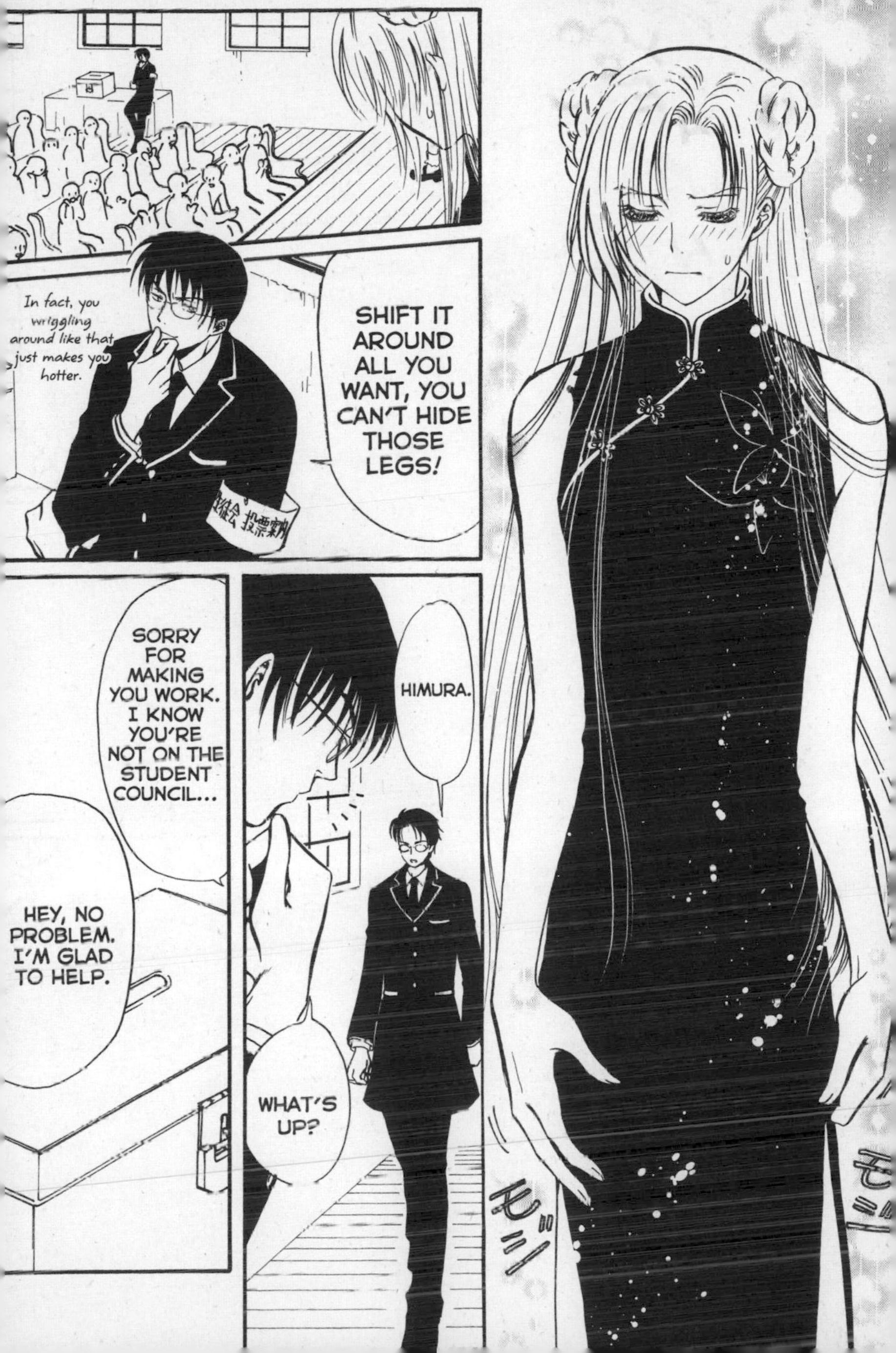
SHIFT IT AROUND ALL YOU WANT, YOU CAN'T HIDE THOSE LEGS!
In fact, you wriggling around like that just makes you hotter.
HIMURA.
WHAT'S UP?
SORRY FOR MAKING YOU WORK. I KNOW YOU'RE NOT ON THE STUDENT COUNCIL...
HEY, NO PROBLEM. I'M GLAD TO HELP.

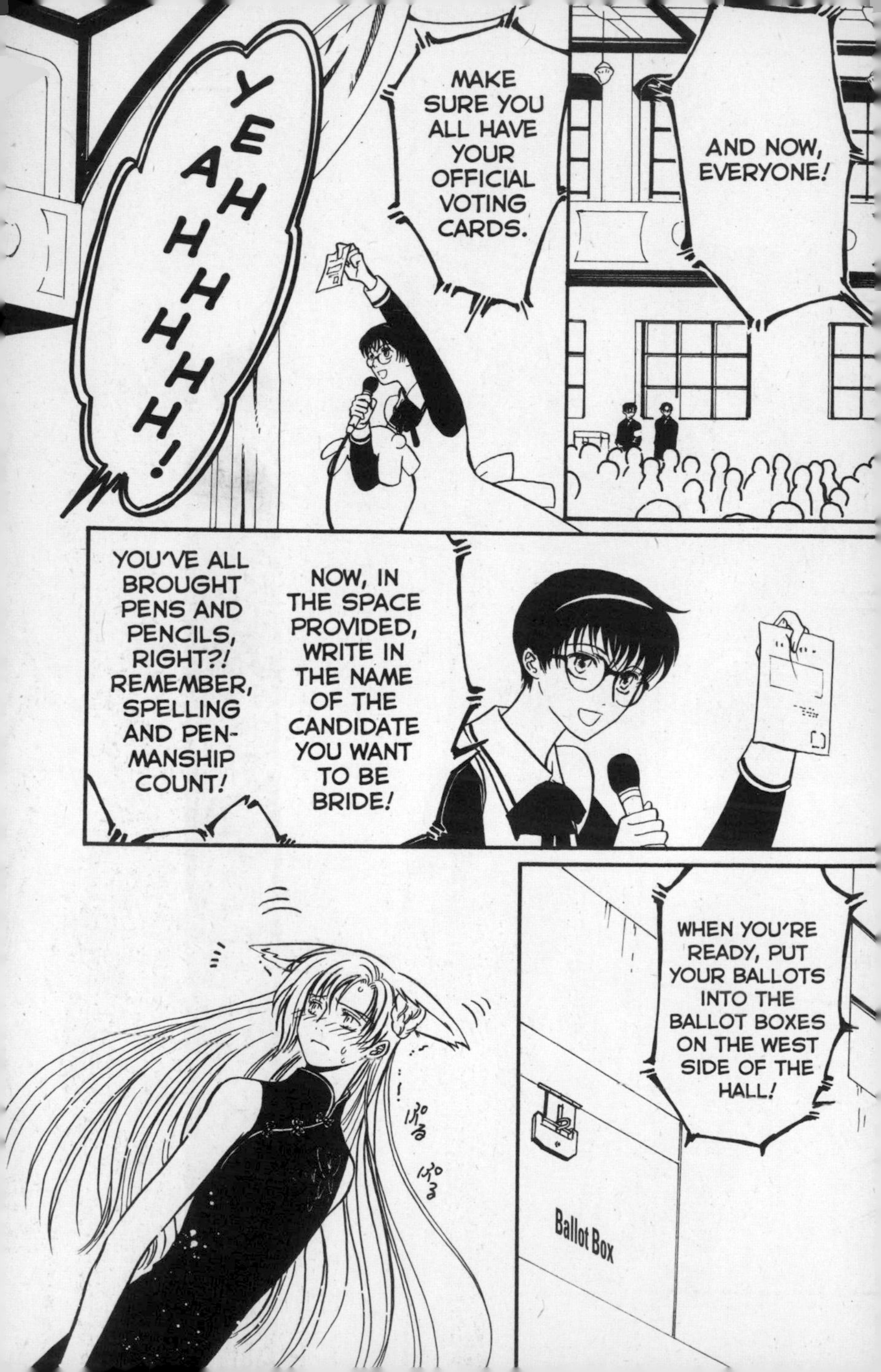
AND NOW, EVERYONE!
MAKE SURE YOU ALL HAVE YOUR OFFICIAL VOTING CARDS.
YEAHHHHHH!
NOW, IN THE SPACE PROVIDED, WRITE IN THE NAME OF THE CANDIDATE YOU WANT TO BE BRIDE!
YOU'VE ALL BROUGHT PENS AND PENCILS, RIGHT?! REMEMBER, SPELLING AND PEN-MANSHIP COUNT!
WHEN YOU'RE READY, PUT YOUR BALLOTS INTO THE BALLOT BOXES ON THE WEST SIDE OF THE HALL!
Ballot Box
ぷる
ぷる

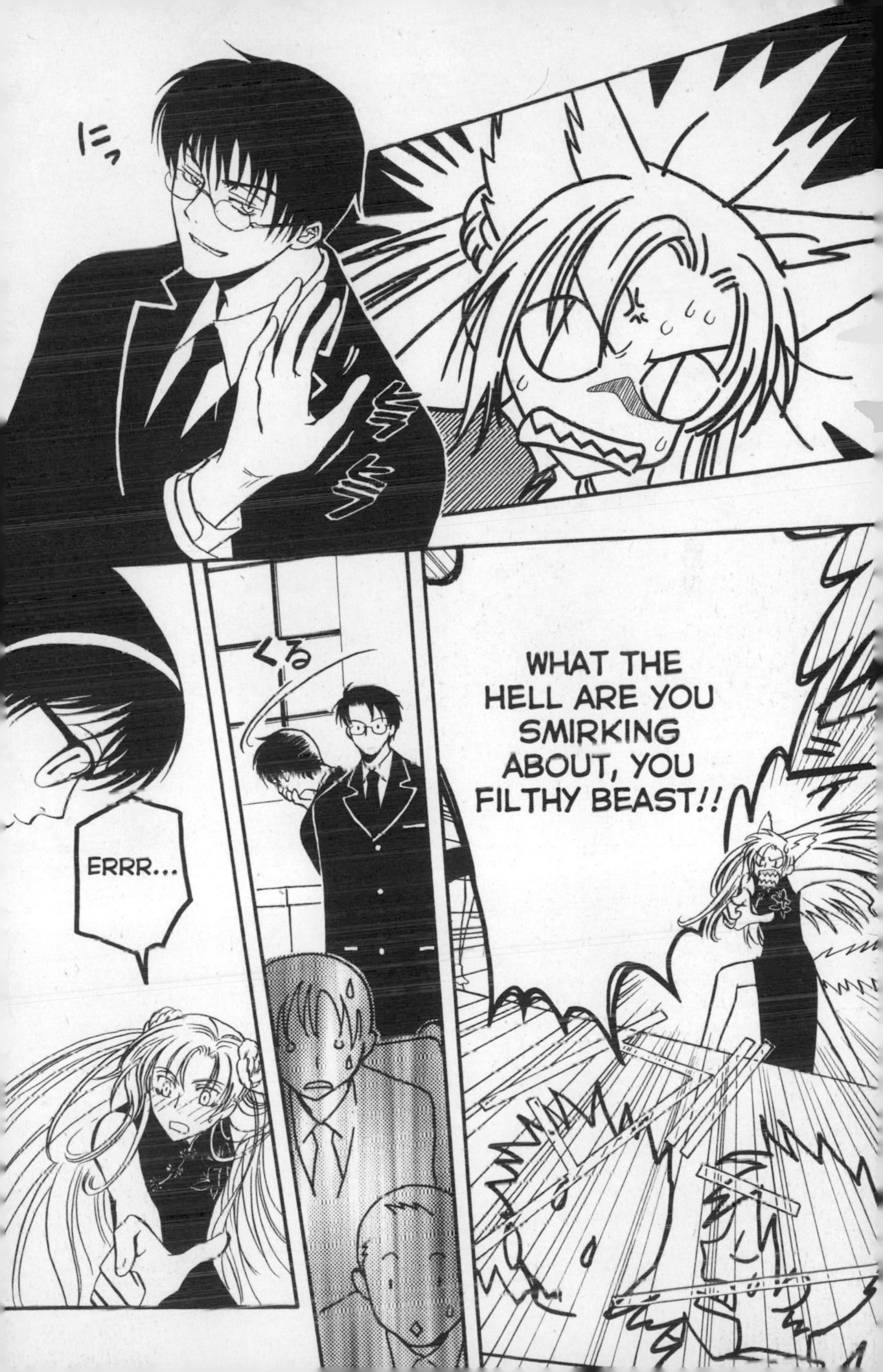
にっ
WHAT THE HELL ARE YOU SMIRKING ABOUT, YOU FILTHY BEAST!!
くる
ERRR...

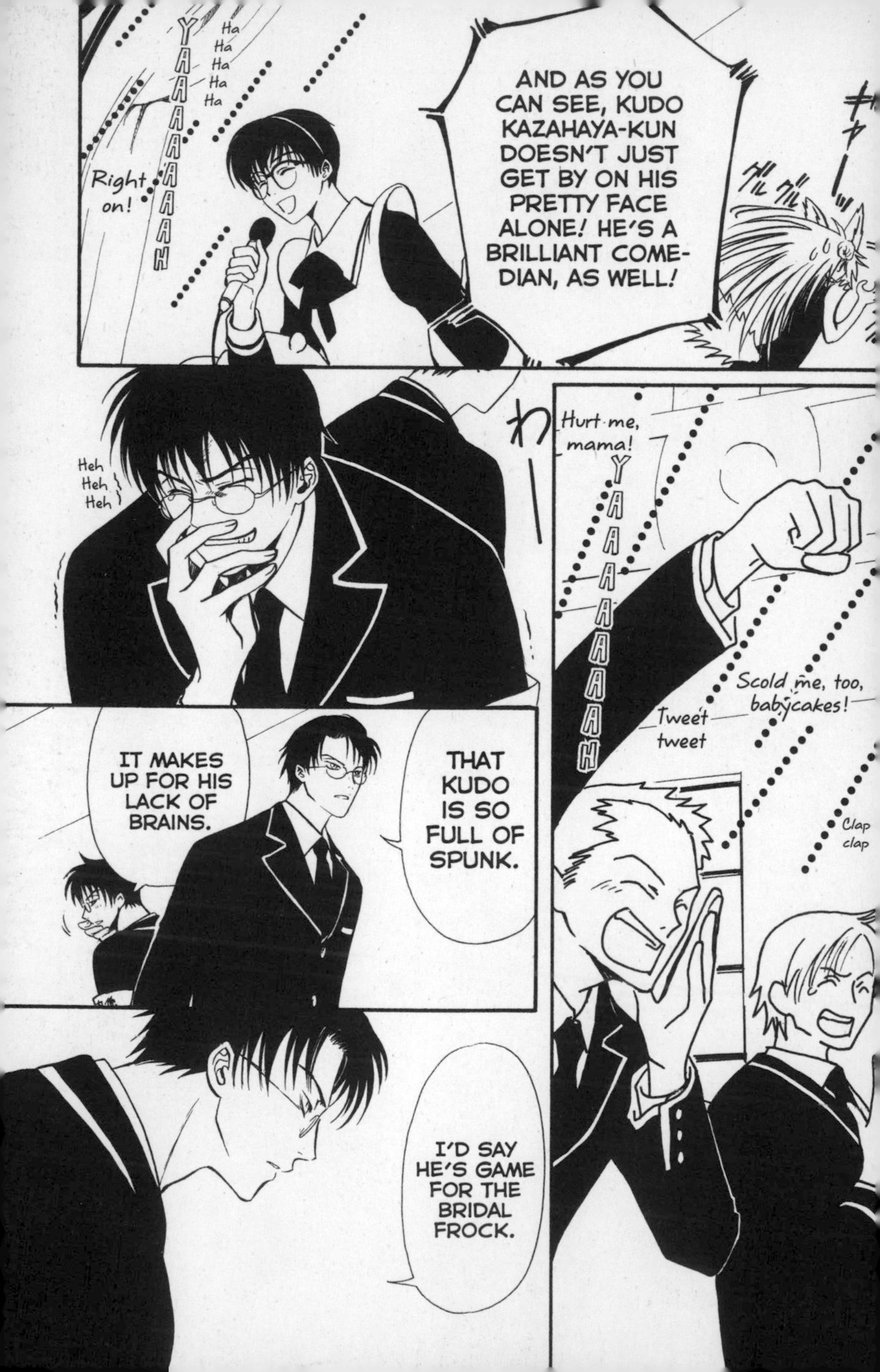
AND AS YOU CAN SEE, KUDO KAZAHAYA-KUN DOESN'T JUST GET BY ON HIS PRETTY FACE ALONE! HE'S A BRILLIANT COMEDIAN, AS WELL!
Ha Ha Ha Ha Ha
YAAAAAAAAAAH
Right on!
Hurt me, mama!
YAAAAAAAAAAH
Scold me, too, babycakes!
Tweet tweet
Clap clap
Heh Heh Heh
THAT KUDO IS SO FULL OF SPUNK.
IT MAKES UP FOR HIS LACK OF BRAINS.
I'D SAY HE'S GAME FOR THE BRIDAL FROCK.

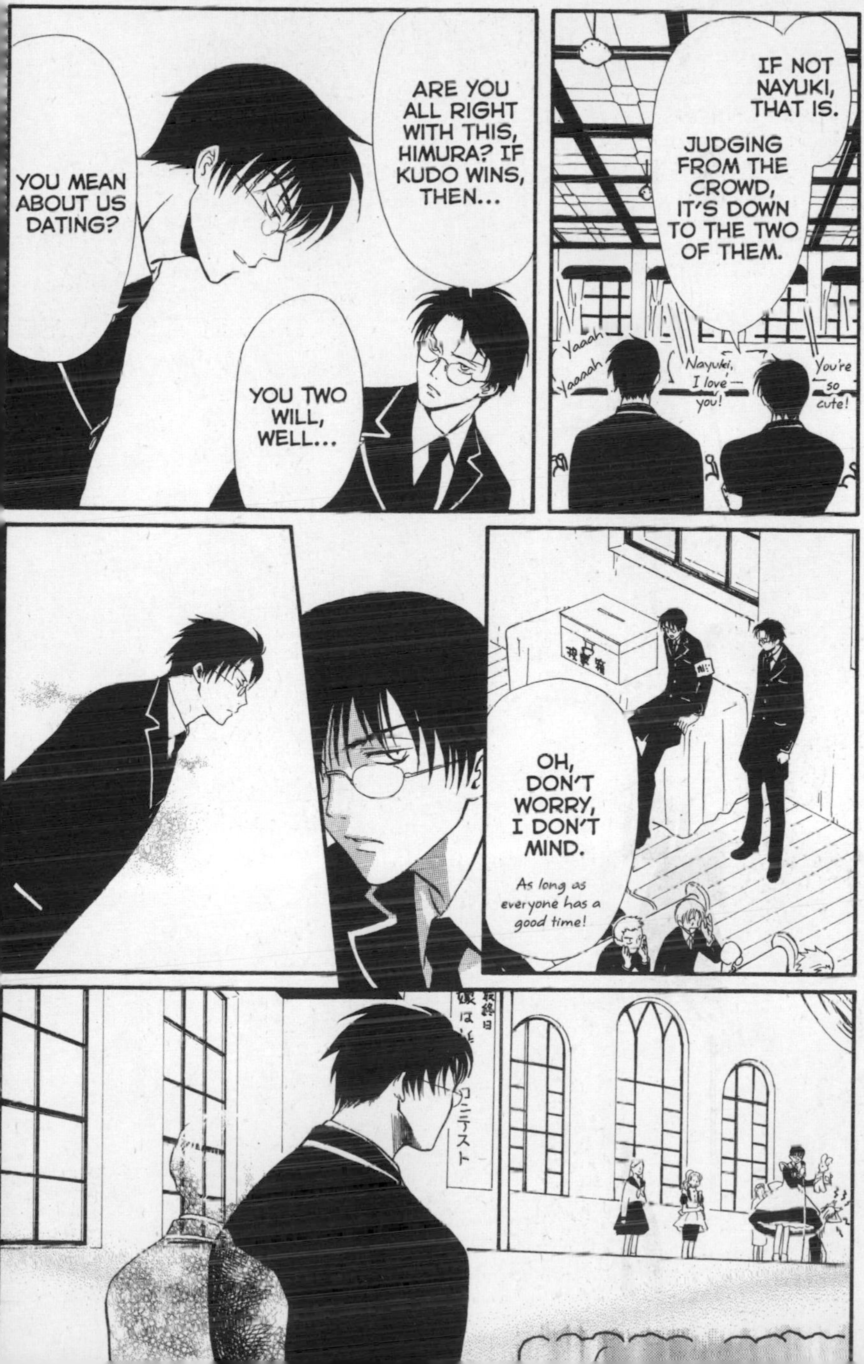
IF NOT NAYUKI, THAT IS.
JUDGING FROM THE CROWD, IT'S DOWN TO THE TWO OF THEM.
Yaaah
Yaaaah
Nayuki, I love you!
You're so cute!
ARE YOU ALL RIGHT WITH THIS, HIMURA? IF KUDO WINS, THEN...
YOU TWO WILL, WELL...
YOU MEAN ABOUT US DATING?
OH, DON'T WORRY, I DON'T MIND.
As long as everyone has a good time!

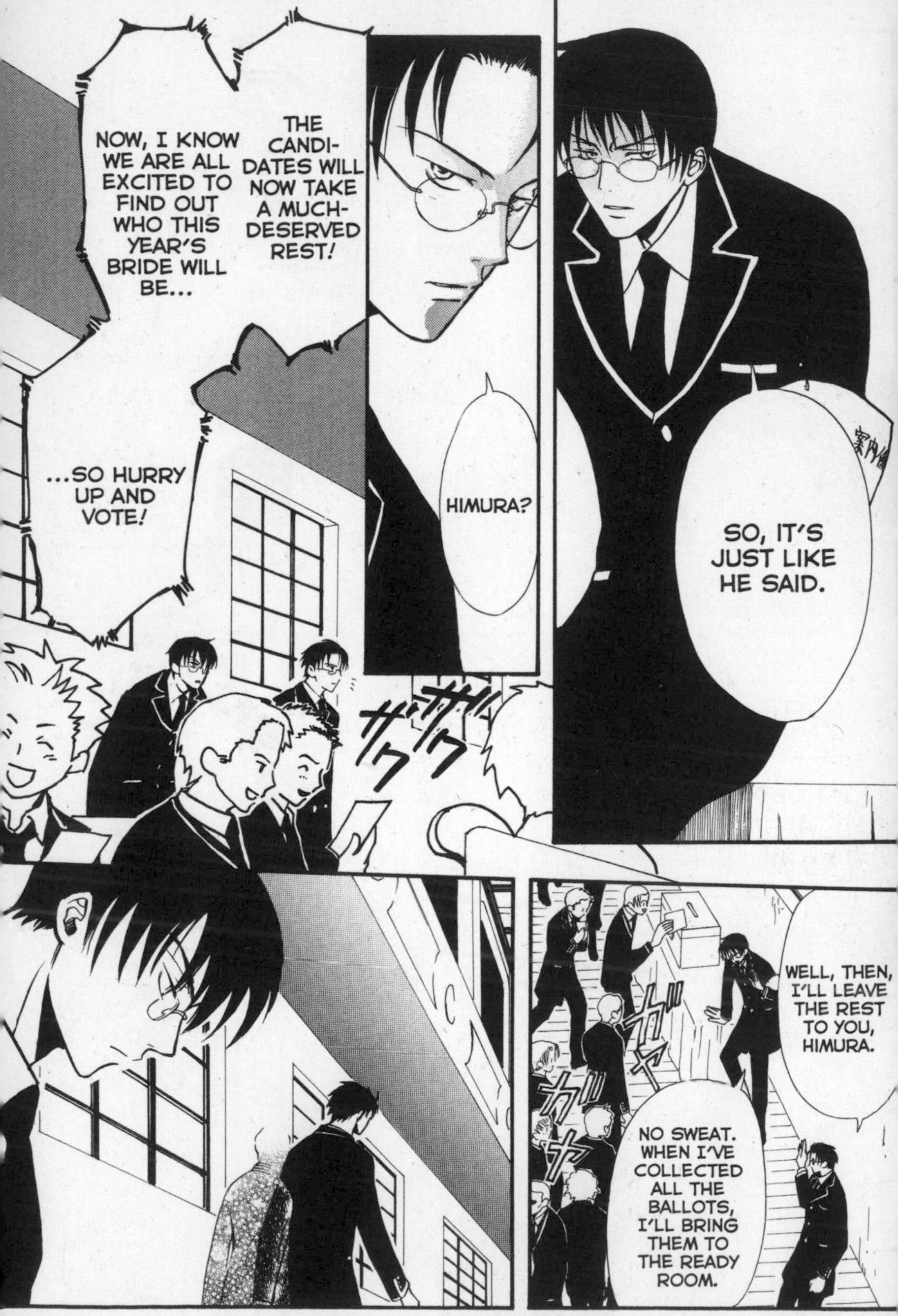
SO, IT'S JUST LIKE HE SAID.
HIMURA?
THE CANDIDATES WILL NOW TAKE A MUCH-DESERVED REST!
NOW, I KNOW WE ARE ALL EXCITED TO FIND OUT WHO THIS YEAR'S BRIDE WILL BE...
...SO HURRY UP AND VOTE!
ザワ
ザワ
WELL, THEN, I'LL LEAVE THE REST TO YOU, HIMURA.
NO SWEAT. WHEN I'VE COLLECTED ALL THE BALLOTS, I'LL BRING THEM TO THE READY ROOM.
ガヤ
ガヤ

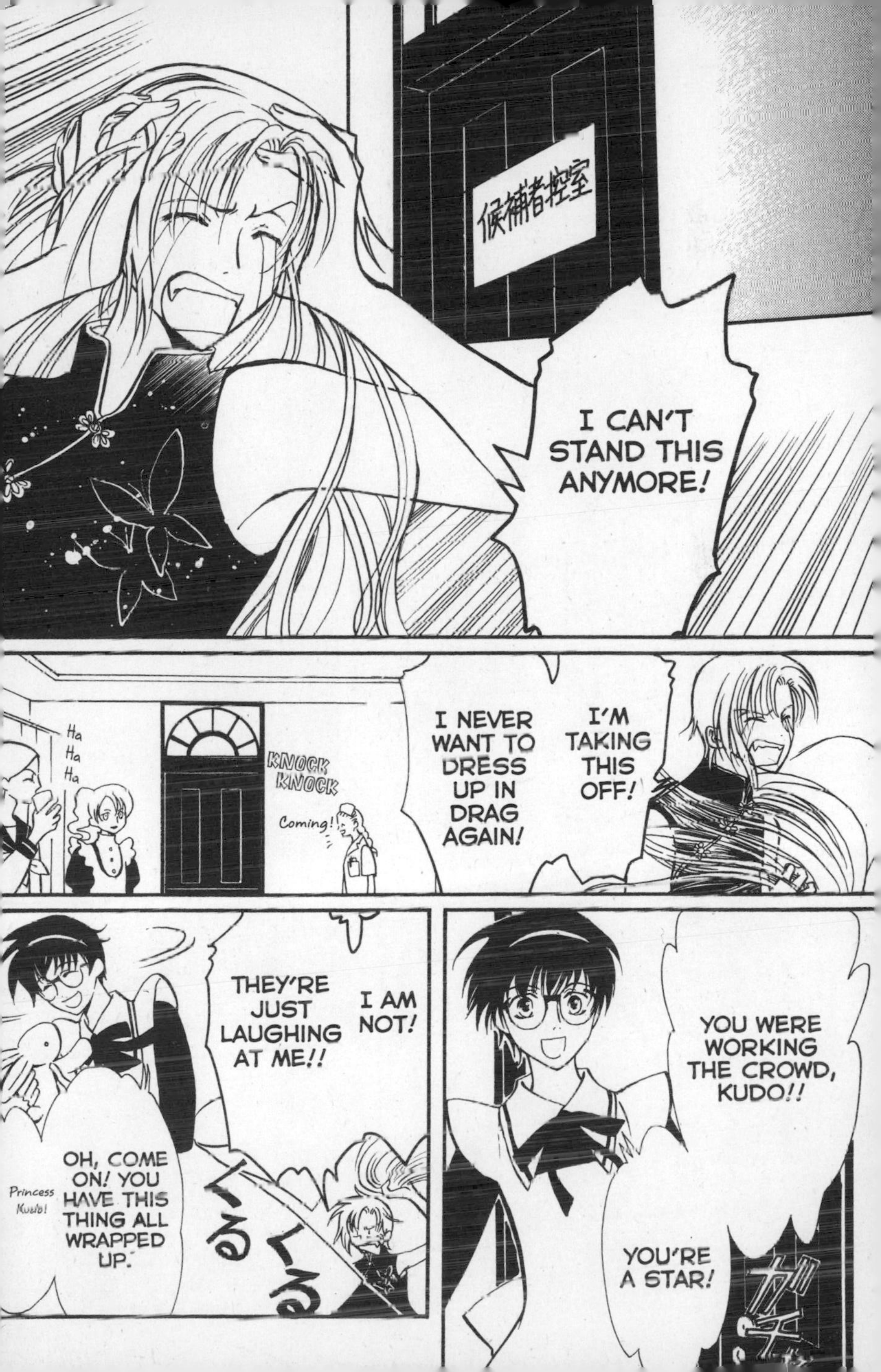
候補者控室
I CAN'T STAND THIS ANYMORE!
I'M TAKING THIS OFF!
I NEVER WANT TO DRESS UP IN DRAG AGAIN!
KNOCK KNOCK
Coming!
Ha Ha Ha
YOU WERE WORKING THE CROWD, KUDO!!
YOU'RE A STAR!
I AM NOT!
THEY'RE JUST LAUGHING AT ME!!
くるくる
OH, COME ON! YOU HAVE THIS THING ALL WRAPPED UP.
Princess Kudo!

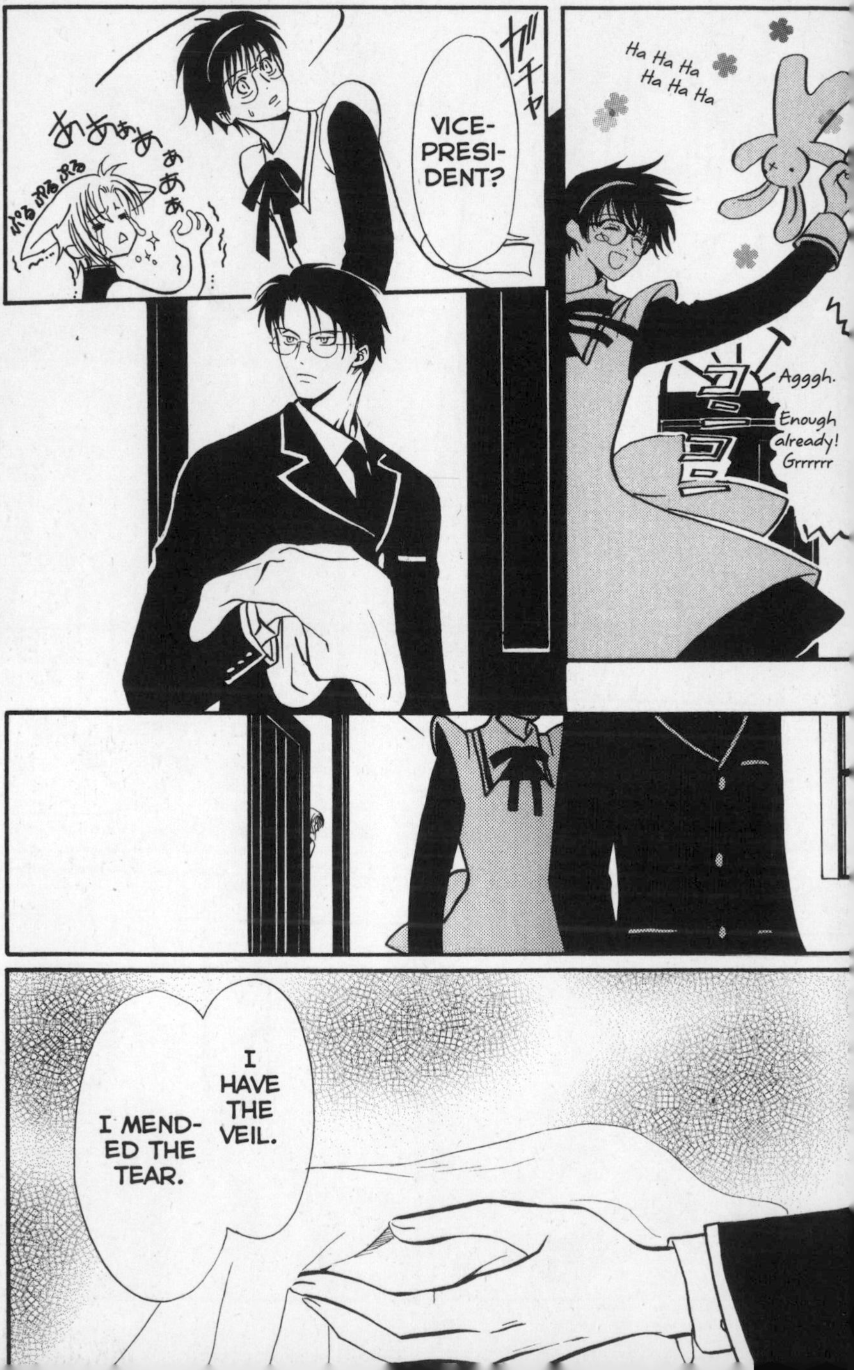
Ha Ha Ha
Ha Ha Ha
Agggh.
Enough already! Grrrrrr
ガチャ
VICE-PRESIDENT?
ぷるぷるぷる
I HAVE THE VEIL.
I MENDED THE TEAR.

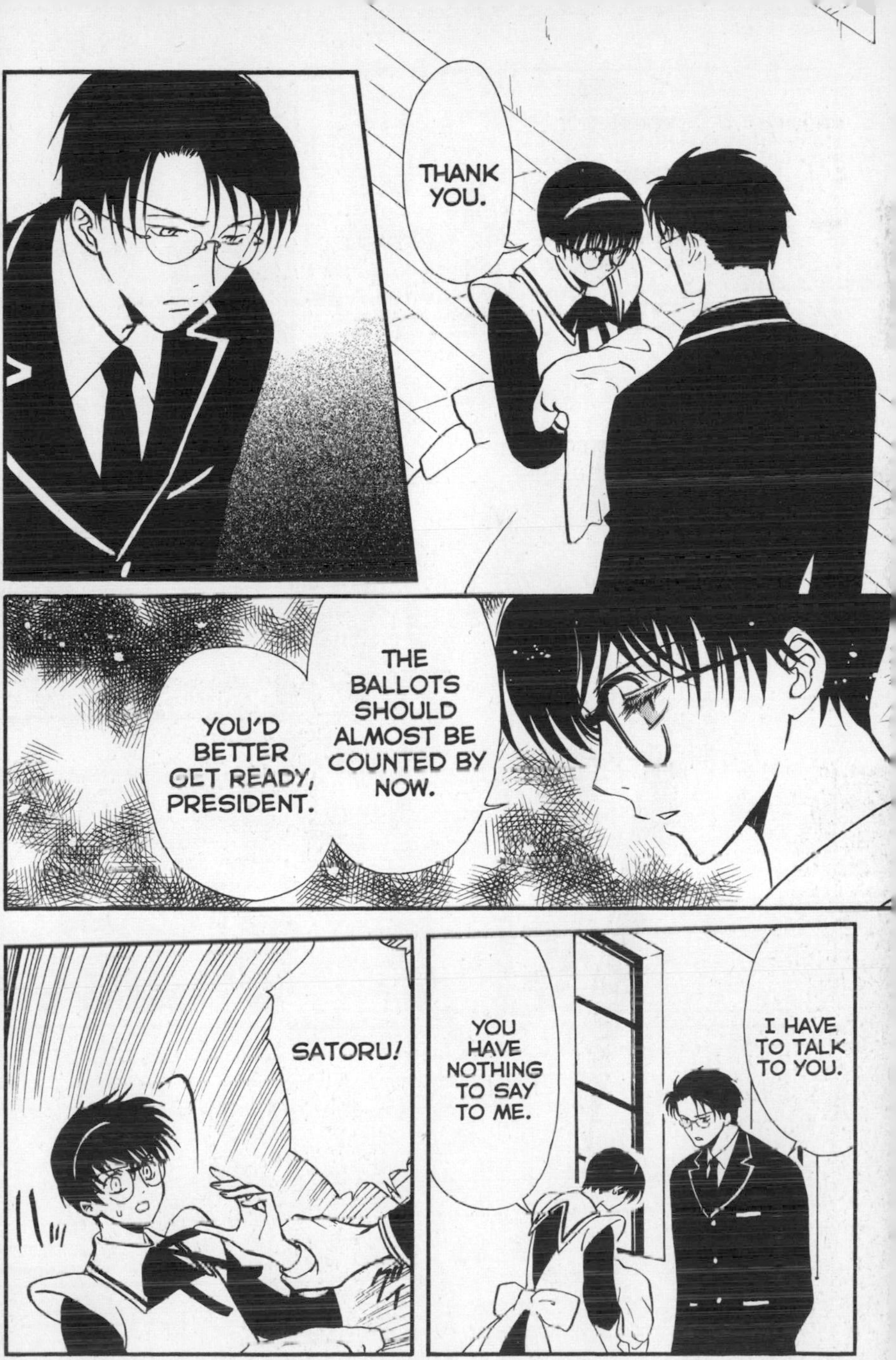
THANK YOU.
THE BALLOTS SHOULD ALMOST BE COUNTED BY NOW.
YOU'D BETTER GET READY, PRESIDENT.
I HAVE TO TALK TO YOU.
YOU HAVE NOTHING TO SAY TO ME.
SATORU!

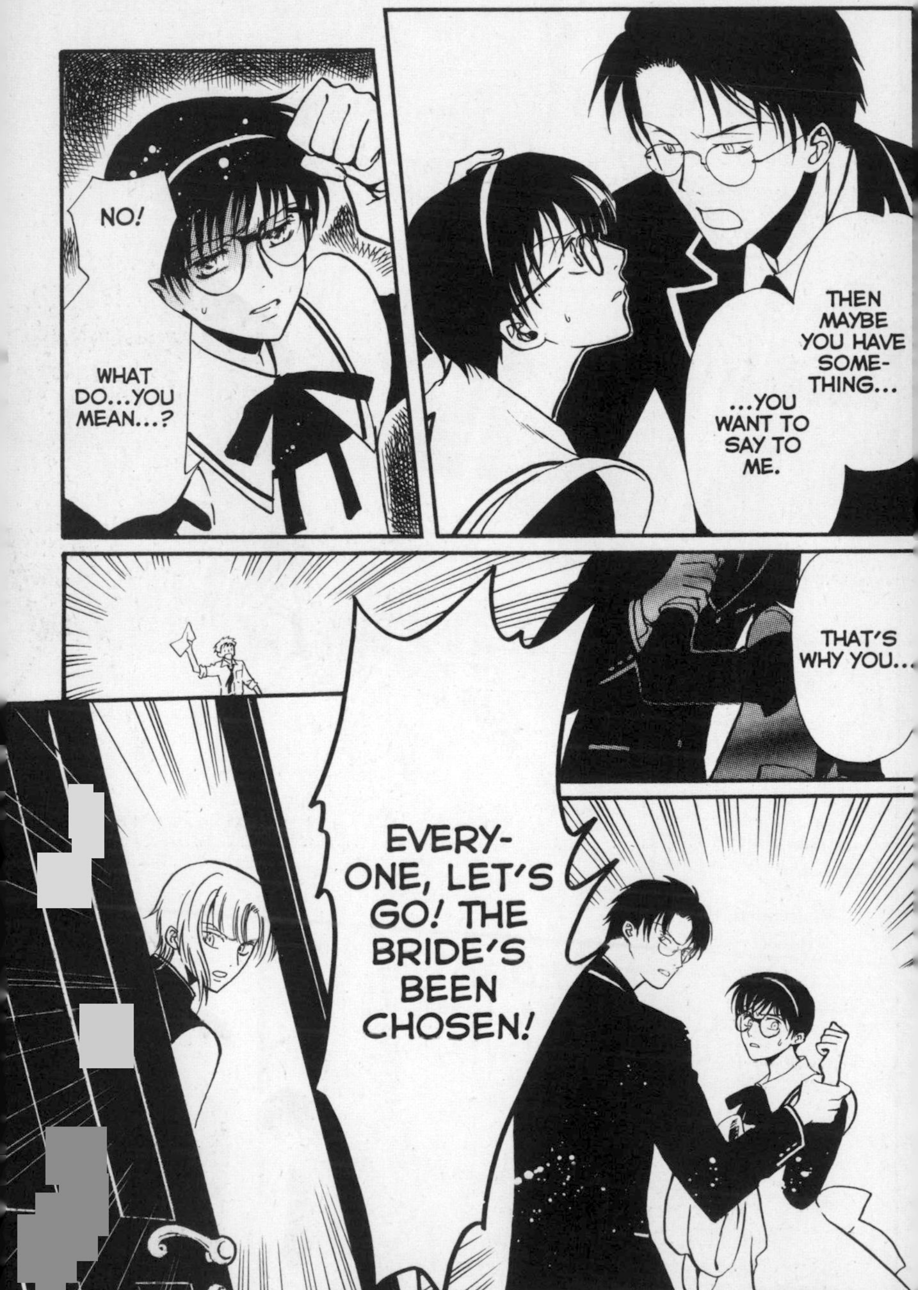
THEN MAYBE YOU HAVE SOMETHING...
...YOU WANT TO SAY TO ME.
NO!
WHAT DO...YOU MEAN...?
THAT'S WHY YOU...
EVERY-ONE, LET'S GO! THE BRIDE'S BEEN CHOSEN!

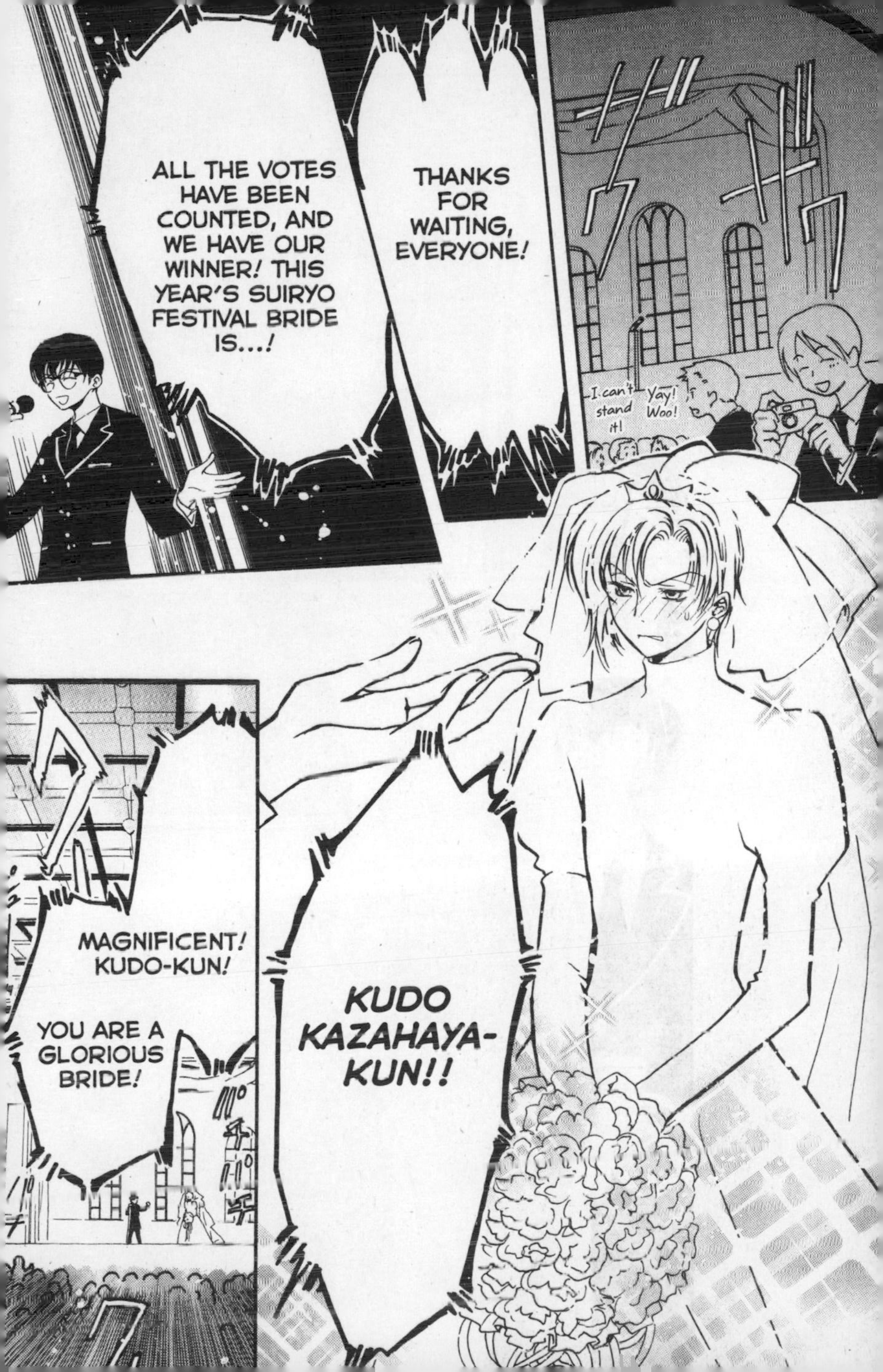
Yay! Woo!
I can't stand it!
THANKS FOR WAITING, EVERYONE!
ALL THE VOTES HAVE BEEN COUNTED, AND WE HAVE OUR WINNER! THIS YEAR'S SUIRYO FESTIVAL BRIDE IS...!
KUDO KAZAHAYA-KUN!!
MAGNIFICENT! KUDO-KUN!
YOU ARE A GLORIOUS BRIDE!

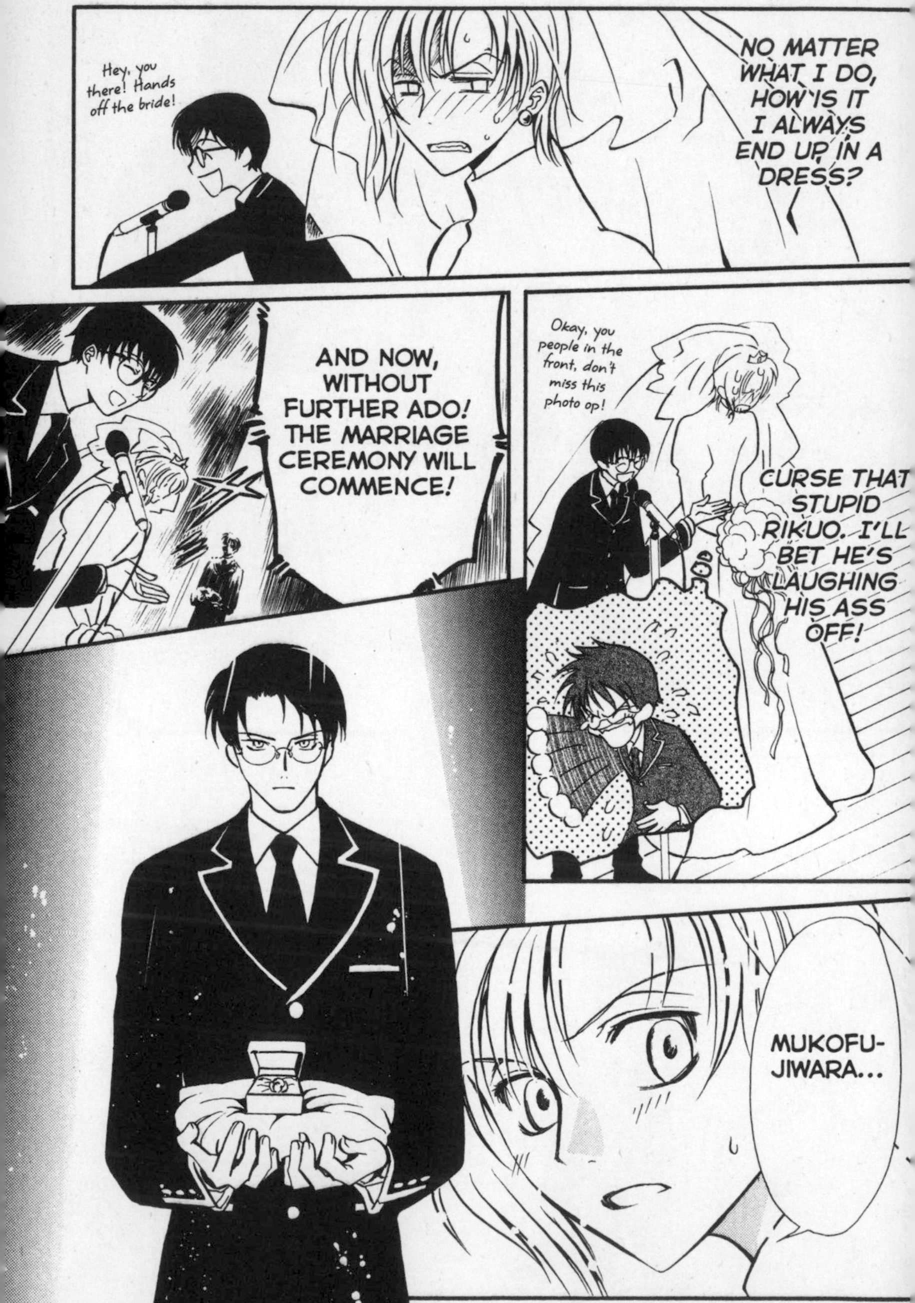
NO MATTER WHAT I DO, HOW IS IT I ALWAYS END UP IN A DRESS?
Hey, you there! Hands off the bride!
Okay, you people in the front, don't miss this photo op!
CURSE THAT STUPID RIKUO. I'LL BET HE'S LAUGHING HIS ASS OFF!
AND NOW, WITHOUT FURTHER ADO! THE MARRIAGE CEREMONY WILL COMMENCE!
MUKOFUJIWARA...

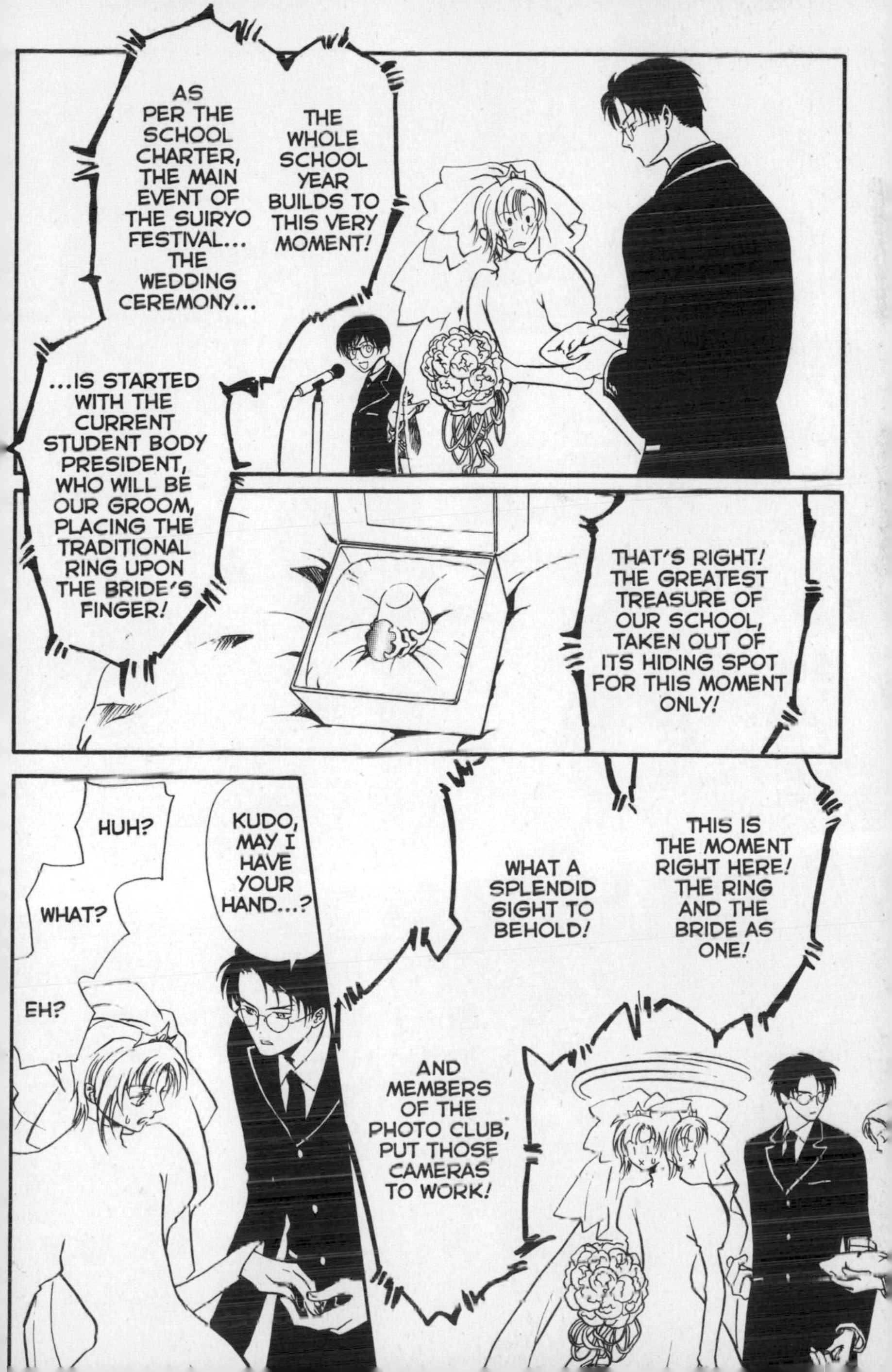
THE WHOLE SCHOOL YEAR BUILDS TO THIS VERY MOMENT!
AS PER THE SCHOOL CHARTER, THE MAIN EVENT OF THE SUIRYO FESTIVAL... THE WEDDING CEREMONY...
...IS STARTED WITH THE CURRENT STUDENT BODY PRESIDENT, WHO WILL BE OUR GROOM, PLACING THE TRADITIONAL RING UPON THE BRIDE'S FINGER!
THAT'S RIGHT! THE GREATEST TREASURE OF OUR SCHOOL, TAKEN OUT OF ITS HIDING SPOT FOR THIS MOMENT ONLY!
THIS IS THE MOMENT RIGHT HERE! THE RING AND THE BRIDE AS ONE!
WHAT A SPLENDID SIGHT TO BEHOLD!
AND MEMBERS OF THE PHOTO CLUB, PUT THOSE CAMERAS TO WORK!
KUDO, MAY I HAVE YOUR HAND...?
HUH?
WHAT?
EH?

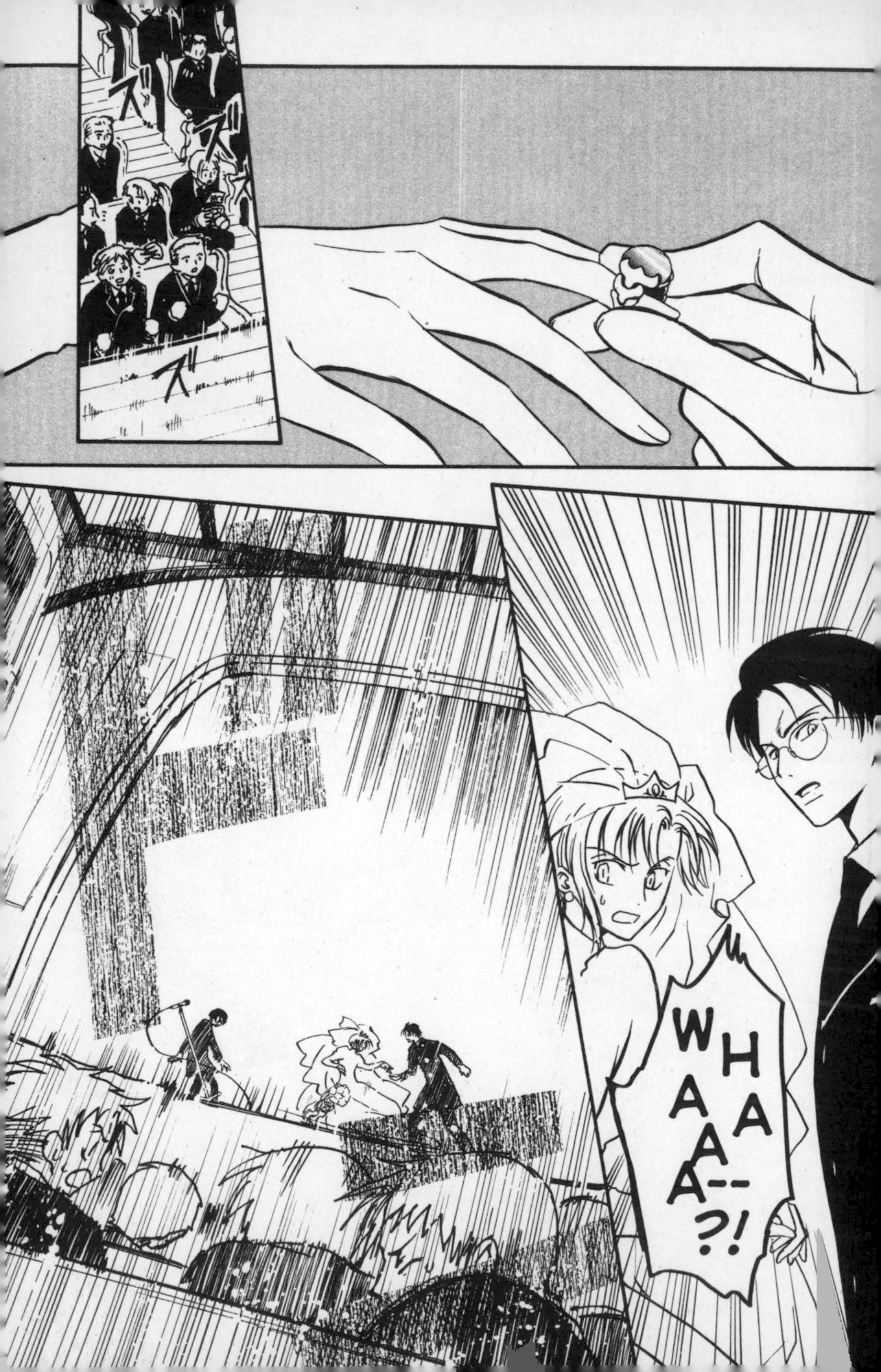
WHAAAA--?!

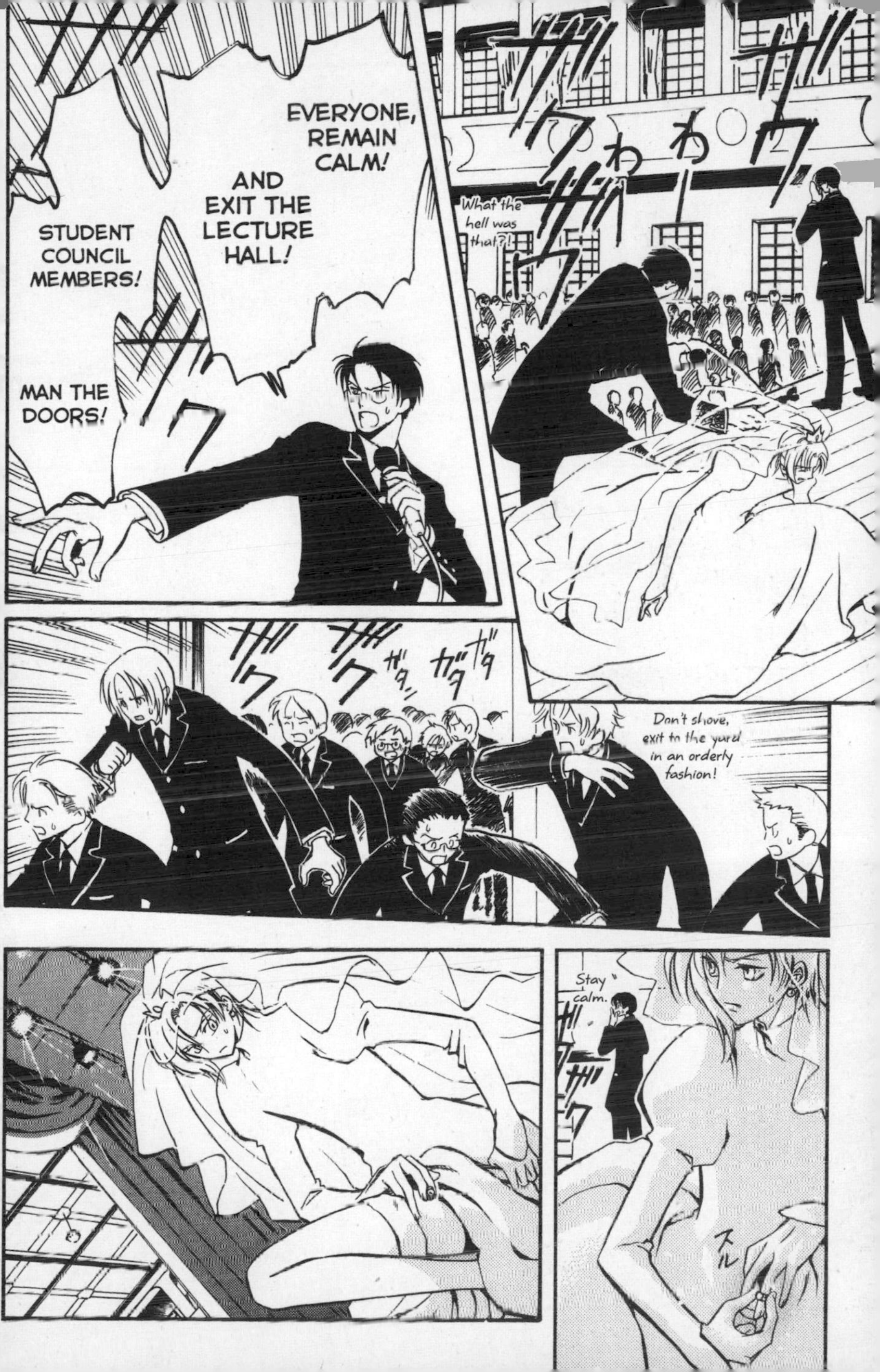
What the hell was that?!
EVERYONE, REMAIN CALM!
AND EXIT THE LECTURE HALL!
STUDENT COUNCIL MEMBERS!
MAN THE DOORS!
Don't shove, exit to the yard in an orderly fashion!
Stay calm.

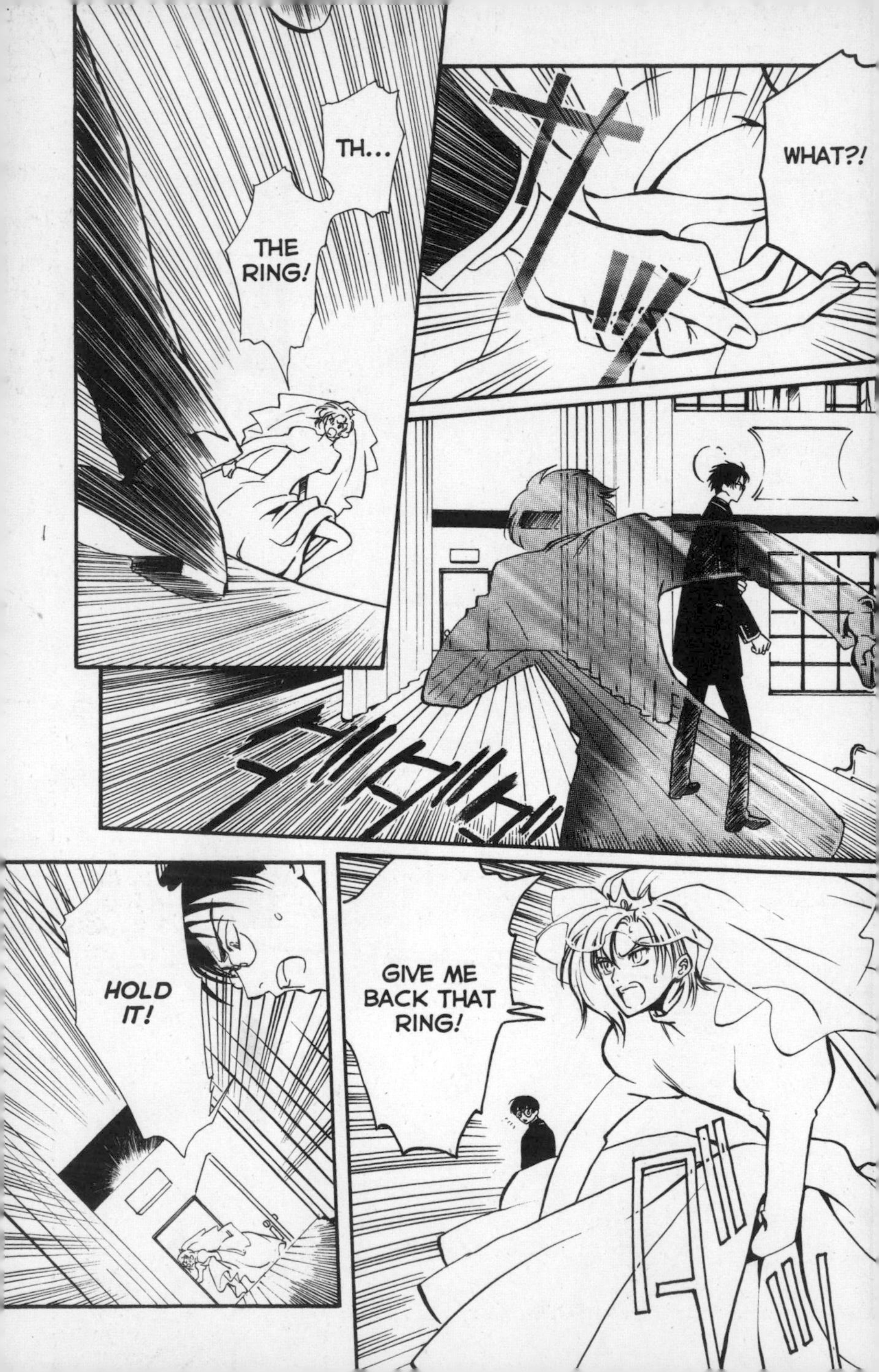
WHAT?!
TH...
THE RING!
GIVE ME BACK THAT RING!
HOLD IT!

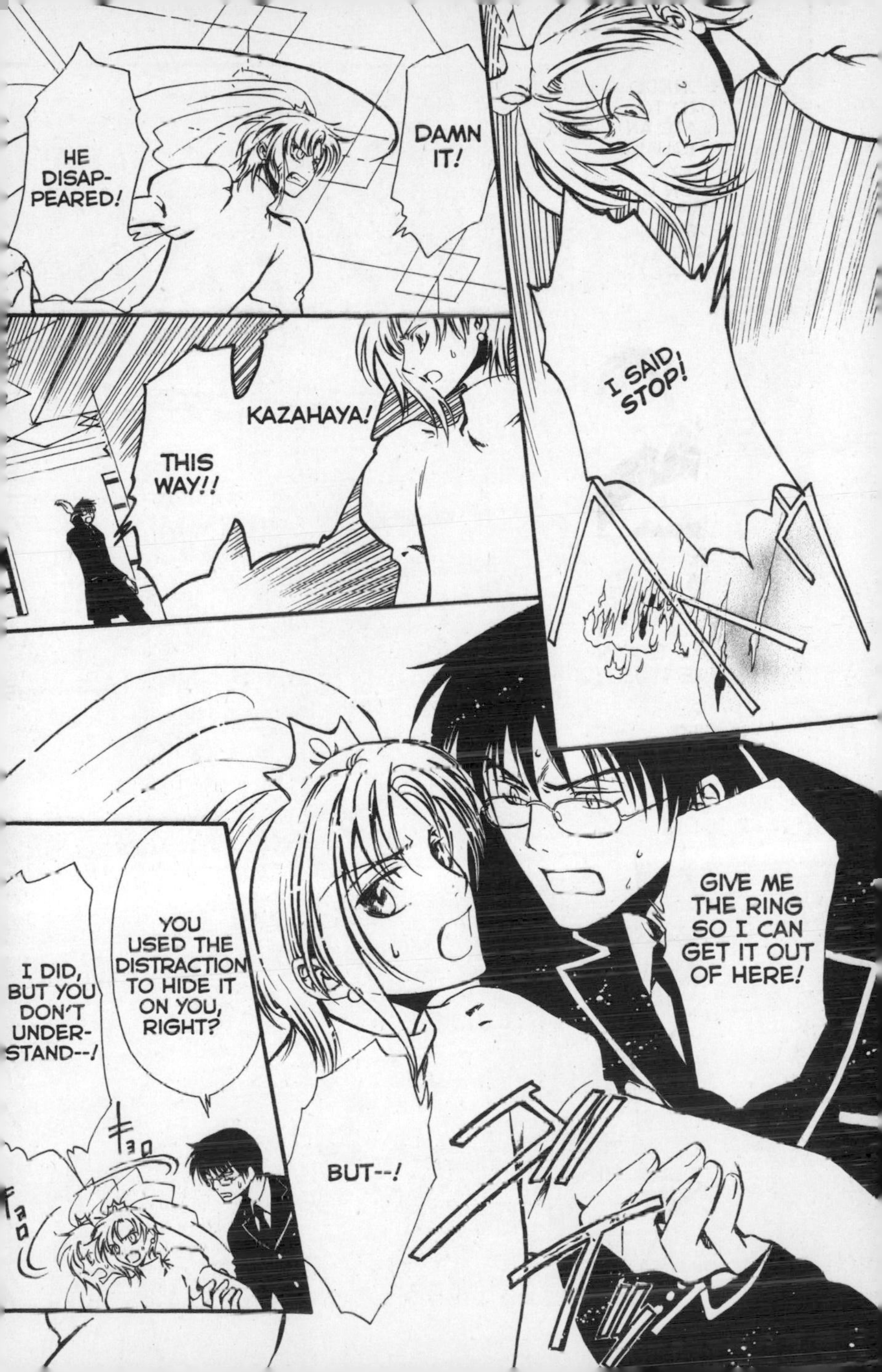
I SAID STOP!
DAMN IT!
HE DISAPPEARED!
KAZAHAYA!
THIS WAY!!
GIVE ME THE RING SO I CAN GET IT OUT OF HERE!
YOU USED THE DISTRACTION TO HIDE IT ON YOU, RIGHT?
BUT--!
I DID, BUT YOU DON'T UNDERSTAND--!

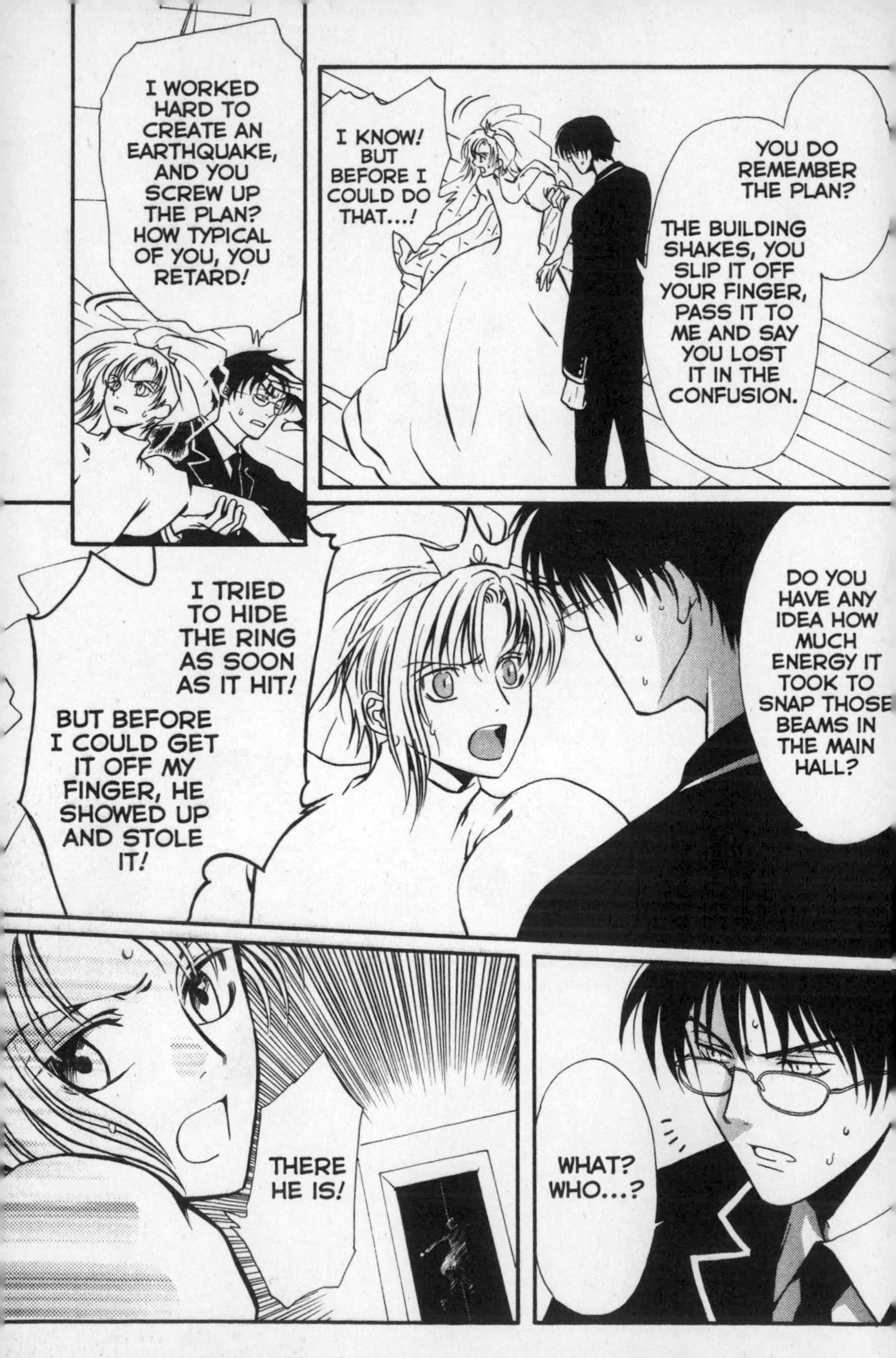
YOU DO REMEMBER THE PLAN?
THE BUILDING SHAKES, YOU SLIP IT OFF YOUR FINGER, PASS IT TO ME AND SAY YOU LOST IT IN THE CONFUSION.
I KNOW! BUT BEFORE I COULD DO THAT...!
I WORKED HARD TO CREATE AN EARTHQUAKE, AND YOU SCREW UP THE PLAN? HOW TYPICAL OF YOU, YOU RETARD!
DO YOU HAVE ANY IDEA HOW MUCH ENERGY IT TOOK TO SNAP THOSE BEAMS IN THE MAIN HALL?
I TRIED TO HIDE THE RING AS SOON AS IT HIT!
BUT BEFORE I COULD GET IT OFF MY FINGER, HE SHOWED UP AND STOLE IT!
WHAT? WHO...?
THERE HE IS!

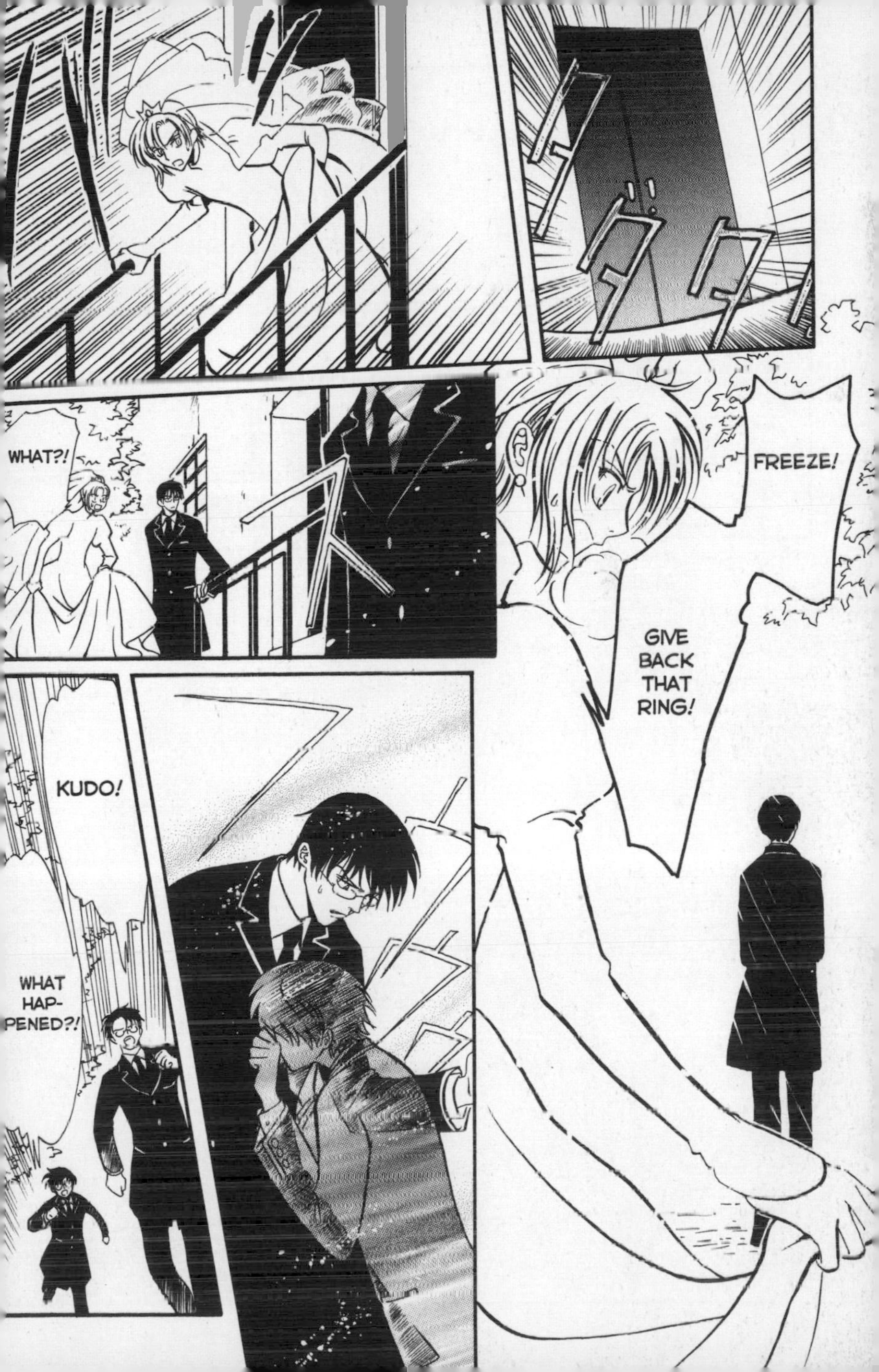
FREEZE!
GIVE BACK THAT RING!
WHAT?!
KUDO!
WHAT HAP-PENED?!

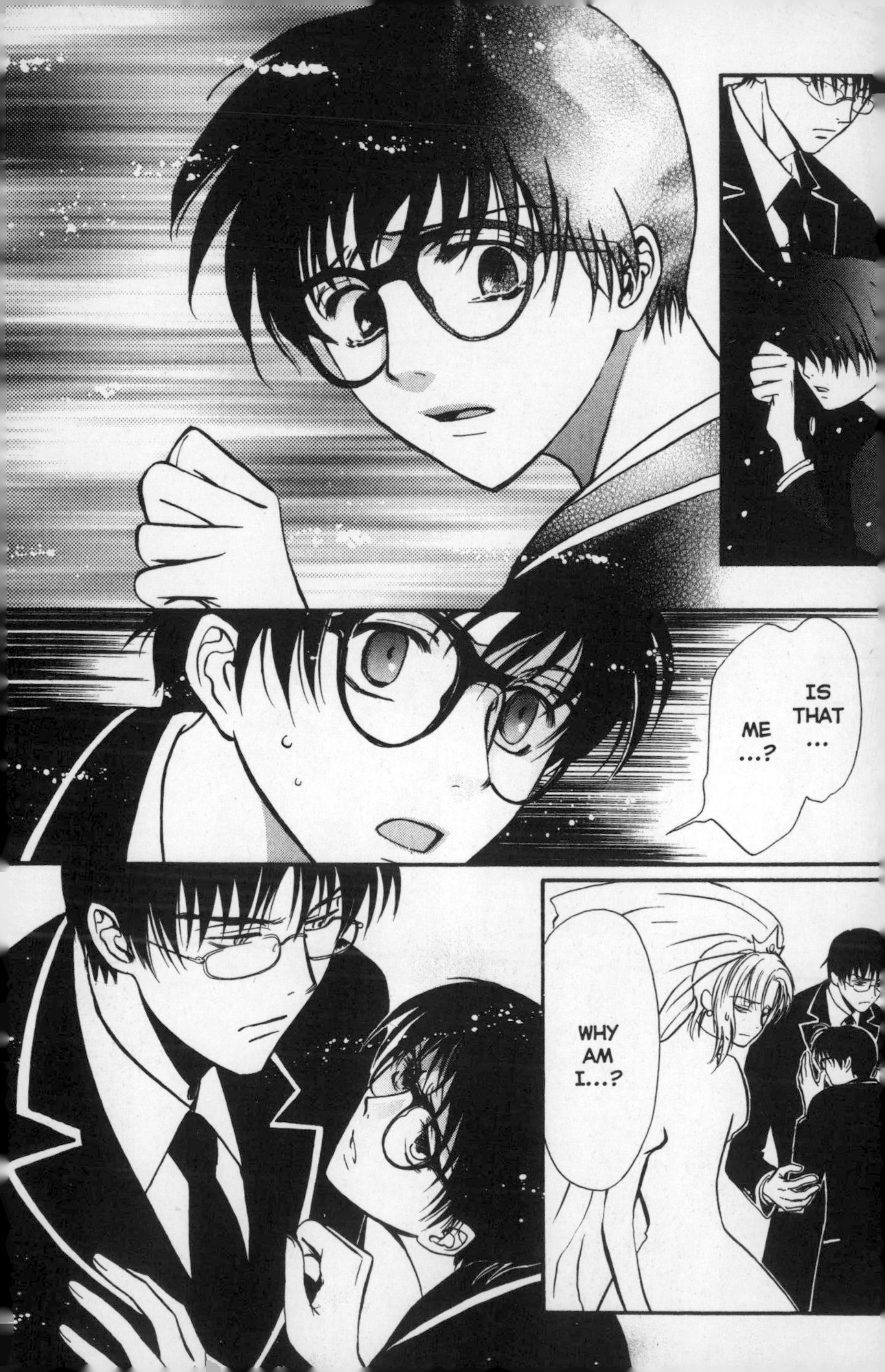
IS THAT ...
ME ...?
WHY AM I...?

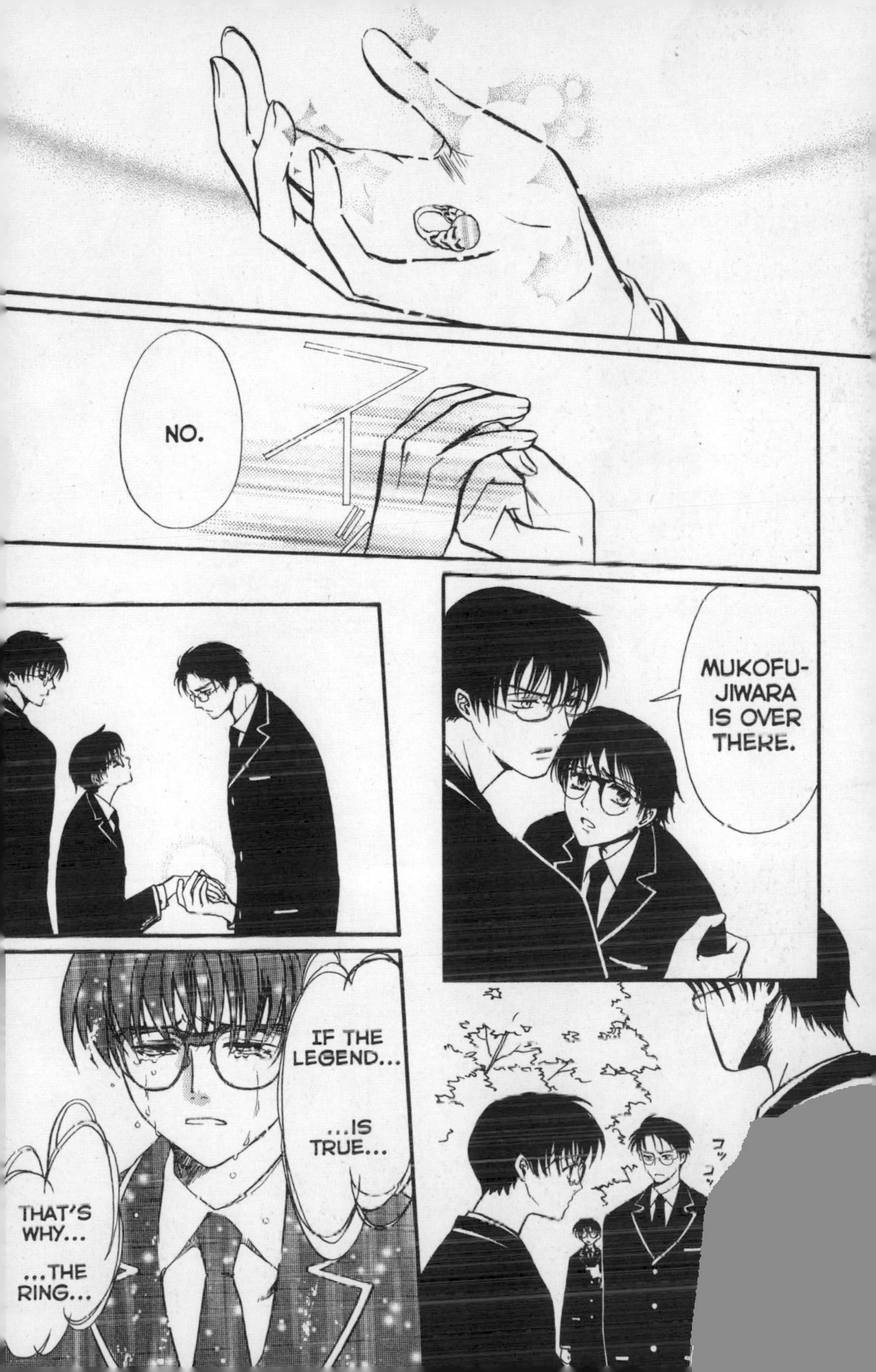
NO.
MUKOFU-JIWARA IS OVER THERE.
コッ コッ
IF THE LEGEND...
...IS TRUE...
THAT'S WHY...
...THE RING...

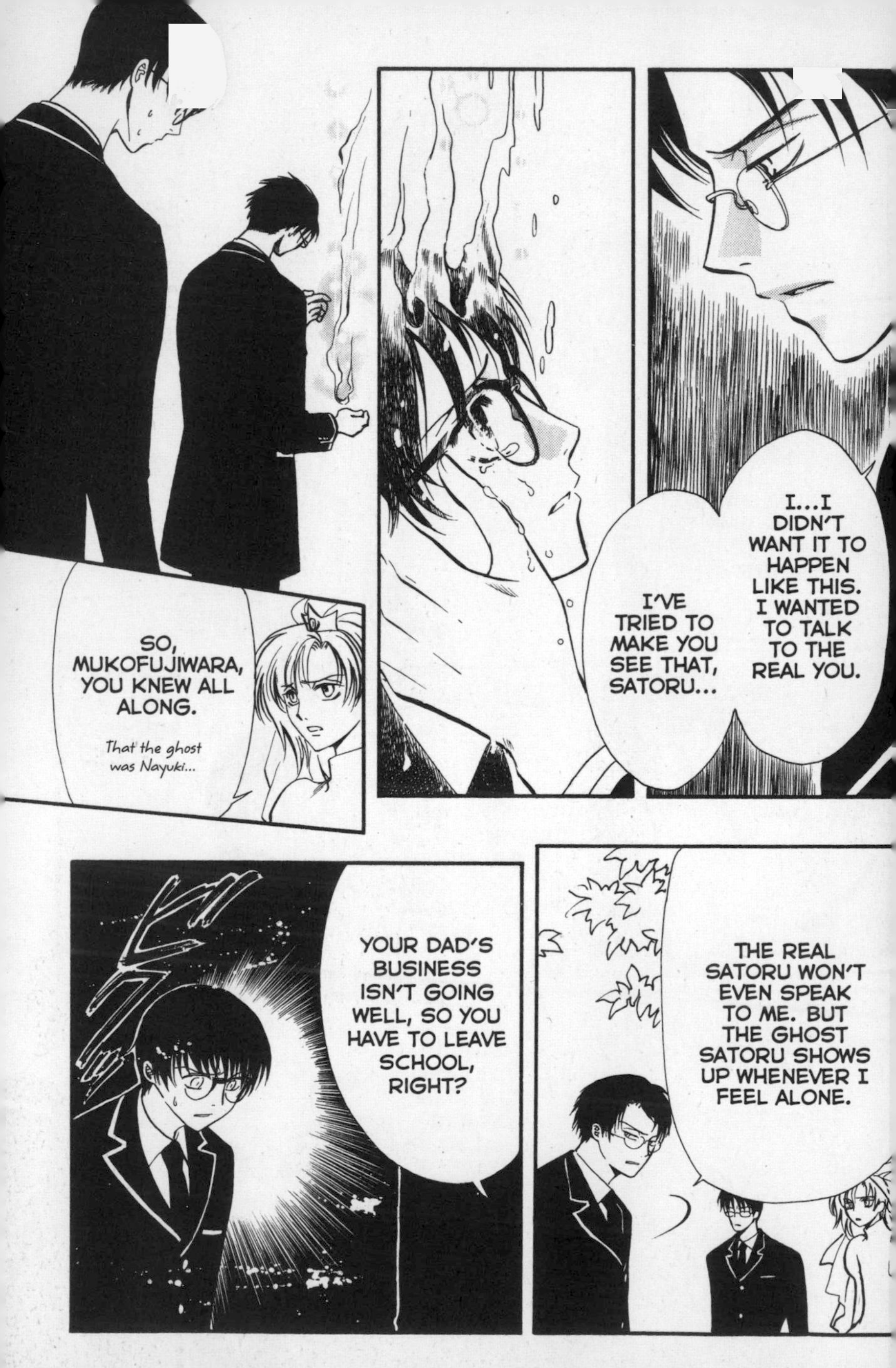
I...I DIDN'T WANT IT TO HAPPEN LIKE THIS. I WANTED TO TALK TO THE REAL YOU.
I'VE TRIED TO MAKE YOU SEE THAT, SATORU...
SO, MUKOFUJIWARA, YOU KNEW ALL ALONG.
That the ghost was Nayuki...
THE REAL SATORU WON'T EVEN SPEAK TO ME. BUT THE GHOST SATORU SHOWS UP WHENEVER I FEEL ALONE.
YOUR DAD'S BUSINESS ISN'T GOING WELL, SO YOU HAVE TO LEAVE SCHOOL, RIGHT?

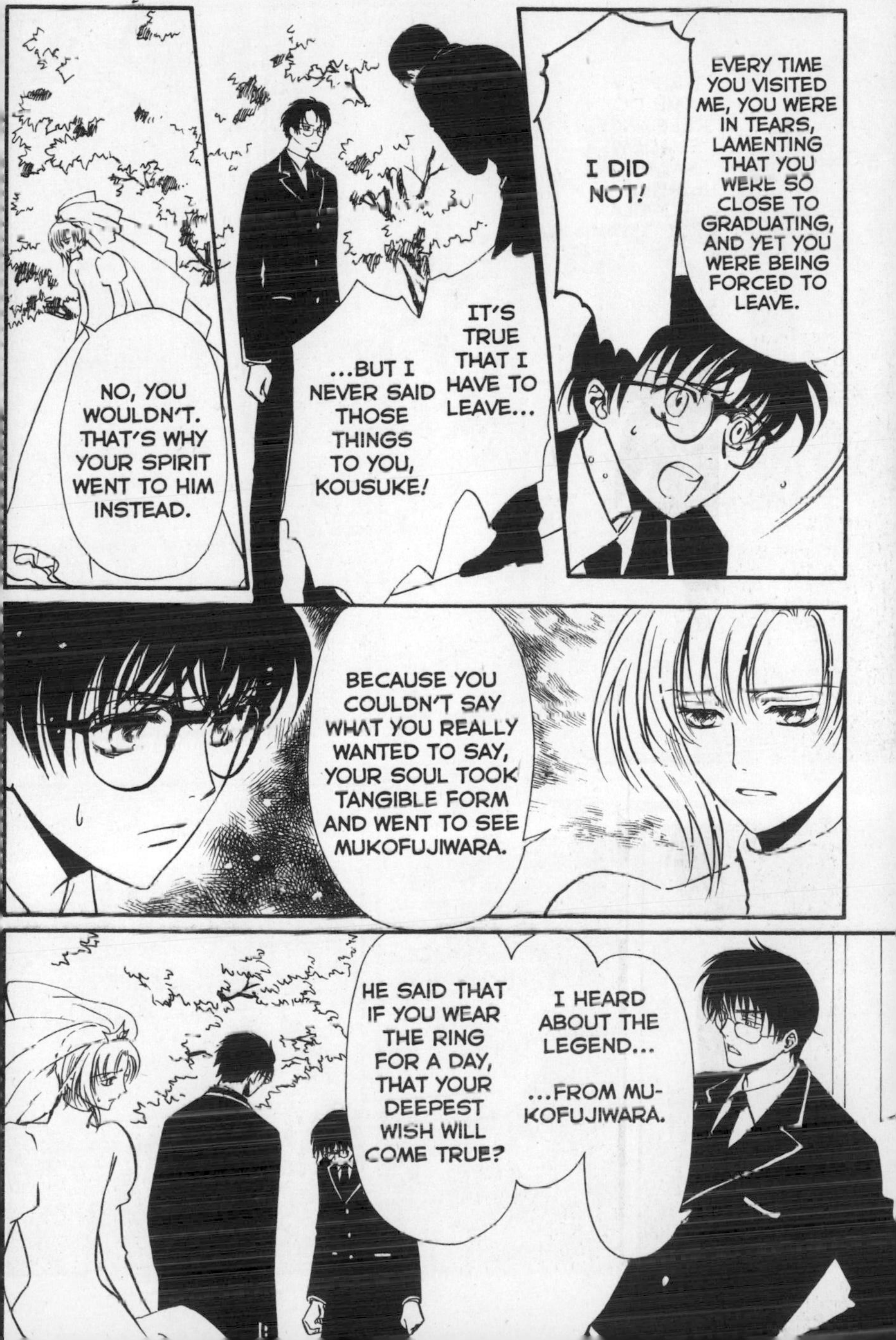
EVERY TIME YOU VISITED ME, YOU WERE IN TEARS, LAMENTING THAT YOU WERE SO CLOSE TO GRADUATING, AND YET YOU WERE BEING FORCED TO LEAVE.
I DID NOT!
IT'S TRUE THAT I HAVE TO LEAVE...
...BUT I NEVER SAID THOSE THINGS TO YOU, KOUSUKE!
NO, YOU WOULDN'T. THAT'S WHY YOUR SPIRIT WENT TO HIM INSTEAD.
BECAUSE YOU COULDN'T SAY WHAT YOU REALLY WANTED TO SAY, YOUR SOUL TOOK TANGIBLE FORM AND WENT TO SEE MUKOFUJIWARA.
I HEARD ABOUT THE LEGEND...
...FROM MU-KOFUJIWARA.
HE SAID THAT IF YOU WEAR THE RING FOR A DAY, THAT YOUR DEEPEST WISH WILL COME TRUE?

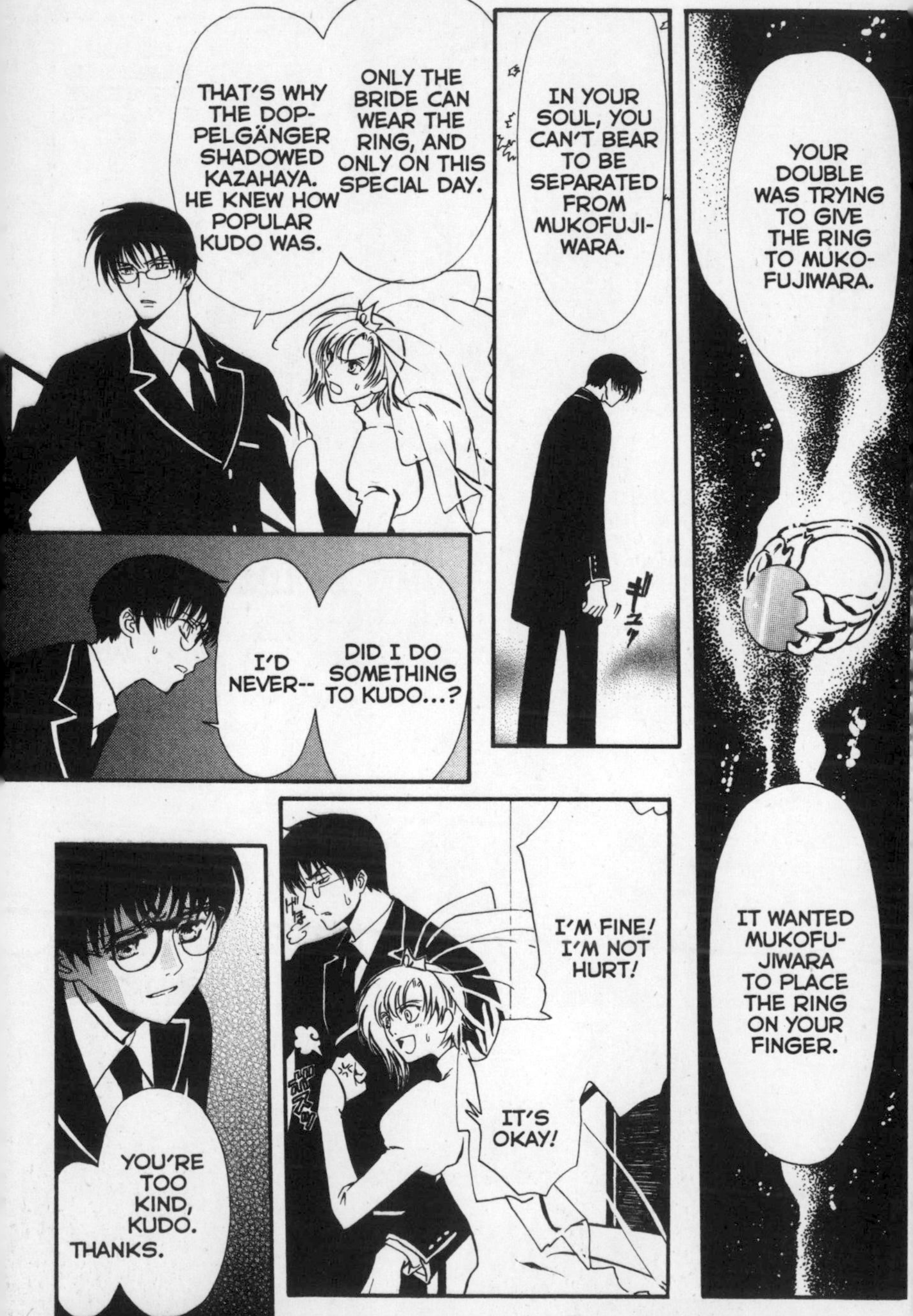
YOUR DOUBLE WAS TRYING TO GIVE THE RING TO MUKO-FUJIWARA.
IT WANTED MUKOFU-JIWARA TO PLACE THE RING ON YOUR FINGER.
IN YOUR SOUL, YOU CAN'T BEAR TO BE SEPARATED FROM MUKOFUJI-WARA.
ONLY THE BRIDE CAN WEAR THE RING, AND ONLY ON THIS SPECIAL DAY.
THAT'S WHY THE DOP-PELGÄNGER SHADOWED KAZAHAYA. HE KNEW HOW POPULAR KUDO WAS.
DID I DO SOMETHING TO KUDO...?
I'D NEVER--
I'M FINE! I'M NOT HURT!
IT'S OKAY!
YOU'RE TOO KIND, KUDO.
THANKS.

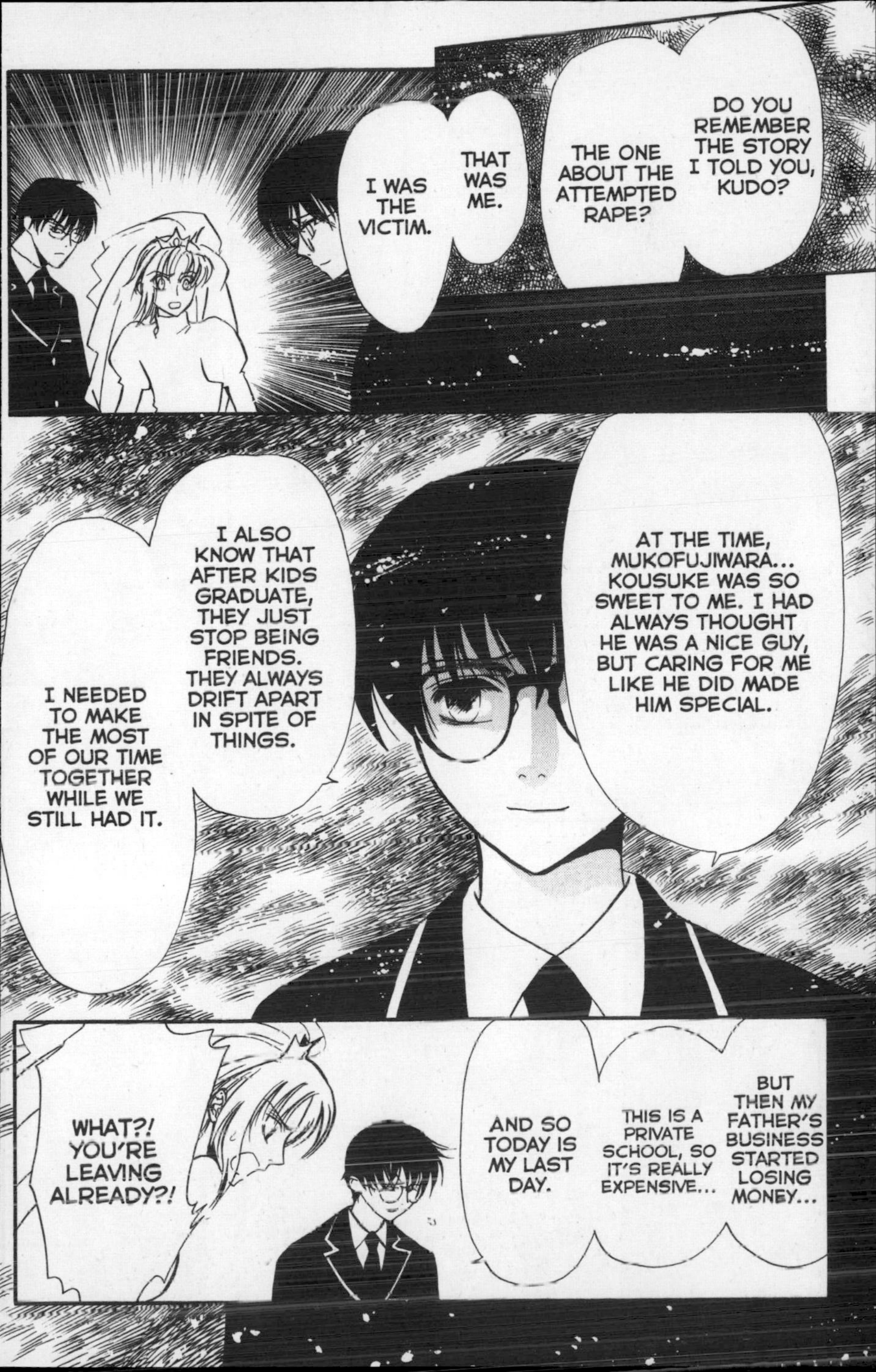
DO YOU REMEMBER THE STORY I TOLD YOU, KUDO?
THE ONE ABOUT THE ATTEMPTED RAPE?
THAT WAS ME.
I WAS THE VICTIM.
AT THE TIME, MUKOFUJIWARA... KOUSUKE WAS SO SWEET TO ME. I HAD ALWAYS THOUGHT HE WAS A NICE GUY, BUT CARING FOR ME LIKE HE DID MADE HIM SPECIAL.
I ALSO KNOW THAT AFTER KIDS GRADUATE, THEY JUST STOP BEING FRIENDS. THEY ALWAYS DRIFT APART IN SPITE OF THINGS.
I NEEDED TO MAKE THE MOST OF OUR TIME TOGETHER WHILE WE STILL HAD IT.
BUT THEN MY FATHER'S BUSINESS STARTED LOSING MONEY...
THIS IS A PRIVATE SCHOOL, SO IT'S REALLY EXPENSIVE...
AND SO TODAY IS MY LAST DAY.
WHAT?! YOU'RE LEAVING ALREADY?!

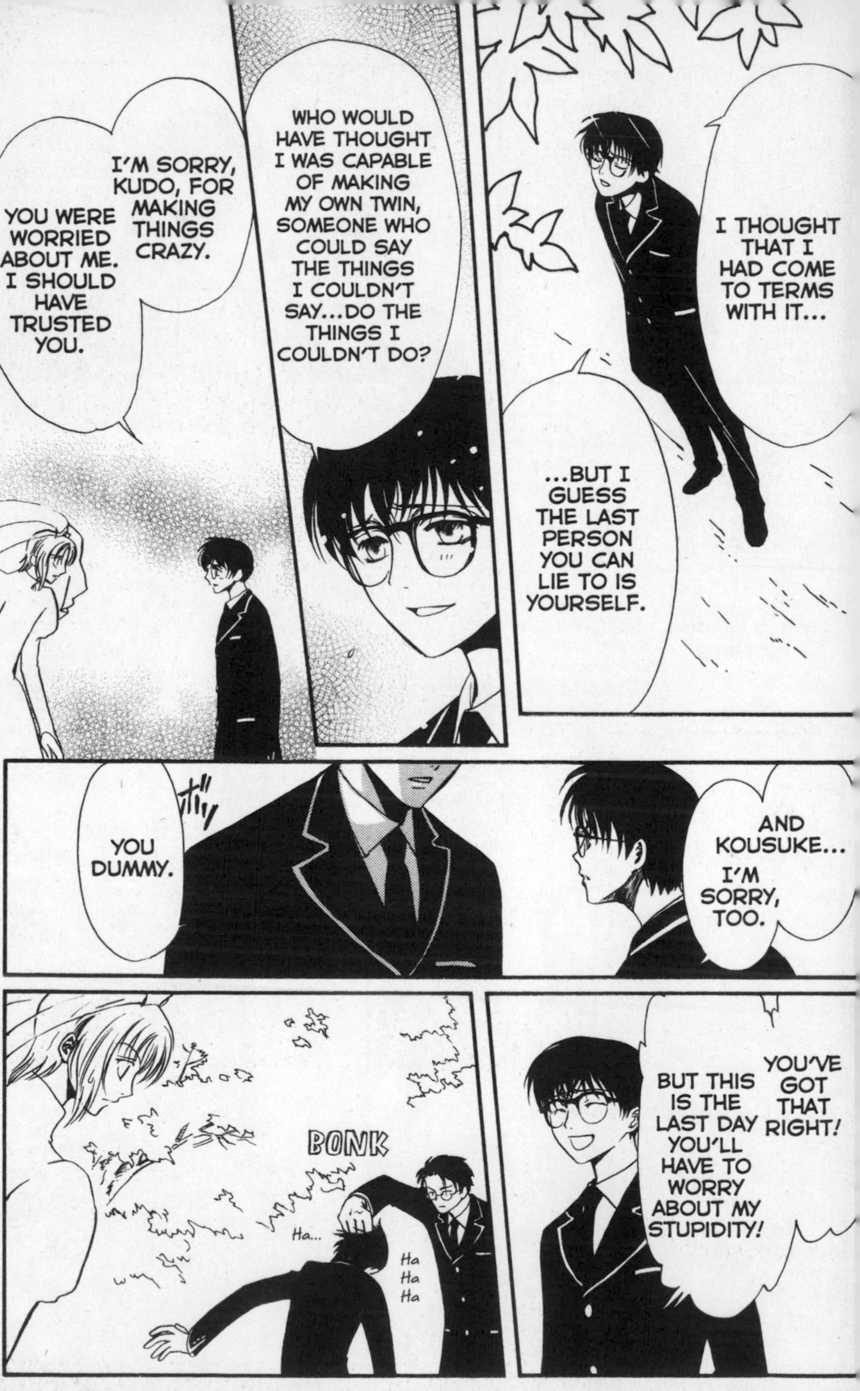

I THOUGHT THAT I HAD COME TO TERMS WITH IT...
...BUT I GUESS THE LAST PERSON YOU CAN LIE TO IS YOURSELF.
WHO WOULD HAVE THOUGHT I WAS CAPABLE OF MAKING MY OWN TWIN, SOMEONE WHO COULD SAY THE THINGS I COULDN'T SAY...DO THE THINGS I COULDN'T DO?
I'M SORRY, KUDO, FOR MAKING THINGS CRAZY.
YOU WERE WORRIED ABOUT ME. I SHOULD HAVE TRUSTED YOU.
AND KOUSUKE... I'M SORRY, TOO.
YOU DUMMY.
YOU'VE GOT THAT RIGHT!
BUT THIS IS THE LAST DAY YOU'LL HAVE TO WORRY ABOUT MY STUPIDITY!
BONK
Ha...
Ha Ha Ha

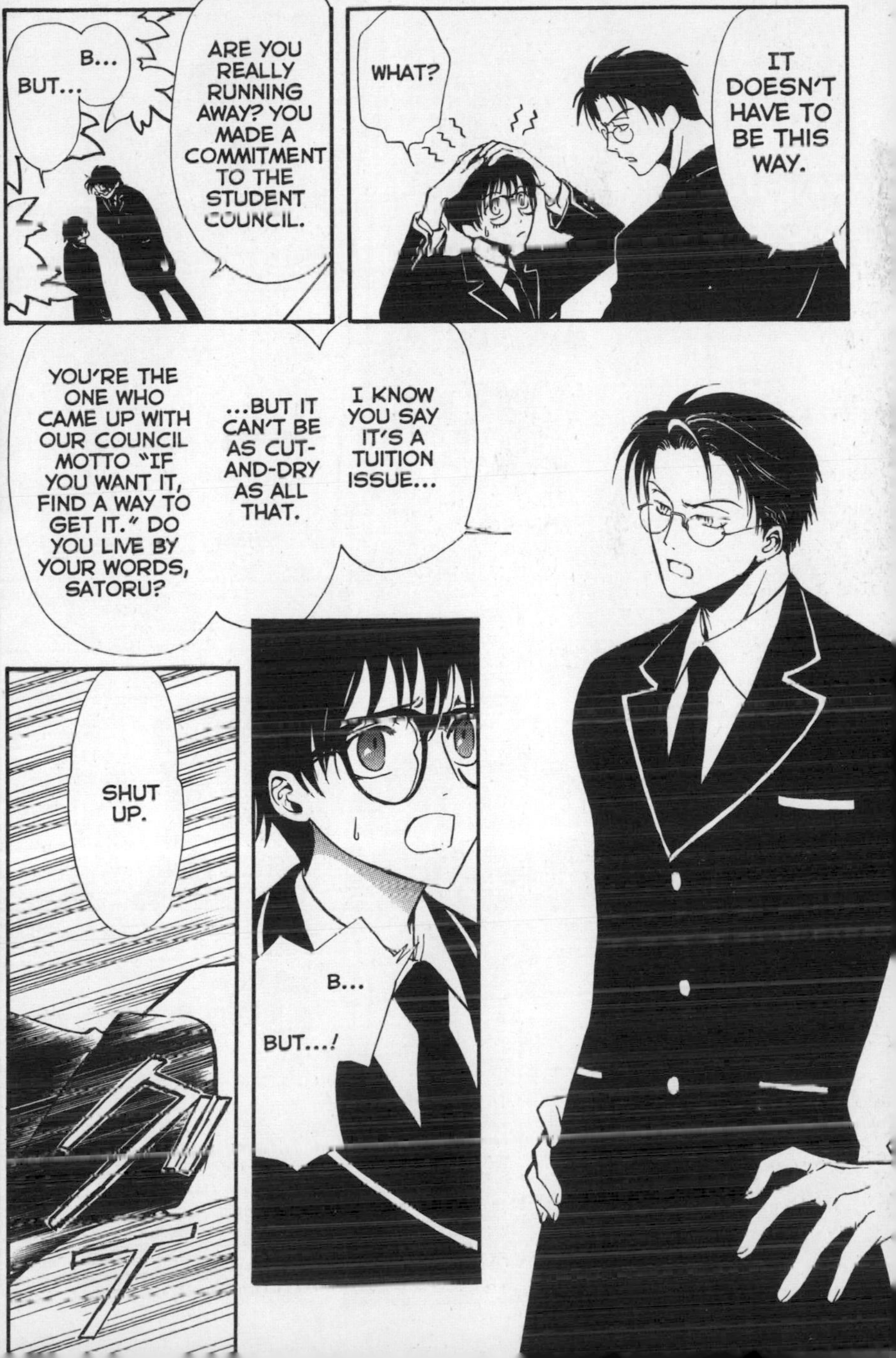
IT DOESN'T HAVE TO BE THIS WAY.
WHAT?
ARE YOU REALLY RUNNING AWAY? YOU MADE A COMMITMENT TO THE STUDENT COUNCIL.
B... BUT...
I KNOW YOU SAY IT'S A TUITION ISSUE...
...BUT IT CAN'T BE AS CUT-AND-DRY AS ALL THAT.
YOU'RE THE ONE WHO CAME UP WITH OUR COUNCIL MOTTO "IF YOU WANT IT, FIND A WAY TO GET IT." DO YOU LIVE BY YOUR WORDS, SATORU?
B...
BUT...!
SHUT UP.

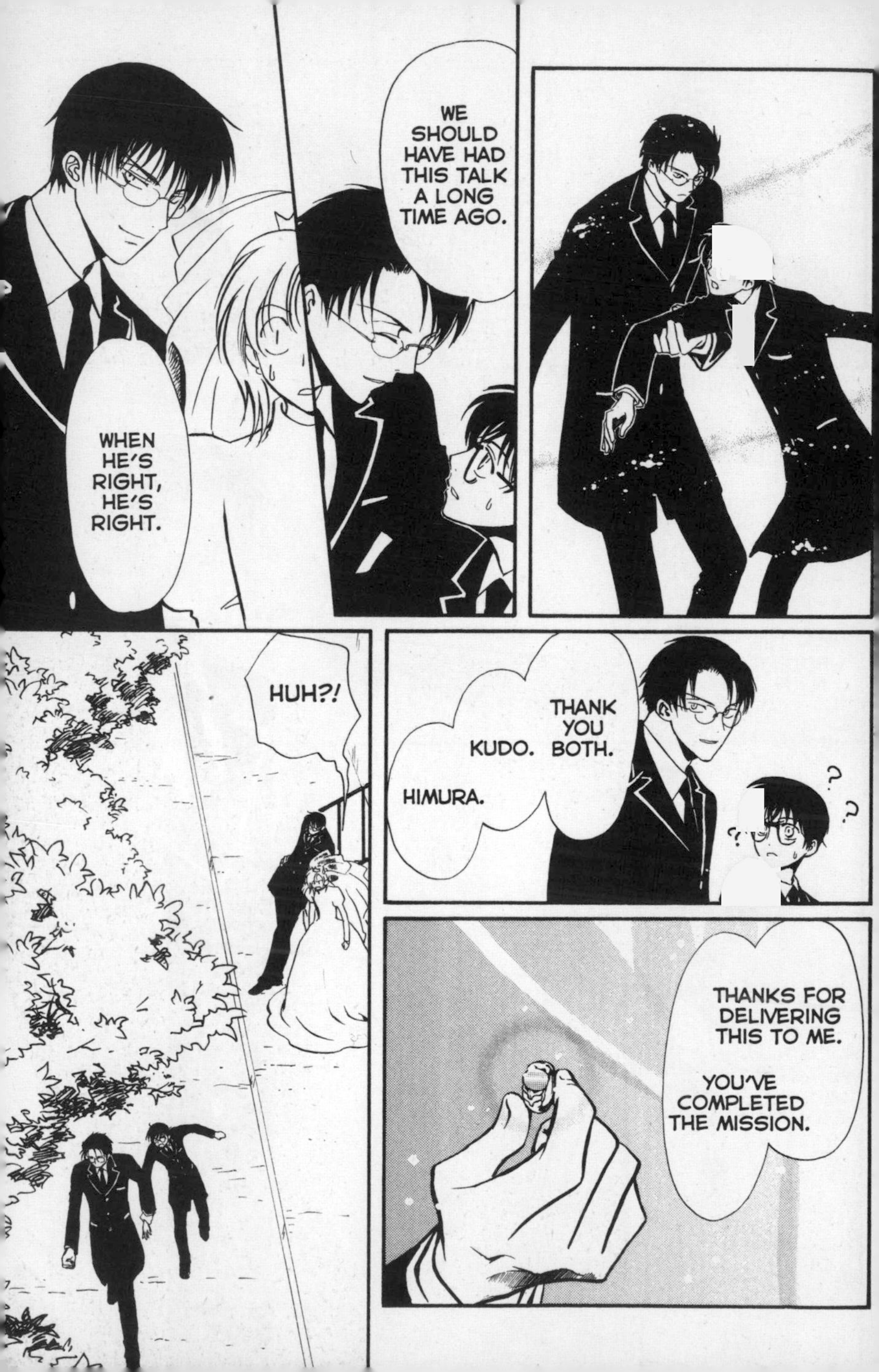
WE SHOULD HAVE HAD THIS TALK A LONG TIME AGO.
WHEN HE'S RIGHT, HE'S RIGHT.
THANK YOU BOTH.
KUDO.
HIMURA.
THANKS FOR DELIVERING THIS TO ME.
YOU'VE COMPLETED THE MISSION.
HUH?!

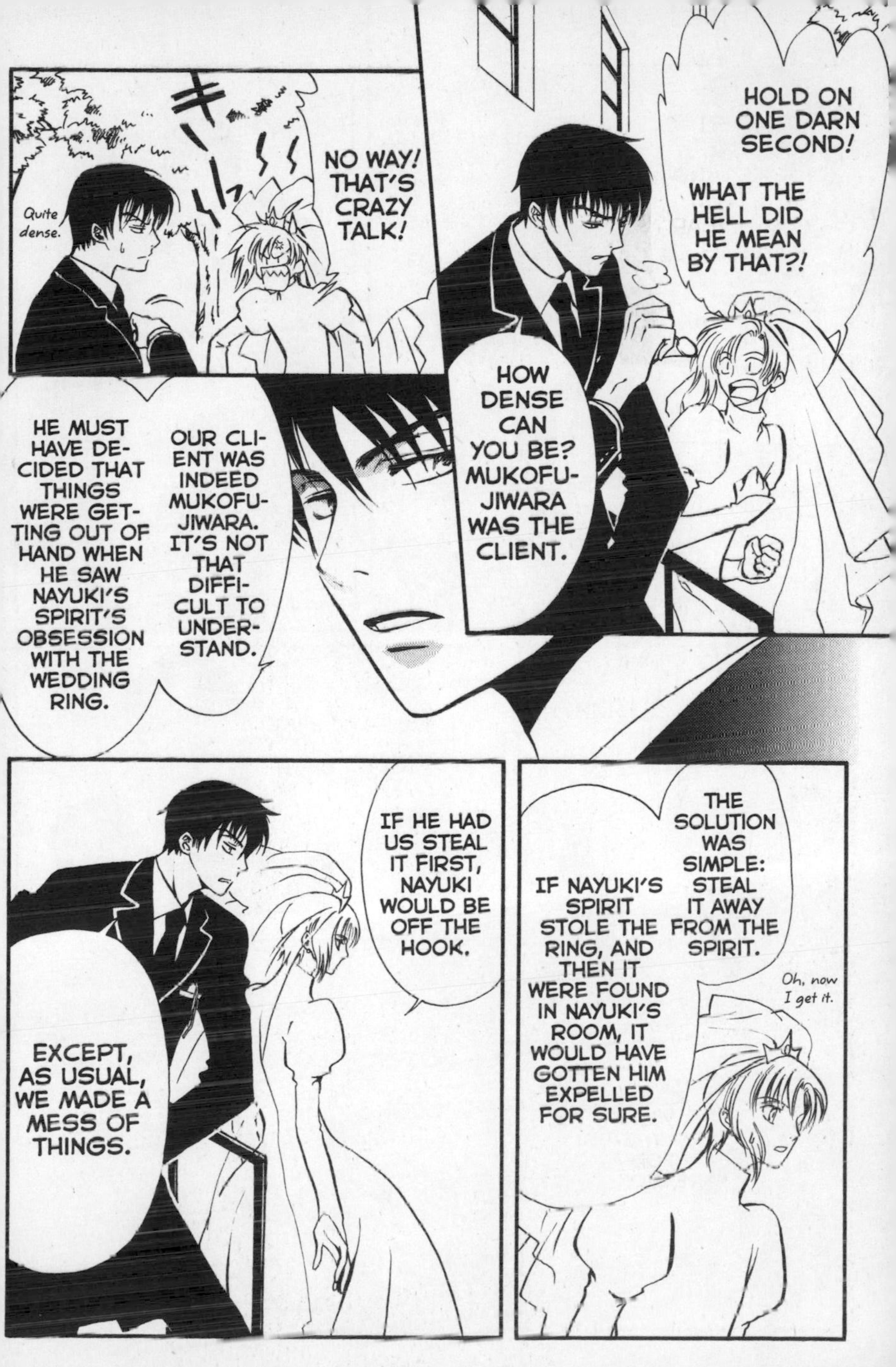
HOLD ON ONE DARN SECOND!
WHAT THE HELL DID HE MEAN BY THAT?!
HOW DENSE CAN YOU BE? MUKOFUJIWARA WAS THE CLIENT.
NO WAY! THAT'S CRAZY TALK!
Quite dense.
OUR CLIENT WAS INDEED MUKOFUJIWARA. IT'S NOT THAT DIFFICULT TO UNDERSTAND.
HE MUST HAVE DECIDED THAT THINGS WERE GETTING OUT OF HAND WHEN HE SAW NAYUKI'S SPIRIT'S OBSESSION WITH THE WEDDING RING.
THE SOLUTION WAS SIMPLE: STEAL IT AWAY FROM THE SPIRIT.
IF NAYUKI'S SPIRIT STOLE THE RING, AND THEN IT WERE FOUND IN NAYUKI'S ROOM, IT WOULD HAVE GOTTEN HIM EXPELLED FOR SURE.
Oh, now I get it.
IF HE HAD US STEAL IT FIRST, NAYUKI WOULD BE OFF THE HOOK.
EXCEPT, AS USUAL, WE MADE A MESS OF THINGS.

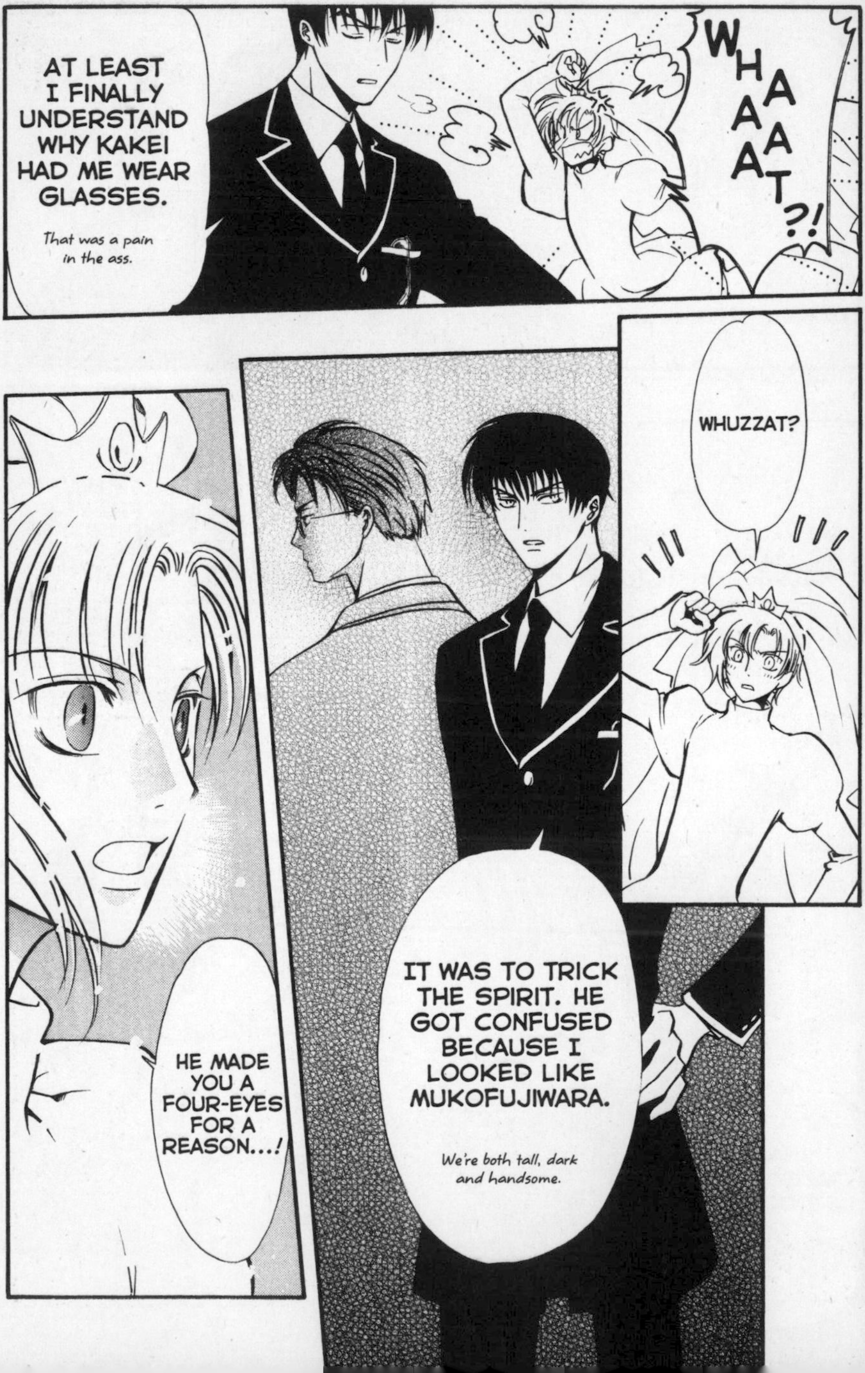
AT LEAST I FINALLY UNDERSTAND WHY KAKEI HAD ME WEAR GLASSES.
That was a pain in the ass.
WHAAAAAT?!
WHUZZAT?
IT WAS TO TRICK THE SPIRIT. HE GOT CONFUSED BECAUSE I LOOKED LIKE MUKOFUJIWARA.
We're both tall, dark and handsome.
HE MADE YOU A FOUR-EYES FOR A REASON...!

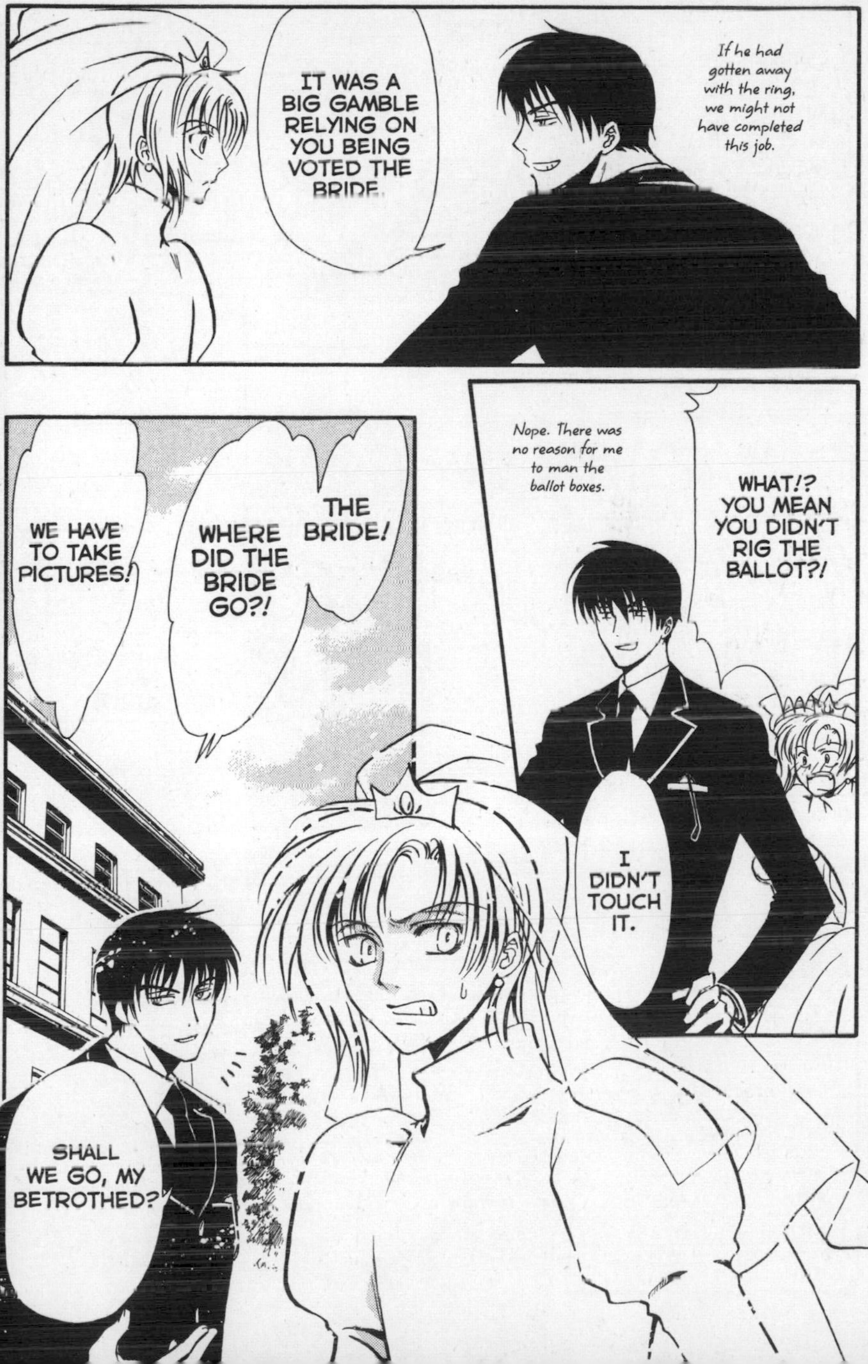
If he had gotten away with the ring, we might not have completed this job.
IT WAS A BIG GAMBLE RELYING ON YOU BEING VOTED THE BRIDE.
WHAT!? YOU MEAN YOU DIDN'T RIG THE BALLOT?!
Nope. There was no reason for me to man the ballot boxes.
I DIDN'T TOUCH IT.
THE BRIDE!
WHERE DID THE BRIDE GO?!
WE HAVE TO TAKE PICTURES!
SHALL WE GO, MY BETROTHED?

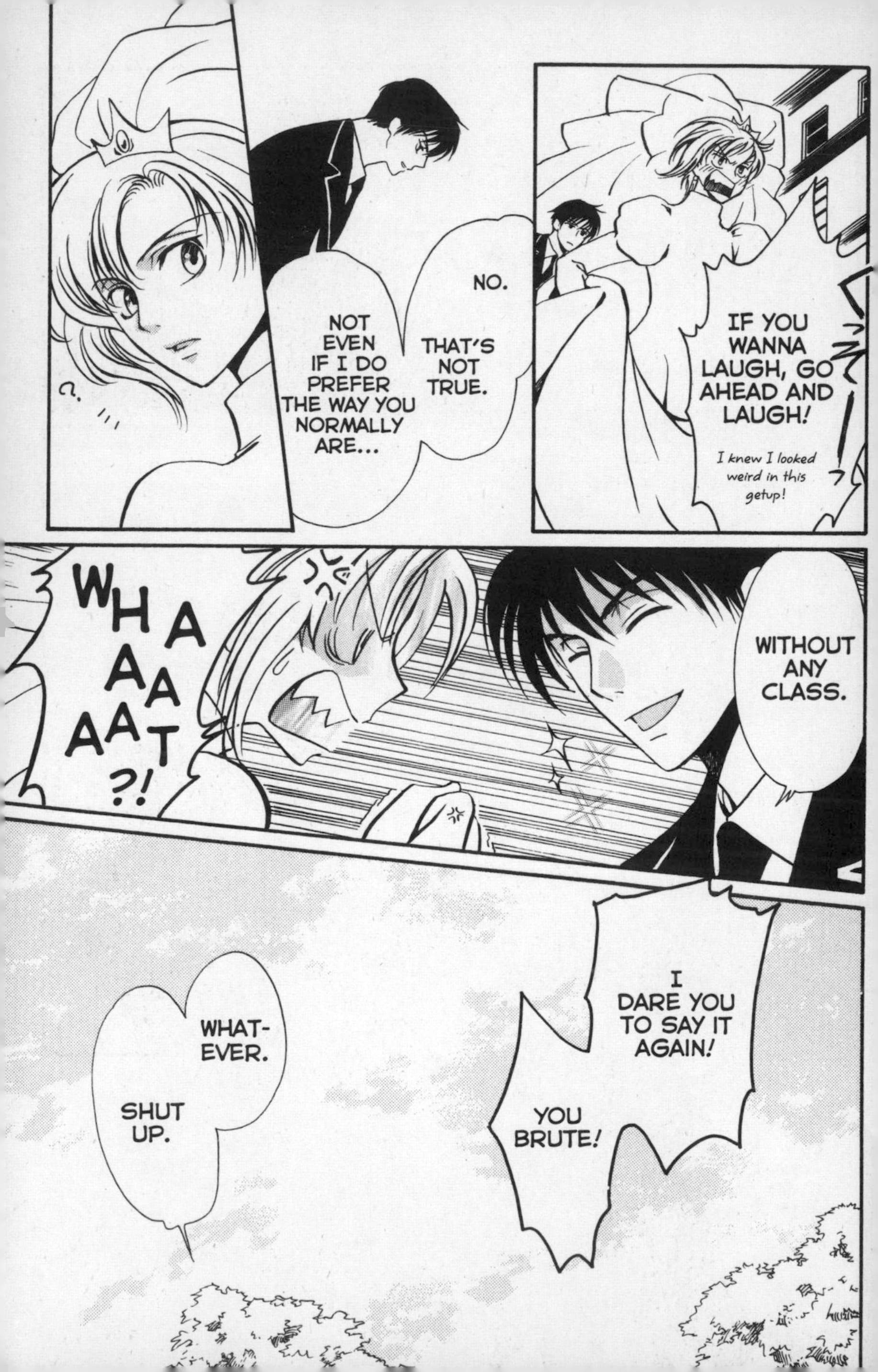
IF YOU WANNA LAUGH, GO AHEAD AND LAUGH!
I knew I looked weird in this getup!
NO.
THAT'S NOT TRUE.
NOT EVEN IF I DO PREFER THE WAY YOU NORMALLY ARE...
WITHOUT ANY CLASS.
WHAAAAAT?!
I DARE YOU TO SAY IT AGAIN!
YOU BRUTE!
WHAT-EVER.
SHUT UP.

合法ドラッグ
LEGAL DRUG

TO BE CONTINUED

合法ドラッグ
LEGAL DRUG

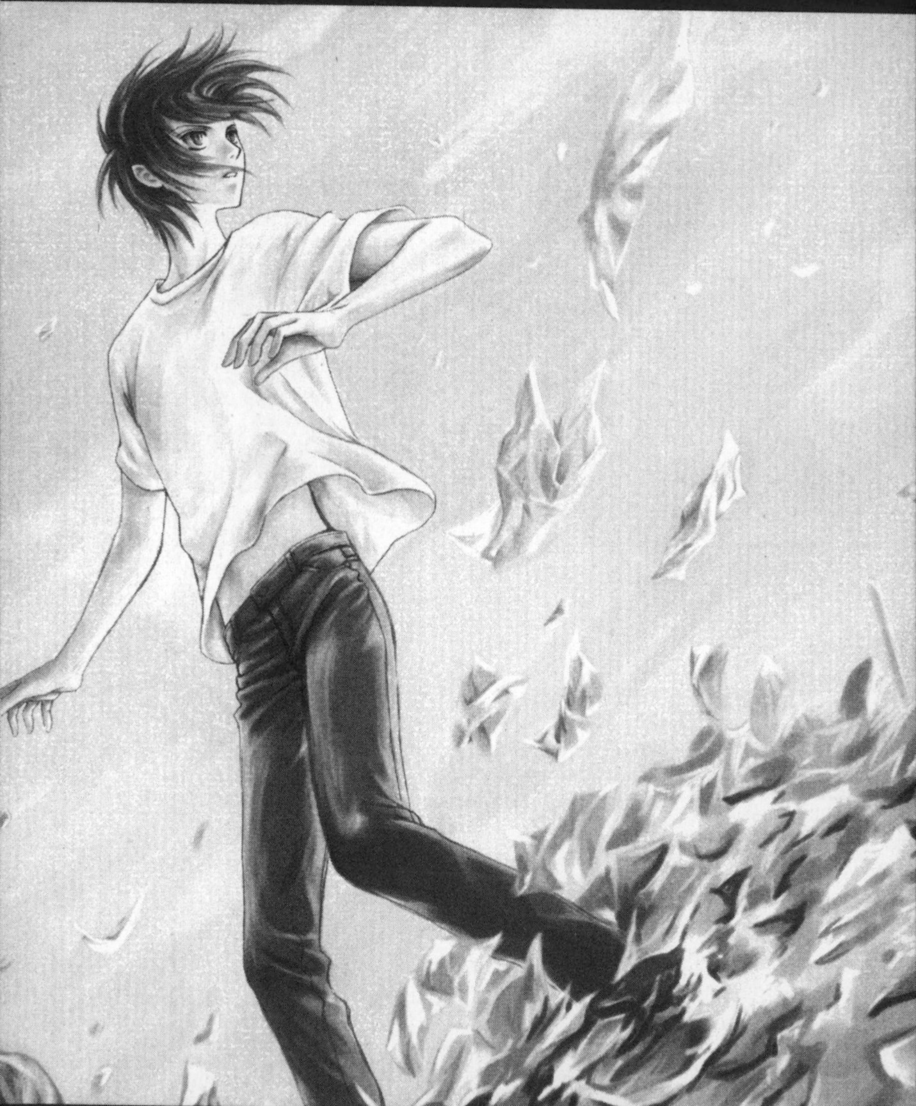

DRUG EXTRA Daily use of the drug may cause poisoning

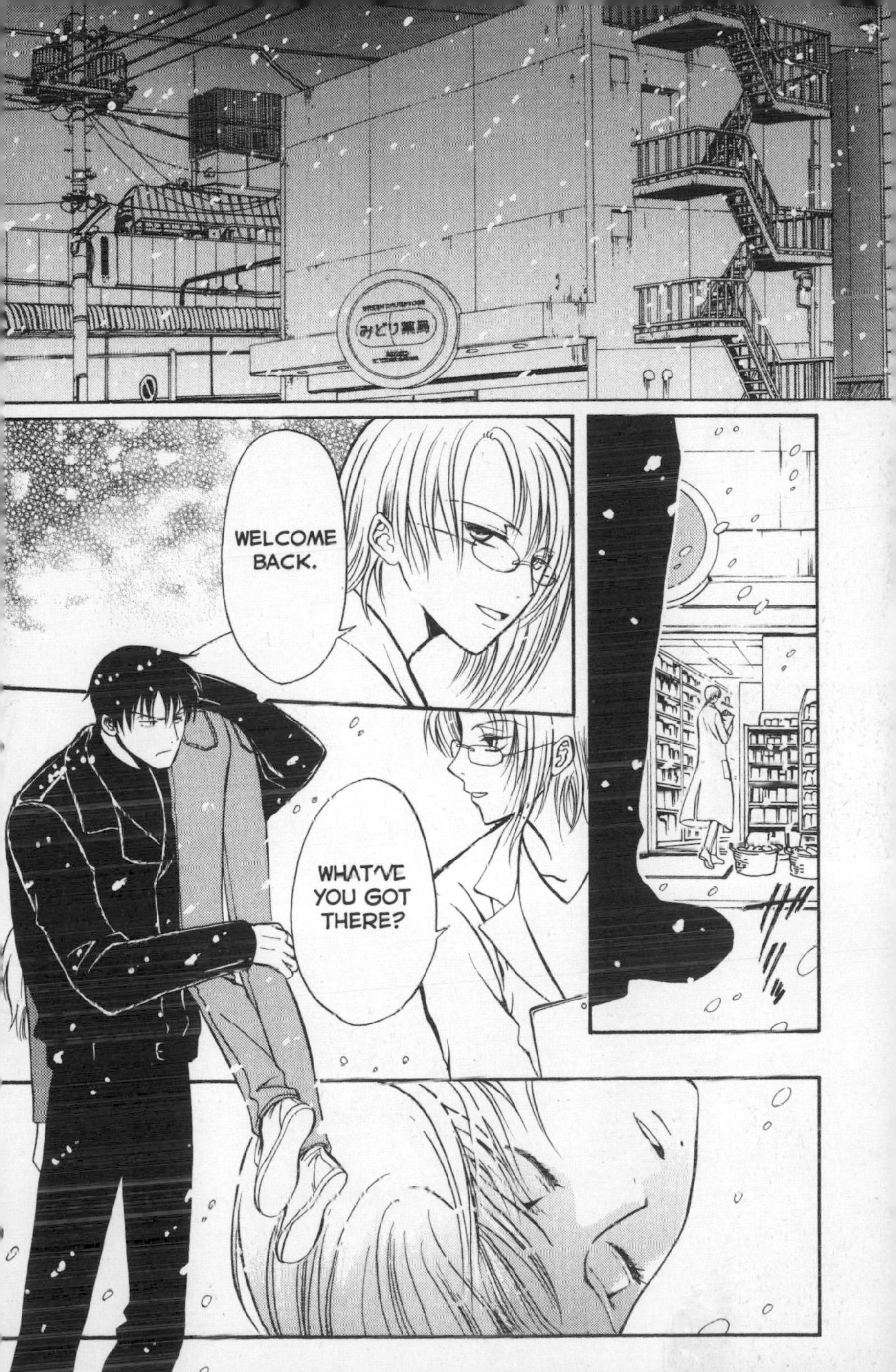
みどり薬局
WELCOME BACK.
WHAT'VE YOU GOT THERE?

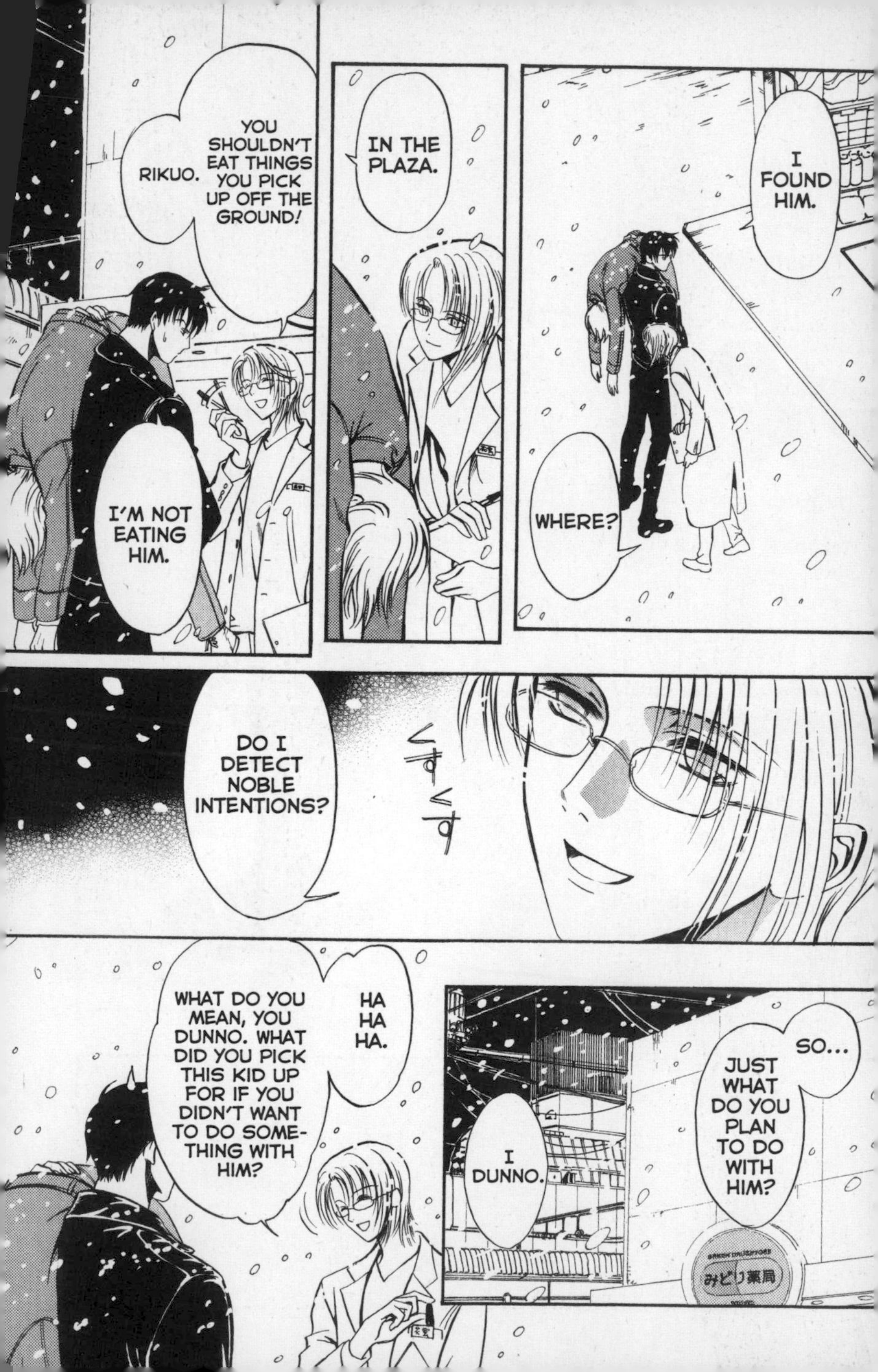
I FOUND HIM.
WHERE?
IN THE PLAZA.
RIKUO. YOU SHOULDN'T EAT THINGS YOU PICK UP OFF THE GROUND!
I'M NOT EATING HIM.
くすくす
DO I DETECT NOBLE INTENTIONS?
SO... JUST WHAT DO YOU PLAN TO DO WITH HIM?
I DUNNO.
みどり薬局
HA HA HA.
WHAT DO YOU MEAN, YOU DUNNO. WHAT DID YOU PICK THIS KID UP FOR IF YOU DIDN'T WANT TO DO SOME-THING WITH HIM?

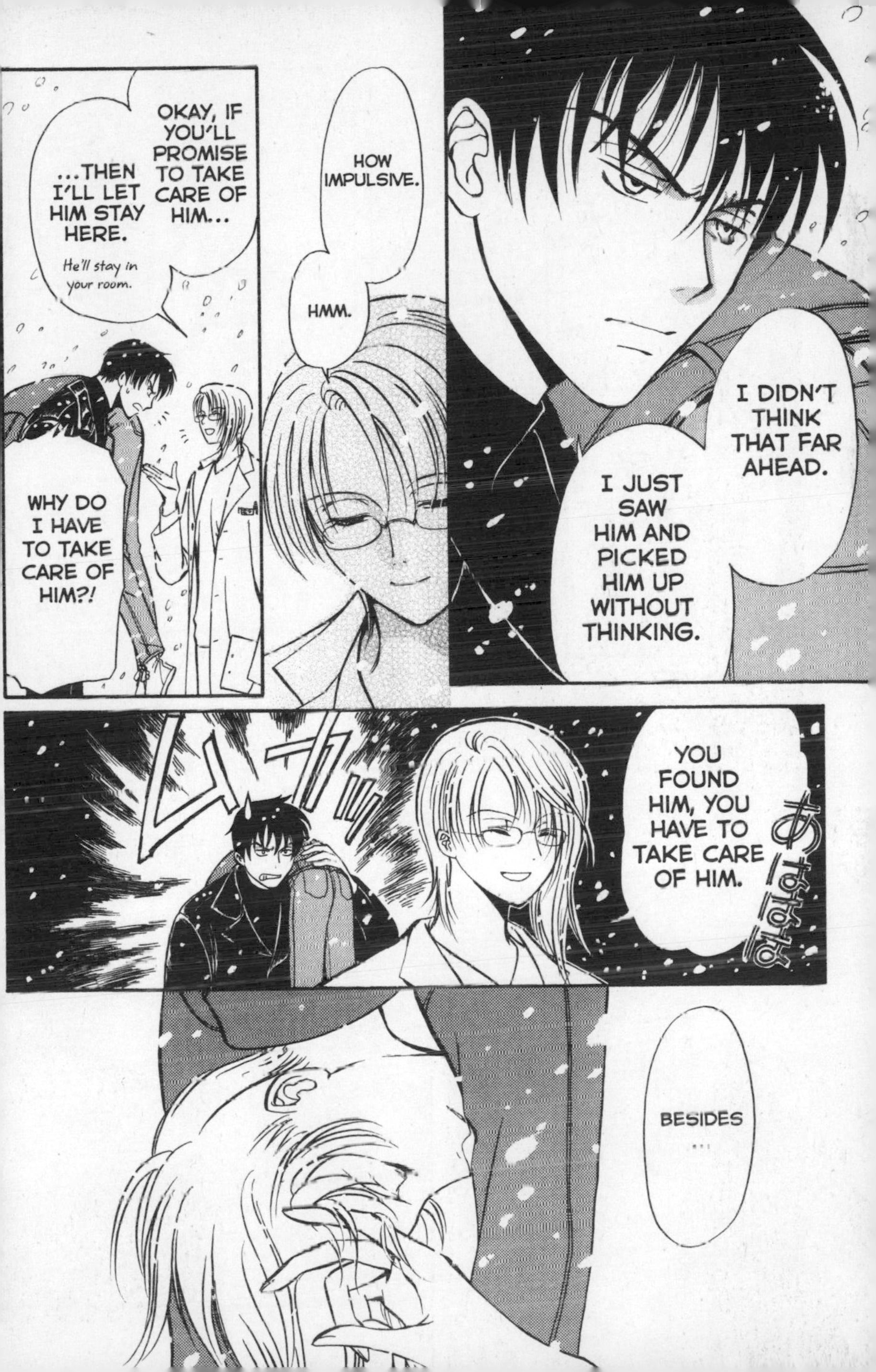
I DIDN'T THINK THAT FAR AHEAD.
I JUST SAW HIM AND PICKED HIM UP WITHOUT THINKING.
HOW IMPULSIVE.
HMM.
OKAY, IF YOU'LL PROMISE TO TAKE CARE OF HIM...
...THEN I'LL LET HIM STAY HERE.
He'll stay in your room.
WHY DO I HAVE TO TAKE CARE OF HIM?!
YOU FOUND HIM, YOU HAVE TO TAKE CARE OF HIM.
BESIDES ...

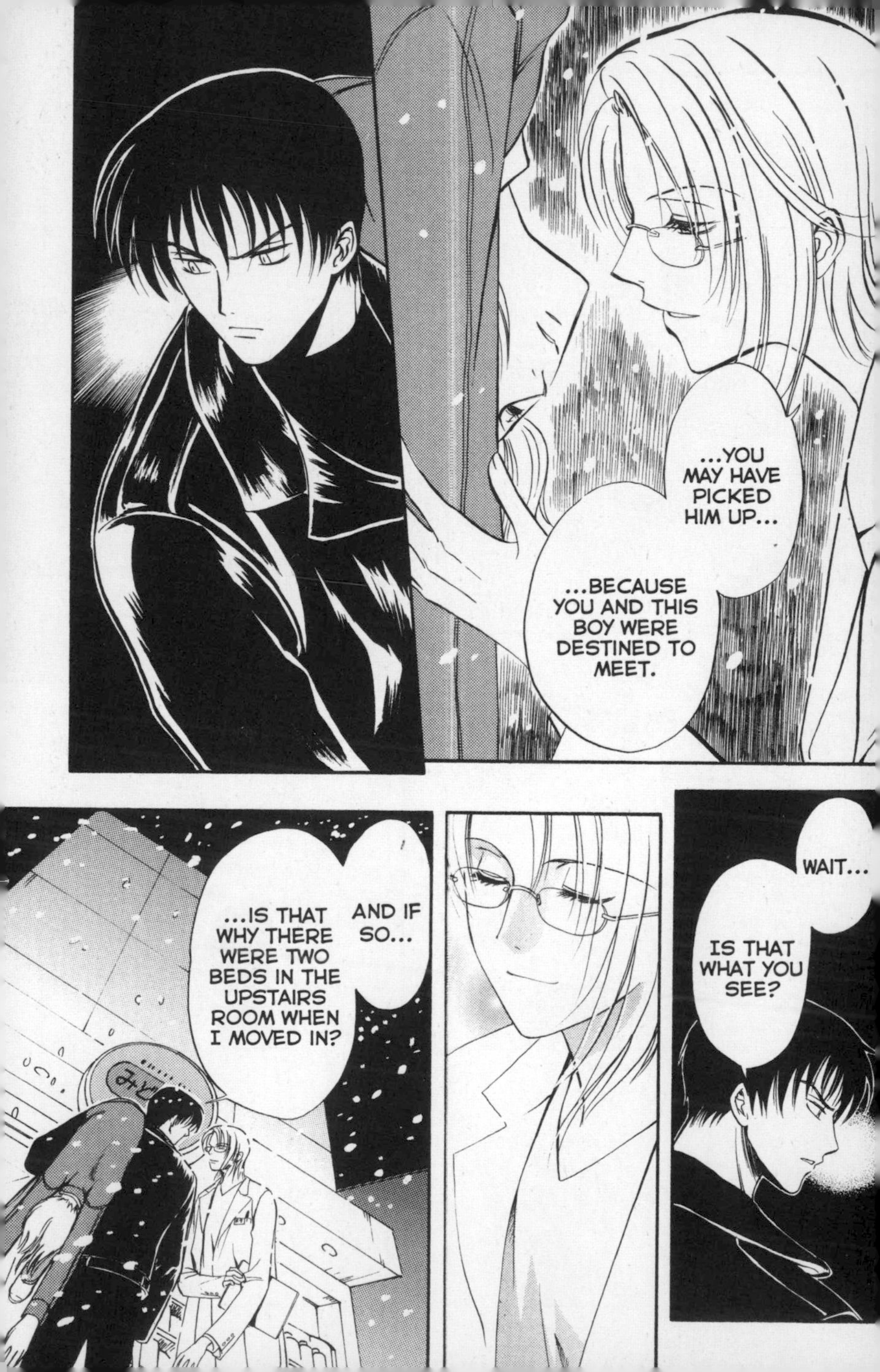
...YOU MAY HAVE PICKED HIM UP...
...BECAUSE YOU AND THIS BOY WERE DESTINED TO MEET.
WAIT...
IS THAT WHAT YOU SEE?
AND IF SO...
...IS THAT WHY THERE WERE TWO BEDS IN THE UPSTAIRS ROOM WHEN I MOVED IN?

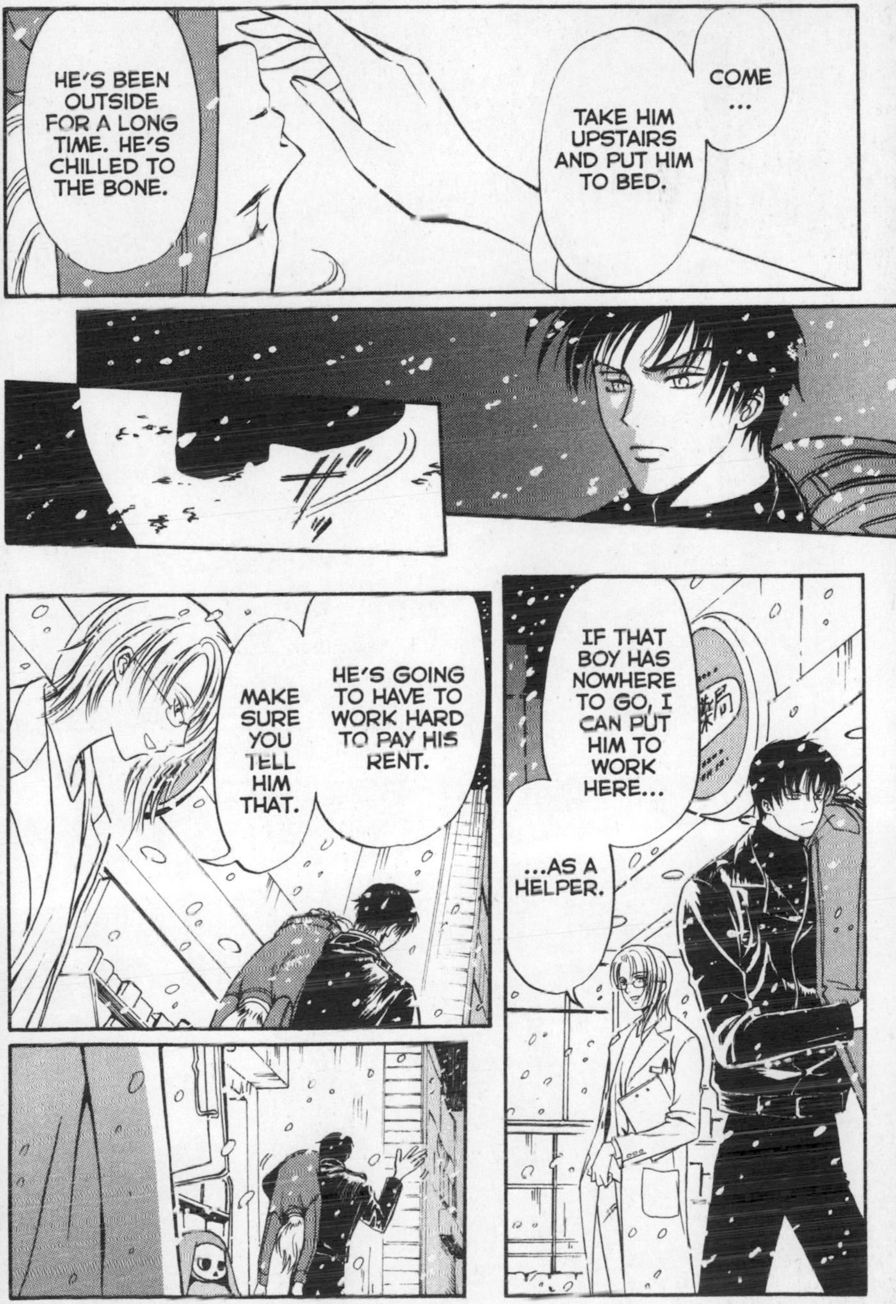
COME ... TAKE HIM UPSTAIRS AND PUT HIM TO BED.
HE'S BEEN OUTSIDE FOR A LONG TIME. HE'S CHILLED TO THE BONE.
IF THAT BOY HAS NOWHERE TO GO, I CAN PUT HIM TO WORK HERE...
...AS A HELPER.
HE'S GOING TO HAVE TO WORK HARD TO PAY HIS RENT.
MAKE SURE YOU TELL HIM THAT.

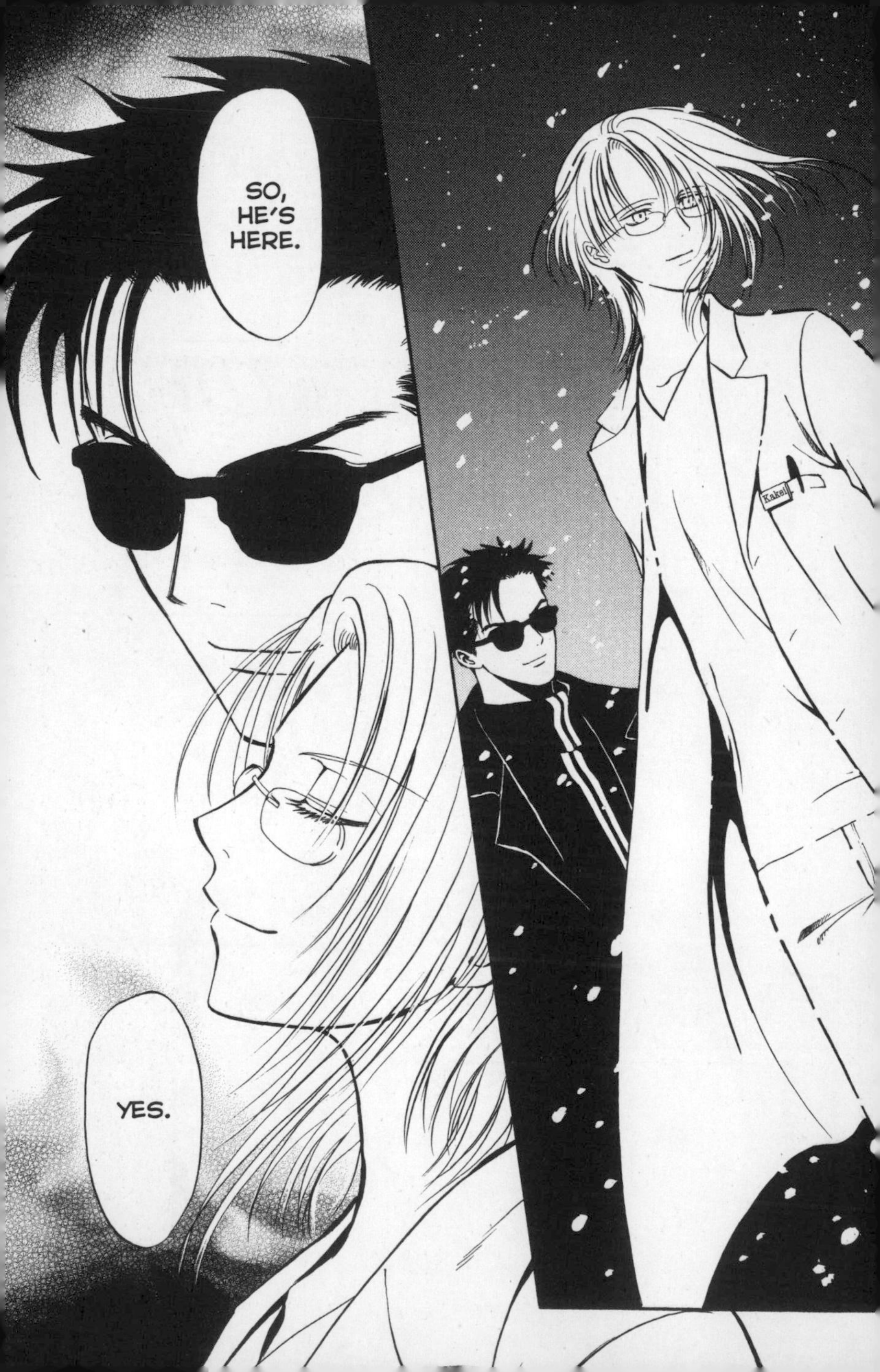
Kakei
SO, HE'S HERE.
YES.

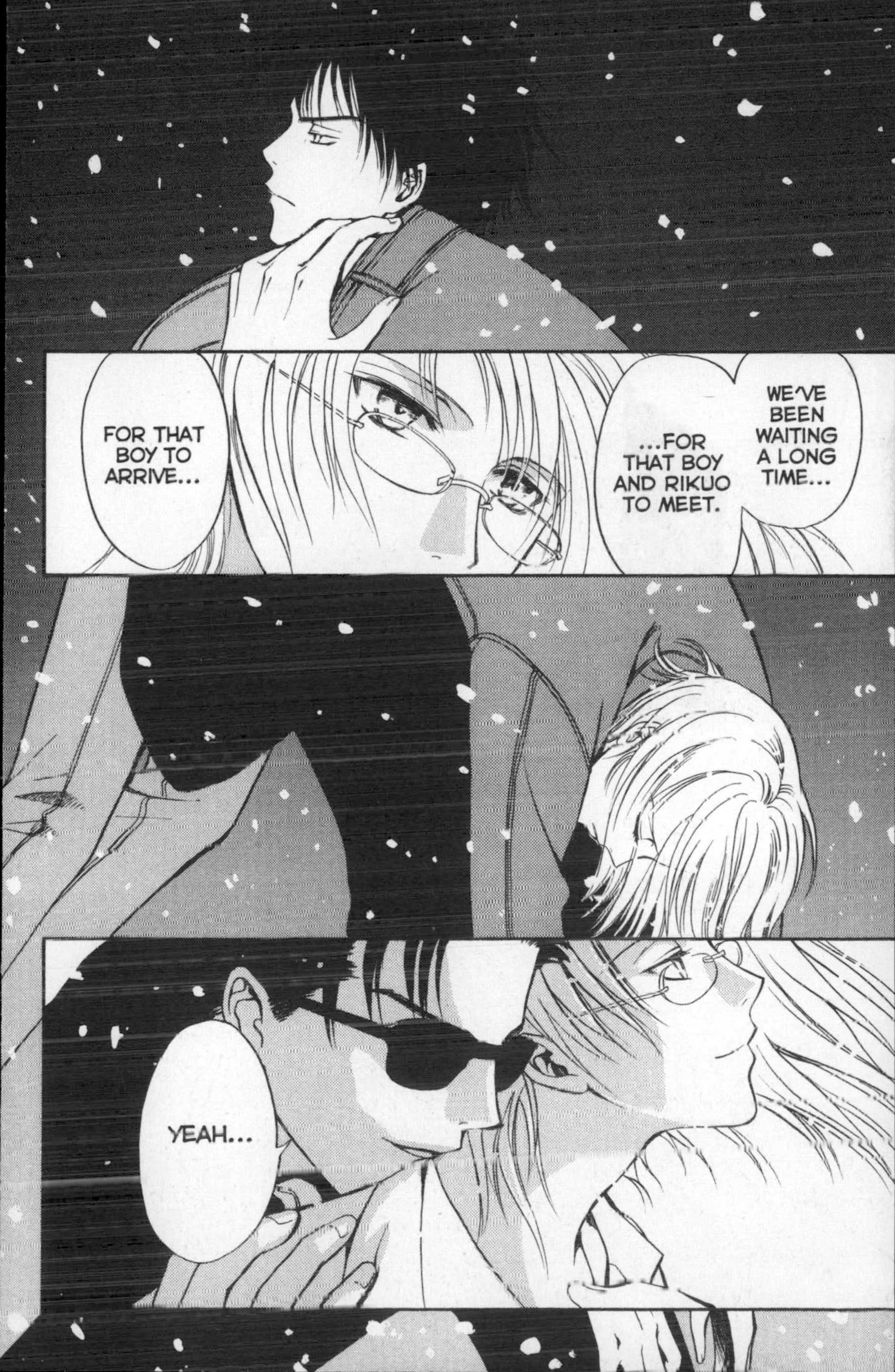
WE'VE BEEN WAITING A LONG TIME...
...FOR THAT BOY AND RIKUO TO MEET.
FOR THAT BOY TO ARRIVE...
YEAH...

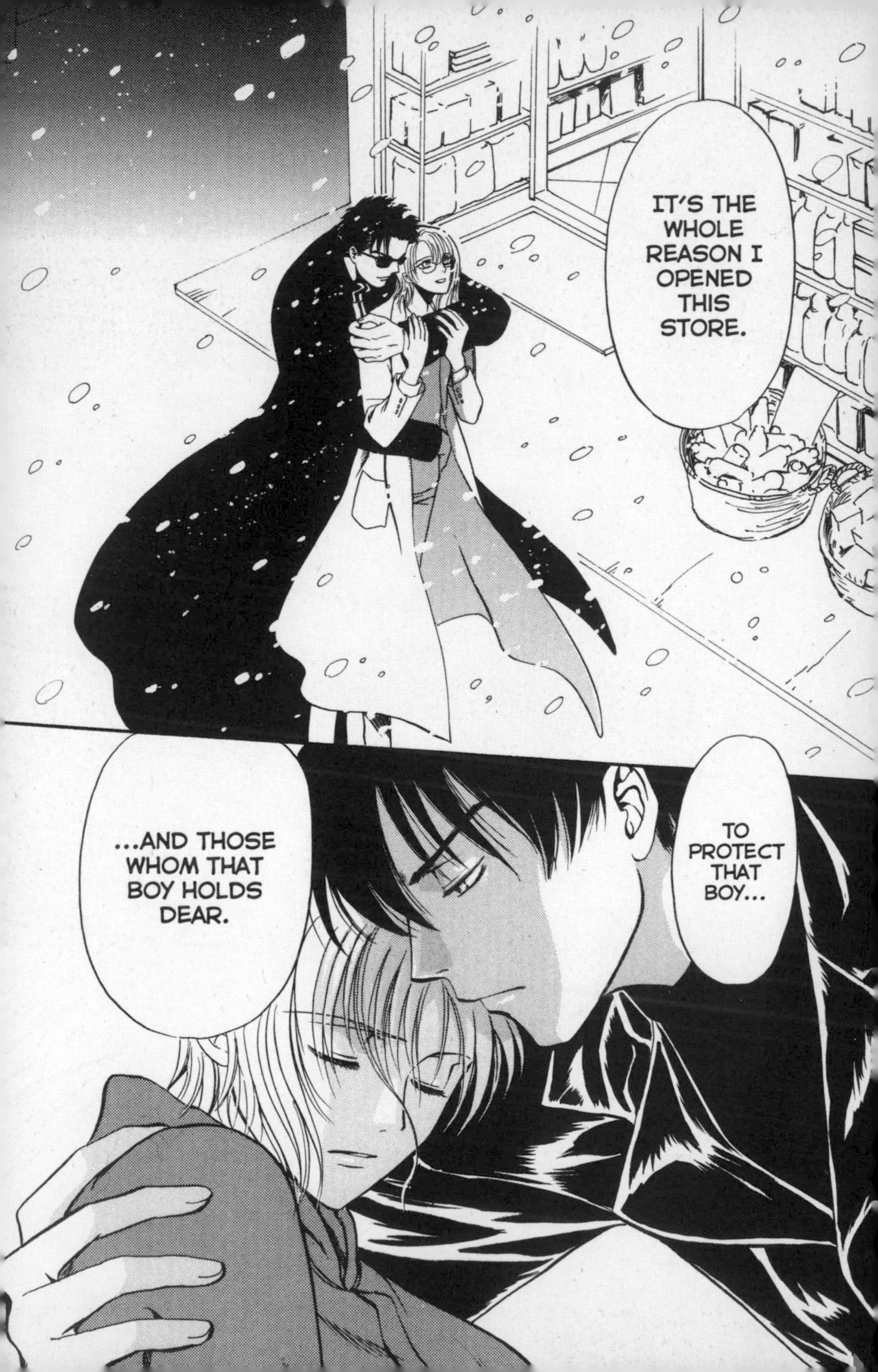
IT'S THE WHOLE REASON I OPENED THIS STORE.
TO PROTECT THAT BOY...
...AND THOSE WHOM THAT BOY HOLDS DEAR.

STAFF DRUG

PLANNING AND PRESENTED BY
CLAMP

STORY
NANASE OHKAWA

COMIC
MICK NEKOI

ART ASSISTANT
SATSUKI IGARASHI
MOKONA APAPA

BOOK DESIGN
CLAMP

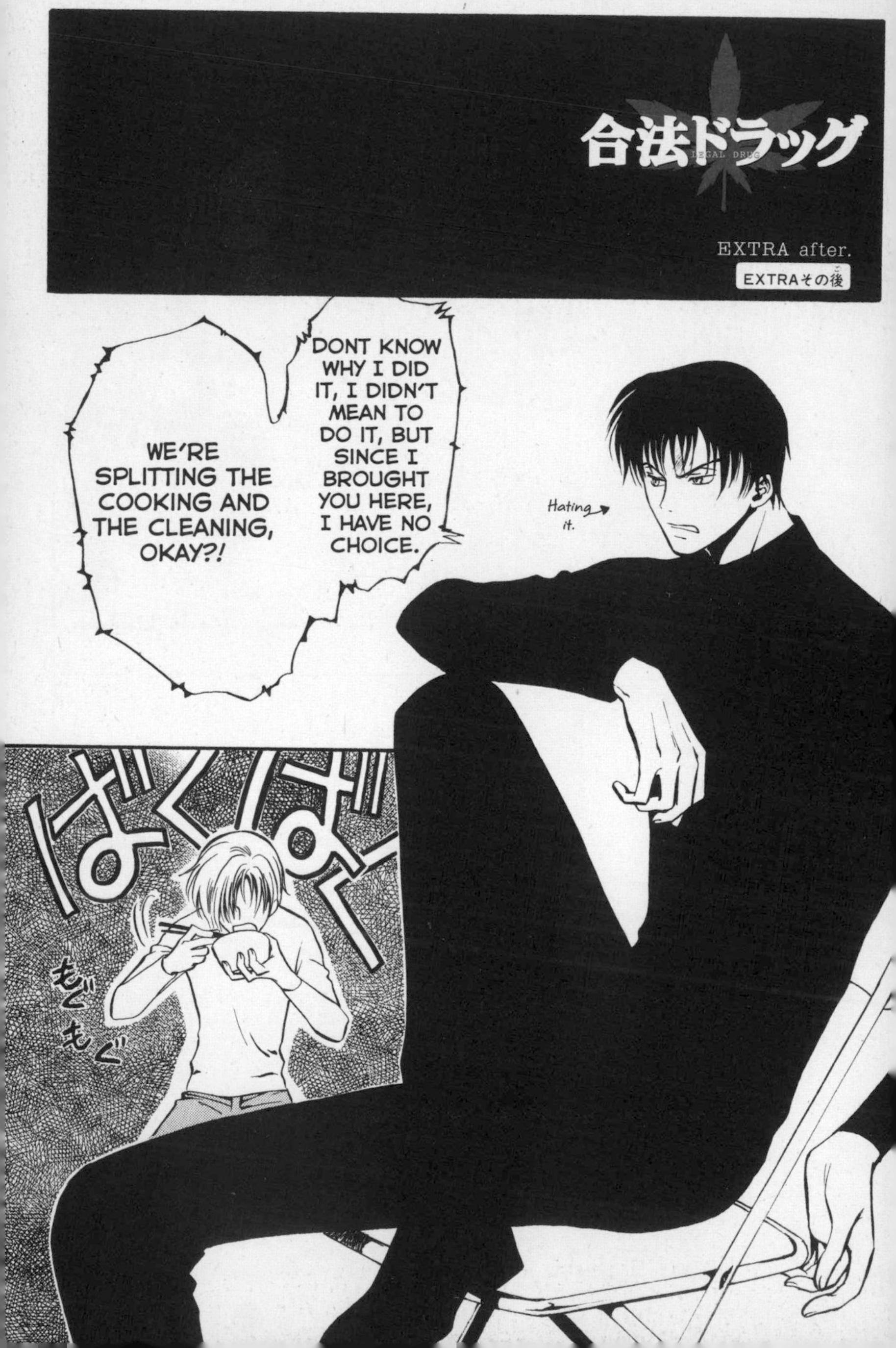
合法ドラッグ
LEGAL DRUG
EXTRA after.
EXTRAその後
DONT KNOW WHY I DID IT, I DIDN'T MEAN TO DO IT, BUT SINCE I BROUGHT YOU HERE, I HAVE NO CHOICE.
WE'RE SPLITTING THE COOKING AND THE CLEANING, OKAY?!
Hating it.
もぐもぐ

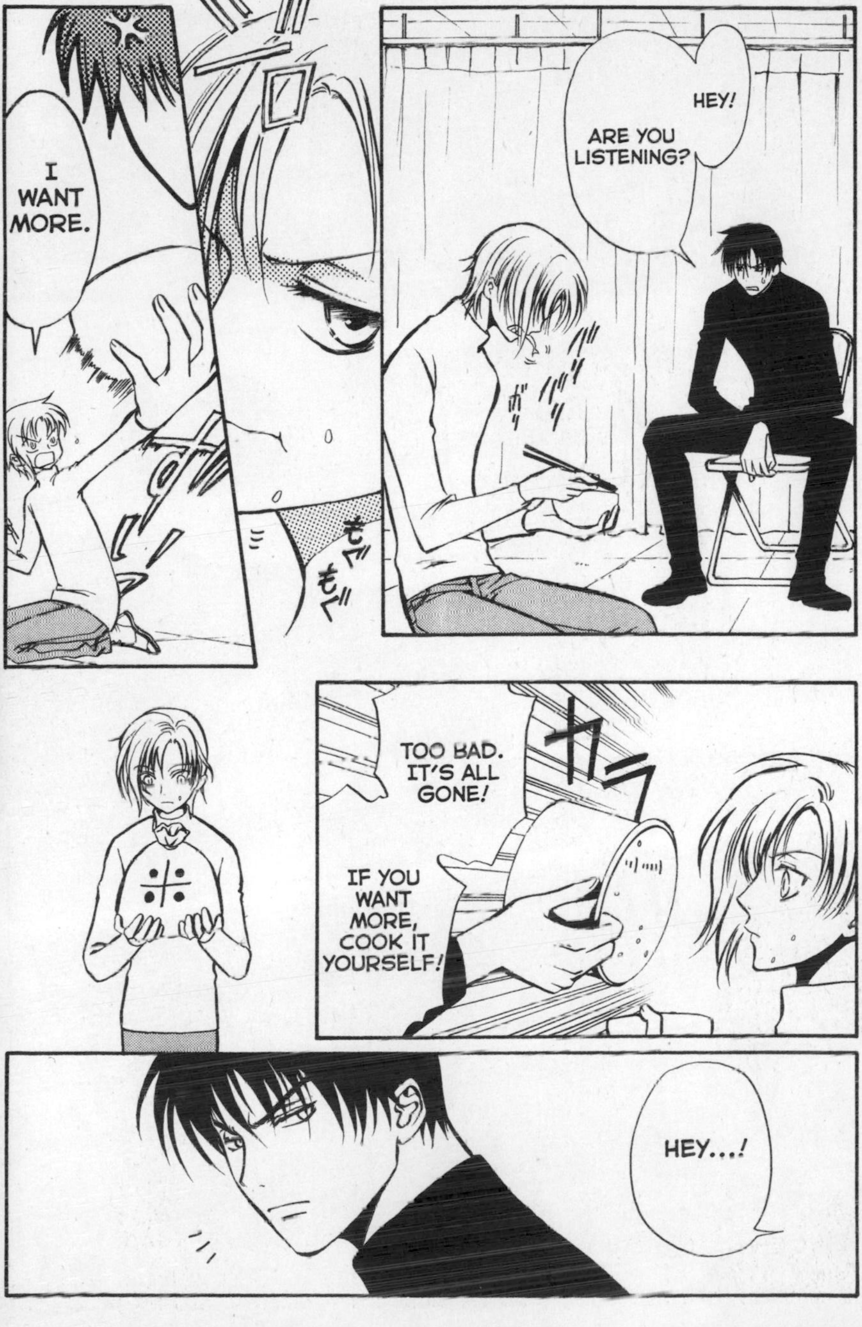
HEY!
ARE YOU LISTENING?
I WANT MORE.
もぐ もぐ
カラ
TOO BAD. IT'S ALL GONE!
IF YOU WANT MORE, COOK IT YOURSELF!
HEY...!

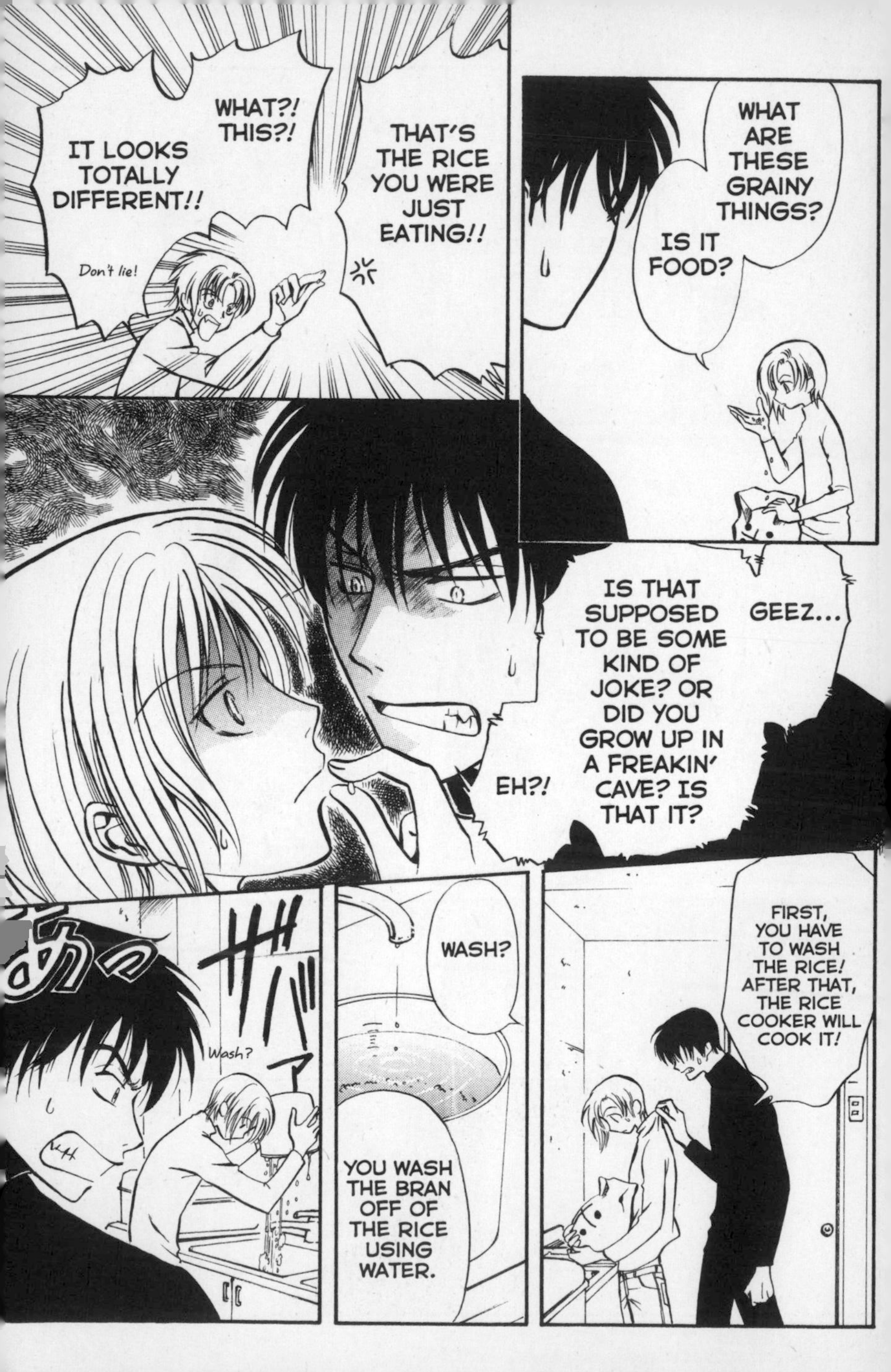
WHAT ARE THESE GRAINY THINGS?
IS IT FOOD?
THAT'S THE RICE YOU WERE JUST EATING!!
WHAT?! THIS?!
IT LOOKS TOTALLY DIFFERENT!!
Don't lie!
GEEZ...
IS THAT SUPPOSED TO BE SOME KIND OF JOKE? OR DID YOU GROW UP IN A FREAKIN' CAVE? IS THAT IT?
EH?!
FIRST, YOU HAVE TO WASH THE RICE! AFTER THAT, THE RICE COOKER WILL COOK IT!
WASH?
YOU WASH THE BRAN OFF OF THE RICE USING WATER.
ザバア
あっ
Wash?

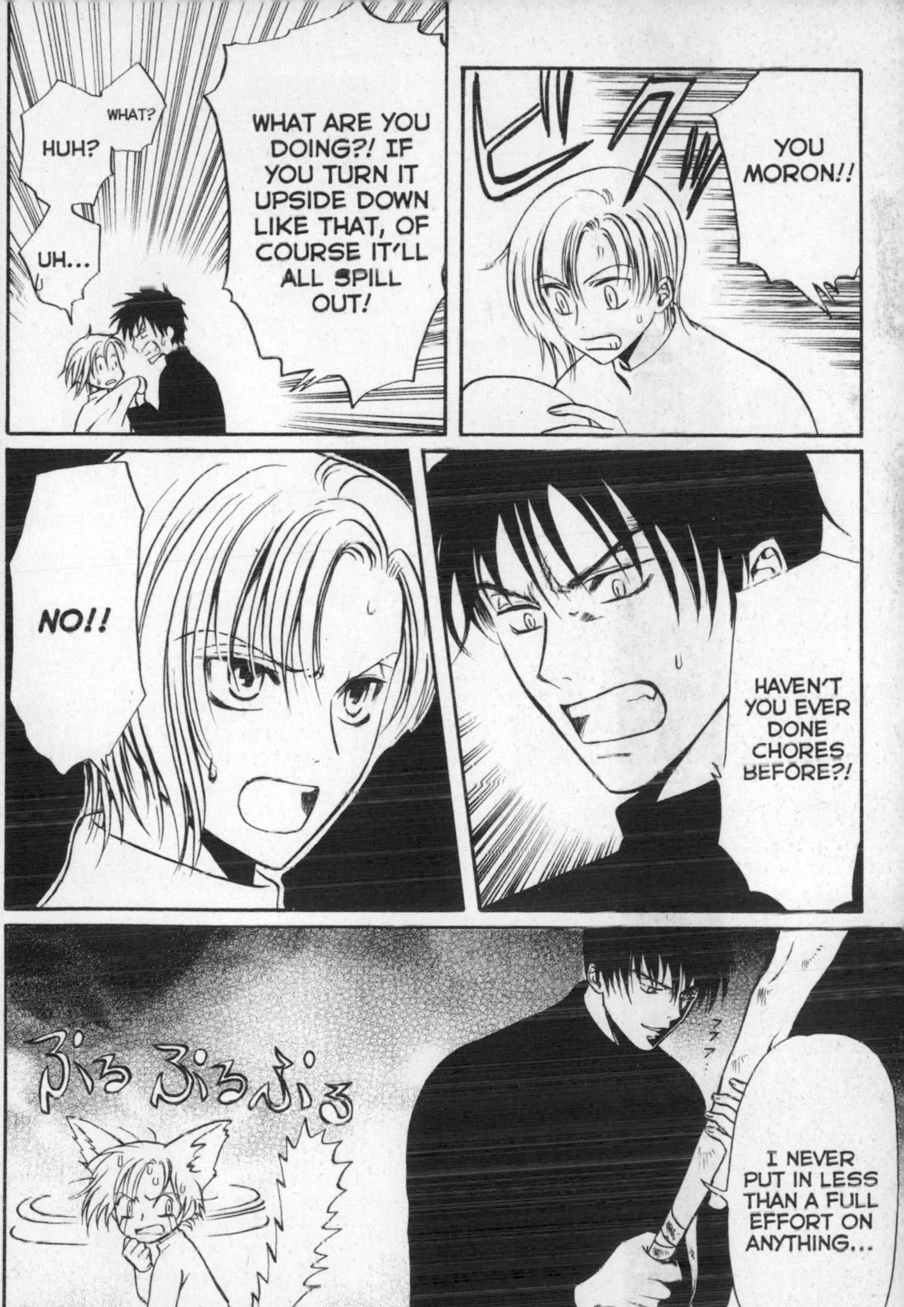
YOU MORON!!
WHAT ARE YOU DOING?! IF YOU TURN IT UPSIDE DOWN LIKE THAT, OF COURSE IT'LL ALL SPILL OUT!
WHAT?
HUH?
UH...
HAVEN'T YOU EVER DONE CHORES BEFORE?!
NO!!
I NEVER PUT IN LESS THAN A FULL EFFORT ON ANYTHING...

And so Kazahaya learned to wash rice!

合法ドラッグ
LEGAL DRUG

"TO BE CONTINUED?"

Legal Drug Vol. 3
Created by CLAMP

Translation - Ray Yoshimoto
English Adaptation - Jamie S. Rich
Associate Editor - Lillian Diaz-Przybyl
Retouch and Lettering - Irene Worri Choi
Production Artist - Vicente Rivera, Jr.
Cover Layout - Matt Alford

Editor - Luis Reyes
Imaging Manager - Chris Buford
Production Managers - Jennifer Miller and Mutsumi Miyazaki
Managing Editor - Jill Freshney
VP of Production - Ron Klamert
Publisher and E.I.C. - Mike Kiley
President and C.O.O. - John Parker

A 🔲 TOKYOPOP Manga

TOKYOPOP Inc.
5900 Wilshire Blvd. Suite 2000
Los Angeles, CA 90036

E-mail: info@TOKYOPOP.com
Come visit us online at www.TOKYOPOP.com

ISBN: 1-59532-422-4
First TOKYOPOP printing: June 2005
10 9 8 7 6 5
Printed in the USA

TOKYOPOP SHOP

PRINCESS AI

A Diva Torn from Chaos
A Savior Doomed to Love

Volume 2
Lumination

Ai continues to search for her place in our world on the streets of Tokyo. Using her talent to support herself, Ai signs a contract with a top record label and begins her rise to stardom. But fame is unpredictable—as her talent blooms, all eyes are on Ai. When scandal surfaces, will she burn out in the spotlight of celebrity?

Preview the manga at:
www.TOKYOPOP.com/princessai

P9-DDH-229

STOP DRUG

This book is printed "manga-style," in the authentic Japanese right-to-left format. Since none of the artwork has been flipped or altered, readers get to experience the story just as the creator intended. You've been asking for it, so TOKYOPOP® delivered: authentic, hot-off-the-press, and far more fun!

DIRECTIONS

If this is your first time reading manga-style, here's a quick guide to help you understand how it works.

It's easy...just start in the top right panel and follow the numbers. Have fun, and look for more 100% authentic manga from TOKYOPOP®!